D0442774

The Law of Affirmative Action

*Twenty-Five Years of Supreme Court
Decisions on Race and Remedies*

Girardeau A. Spann

NEW YORK UNIVERSITY PRESS

New York and London

NEW YORK UNIVERSITY PRESS
New York and London

© 2000 by New York University
All rights reserved

Library of Congress Cataloging-in-Publication Data
Spann, Girardeau A., 1948–
The law of affirmative action : twenty-five years of Supreme Court
decisions on race and remedies / Girardeau A. Spann.
p.   cm.
Includes bibliographical references and index.
ISBN 0-8147-8140-3 (cloth : acid-free paper)
1. Affirmative action programs—Law and legislation—United
States—History. 2. United States. Supreme Court.   I. Title.
KF4755.5 .S65 1999
342.73'087—dc21   99-050402
                            CIP

New York University Press books are printed on acid-free paper,
and their binding materials are chosen for strength and durability.

Manufactured in the United States of America

10 9 8 7 6 5 4 3 2 1

Contents

Acknowledgments

I would like to thank Bob Drinan, Steve Goldberg, Chuck Lawrence, Mari Matsuda, Elizabeth Patterson, Jill Ramsfield, and Mike Seidman for their help in developing the ideas expressed in this book. I am grateful for the research assistance and support provided by Derreck Brown, Marcia Carlson, Rebecca Kamp, Justin Murphy, Erica Niezgoda, Jeffrey Rudd, Nick Sanservino, and Karen Summerhill. Portions of chapters 1 and 5 contain updated versions of material that was originally published in *Affirmative Action and Discrimination*, 39 Howard Law Journal 1 (1995). Support for this book was provided by a research grant from the Georgetown University Law Center.

1

Affirmative Action

The contemporary debate about race in the United States is perplexing.[1] Each side seems genuinely to feel distressed at the demands being made by the other. Racial minorities point to *Dred Scott's*[2] insistence on racial castes, *Plessy's*[3] endorsement of official segregation, and *Brown's*[4] reluctance to remedy unlawful discrimination as evidence that the white majority is inevitably inclined to advance its own interests at minority expense. Minority group members, therefore, tend to argue that the only way to arrest this majoritarian inclination is through the use of race-conscious remedial programs that will ensure an equitable distribution of resources. Most members of the white majority concede past transgressions but warn of the need for fairness in fashioning remedies, asserting that members of the present majority rarely commit acts of overt discrimination, and that members of the present minority are rarely among the actual victims of past discrimination. Members of the white majority, therefore, tend to argue that the only way to end racial discrimination is through a prospective commitment to race neutrality, stressing the irony inherent in using racial classifications to remedy the racial discrimination of the past. Accordingly, the nation's debate about the significance of race, which began with slavery and persisted through the era of official segregation, has now converged on the contentious issue of affirmative action. In the early years, the Supreme Court gave qualified support to the concept of racial affirmative action, but in recent years, a majority of the Court has consistently opposed affirmative action programs.

This book attempts to chronicle the evolution of the Supreme Court's law of affirmative action during the past twenty-five years—the years during which the Court first began to struggle with the affirmative action issue. The Supreme Court's 1974 decision in *DeFunis v. Odegaard*[5] marked the beginning of the modern Court's entanglement with what has now come to be known as racial affirmative action. And the controversy that the Court initially left unresolved in *DeFunis* has thus far persisted through the

Court's 1998–99 Term. The law of affirmative action established by these twenty-five years of Supreme Court decisions reflects the formal culture of contemporary race relations in the United States. By "culture," I mean the set of organizing and interpretive categories that a group of people use to understand the world in which they live. The rhetorical content of Supreme Court affirmative action decisions makes pronouncements about when racial considerations are legitimate in contemporary culture, and when the consideration of race is improper. On a deeper level, the Supreme Court opinions designate which subcultural perspectives on race are to be deemed "real" aspects of the dominant culture, and which are to be relegated to the status of unsubstantiated mythology.

Contemporary anthropologists have argued that claims of objectivity in the observation and description of a culture are no longer plausible. Observers necessarily filter their observations through their own cultural biases, and only imperfectly appreciate the significance of actions that they observe in other cultures.[6] One anthropological response to this skepticism about objectivity has been to offer "thick descriptions" of the cultures that are being observed. Thick descriptions are characterized by conscious efforts to guard against bias and reification through a focus on context and particularity. This, in turn, enhances the "texture" of the behavior being observed.[7] Thick description can serve as the basis for the formulation of local—as opposed to grandiose—theoretical accounts of observed cultures.[8] However, thick description also permits readers to generate a multiplicity of interpretations, rather than steering readers to a single interpretation privileged by the observer who offers the description. Although the danger of subjective predispositions inherent in the observer's own categorizations necessarily remains, at least the observer's motives are more likely to be pure and nonstrategic.

In a sense, this book attempts a "thick description" of the Supreme Court culture of affirmative action. In writing the book, I have made conscious efforts to minimize my normative evaluations of the Court's decisions, so that readers can formulate their own interpretations of the Court's affirmative action jurisprudence. Although my descriptions of the Supreme Court's affirmative action opinions are substantially shorter than the opinions themselves, I have tried to describe the opinions in a uniform, systematic manner that gives the opinions enough context and texture to permit easy comparisons among them. I have focused greatest attention on the Court's constitutional decisions, but I have given enough consideration to the Court's Title VII and Voting Rights Act decisions to permit readers to contrast the

Court's constitutional jurisprudence with its statutory jurisprudence in the area of racial affirmative action. I have also focused more attention on recent cases than on older cases, reasoning that the opinions written by justices who currently sit on the Supreme Court are likely to have a higher present value than opinions written by justices who are no longer on the Court.

I have tried to make my distillations of the Court's opinions more accessible to more people with limited patience and technical expertise than the opinions themselves would be without such distillations. And although there is an obvious danger of subjective filtering in my distillations, I believe that my descriptions of the Court's opinions are less instrumental than the opinions are themselves. I have tried to describe each opinion in each affirmative action case in a way that provides a reliable data stream enabling readers to "experience" the emergence and development of doctrinal issues, and to "witness" the evolving relationships that have developed among the justices with respect to the issue of affirmative action. I hope that these descriptions will have useful reference value, and that they will permit readers to form their own opinions about the Supreme Court and affirmative action. Although I have strong normative views of my own about the Supreme Court and its affirmative action decisions, I have tried to confine the expression of those views to chapter 5 and to other works.[9] Nevertheless, my primary hope is that this "case study" of affirmative action will prompt a reevaluation of the romanticized view that is customarily held of the Supreme Court as a social institution.

1. Racial Affirmative Action

Racial affirmative action is the race-conscious allocation of resources—resources such as jobs, educational opportunities, and voting strength—that is motivated by an intent to benefit racial minorities. The nation's first racial affirmative action programs were adopted during the post–Civil War Reconstruction period—contemporaneous with the adoption of the Fourteenth Amendment—when Congress created the Freedmen's Bureau to administer a series of race-conscious social welfare programs designed to benefit blacks.[10] Those programs included assistance to blacks in the form of food, educational benefits, regulation of labor contracts, distribution of abandoned lands, adjustment of real estate disputes, special freedmen's courts, aid to orphans, medical care, special protective legislation for black servicemen, and special laws prohibiting discrimination against freedmen.[11] Although the term "affirmative action" was not then in use, the Reconstruction programs shared with contemporary race-conscious programs a certain skepticism about the ability of race-neutrality alone to provide adequate protection for racial minorities.

The term "affirmative action" was originally coined in the era following *Brown v. Board of Education*,[12] as a response to subtle forms of societal discrimination that continued to operate against racial minorities. Despite the invalidation of segregation laws in *Brown*,[13] whites were still customarily granted priority over minorities in the allocation of jobs and educational opportunities, even when minorities possessed qualifications that were the same as or better than the qualifications of the whites receiving preferential treatment. In 1961, Vice-President Lyndon Johnson oversaw the drafting for President John F. Kennedy of Executive Order 10,925, which prohibited racial discrimination in civil service hiring and government contracting. Executive Order 10,925 stated in part: "The contractor will not discriminate against any employee or applicant for employment because of race, creed, color, or national origin. The contractor will take *affirmative action* to ensure that applicants are employed, and that employees are treated during employment, without regard to their race, creed, color, or national origin."[14]

In its early years, affirmative action received little attention, and debate about race relations centered on the legitimacy of formal and informal methods of discriminating against racial minorities. Over time, however, controversy developed over the use of race-conscious efforts to reduce the underrepresentation of minorities in various social roles.[15] Now, affirmative action has become the hot topic in contemporary racial politics. Black leaders have insisted on a continued national commitment to affirmative action;[16] the University of California has terminated its three decades of affirmative action in hiring and admissions;[17] the states of California and Washington have both adopted ballot initiatives that ban affirmative action;[18] bills have been introduced in Congress to make affirmative action illegal;[19] Republican presidential hopefuls chose to run against affirmative action in the 1996 election;[20] the Clinton Administration chose to "review,"[21] and then rhetorically to "reaffirm" affirmative action;[22] steadfast liberal Democrats have loyally defended affirmative action;[23] and the American public has become profoundly ambivalent about the social utility of affirmative action.[24] As with the defining race-relations issues for earlier generations—issues including miscegenation,[25] integrated education,[26] official segregation,[27] and slavery[28]—the Supreme Court has endeavored to determine the social acceptability of affirmative action. In seeking to make this determination, the Court has consulted the equal protection clause of the Constitution,[29] as well as federal antidiscrimination statues such as Title VII of the Civil Rights Act of 1964[30] and the Voting Rights Act of 1965.[31]

This book is limited to the consideration of programs involving racial affirmative action. Other types of affirmative action programs exist for characteristics such as gender, religion, sexual orientation, and physical impairment. Still other affirmative action programs exist for athletes, residents of particular states, children of alumni, and the like. I have focused on the Supreme Court's racial affirmative action decisions because race has special significance in constitutional analysis. This special significance derives from the Thirteenth, Fourteenth, and Fifteenth Amendments, which were added to the Constitution after the Civil War. The Thirteenth Amendment abolished slavery;[32] the Fourteenth Amendment accorded citizenship, with due process and equal protection rights, to former black slaves;[33] and the Fifteenth Amendment gave blacks the right to vote.[34] Each of these amendments can be viewed as an affirmative action enactment for blacks that is relevant to the constitutionality of contemporary affirmative action programs. As this book reveals, however, analyzing the constitutionality of racial affirmative action has proved to be quite difficult in its own right. Affirmative action programs based on factors such as gender, religion, or sexual orientation raise additional complexities under the Constitution that can be better analyzed once the paradigmatic issue of racial affirmative action has been resolved in an acceptable manner. Therefore, focusing on racial affirmative action seems to be a sensible place to start. The present debate over racial affirmative action in the United States is not only a long-standing debate but also a debate that has become intensely controversial.

2. The Affirmative Action Debate

The arguments favoring and opposing racial affirmative action are easy enough to state in ways that make them sound appealing. However, because neither the Constitution nor federal statutes speak unambiguously to the issue, the Supreme Court has had great difficulty in its efforts to produce a stable resolution of the affirmative action debate. The arguments favoring and opposing affirmative action are both rooted in the belief that racial discrimination is morally wrong, constitutionally impermissible under the

Fifth and Fourteenth Amendments, and prohibited by federal antidiscrimination statutes such as Title VII and the Voting Rights Act. Although each side in the affirmative action debate claims that its position is traceable to the *a priori* proposition that race is virtually always an impermissible legislative classification, the two sides diverge when confronted with the problem of how to deal with the issue of past discrimination. I do not intend to suggest that compensation for past discrimination is the only, or even the best, potential justification for affirmative action. Indeed, some commentators argue that the best justification for affirmative action is the need to avoid a permanent underclass that is identified by race, regardless of the reason for the initial emergence of that underclass.[35] Nevertheless, the remedy-for-past-discrimination justification is the justification on which the Supreme Court, and most members of the public, appear to have focused. Ultimately, the way that one feels about the competing arguments is likely to be determined by one's metaphysical conception of equality, and by the instrumental consequences of favoring one argument over the other.

i. Proponents

Proponents of affirmative action begin with the proposition that racial discrimination is wrong because race is rarely, if ever, a legitimate basis on which to rest governmental classifications.[36] Unfortunately, however, racial discrimination has been persistently present since the founding of the nation.[37] Much of this discrimination has been officially mandated, such as the laws regulating slavery[38] and the laws requiring official segregation in the use of public facilities.[39] Although the Supreme Court has been charged with the obligation of defending the rights of racial minorities,[40] the Supreme Court has not always done so.

The Court upheld and protected the institution of slavery in *Dred Scott v. Sandford*.[41] When that case was "overruled" by the Civil War and the subsequent Reconstruction amendments to the Constitution, the Court adopted narrow readings of the Reconstruction amendments in *The Slaughter-House Cases*[42] and narrow interpretations of Reconstruction statutes in subsequent cases.[43] The Court even invalidated a major piece of Reconstruction legislation in *The Civil Rights Cases*.[44] This permitted Jim Crow laws to perpetuate the economic and social disadvantage of former black slaves. The Jim Crow laws matured into a regime of official segregation that the Supreme Court then upheld in *Plessy v. Ferguson*,[45] which endorsed the constitutionality of separate-but-equal public facilities.[46] During World

War II, the Court again acquiesced in the country's xenophobic aggression by validating the internment of Japanese-American citizens in *Korematsu v. United States*.[47] Although the Court nominally rejected *Plessy* in *Brown v. Board of Education*,[48] invalidating the practice of *de jure* segregated education, the Court delayed implementation of any meaningful remedy for *Brown*,[49] and ultimately interpreted *Brown* to permit the continued education of minority children in *de facto* segregated schools that were measurably inferior to the schools in which white children were educated.[50]

This historical treatment of racial minorities as inferior has had a pervasive effect on society, causing race to remain either a conscious or an unconscious factor in virtually all societal decision making.[51] The racial attitudes that continue to emanate from the nation's long history of discrimination have placed racial minorities in a disadvantaged position in the competition for societal resources. As a result, minorities continue to be systematically underrepresented relative to their proportion of the population in the allocation of educational, employment, and political opportunities.[52] This, in turn, has caused racial minorities to have lower standards of living, poorer health, higher vulnerability to crime, and shorter life expectancies than members of the white majority.[53]

Proponents of affirmative action contend that the only way to compensate for the historical disadvantage of racial minorities is through the prospective race-conscious allocation of educational, employment, and political resources to minorities through affirmative action programs. Mere prospective race neutrality does not provide adequate compensation for past inequities but simply freezes the existing advantages that the white majority has over racial minorities.[54] Once affirmative action programs have neutralized this unfair advantage, those programs can be terminated and all races can coexist on equal terms in a color-blind society.[55]

ii. Opponents

Opponents of affirmative action also begin with the proposition that racial discrimination is wrong because race is rarely, if ever, a legitimate basis on which to rest governmental classifications.[56] It is true that there have been ugly periods in American history during which the nation has failed to honor this fundamental principle of racial equality by tolerating the institutions of slavery and official segregation.[57] It is also true that the Supreme Court has been implicated in unfortunate acts of racial discrimination through the issuance of decisions such as *Dred Scott*, *Plessy*, and

Korematsu.[58] However, those decisions serve as embarrassing reminders that the nation must exercise constant vigilance to avoid a recurrence of the racial discrimination that characterized the dark side of the nation's history.[59]

The principle of racial equality reflects the need to treat people as individuals rather than as mere members of racial groups.[60] Accordingly, the disadvantages that individual members of racial minority groups have suffered as a result of identifiable acts of past discrimination should be neutralized through the implementation of make-whole remedies that will fully compensate those individuals for the racial discrimination that they have been forced to endure.[61] But, remedies that go beyond compensation for identifiable acts of racial discrimination, and accord preferential treatment based on mere membership in a racial minority group, constitute the very same type of racial discrimination that caused the need for a remedy in the first place.[62] In addition, such remedies harm the beneficiaries of affirmative action by promoting dependence on government largess rather than self-sufficiency, and by stigmatizing beneficiaries as undeserving of the benefits and accomplishments that they secure.[63]

The types of official race discrimination that existed in the past are now unconstitutional, and have been unconstitutional since 1954 when the Supreme Court rejected *Plessy* in *Brown*.[64] As a result, present affirmative action programs that divert resources from whites in order to benefit members of historically disadvantaged racial minority groups actually end up punishing innocent whites who were not the perpetrators of pre-*Brown* racial discrimination in order to benefit contemporary minority group members who were not the actual victims of pre-*Brown* discrimination.[65] Such a race-conscious allocation of societal resources produces resentment in the minds of the innocent whites who are burdened, and feelings of inferiority and self-doubt in the minds of the racial minority group members who benefit from such arbitrary governmental action. This, in turn, generates friction between whites and minority groups, as well as intergroup friction between the various minority groups that must compete with one another for the resources set aside under race-based affirmative action programs.[66] Ultimately, such frictions exacerbate rather than ameliorate race-relations problems in contemporary culture.[67]

Opponents of affirmative action contend that the vision of society emerging from the toleration of affirmative action programs that go beyond what is necessary to compensate the actual victims of discrimination is not an appealing one. Not only is individuality subordinated to group identification, but the concept of merit is supplanted by quotas.[68] In a Brave New World[69] of racial engineering, population proportionality will be politically correct, but jobs will cease to be performed by those who are best qualified to perform them.[70] In addition, educational opportunities will cease to go to those who are best equipped to make good use of them,[71] and political representation will be distorted by the artificial elevation of racial considerations over more substantive interests.[72] The forced racial proportionality that exists in such a society will have been purchased at the price of internal disaffection and racial balkanization.[73]

iii. Perspective

The arguments favoring affirmative action and the arguments opposing it have considerable appeal, with the ultimate persuasiveness of those arguments being a function of the analytical perspective that one adopts when evaluating them. Each set of arguments can be framed in a manner that makes it seem consistent with general principles of equality and race neutrality. If one views equality as a concept that is to be measured against an ideal or aspirational baseline, race-conscious affirmative action seems necessary to equalize imbalances caused by slavery and segregation, and thereby does more to promote equality than would mere prospective neutrality. However, if one elects to adopt the status quo as the baseline for making equality determinations, thereby taking preexisting differences in the allocation of resources as a given, affirmative action seems like a racially discriminatory deviation from the principle of prospective neutrality. As the current controversy surrounding affirmative action attests,[74] one's stake in the outcome is likely to affect which conception of equality has the greater appeal. Because the culture has been unable to reach consensus on the appropriate analytical baseline, the debate about affirmative action has remained intractable. The intractability of the debate, and the intensity of the political controversy surrounding it, have made it difficult for the Supreme Court to achieve a satisfactory resolution of the affirmative action problem.

2

The Early Cases

The Supreme Court adopted its present law of affirmative action after an extended period of experimentation. In a series of plurality decisions, various justices and coalitions of justices toyed with a variety of legal standards to govern the use of racial classifications for the benefit of racial minorities. In the course of the deliberations that occurred among the justices, a number of legal issues emerged as having potential constitutional significance. Finally, after a series of Reagan and Bush appointments, the Supreme Court was able to speak through majority opinions in issuing its formula for constitutionally acceptable affirmative action. Under current law, most forms of race-conscious affirmative action now appear to be unconstitutional.

The Court's constitutional decisions are directly applicable only to governmental use of affirmative action programs because the state-action requirement of the Fourteenth Amendment—the legal provision on which the Court's decisions are based—does not apply to purely private action. Private affirmative action programs, however, must comply with the congressional statutes that govern the private use of racial classifications, such as the Civil Rights Act of 1964, which prohibits, *inter alia*, discrimination in education, employment, and public accommodations. It is unclear whether the Supreme Court will ultimately adopt the same standards for statutory and constitutional analysis of affirmative action.[1]

The problems posed by affirmative action are directly traceable to *Brown v. Board of Education*.[2] In *Brown I*, the Supreme Court invalidated the separate-but-equal doctrine of *Plessy v. Ferguson*,[3] and held that, under the equal protection clause of the Fourteenth Amendment, governmental use of racial classifications was constitutionally suspect.[4] Then, in *Brown II* and its progeny, the Court not only held that the Constitution required a remedy for the continuing effects of past discrimination but stressed that the use of racial classifications was constitutionally compelled where necessary to provide an effective remedy for the prior constitutional violation. As a result,

Brown can be read to support each of the following propositions: racial classifications are constitutionally prohibited; racial classifications are constitutionally permissible; and racial classifications are constitutionally required. The uncertainty concerning proper characterization of affirmative action initiatives caused the Supreme Court to enter into an extended period of doctrinal instability and confusion before adopting its current position on affirmative action.[5]

1. Pre-Bakke Cases

The school desegregation cases decided in the aftermath of *Brown* are not traditionally viewed as affirmative action cases, but those cases were nevertheless the modern harbingers of contemporary affirmative action. The post-*Brown* school desegregation cases generally produced majority opinions that authorized the use of race-conscious remedies to dismantle formally segregated school systems. The 1955 decision in *Brown II* required desegregation of previously segregated school systems "with all deliberate speed."[6] Subsequent cases emphasized that contemplated desegregation strategies had to be effective in order to be acceptable.[7] In the 1971 *Swann v. Charlotte-Mecklenburg Board of Education*[8] decision, the Court explicitly authorized the use of race-based pupil assignment as a permissible remedy for prior constitutional violations.[9] Chief Justice Burger, writing for a unanimous Court, also endorsed—albeit reluctantly—the use of mathematical ratios reflecting racial proportionality in the school district population as targets in formulating desegregation plans to remedy constitutional violations, and he did so in the face of a congressional statute that arguably prohibited pupil assignment for the purpose of achieving racial balance.[10] In a companion case named *North Carolina State Board of Education v. Swann*,[11] the Court held that a prohibition on race-based pupil assignment in favor of color-blind pupil assignment was also unconstitutional because it interfered with the school board's ability to fashion an effective remedy for past segregation.[12] The Supreme Court remained supportive of affirmative efforts to promote school desegregation while the desegregation effort remained in the South, but the Court seemed to lose its resolve as the desegregation effort moved north in the 1970s.[13]

In the 1973 Supreme Court decision in *Keys v. School District No. 1, Denver, Colorado*,[14] the Court limited court-ordered desegregation to *de jure* rather than *de facto* segregated school districts.[15] In the 1974 *Milliken v.*

Bradley[16] decision, the Court held that race-conscious desegregation remedies could not be imposed on suburban Detroit schools because segregation in the Detroit suburbs had resulted from *de facto* residential segregation rather than *de jure* school policies.[17] This was the first time in the twenty years since *Brown I* that the Supreme Court had invalidated a school desegregation plan.[18] *Milliken* also precluded the possibility of meaningful desegregation in many northern metropolitan areas because the inability to reach white suburban students meant that there were no white students available to desegregate the predominantly black inner-city schools.[19] The erosion of Supreme Court support for school desegregation seemed to reflect a loss of public support for desegregated schools in the North. In the 1970s, racial violence accompanied efforts to desegregate the Boston public schools. Richard Nixon, who had been elected president in 1968 on a platform that included opposition to busing, was reelected in 1972. And Congress not only passed antibusing legislation in 1972 and 1974 but also began to consider constitutional amendments that would prohibit busing.[20] In this climate of decreasing public support for school desegregation, the Supreme Court also began to consider the constitutionality of affirmative action plans that adopted race-conscious strategies for achieving societal goals other than the elimination of *de jure* school segregation. In the mid-1970s, the Supreme Court began to issue fractured decisions when called upon to evaluate the politically controversial use of these plans that have now come to be known as "affirmative action." And it would be fifteen years before the Supreme Court would be able to issue a majority opinion in an affirmative action case.[21]

i. *DeFunis* (1974)

The Supreme Court first explicitly addressed the issue of racial affirmative action in the 1974 case of *DeFunis v. Odegaard.*[22] However, the Court shied away from ruling on the constitutionality of affirmative action. *DeFunis* involved a preferential admissions program for minority applicants that had been adopted by the University of Washington School of Law. When the program was challenged by a white applicant who had allegedly been rejected in favor of a less-qualified minority applicant, the Supreme Court held in a per curiam opinion that the case had become moot because of the plaintiff's impending graduation from law school.[23] As a result, the Court vacated a decision by the Supreme Court of Washington upholding the challenged program, even though the case was not moot as a matter of Washington state law.[24]

Four justices dissented from the Supreme Court's mootness holding in *DeFunis*—Justices Brennan, Douglas, White, and Marshall.[25] The dissenters agreed with *both* parties that the case was not moot. They asserted that the "voluntary cessation" doctrine precluded a finding of mootness where the school refused to concede the illegality of the challenged program, even though the school had exercised its discretion to permit the student to register for his final semester. The dissenters also argued that the public interest in avoiding repetitive litigation required the Court to address the merits of the affirmative action issue promptly rather than sidestep the constitutional issue because of its difficulty.[26] Only Justice Douglas addressed the merits, arguing that even benign racial classifications should be subject to strict scrutiny.[27] Douglas emphasized that benign racial classifications could have the unintended effect of stigmatizing their intended beneficiaries by suggesting that those beneficiaries lacked the capacity to achieve on their own merit. However, Douglas did believe that race-neutral consideration of an applicant's ability to overcome a deprived background would be constitutionally permissible. Justice Douglas also favored abolition of the Law School Admission Test (LSAT).[28]

Under the *Munsingwear* doctrine,[29] the Supreme Court's vacation of the Supreme Court of Washington decision on mootness grounds nullified the lower court decisions and technically left the University of Washington Law School affirmative action program in place. For this reason, *DeFunis* is designated a decision that facilitates rather than frustrates affirmative action in the Affirmative Action Voting Chart that is included on pages 162–63. Because the positions of Justices Brennan, White, and Marshall on the merits of affirmative action were not disclosed in their dissenting opinion, their votes are designated indeterminate in the Voting Chart.

ii. *United Jewish Organizations* (1977)

In the 1977 case of *United Jewish Organizations v. Carey*,[30] the Court considered the constitutionality of a race-conscious legislative apportionment scheme adopted by the state of New York that was designed to increase the voting strength of blacks in order to comply with the Voting Rights Act of 1965. The constitutionality of the apportionment scheme was challenged by members of a Hasidic Jewish community whose voting strength had been diluted under the plan.[31] Although the Court rejected the constitutional challenge, it was unable to agree upon a majority opinion. Four members of the Court—Justices White, Stevens, Brennan, and Blackmun—stated that the racial classifications used in the plan were constitutionally permissible because they were adopted in order to comply with a congressional statute; that they were permissible even though no past constitutional violation had been established mandating the use of a remedial plan; and that they were not invalid because of their utilization of numerical quotas as targets.[32] Three justices—Justices White, Stevens, and Rehnquist—stated that the plan was constitutionally permissible because it did not stigmatize either minorities or whites, and because it did not burden whites by "minimiz[ing] or unfairly cancel[ing] out white voting strength."[33] Two justices—Justices Stewart and Powell—voted to uphold the reapportionment plan because, even though it rested upon a racial classification, there was no indication that the plan was adopted with the intention of disadvantaging white voters, as would be required for a Fourteenth Amendment violation under *Washington v. Davis*.[34] Justice Brennan wrote a concurring opinion arguing that even benign racial classifications should typically be treated as "suspect" because they posed the danger of concealing what might in fact amount to a disadvantageous classification; because they might stigmatize the beneficiaries and stimulate society's latent race consciousness; and because they might create a general impression of injustice in society that would ultimately injure "discrete and insular" groups of whites, such as the Hasidic Jews who challenged the reapportionment plan in *United Jewish Organizations*. However, Justice Brennan voted to uphold the plan because he viewed congressional authorization under the Voting Rights Act as a sufficient precaution against these dangers, and because the plan was not intended to inflict racial insult or injury on the white voters who were adversely affected.[35] Justice Burger dissented, finding the percentage targets of the apportionment plan to constitute impermissible racial quotas that were inconsistent with the "melting pot" objective of achieving a homogeneous society.[36] Justice Marshall did not participate in the decision.

These two pre-*Bakke* cases set the terms of the affirmative action debate that was to follow. *DeFunis* foreshadowed the fact that a majority of the Court would be unable to agree upon anything other than the contentiousness of the affirmative action issue.[37] *United Jewish Organizations* indicated that all of the justices except Justice Burger were prepared to accept the constitutionality of some race-conscious affirmative action plans.[38] In *DeFunis*,

Justice Douglas introduced both the idea that benign affirmative action should be subjected to heightened judicial scrutiny and the concern that affirmative action might inadvertently stigmatize its intended minority beneficiaries.[39] These concerns were endorsed and enlarged upon by Justice Brennan in *United Jewish Organizations*.[40] In *United Jewish Organizations* also, Justice White introduced consideration of the degree of burden on innocent whites as a constitutionally significant factor in determining the validity of an affirmative action plan,[41] and Justice Burger introduced the idea of hostility to racial quotas as inconsistent with the American dream of a color-blind society.[42] Moreover, in *United Jewish Organizations*, four members of the Court—Justices White, Stevens, Brennan, and Blackmun—were willing to uphold the use of explicit racial quotas, even in the absence of an adjudicated constitutional violation, because they were authorized by Congress.[43] It is interesting to note that the arguably simple standard endorsed by Justices Stewart and Powell in *United Jewish Organizations*—i.e., subjecting benign racial classifications to the same invidious intent standard that they viewed the Court as having applied to all other racial classifications under *Washington v. Davis*[44]—would prove problematic in subsequent cases.[45]

2. Bakke *(1978)*

The Supreme Court's 1978 decision in *Regents of the University of California v. Bakke*,[46] is one of the Court's most famous affirmative action decisions. In *Bakke*, the Court reached the merits of the racial preference issue that it had sidestepped in *DeFunis*. *Bakke* involved an affirmative action program adopted by the University of California at Davis Medical School that set aside 16 percent of the seats in its entering class for disadvantaged minority students.[47] A five-justice majority voted to invalidate the particular plan that was before the Court, while a different five-justice majority voted to uphold the use of racial preferences in appropriate circumstances. Four justices—Justices Stevens, Burger, Stewart, and Rehnquist—declined to reach the constitutional question, finding that the Davis plan violated Title VI of the Civil Rights Act of 1964,[48] which prohibits federally funded programs from excluding or denying benefits to any person on the grounds of race.[49] The fifth vote to invalidate the plan was provided by Justice Powell, who would have invalidated it on equal protection grounds.[50]

Four justices—Justices Brennan, White, Marshall, and Blackmun—believed that racial classifications designed to remedy disadvantages imposed upon minorities by past societal discrimination should be subjected to an intermediate level of scrutiny. They thought that such classifications should be upheld where they advanced an important and articulated purpose, did not stigmatize any group, and did not force politically underrepresented groups to bear the burden of the remedial action.[51] Although the Brennan opinion referred to the need for appropriate judicial, legislative, or administrative findings, it appears that informal findings concerning the need to address the problems of societal discrimination would be sufficient.[52] Because the four justices joining the Brennan opinion viewed the Davis program as having satisfied the constitutional test, they voted to uphold its constitutionality.[53] The fifth vote to uphold the use of racial classifications in affirmative action programs was again provided by Justice Powell. Although Justice Powell thought that racial preferences were constitutionally permissible in appropriate circumstances, he found that the Davis plan did not satisfy the constitutional standards.[54]

Justice Powell's views concerning the circumstances under which affirmative action was constitutionally permissible were significant because at the time he appeared to possess the swing vote on the affirmative action issue.[55] Indeed, even though he is no longer on the Court, Justice Powell's *Bakke* opinion is still treated with a certain reverence.[56] Powell argued that all racial classifications should be subject to strict scrutiny, rejecting the argument that strict scrutiny should be reserved for classifications that adversely affect discrete and insular minorities.[57] In support of this position, he asserted that it would be difficult to distinguish between benign and burdensome classifications; that reduced scrutiny for benign classifications would reinforce common racial stereotypes; and that it would be inequitable to force innocent whites to bear the burden of redressing injuries for which they themselves were not responsible. Powell then found that none of the four objectives offered to justify the Davis plan satisfied the strict constitutional standard.[58] The goal of securing a specified percentage of minority enrollment not only was insubstantial but was itself an act of facially invalid racial discrimination.[59] Although eliminating the effects of past discrimination could constitute a compelling state interest, remedial classifications had to be accompanied by judicial, legislative, or administrative findings of past discrimination, which were absent with respect to the Davis plan.[60] Although increasing the supply of medical services to deprived minority communities might also constitute a compelling state interest, there was no evidence that the Davis plan would promote that objective better than a plan based upon racially neutral classifications.[61] Finally, although increasing diversity in an academic environment might constitute a compelling state interest, the racial quotas incorporated into the Davis plan were not necessary to the achievement of that end. Diversity could be advanced by using race as one of a variety of factors that went into admissions decisions, thereby preserving the important constitutional objective of treating individuals as individuals rather than as mere members of a racial group the way the Davis plan quotas did.[62] It is this diversity "holding" in Justice Powell's *Bakke* opinion that some lower courts have now rejected in recent anti-affirmative-action decisions.[63]

Justice Marshall wrote a separate opinion asserting that it would be anomalous to read the Constitution, which had permitted ownership of and overt discrimination against black slaves, to prohibit affirmative action efforts to remedy that history of discrimination on the grounds that the remedies were race-conscious. Marshall also stressed the irony inherent in the Court's use of the Fourteenth Amendment, which had been enacted after the Civil War to protect blacks from continued exploitation by whites, to advance the interests of whites at minority expense. Marshall stated his fear that the Court had come full circle and was once again impeding the realization of racial equality by invalidating affirmative action measures just as it had done after the Civil War in the infamous *Civil Rights Cases* and *Plessy v. Ferguson*.[64] Justice Blackmun also wrote a separate opinion, stressing that the government frequently dispenses benefits through the use of special interest preferences, and arguing that there was no important difference between the Davis quota plan and the Harvard plan of which Justice Powell approved.[65]

In *Bakke*, four justices—Justices Brennan, White, Marshall, and Blackmun—committed themselves to a standard of intermediate scrutiny for racial classifications that were intended to remedy the effects of past discrimination.[66] Justice Powell emerged as the potential fifth vote to uphold affirmative action plans, but he insisted on a standard of strict scrutiny that required both a compelling state interest and a tight fit between the plan and that interest.[67] Justice Powell also insisted on formal findings concerning each prong of the constitutional test by a legislative or administrative body that was institutionally competent to make such findings.[68] Although Justice Powell was willing to accept both the goals of ameliorating the effects of past discrimination and of promoting prospective diversity as sufficiently compelling interests, he insisted that an affirmative action plan treat people as individuals rather than mere members of a racial group.[69] Justice Marshall introduced the irony inherent in reading the Fourteenth Amendment to protect whites from race-conscious affirmative action that benefited minorities.[70]

3. Fullilove *(1980)*

In 1980, the Court issued another plurality decision in *Fullilove v. Klutznick*,[71] upholding the constitutionality of a congressionally enacted set-aside program for minority contractors. Under the program established by the Public Works Employment Act of 1977,[72] recipients of federal funds appropriated for local public works projects were required to use 10 percent of those funds to procure goods or services from minority contractors—formally known as minority business enterprises or MBEs. The 10 percent requirement was subject to administrative waiver if minority firms were unavailable, and the agency implementing the act was charged with ensuring that the funds were allocated to *bona fide* minority firms that had been disadvantaged by past discrimination.[73]

By a vote of 6–3, the Court rejected a facial challenge to the set-aside program filed by nonminority contractors, thereby reaffirming the constitutionality of remedial racial classifications, and establishing the constitutionality of racial quotas in appropriate circumstances. Chief Justice Burger, in an opinion joined by Justices White and Powell, did not take a position on the standard-of-review issue that had crystallized in *Bakke*, but rather stated that the congressional set-aside program would survive either intermediate or strict scrutiny.[74] After rejecting the argument that Congress was required to act in a color-blind manner, the Burger opinion asserted that Congress was authorized to adopt the set-aside program under its spending power, its commerce power, and its implementation power under § 5 of the Fourteenth Amendment.[75] The opinion also asserted that it was permissible to require innocent nonminority contractors to share the burden of remedying past discrimination through the disappointment of their contractual expectations.[76] Finally, the opinion rejected the argument that the program was both overinclusive and underinclusive, finding that the statutory administrative apparatus designed to effect appropriate waivers and ensure the *bona fides* of minority fund recipients made the program sufficiently narrow.[77] Although Justice Powell signed Justice Burger's opinion, he also wrote a concurring opinion emphasizing the importance of strict scrutiny and the need for adequate findings concerning a past constitutional violation made by a competent governmental body.[78]

The additional three votes to uphold the set-aside program came from Justices Marshall, Brennan, and Blackmun.[79] Justice Marshall's opinion reasserted the desirability of intermediate scrutiny for benign racial classifications adopted by the Brennan plurality in *Bakke*, and found that the set-aside program easily survived such scrutiny.[80] Justice Marshall, citing Justice Brennan's *Bakke* opinion, emphasized that although the set-aside program utilized racial quotas, it did not "establish a quota in the invidious sense of a ceiling" on minority firms.[81] In addition, because only qualified minority contractors were eligible to receive funds under the Public Works Employment Act, there was no serious danger of racial stigmatization.[82]

The three votes to invalidate the set-aside program came from Justices Stewart, Rehnquist, and Stevens. Justice Stewart, in an opinion signed by Justice Rehnquist, argued that the Constitution was color-blind, and that Congress was not authorized to act to the detriment of an individual solely because of that individual's race. It did not matter that those injured by the congressional set-aside were members of the majority rather than members of a racial minority; in upholding the set-aside, the Court was making the same mistake that the Supreme Court had made in *Plessy v. Ferguson*.[83] Justice Stewart also argued that congressional power to remedy the effects of past discrimination could not justify the set-aside program because there was no finding that Congress had discriminated in the disbursement of federal contract funds. Rather than seeking to remedy past racial discrimination, the program was designed to promote racial balance by channeling a certain percentage of funds to minorities, and to counteract the effects of past social, educational and economic disadvantage—something that was not limited to minorities.[84]

Justice Stevens did not believe that the Constitution required race neutrality, but in his dissent, he argued that racial classifications were so pernicious that a tight fit between racial classifications and their justifications was necessary to establish their constitutionality.[85] Justice Stevens did not explicitly discuss the applicable standard of review, but he implied that strict scrutiny was appropriate.[86] Although Justice Stevens believed that the set-aside program was insufficiently narrow,[87] and that it constituted an impermissible minority effort to obtain "a piece of the action,"[88] he did not favor setting the program aside on substantive grounds as Justice Stewart did. Rather, Justice Stevens thought the program was unconstitutional because it contained too many serious questions that Congress had not adequately addressed, including the danger that the program would promote counterproductive resentment and racial stereotyping.[89] Justice Stevens seems to have been motivated by the belief that the statute was simply a product of partisan political pressure designed to create a spoils system for specified minority groups.[90]

Despite its fragmented opinions, *Fullilove* did seem to settle certain doctrinal matters. Although a majority was unable to agree on a standard of scrutiny, seven members of the Court—Justices Burger, White, Powell, Marshall, Brennan, Blackmun, and Stevens—did endorse the use of race-conscious remedies for past discrimination,[91] as well as the permissibility of using racial quotas in furtherance of such remedies.[92] As a result, every member of the Court had at one time or another endorsed the constitutionality of race-conscious affirmative action remedies, even outside the school desegregation context. Only Justices Stewart and Rehnquist contested the use of such remedies in *Fullilove*, and neither made any serious effort to distinguish his earlier tolerance of race-conscious remedies in *United Jewish Organizations*.[93] In addition, although virtually all of the justices had at times expressed apprehensions about the promotion of racial stereotyping and stigmatization, those apprehensions were overcome by the six justices who voted to uphold the congressional set-aside in *Fullilove*.[94] Moreover, Justice Powell's insistence on treating people as individuals rather than as members of a particular racial group, first articulated in *Bakke*,[95] was explicitly endorsed by only two additional justices in *Fullilove*—Justices Stewart and Rehnquist.[96] Further, although many of the justices spoke about the importance of findings, in actuality, very informal findings were deemed sufficient to uphold the *Fullilove* set-aside plan, including findings made in connection with different pieces of legislation.[97] The goal of providing a remedy for the effects of societal discrimination in general, rather than identifiable sources of discrimination in particular, was sufficient for the six justices who upheld the use of race-conscious remedies in *Fullilove*.[98] Justice Stewart, however, introduced the argument that remedial use of affirmative action should be limited to circumstances in which the governmental unit implementing the plan was itself guilty of past discrimination, and that affirmative action should not be used merely to promote racial balance.[99] Justice Burger's opinion announcing the judgment of the Court noted that Congress possessed special powers under § 5 of the Fourteenth Amendment but did not rest on § 5 alone, invoking the commerce and spending powers as well as authority for the set-asides.[100] Finally, *United Jewish Organizations* and *Fullilove* combined suggested that congressional affirmative action plans were likely to fare better than state plans.[101] `

4. *Post*-Fullilove

The tone of the early Supreme Court cases was generally hospitable to the concept of affirmative action. The mootness holding of *DeFunis*, issued after a series of school desegregation cases upholding race-conscious pupil assignment plans, may well have constituted an effort by a majority of the Court to delay the issuance of *any* Supreme Court order that would for the first time have invalidated a race-conscious remedy. Moreover, when that ruling did come four years later in *Bakke*, a majority of the Court was careful not to invalidate all forms of affirmative action, insisting instead that affirmative action remedies would remain constitutionally tolerable if they satisfied certain requirements. The Supreme Court cases decided after *Bakke*, however, exhibited a tone that was markedly less receptive to the concept of affirmative action than the earlier cases had been. As popular hostility to affirmative action increased, so did Supreme Court impatience with race-conscious remedies. Even the decisions upholding affirmative action plans seemed to do so grudgingly and with little sense of conviction.

i. *Wygant* (1986)

In *Wygant v. Jackson Board of Education*,[102] decided in 1986, the Court invalidated by a vote of 5–4 an affirmative action consent decree that was designed to preserve the number of minority schoolteachers in Jackson, Michigan, by protecting minority teachers with limited seniority from layoffs at the expense of white teachers who had greater seniority.[103] The affirmative action consent decree was the result of a decision by the school board to settle rather than litigate discrimination proceedings that had been commenced against it, thereby rendering the affirmative action plan at issue technically voluntary, although not magnanimous.[104] Justice Powell wrote a plurality opinion signed by four justices—Justices Powell, Burger, Rehnquist, and O'Connor—that applied strict scrutiny to the school board's voluntary affirmative action plan.[105] The lower courts had upheld the plan based on the need to remedy past societal discrimination through the provision of role models for minority students, but Justice

Powell rejected that justification. Not only was neutralizing the effects of past societal discrimination insufficiently compelling to withstand strict scrutiny, but the plan was insufficiently narrow because it linked the target number of minority *teachers* to the percentage of minority *students*—something that did not bear a necessary relationship to the scope of any remedy that might be required.[106] Although remediation of past discrimination by the Jackson school board could constitute a compelling state interest, there were no findings of past discrimination by the school board. Indeed, during earlier phases of the litigation, the school board had denied engaging in any racial discrimination at all, arguing that statistical disparities between minority and nonminority teachers were the result of general societal discrimination. Moreover, there was no need for a remand to permit additional findings.[107]

Three justices—Justices Powell, Burger, and Rehnquist—found no need for a remand because they viewed layoffs as simply too heavy a burden to be imposed on innocent whites. Remedies for past discrimination could be achieved through less-burdensome alternatives, such as hiring goals. As a result, the preferential layoff plan at issue in *Wygant* did not satisfy the narrowness demands of strict scrutiny.[108] Justices Powell, Burger, and Rehnquist did, however, concede the constitutionality of using layoffs as a make-whole remedy for identifiable victims of particular acts of discrimination.[109]

Justice O'Connor wrote a concurring opinion.[110] Although she was unwilling to rule out completely the use of race-conscious layoffs as a remedy, she too viewed a remand as unnecessary because the school board had pursued a goal that could not satisfy the narrowness requirement of strict scrutiny. By using the percentage of minority *students* in the school district rather than the percentage of minority teachers in the *labor pool* as the target figure for its hiring goals, the school board could not have been acting in a narrowly tailored way to remedy employment discrimination, as opposed to general societal discrimination.[111] Justice O'Connor, however, did not believe that formal findings of past discrimination were required. Unlike Justice Powell, she was not willing to permit the absence of formal findings to preclude recognition of the past school board discrimination that appears to have existed.[112] Justice O'Connor was also willing to concede that prospective racial diversity could constitute a compelling governmental interest, at least in an educational context.[113] However, although Justice O'Connor was willing to view prospective diversity as a potentially compelling governmental interest, she was careful to distinguish diversity from the role-model rationale relied on by the lower courts to uphold the plan.[114]

The fifth vote to invalidate the preferential layoff plan came from Justice White. In a very brief opinion, Justice White simply asserted that the Constitution did not permit the discharge of white teachers in order to hire minority teachers who were not themselves the actual victims of particular acts of discrimination. Further, he viewed the Jackson preferential layoff plan as the functional equivalent of a plan discharging white teachers in order to hire minority teachers. In this regard, Justice White constituted a fourth vote—combined with those of Justices Powell, Burger, and Rehnquist—for the proposition that layoffs were a constitutionally impermissible burden to impose on innocent whites.[115] Justice White's aversion to layoffs appears traceable to his majority opinion in *Firefighters Local Union No. 1784 v. Stotts*,[116] a Title VII case in which the Court invalidated a preferential layoff plan embodied in a judicially modified consent decree on the grounds that the plan imposed impermissible burdens on innocent whites.[117]

The four justices who voted to uphold the Jackson preferential layoff plan issued two opinions. Justice Marshall wrote a dissent signed by three justices—Justices Marshall, Brennan, and Blackmun. They favored the intermediate scrutiny that they had advocated in *Bakke* and *Fullilove*, but believed that the Jackson preferential layoff plan could survive either intermediate or strict scrutiny.[118] They thought that the state's interest in preserving the level of faculty integration that had been secured through tense negotiations during a racially volatile period was a sufficient state interest for equal protection purposes,[119] and the use of preferential layoffs as part of a voluntarily agreed upon settlement was sufficiently narrow to survive constitutional scrutiny.[120] Justice Marshall argued that the Jackson plan was less burdensome than a plan that did not consider seniority at all; a lottery-based layoff plan; or a total freeze on minority layoffs.[121] Justice Marshall also argued that if the plurality believed formal findings to be essential, it should remand the case for such findings.[122]

Justice Stevens supplied the fourth vote to uphold the Jackson plan, appearing to apply only minimal, rational-basis scrutiny. Justice Stevens rejected the argument that benign racial classifications could be used only to remedy the effects of past discrimination, and argued that the constitutional test should be whether the racial classification at issue advanced some prospective public interest.[123] Justice Stevens thought that the faculty-diversity and role-model justifications offered to support the layoff plan were constitutionally sufficient.[124] In addition, although Justice Stevens believed that it was necessary to scrutinize the burden imposed on whites, the preferential layoff plan did not impose an impermissible burden. The plan was voluntarily adopted by the school board and the teachers union in a manner that was procedurally fair, and the plan did not stigmatize or stereotype disadvantaged whites. Justice Stevens distinguished *Fullilove*—a case in which he had voted to invalidate the affirmative action plan at issue—as a case in which the racial classification was not selected by Congress in a manner that was procedurally adequate.[125]

ii. *Sheet Metal Workers* (1986)

After *Wygant*, the Supreme Court considered the constitutionality of two affirmative action plans that were not adopted voluntarily, but rather were imposed by lower courts as remedial measures on defendants found to have engaged in aggravated forms of racial discrimination. The first plan was imposed in *Local 28, Sheet Metal Workers International Association v. Equal Employment Opportunity Commission*,[126] which like *Wygant* was decided in 1986. A federal district court initially found in 1975 that a New York local of the sheet metal workers' union had engaged in a long history of racial exclusion that violated the employment discrimination provisions of Title VII of the Civil Rights Act of 1964. For more than a decade thereafter, the district court attempted to implement an effective remedial order. During that period of time, the district court attempted to get the union to comply with hiring goals that reflected the percentage of minority workers in the local labor force. Because the union repeatedly failed to comply with those hiring goals, the district court issued two separate civil contempt citations and fined the union $150,000. The court placed the proceeds of the fine in a special fund that was to be used for the recruitment and training of minority workers, and the court required the union to replenish the fund at a certain specified rate. The court of appeals upheld these remedial measures, and the Supreme Court affirmed in a 5–4 decision.[127] A five-justice majority of the Supreme Court—consisting of Justices Brennan, Marshall, Blackmun, Powell, and Stevens—upheld the district court's use of statistical evidence, and upheld the district court's use of its civil contempt power to impose a fine for the establishment of a remedial fund.[128] Other aspects of the case were resolved by plurality opinion.

Justice Brennan wrote a plurality opinion that was signed by four members of the Court—Justices Brennan, Marshall, Blackmun, and Stevens.[129] Justice Brennan first addressed the validity of the district court order under Title VII.[130] The union claimed that the race-conscious district court hiring goals were unlawful because Title VII limited the use of race-conscious measures to make-whole remedies for actual victims of discrimination, and did not therefore permit courts to order preferential treatment for members of a racial group simply because other members of that group had suffered discrimination in the past. Justice Brennan rejected this argument after a lengthy discussion of the pertinent legislative history. Although Title VII prohibited the use of quotas or evidence of racial imbalance to establish *liability* for employment discrimination, it did not prohibit the use of race-conscious measures for *remedial* purposes once Title VII liability had been established.[131]

Justice Brennan distinguished the Court's prior decision in *Firefighters Local Union No. 1784 v. Stotts*[132]—a case that is discussed later in this chapter—where the Court had read Title VII to permit the use of race-conscious remedies to override *bona fide* seniority systems only when necessary to provide remedies for actual victims of discrimination. Justice Brennan stated that *Stotts* applied to the *retrospective* award of *make-whole* remedies to *individuals*. It did not limit the *prospective* use of race-conscious affirmative action remedies for a whole *class* of workers where such remedies were necessary to provide meaningful redress for systemic past discrimination. Such remedies were not the type of *make-whole* remedies to which the *Stotts* actual-victim limitation applied.[133] Justice Brennan noted that race-conscious affirmative action should not be ordered unnecessarily, but the district court's use of hiring goals, fines, and the remedial fund was proper. Those remedies were proper because of the union's pervasive and egregious discrimination, and the need to counteract the lingering effects of the union's past discrimination. In addition, the district court used the hiring goals as a temporary benchmark rather than as a means of achieving and retaining racial balance, and the goals did not impermissibly interfere with the interests of white employees.[134]

Justice Brennan next addressed the validity of the district court affirmative action remedies under the equal protection component of the Fifth Amendment due process clause.[135] He noted the Supreme Court's disagreement over the proper constitutional standard to govern the use of benign racial classifications, but found that the district court order would satisfy even the most rigorous test.[136] The district court remedies were designed to eliminate the lingering effects of egregious discrimination, and were narrowly tailored to accomplish that objective.[137] Justice Brennan also stressed that the district court remedies would have only a marginal effect on the interests of white workers. They did not disadvantage any existing union members, and they did not completely preclude whites from securing union membership.[138] Justice Brennan finally stressed once again that six members of the Court—the four justices in the Brennan plurality, as well as Justices Powell and White—agreed that both Title VII and the equal protection clause permitted remedial racial classifications that benefited individuals who were not themselves actual victims of discrimination.[139]

The fifth vote to uphold the district court order was supplied by Justice Powell, who wrote separately in order to emphasize the need for strict scrutiny of even remedial classifications.[140] Justice Powell stated that the egregious facts of *Sheet Metal Workers* permitted the use of race-conscious affirmative action remedies even for those who were not the actual victims of discrimination. The language in *Stotts* asserting that Title VII remedies should *always* be limited to actual victims of discrimination was dicta because that broad issue was not before the Court.[141] Although Justice Powell believed that strict scrutiny should be applied to benign racial classifications, he also believed that the district court remedies survived strict scrutiny because they served the compelling interest of neutralizing the union's bad-faith discrimination, and they were narrowly tailored to serve that interest.[142] Justice Powell also emphasized that the district court order did not directly burden white employees.[143]

Four justices—Justices O'Connor, White, Rehnquist, and Burger—declined to address the equal protection issue, voting instead to reverse the district court order as beyond the scope of permissible remedies under Title VII.[144] Justice O'Connor wrote an opinion, concurring in part and dissenting in part, which argued that the district court hiring goals and remedial fund were not authorized by Title VII.[145] She believed that Title VII, as construed by *Stotts*, prohibited a court from using race-conscious remedial preferences to benefit individuals who were not themselves the actual victims of discrimination. She also rejected Justice Brennan's claim that the Title VII actual-victim limitation on race-conscious relief was limited to make-whole remedies, arguing that important dicta in *Stotts* had squarely rejected that claim and had read Title VII to impose an actual-victim limitation on prospective affirmative action remedies as well.[146] Even if race-conscious remedies could properly be applied to individuals who were not the actual victims of discrimination, Justice O'Connor believed that the district court hiring goals were still invalid. Justice O'Connor conceded that a majority of the Court now permitted some race-conscious relief for nonvictims of discrimination, but she believed that the hiring goals still violated Title VII because they constituted racial quotas. They inflicted harm on nonminority workers, and they did not adequately take account of the compliance difficulties that the union would face in light of economic conditions and the number of qualified minority applicants.[147] Justice O'Connor also believed that the remedial fund constituted an impermissible racial quota because it created benefits for minority workers that nonminority workers were precluded from sharing.[148]

Justice White wrote a dissenting opinion arguing that the general policy of Title VII was to limit race-conscious relief to the actual victims of discrimination, but that in some circumstances such relief was appropriate for nonvictims.[149] Although the unusual facts of *Sheet Metal Workers* might have made some nonvictim relief appropriate, the district court order was excessive. The cumulative effect of the district court hiring goals and contempt citation was to create a strict racial quota that the union was required to comply with despite an economic decline in the construction industry. As a result, the union could comply only by displacing nonminority workers, and a judicial order compelling such displacement constituted an inequitable remedy.[150] Justice Rehnquist wrote a brief dissent for himself and Chief Justice Burger arguing that Title VII, as construed in *Stotts*, precluded the use of judicial remedies that effectively displaced nonminority workers unless such displacement was necessary to provide relief for actual victims of discrimination.[151]

iii. *Paradise* (1987)

The second post-*Wygant* case in which the Supreme Court considered the constitutionality of a judicially imposed affirmative action plan was the 1987 case of *United States v. Paradise*.[152] In 1972, a federal district court found that the Alabama Department of Public Safety had engaged in a "blatant and continuous pattern" of discrimination so egregious that not a single black state trooper had ever been hired during the thirty-seven-year history of the state troopers.[153] For the next twelve years, the district court entered a series of orders attempting to get the repeatedly recalcitrant department to hire and promote black state troopers. The district court order that ultimately reached the Supreme Court required the department to promote one qualified black state trooper for every white state trooper promoted until the department developed a permanent promotion plan that would not have a racially discriminatory impact, or until blacks comprised 25 percent of each trooper rank—a number that reflected the proportion of blacks in the relevant labor pool. The district court phased out the promotion quota as the department finally began to promote blacks to higher ranks.[154] The court of appeals affirmed the district court order, and the Supreme Court affirmed in a 5–4 plurality decision.[155]

Justice Brennan wrote a plurality opinion that was joined by four justices—Justices Brennan, Marshall, Blackmun, and Powell.[156] As in *Sheet Metal Workers*, Justice Brennan's opinion noted the Court's historical inability to agree on a constitutional standard to govern the use of benign racial classifications, but found that the district court remedy in *Paradise* satisfied even strict scrutiny.[157] Justice Brennan found that the district court order advanced the compelling state interest of providing a remedy for the department's "pervasive, systematic, and obstinate" past discrimination,[158] and rejected the argument that the district court order was really designed to impose a particular racial balance on the department.[159] Justice Brennan also concluded that the district court order was narrowly tailored in light of the order's temporary and flexible nature; the Department's continual resistance to the court's prior antidiscrimination orders; the need to provide some form of meaningful remedy for black troopers; the order's application only where qualified black troopers were available; and the fact that the order was contingent on the department's own failure to adopt a nondiscriminatory promotion plan.[160] Justice Brennan believed that the district court's use of a 25 percent black promotion goal was constitutionally permissible, and that the district court's use of a 50 percent promotion quota was also a constitutionally permissible means of speeding up compliance with the 25 percent goal in the absence of the department's adoption of its own nondiscriminatory promotion plan.[161] Moreover, the one-for-one quota did not impermissibly burden white troopers because no white troopers were discharged as a result of the quota, and half of the promotions made under the quota went to whites.[162] Finally, Justice Brennan stressed that the equitable discretion of the district court in fashioning an effective remedy was owed deference after a Fourteenth Amendment violation had been established, and here the district court had not abused its discretion.[163]

Justice Powell, who joined Justice Brennan's plurality opinion, also wrote a separate concurrence emphasizing the narrowness of the district court order and the limited burden that it imposed on innocent whites.[164] He stressed the need for strict scrutiny of race-conscious remedies even when those remedies were imposed by a court after an adjudicated constitutional violation, and he rejected the suggestion made in Justice Stevens's concurrence that the district court should have the same broad remedial discretion that the Supreme Court had accorded federal district courts in school desegregation cases.[165] Justice Powell also listed five factors that he found relevant to the strict-scrutiny, narrow-tailoring inquiry: (i) the efficacy of alternative remedies; (ii) the duration of the remedy, (iii) the correspondence between percentage hiring goals and relevant minority population percentages; (iv) the availability of waiver provisions; and (v) the effect on innocent third parties.[166] For Justice Powell, therefore, the equal protection clause imposed the same restrictions on race-conscious judicial remedies for constitutional violations that it imposed on state officials wishing to use racial classifications for invidious reasons.[167]

The fifth vote to uphold the district court order was provided by Justice Stevens, whose opinion concurring in the judgment viewed the district court order as within the court's equitable discretion to fashion an appropriate remedy for an established constitutional violation.[168] Justice Stevens disagreed with the plurality's application of strict scrutiny to a judicial remedial order, arguing that Supreme Court school desegregation cases such as *Swann v. Charlotte-Mecklenburg Board of Education*[169] granted the district court broad equitable discretion to fashion effective remedies for adjudicated equal protection violations.[170] For Justice Stevens, therefore, the equal protection clause imposed more stringent constraints on both invidious discrimination and voluntary affirmative action than it imposed on court-ordered remedial affirmative action.[171]

Justice White dissented on the ground that the district court had exceeded its equitable powers. He also endorsed much of Justice O'Connor's dissenting opinion, although he did not join that opinion.[172]

Justice O'Connor dissented, in an opinion signed by Justices Rehnquist and Scalia, on the ground that the district court's remedial order was not sufficiently narrow.[173] Justice O'Connor cited *Wygant* for the proposition that strict scrutiny applied even to racial classifications that disadvantaged the white majority rather than racial minorities. Although the district court had a compelling interest in fashioning a remedy for the defendant's egregious discriminatory conduct, the district court remedy was not narrowly tailored enough to satisfy strict scrutiny. The district court's one-for-one promotion quota was not designed to remedy the effects of past discrimination, but rather was designed to coerce the department into adopting a nondiscriminatory promotion plan. Even if the goal of the quota was to eradicate the effects of past discrimination, the 50 percent quota was not narrowly tailored to that end because blacks made up only 25 percent of the relevant workforce. The plurality's argument that the 50 percent quota was permissible as a means of speeding compliance with the district court's ultimate goal of increasing black representation to 25 percent in each trooper rank was inadequate because that same argument could have been used to justify even a 100 percent minority promotion quota. Quotas that departed from relevant population percentages imposed too great a burden on nonminority workers.[174] Justice O'Connor believed that there were less restrictive, nonracial alternatives for getting the department to develop a nondiscriminatory promotion plan. The district court could have appointed a trustee to oversee the development of such a plan, or it could have imposed fines or other contempt penalties for continued noncompliance with district court remedial orders. However, the district court did not even *consider* nonracial alternatives, which a court must do in order to satisfy the requirements of strict scrutiny.[175]

The Court's post-*Fullilove* cases suggested the emergence of certain trends in the views of particular justices concerning the issue of affirmative action. By the time *Wygant* was decided, Justice O'Connor had replaced Justice Stewart on the Supreme Court, and like Justice Stewart, she was relatively unreceptive to affirmative action plans. In *Wygant,* four justices—Justices Powell, Burger, Rehnquist, and O'Connor—favored strict scrutiny; rejected both the role-model and general-societal-discrimination justifications for affirmative action; insisted on a very tight fit between the state interest and the nature of the remedy; and disfavored layoffs of innocent whites.[176] Justices Powell, Burger, and Rehnquist simply ruled out layoffs for affirmative action because they were excessively burdensome.[177] Justice O'Connor became the champion of the narrowness requirement by emphasizing the need for careful scrutiny of the relationship between target populations and prior injuries, although she did recognize the goal of diversity as a potentially compelling state interest.[178] Justice Stevens endorsed both the diversity and role-model justifications for affirmative action, exhibiting an inclination to focus more on the prospective benefits of affirmative action than on the relationship between the remedy and past violations.[179] Five justices—Justices Brennan, Marshall, Blackmun, Stevens, and Powell—voted to uphold fairly stringent racial quotas against recalcitrant defendants in *Sheet Metal Workers*[180] and *Paradise*[181] after the defendants had been adjudicated guilty of past discrimination. In *Paradise*, Justice Scalia had the opportunity to cast his first vote in an affirmative action case after replacing Justice Burger on the Supreme Court, voting to invalidate the plan because it was not sufficiently narrow.[182] Considered together, *Wygant, Sheet Metal Workers,* and *Paradise* suggested that court-ordered remedial plans were likely to fare better than voluntary affirmative action plans adopted without a finding of past constitutional or statutory violations.[183] However, that generalization did not seem to hold under the Supreme Court's Title VII cases.

5. *Title VII*

In addition to the Court's string of plurality decisions concerning application of the equal protection clause to benign racial classifications, the Court has decided a line of Title VII cases that have potential equal protection implications. In fact, some of the Court's decisions, such as *Sheet Metal Workers*,[184] expressly consider both Title VII and equal protection issues. Title VII prohibits certain types of discrimination in employment, including race and gender discrimination in hiring, promotions, and admission to apprenticeship or other training programs. Because Title VII is not subject to the state-action restriction of the Fourteenth Amendment, the Title VII antidiscrimination provisions apply to both private and governmental employers.[185] Several of the Supreme Court's Title VII cases are interesting because of what they reveal about the justices' views concerning the imposition of burdens on innocent whites and about the permissibility of voluntary affirmative action initiatives. Unlike the early equal protection cases, most of the pertinent Title VII cases were decided by majority opinions.

i. *Weber* (1979)

In *United Steelworkers of America v. Weber*,[186] decided in 1979, the Supreme Court held that Title VII permitted a private union and a private employer to adopt a voluntary, race-conscious affirmative action plan. The employer, Kaiser Aluminum & Chemical Corp., had a long history of racial segregation in its skilled-craft job categories. This segregation resulted in large part from the fact that blacks had traditionally been excluded from the craft unions that trained workers for skilled jobs. In order to remedy the conspicuous racial imbalance in plants, and to avoid potential litigation and the loss of federal contract funds, Kaiser entered into a 1974 collective bargaining agreement with the United Steelworkers union establishing the affirmative action plan at issue. The plan provided hiring goals for blacks that reflected the percentage of blacks in the local labor force for each Kaiser plant. Kaiser was to meet these goals by establishing on-the-job training programs for unskilled Kaiser production workers, and by reserving 50 percent of the openings in those training programs for black workers until the hiring goals were met. A white worker at Kaiser's Gramercy, Louisiana, plant filed a class action challenge to the program under Title VII, arguing that the plan impermissibly admitted to the training program black workers who had less seniority than white workers who were not admitted. The district court and court of appeals held that the racial preference violated Title VII, but the Supreme Court reversed in a 5-2 decision.[187]

The Court's majority opinion—written by Justice Brennan and signed by Justices Stewart, White, Marshall, and Blackmun—held that the voluntary nature of the challenged plan and its goal of redressing past racial discrimination in traditionally segregated job categories made it consistent with Title VII's primary concern for improving the economic plight of blacks in the nation by increasing black employment opportunities.[188] Justice Brennan stated that neither the race-conscious nature of the plan nor its utilization of numerical quotas designed to achieve racial proportionality rendered the plan illegal. Moreover, the plan did not "unnecessarily trammel the interests of the white employees" because it did not require the discharge of any white workers; it did not totally preclude whites from securing positions in the training program; and it was a temporary plan that was intended to cure past discrimination rather than maintain racial balance.[189] The effect of the decision was to establish that an adjudicated Title VII violation is not a prerequisite to voluntary race-conscious remedies, at least with respect to traditionally segregated job categories.[190]

Justice Blackmun concurred, suggesting that an arguable violation of Title VII might properly be required as a prerequisite to a valid voluntary remedy. He perceived a tension to be embedded in Title VII's concern with improving employment opportunities for blacks on the one hand and prohibiting employment discrimination against whites on the other. Accordingly, Justice Blackmun viewed an arguable-violation limitation on the scope of permissible voluntary affirmative action as a proper way of mediating this tension.[191] However, equitable considerations raised by the need to provide an effective remedy for past discrimination caused Justice Blackmun to conclude that the voluntary plan at issue in *Weber* was permissible under Title VII even though it remedied some past discrimination that did not technically violate Title VII.[192]

Justices Burger and Rehnquist wrote separate dissents asserting that Title VII simply prohibited race-conscious affirmative action.[193] Chief Justice Burger's brief dissent argued that the language of Title VII prohibited race-conscious affirmative action programs such as the program involved in *Weber* because the language of Title VII expressly prohibited racial discrimination in the selection of employees for training programs. Although remedial affirmative action measures might be desirable as a policy matter, Congress—not the Supreme Court—would have to amend Title VII in order to make such programs permissible under the statute.[194] Justice Rehnquist wrote a long dissent, joined by Chief Justice Burger, arguing that the language of Title VII, its legislative history, and Supreme Court precedents interpreting that statute all established that Title VII precluded voluntary race-conscious affirmative action.[195] Justice Rehnquist's opinion contained an extensive discussion of the legislative history of Title VII, concluding that Title VII did not permit the use of racial preferences or quotas in order to correct racial imbalance.[196]

Justices Powell and Stevens did not participate in the decision.[197]

ii. *Stotts* (1984)

In 1984, the Supreme Court decided *Firefighters Local Union No. 1784 v. Stotts*,[198] which held that Title VII prohibited an affirmative action consent decree from overriding the seniority rights of nonminority workers.[199] Between 1977 and 1979, the United States and individual black firefighters filed three separate lawsuits suits against the Memphis, Tennessee, Fire Department, alleging that the department had engaged in a pattern and practice of race and gender discrimination in its hiring and promotion decisions. After *Stotts* was certified as a class action, the discrimination claims were settled and incorporated into a judicial consent decree that adopted numerical hiring and promotion goals designed to remedy the effects of past discrimination. The ultimate goal of the consent decree was to increase minority representation in the Memphis Fire Department so that it would reflect the proportion of minorities in the Memphis workforce. Then, however, a projected budget deficit caused the city to lay off municipal employees, including firefighters. The district court enjoined the city from using seniority as the sole criterion in making layoffs because the use of seniority would have a discriminatory impact on the minority firefighters who had been newly hired and promoted under the consent decree.[200] The Sixth Circuit affirmed the district court ruling,[201] but the Supreme Court reversed in a 6-3 decision.[202]

Justice White wrote a majority opinion for five members of the Supreme Court—Justices White, Burger, Powell, Rehnquist, and O'Connor.[203] Justice Stevens, concurring in the judgment, provided the sixth vote for the Court's holding.[204] Justice White's majority opinion held that the case was not moot, even though all of the laid-off white firefighters had been rehired after one month, because those firefighters continued to suffer the loss of one month's back pay and seniority.[205] The majority opinion did not discuss the fact that the layoffs were actually made in reverse alphabetical order because all affected black and white workers were hired on the same day and had accumulated the same seniority.[206] Addressing the merits, the majority opinion stated that the consent decree did not by its terms permit affirmative action concerns to override seniority.[207] In addition, the Court held that the district court lacked the authority to modify the Title VII consent decree in a way that would protect the minority beneficiaries of the original decree from unanticipated layoffs.[208] Justice White cited the Court's prior decision in *Teamsters v. United States*[209] for the proposition that special Title VII protections accorded *bona fide* seniority plans under § 703(h),[210] as well as the Title VII restriction in § 706(g)[211] prohibiting courts from making particular remedies available to anyone other than the actual victims of discrimination, precluded the district court from adopting a plan that would lay off white firefighters with greater seniority than the minority firefighters who would retain their jobs.[212] Justice White's opinion had the effect of limiting race-conscious affirmative action remedies under Title VII to the *actual victims* of identifiable discrimination, rather than to members of *racial groups* who had historically been targets of discrimination.[213]

Justice O'Connor concurred, emphasizing her belief that the district court had abused its discretion in seeking to maintain a particular racial balance.[214] Justice O'Connor did not think that the case had become moot, because the one-month enhanced seniority that the black firefighters received as a result of the district court injunction constituted a collateral effect of the lower court judgments that could not be eliminated merely by vacating those judgments as moot under the *Munsingwear* doctrine.[215] On the merits, Justice O'Connor believed that the seniority claims of the laid-off white firefighters outweighed the affirmative action claims of the retained black firefighters because the seniority system was not adopted with racial animus in a way that violated Title VII; race-conscious remedies could not be used in the absence of a Title VII violation merely to preserve racial balance; the consent decree itself did not bar the use of seniority; and the district court could not modify the consent decree to give a preference to black firefighters who were not themselves actual victims of discrimination.[216]

Justice Stevens concurred in the judgment.[217] He did not think that the case was moot because the district court injunction continued to prohibit the city from giving effect to seniority in a way that would upset racial balance.[218] However, Justice Stevens did distance himself from the Court's discussion of Title VII, arguing that Title VII was not relevant to the validity of any affirmative action that might have been authorized by a voluntary consent decree.[219] Nevertheless, Justice Stevens did not believe that the consent decree authorized preferential protection from seniority-based layoffs, and the district court did not have the power to modify the decree because there were no unanticipated changed circumstances that would justify such a modification.[220]

Justice Blackmun dissented in an opinion joined by Justices Brennan and Marshall that accused the majority of straining to make novel Title VII law in a moot case that did not present a justiciable controversy.[221] Justice Blackmun believed the case to be moot because all of the laid-off firefighters had been re-hired after one month—well before the case had been argued in the Supreme Court. Moreover, any collateral consequences of the district court order could be eliminated by vacating the lower court judgments under the *Munsingwear* doctrine because nothing precluded the city from voluntarily awarding back pay or lost seniority to laid-off white firefighters.[222]

On the merits, Justice Blackmun did not believe that any conflict existed between the city's seniority plan and the district court's affirmative action plan that was properly before the Supreme Court. The Supreme Court should have considered only whether the district court had abused its discretion in entering a *preliminary* injunction. No permanent injunction had ever been entered resolving the merits of the underlying issues, and those issues were not before the Supreme Court.[223] Moreover, nothing in the preliminary injunction *required* the city to lay off white workers. For example, the city was free to reduce the working hours of all workers in order to avoid layoffs altogether. Therefore, the city—not the district court—had decided to place seniority in conflict with affirmative action.[224] Justice Blackmun also argued that the terms of the consent decree explicitly authorized the district court's preferential layoff policy in order to "effectuate the purposes" of the decree.[225] He also argued that the city's budget deficit constituted changed circumstances that permitted the district court to modify the consent decree, and that Title VII seniority protections did not prohibit such a modification.[226] Finally, Justice Blackmun read *Teamsters v. United States*[227] to mean that any actual-victim limitations contained in Title VII applied only in the context of make-whole, individual remedies. There was no actual-victim limitation that prohibited the use of classwide, race-conscious affirmative action remedies.[228]

After *Stotts* it appeared that five members of the Court were unwilling to permit a district court to order race-conscious affirmative action remedies in a Title VII pattern-and-practice case—the typical Title VII case, which is based on statistical disparities between white and minority workers. Rather, it seemed that the Court would limit the availability of race-conscious remedies to suits filed by individuals who were the actual victims of discriminatory employment practices.[229] Justice Blackmun's dissent argued that such an actual-victim limitation applied only to individual, make-whole remedies, and not to classwide, affirmative action remedies. Subsequently, a majority of the Court would go on to adopt Justice Blackmun's view in *Local 28, Sheet Metal Workers International Association v. Equal Employment Opportunity Commission*.[230] Even Justice White, the author of the majority opinion in *Stotts*, would concede in *Sheet Metal Workers* that some race-conscious remedies were permissible under Title VII for nonvictims.[231]

iii. *Firefighters v. Cleveland* (1986)

In 1986—on the same day that the Supreme Court decided *Sheet Metal Workers*[232]—the Court also decided *Local 93, International Association of Firefighters v. Cleveland*.[233] In *Firefighters v. Cleveland*, the Court upheld by a vote of 6–3 a consent decree calling for race-conscious promotions in the Cleveland Fire Department. The consent decree settled a suit filed by minority firefighters who had alleged discrimination in the city's hiring, assignment, and promotion of firefighters. Although the minority firefighters and the city agreed to the use of affirmative action quotas to remedy the city's admitted prior discrimination, the firefighters union intervened in the district court to oppose the proposed consent decree. The United States intervened in support of the union, even though it had previously rejected the union's position in *Weber*.[234] The district court approved the consent decree; the court of appeals affirmed; and the Supreme Court affirmed.[235]

Justice Brennan wrote a majority opinion signed by six members of the Court—Justices Brennan, Marshall, Blackmun, Powell, Stevens, and O'Connor—rejecting the union intervenor's argument that Title VII precluded race-conscious remedies designed to benefit those who were not themselves actual victims of discrimination by the city.[236] Justice Brennan's opinion first held that whatever limitations Title VII might impose on judicially imposed remedies, those limitations did not apply to a settlement that was voluntarily entered into by the parties. This was because the legislative history revealed that Title VII rested on a congressional policy favoring the voluntary settlement of employment discrimination claims. Moreover, it was the *voluntary nature* of a settlement that mattered, not whether the settlement took the *form* of a private contract or a judicial consent decree.[237]

Justice Brennan next addressed the union's argument that Title VII imposed an actual-victim limitation on the use of race-conscious remedies. That argument was based on the final sentence of § 706(g), which states in pertinent part that "[n]o order of the court shall require the hiring, reinstatement, or promotion of an individual as an employee . . . if such individual . . . was refused employment or advancement . . . for any reason other than discrimination on account of race, color, religion, sex or national origin or in violation of section 2000e-3(a) of this title."[238] Consistent with *Stotts*,[239] the union argued that this language limited all enumerated Title VII remedies to the actual victims of discrimination. Although the actual-victim limitation of *Stotts* had that same day been rejected by six members of the Court in *Sheet Metal Workers*,[240] the Supreme Court chose to dispose of *Firefighters v. Cleveland* by holding that the scope of permissible consent-decree remedies under Title VII was broader than the scope of permissible judicial orders. The fact that a court might not have been *authorized* to enter a particular order after trial did not preclude the court from entering that same order with the consent of the parties, as long as no statute *prohibited* the court from entering that order. Justice Brennan concluded that Title VII did not prohibit voluntary affirmative action, and he distinguished *Stotts* as a case in which the lower court's *modification* of the subject consent decree violated Title VII.[241]

Finally, Justice Brennan rejected the union intervenor's claim that the case could not be settled without the union's consent. The union could not prevent the other parties from settling their dispute because the consent decree did not impose any obligations on the union or terminate any other legal claims that the union might have. Justice Brennan left it to the district court on remand to determine whether the union had any Fourteenth Amendment or other legal claims against the city emanating from the consent decree.[242]

Justice O'Connor concurred in the majority opinion, emphasizing that third parties affected by consent decrees retained the right to challenge those decrees on constitutional or statutory grounds.[243] She believed that the majority opinion was narrow, and that voluntary race-conscious remedies could still be found on remand to violate the equal protection clause or the antidiscrimination provisions of § 703 of Title VII. Justice O'Connor also asserted that any predicate conditions established by *Weber* for race-conscious affirmative action under Title VII, such as the existence of prior discrimination, remained undisturbed by the Court's holding in *Firefighters v. Cleveland.*[244]

Justice White dissented on the grounds that Title VII applied to voluntary consent decrees as well as to judicially imposed remedies.[245] He did not believe that the scope of voluntary race-conscious remedies could exceed the scope of remedies that a court was authorized to order. Both were subject to the same prior-discrimination predicate adopted by the Supreme Court in *Weber.* Accordingly, an employer could not voluntarily agree to a race-conscious remedy in the absence of prior discrimination, and a court could not adopt such a remedy as part of a consent decree. Justice White stated that, although *Sheet Metal Workers* read Title VII to permit race-conscious remedies for nonvictims in cases of particularly egregious prior discrimination, Title VII did not permit such remedies for nonvictims in the absence of egregious discrimination. Justice White believed that, under the facts of *Firefighters v. Cleveland,* § 706(g) of Title VII prohibited the use of race-conscious promotion quotas because the beneficiaries of those quotas were not the actual victims of prior discrimination. Moreover, the burden imposed on innocent whites in order to achieve racial balance was as serious as the layoffs that had been invalidated on Title VII grounds in *Stotts,* and on equal protection grounds in *Wygant.*[246]

Justice Rehnquist dissented on similar grounds in an opinion joined by Chief Justice Burger, arguing that the *Firefighters v. Cleveland* consent decree was precluded by the Court's decision in *Stotts.*[247] Although the majority believed that a voluntary consent decree could include race-conscious affirmative action that would not be permitted in a judicially imposed order, Justice Rehnquist saw no basis for such a distinction. Under the facts of *Firefighters v. Cleveland,* the plaintiffs and the city may have agreed to certain affirmative action relief, but that relief was coercive rather than voluntary with respect to the union that had opposed it.[248] Justice Rehnquist stated that the legislative history of Title VII might be inconclusive, but the express language of § 706(g) limited judicial remedies to the actual victims of discrimination. For Justice Rehnquist, this was true whether the remedy came in the form of a coercive order or a consent decree.[249]

iv. *Johnson v. Transportation Agency* (1987)

In 1987, the Supreme Court upheld a voluntary affirmative action plan adopted by the Santa Clara County, California, municipal transportation agency in *Johnson v. Transportation Agency.*[250] The plan was adopted unilaterally by the agency, rather than as part of a litigation settlement agreement. Although the plan did not utilize quotas, it established short-term annual hiring and promotion goals for women, minorities, and handicapped individuals after concluding that mere antidiscrimination laws were not sufficient to remedy the effects of past discrimination. The long-term goal of the plan was to attain a workforce whose composition reflected the proportions of those groups in the local labor force. The feature of the plan that was at issue before the Supreme Court was its designation of gender as a preferential factor to be taken into account when making promotions to traditionally segregated job classifications in which women were significantly underrepresented, although the Court stated that its analysis was applicable to racial minorities as well.[251] The plan was challenged by a male employee who was passed over for promotion in favor a female employee possessing similar qualifications. Although the defendant was a government agency, the challenge concerned only Title VII claims and did not encompass Fourteenth Amendment equal protection claims.[252] The district court invalidated the plan, finding that it violated the gender discrimination provisions of Title VII as interpreted by the Supreme Court in *Weber.*[253] The Ninth Circuit Court of Appeals reversed. The Supreme Court then affirmed, upholding the plan by a vote of 6–3.[254]

Justice Brennan wrote a majority opinion signed by five members of the Court—Justices Brennan, Marshall, Blackmun, Powell, and Stevens—that held that the Title VII prohibition on affirmative action was not as stringent as the constitutional prohibition on affirmative action found in the equal protection clause.[255] Justice Brennan first stated that the plaintiff had the burden of proving that the agency's affirmative action plan was invalid under the standards adopted by the Court in *Weber*. He stressed that *Weber* did not require an employer to admit past discrimination, or even an arguable violation of Title VII, as a predicate to adopting a race-conscious affirmative action plan. The only predicate required by Title VII was a "conspicuous . . . imbalance in traditionally segregated job categories."[256] The agency plan satisfied that requirement by seeking to approximate female population percentages in the relevant local labor forces for job classifications that had been strikingly imbalanced.[257]

Justice Brennan next found that the agency plan satisfied the *Weber* requirement that an affirmative action plan not unnecessarily trammel the rights of male employees. The agency plan permitted the consideration of gender as one factor in making employment decisions; it used flexible goals rather than strict quotas to find qualified female workers; and it did not automatically exclude males from any positions. The fact that the plan did not have a specific termination date was inconsequential because the plan was intended to *attain* gender balance in the agency workforce, rather than *maintain* such balance for some indefinite period of time.[258] Justice Brennan concluded by emphasizing that voluntary affirmative action facilitated the Title VII policy favoring voluntary efforts to eliminate the vestiges of discrimination.[259]

Justice Stevens, who signed the Brennan majority opinion, wrote a concurring opinion emphasizing that Title VII should be read to permit voluntary affirmative action plans even in the absence of arguable past violations of Title VII.[260] Although the Supreme Court initially interpreted Title VII to prohibit any type of preferential treatment in employment, since its 1978 and 1979 decisions in *Bakke* and *Weber*, the Court had permitted voluntary preferential treatment for minorities.[261] Although that reading of Title VII was at odds with his view of the actual intent of drafters, Justice Stevens favored adhering to that view in order to promote doctrinal stability and deference to management prerogatives aimed at improving the plight of minorities.[262] Justice Stevens also thought that Title VII permitted employers to use voluntary affirmative action to pursue goals such as prospective diversity, even if those goals were not tied to the need to remedy past violations of Title VII.[263]

Justice O'Connor did not sign Justice Brennan's majority opinion but wrote a separate opinion concurring in the judgment.[264] She argued that both Title VII and the equal protection clause required enough evidence to establish a prima facie case of prior discrimination before a race-conscious remedy would be permissible. This predicate struck the proper balance between the competing interests of minority and nonminority workers affected by a proposed affirmative action plan. Justice O'Connor also emphasized that the desire to remedy the effects of general societal discrimination was not an adequate basis for affirmative action.[265] Justice O'Connor, however, did not favor requiring formal findings of prior discrimination.[266] Like Justice Stevens, Justice O'Connor disagreed with the Supreme Court's earlier construction of Title VII in *Weber* permitting race-conscious affirmative action, but she too believed that *stare decisis* now required adherence to the *Weber* approach.[267] Under the facts of *Johnson v. Transportation Agency*, Justice O'Connor concluded that the agency plan satisfied the standards of *Weber* and *Wygant* because it was predicated on a conspicuous gender imbalance; it had realistic short-term goals based on population percentages of *qualified* women in the labor force for particular job categories; and it considered gender as only one of a number of factors in making the challenged promotion decision.[268]

Justice White dissented, arguing that *Weber* should be overruled because it had come to permit affirmative action remedies based upon mere imbalance in the workforce rather than on a showing of intentional and systematic discrimination.[269] In voting with the majority in *Weber*, Justice White had understood the required predicate to be that the employer's voluntary affirmative action program was adopted to remedy past intentional discrimination. However, a majority of the Court had now interpreted *Weber* to require only a manifest imbalance in the workforce, and this constituted a perversion of Title VII.[270]

Justice Scalia dissented in an opinion that was joined by Chief Justice Rehnquist and joined in part by Justice White.[271] He argued that the majority had transformed Title VII from a statute that prohibited discrimination on the basis of race or gender into a statute guaranteeing that such discrimination would often occur.[272] Justice Scalia emphasized that the purpose of the agency affirmative action plan at issue could not have been to remedy prior discrimination because the district court found that the county had not engaged in prior gender discrimination. Rather, the goal of the plan was to attain the level of race and gender balance that the county deemed desirable. Although the majority and Justice O'Connor suggested that gender was only one of a number of factors that contributed to the promotion decision at issue, the district court found that gender was the dispositive factor—the promoted employee would not have received the promotion if she had not been a woman.[273]

Justice Scalia also argued that the majority disregarded the Supreme Court's prior decision in *Wygant* by permitting affirmative action to be used as a remedy for mere general societal discrimination, rather than as a remedy for particularized acts of prior discrimination committed by the employer adopting the plan at issue. Although this was a Title VII rather than an equal protection case, the societal-discrimination restriction that the Constitution applied under *Wygant* was also relevant under Title VII, because there was no reason to believe that the Constitution and Title VII tolerated different degrees of discrimination.[274] Justice Scalia asserted that the majority ignored *Sheet Metal Workers*, which limited the use of affirmative action for the benefit of nonvictims to cases of unusual or egregious discrimination. Moreover, the majority tacitly rewrote the *Weber* requirement limiting affirmative action to "traditionally segregated job categor[ies]" so that the requirement could now be satisfied by mere imbalance rather than a history of conscious exclusionary discrimination.[275]

Justice Scalia finally argued, in a portion of the opinion signed by Chief Justice Rehnquist, that *Weber* should be overruled. *Weber* was wrong when it was decided, and the majority simply compounded that error by extending *Weber* from private to public employers.[276] In addition, Justice Scalia suggested that the majority opinion inverted the meaning of Title VII because it was now in the interest of employers to hire minimally qualified minority group members—rather than the best qualified workers—in order to avoid statistical imbalances that might result in the filing of Title VII suits.[277] Justice Scalia then offered a Marxist interpretation of the majority opinion, arguing that the burdens of the voluntary affirmative action programs that the Court had authorized would ultimately benefit corporate and bureaucratic interests at the expense of the working-class employees that the majority purported to be helping.[278]

The Title VII cases suggest—contrary to the implications of *Wygant*, *Sheet Metal Workers*, and *Paradise*—that voluntary affirmative action plans may ultimately fare better than court-ordered plans because voluntary plans can exceed the scope of permissible court-ordered remedies, which are available only after adjudicated constitutional or statutory violations. Five justices—Justices Brennan, Marshall, Blackmun, Powell, and Stevens—voted to uphold both the *Firefighters v. Cleveland* and *Johnson v. Transportation Agency* plans, which included statistical goals resembling quotas, while agreeing to explicit language stating that voluntary remedies could exceed the scope of court-ordered remedies even if the voluntary remedies were incorporated into judicially approved consent decrees.[279] In *Firefighters v. Cleveland*, these five justices also rejected the argument that permissible affirmative action remedies had to be limited to the actual victims of discrimination.[280] In addition, *Firefighters v. Cleveland* suggests that the voluntary assumption of an affirmative action burden by innocent whites may make that burden permissible, even when consent to the burden is more constructive than real.[281] Justice O'Connor has resisted the idea that a voluntary affirmative action plan can exceed the scope of court-ordered affirmative action,[282] and Justices White, Rehnquist, and Scalia have objected to the use of affirmative action remedies to benefit anyone other than the actual victims of discrimination, arguing that affirmative action is unavailable to remedy general societal discrimination or to promote racial balance.[283]

In 1997, the Supreme Court granted certiorari in *Taxman v. Piscataway Township Board of Education*[284]—a case that is discussed in chapter 3, part

5, section iii. That case would have given the Court an opportunity to clarify further the meaning of Title VII, but the Court dismissed the writ of certiorari on the grounds of mootness when the parties settled the case prior to oral argument.[285]

6. Transition

Of the six constitutional affirmative action cases that the Supreme Court resolved by plurality decisions between 1974 and 1989, the Court invalidated the affirmative action plans under consideration in two and upheld the affirmative action plans under consideration in four. The Court invalidated the plans presented in *Wygant* and *Bakke*, and upheld the plans in *Paradise*, *Sheet Metal Workers*, *Fullilove*, and *United Jewish Organizations*. A liberal group of justices consisting of Justices Brennan, Marshall, and Blackmun voted to uphold the affirmative action plan at issue in each of the six cases.[286] A conservative group consisting of Justices Burger, Stewart, and Rehnquist voted only once to uphold the constitutionality of the affirmative action plan at issue.[287] Prior to the first constitutional decision that the Supreme Court would be able to resolve by majority opinion, Justices Stewart and Burger left the Court and were replaced by Justices O'Connor and Scalia, both of whom voted to invalidate each affirmative action plan that had been presented to them in a constitutional case.[288] In addition, Justice Powell had been replaced by Justice Kennedy. Accordingly, the Court that would go on to consider the transition cases of *Croson* and *Metro Broadcasting* contained a solid liberal bloc—consisting of Justices Brennan, Marshall, and Blackmun—that was receptive to affirmative action, and a solid conservative bloc—consisting of Justices Rehnquist, O'Connor, and Scalia—that was hostile to affirmative action. Of the remaining three justices, Justice Stevens appeared likely to join with the liberal bloc when he was convinced of the prospective benefit of the racial classification being used and was satisfied with the procedural surroundings out of which that classification had emerged.[289] Justice White, who has been reluctant to impose the burdens of affirmative action on innocent whites,[290] appeared likely to vote with the conservative bloc and to invalidate affirmative action plans when the federal government was not involved in the design of the plan.[291] Justice Kennedy did not sit on any constitutional affirmative action cases prior to the Court's issuance of a majority opinion in *Croson*.

3

The Majority Opinions

In 1989, after President Reagan's appointment of Justices O'Connor, Scalia, and Kennedy to the Supreme Court and his elevation of Justice Rehnquist to the position of chief justice,[1] the Court was able to issue its first majority opinion in a constitutional affirmative action case. The decision, rendered in *City of Richmond v. J.A. Croson Co.*,[2] invalidated a *Fullilove*-type minority set-aside program that had been adopted by the Richmond City Council. Justices Kennedy, White, and Stevens joined with the conservative group comprised of Justices Rehnquist, O'Connor, and Scalia to invalidate the plan 6–3.[3] Although several opinions were issued in the case, portions of Justice O'Connor's opinion attracted a five-justice majority.[4] The following year, in 1990, the Court again issued a majority opinion in an affirmative action case. In *Metro Broadcasting v. FCC*,[5] the Court upheld two broadcast licensing programs adopted by the FCC that were intended to give certain preferences to minorities in obtaining radio and television broadcast licenses. This time, Justices White and Stevens joined with the liberal group consisting of Justices Brennan, Marshall, and Blackmun in issuing a majority opinion that upheld the programs 5–4.[6] *Metro Broadcasting* was the last major decision in which the Supreme Court upheld the constitutionality of a racial affirmative action plan.[7] The Court's subsequent decision in *Northeastern Fla. Chapter of the Associated Gen. Contractors of Am. v. City of Jacksonville*[8] facilitated challenges to affirmative action programs, and the Court's decision in *Adarand Constructors v. Pena*[9] then overruled *Metro Broadcasting*.[10] *Adarand* was followed by a series of constitutional decisions concerning the Voting Rights Act of 1965 and a series of actions on petitions for certiorari that were systematically adverse to the affirmative action plans at issue.[11]

1. Croson *(1989)*

In 1989, the Court invalidated a minority set-aside program for contractors awarded municipal construction contracts in *City of Richmond v. J.A. Croson Co.*[12] The program adopted by the city of Richmond had been modeled after the federal program upheld by the Court in *Fullilove*, except that the Richmond program contained a 30 percent set-aside rather than the 10 percent set-aside contained in the *Fullilove* program.[13] Although the district court and the court of appeals had previously upheld the plan on the basis of *Fullilove*, the Supreme Court remanded the case to the court of appeals for reconsideration in light of its decision in *Wygant*, and then affirmed the court of appeals decision invalidating the plan after the remand.[14]

Justice O'Connor wrote a majority opinion, joined by Justices Rehnquist, White, Stevens, and Kennedy, holding that the Richmond set-aside plan was unconstitutional because the city had not made adequate findings of past discrimination, and because the fit between the racial quota and any past discrimination that might have existed was not sufficiently tight. Although the Richmond City Council had declared the plan to be remedial, there was inadequate evidence of prior discrimination in the construction trades by either the city or by private contractors. As a result, it could not be said that a 30 percent racial quota was necessary to remedy any past discrimination. Rather, the set-aside seemed designed simply to promote racial balance in a way that impermissibly treated contractors as members of racial groups rather than as individuals.[15]

Of the five justices who signed Justice O'Connor's majority opinion, only four—Justices O'Connor, Rehnquist, White, and Kennedy—agreed that strict scrutiny was appropriate for benign racial classifications.[16] Nevertheless, Justice Scalia provided a fifth vote for strict scrutiny, even though he was unwilling to sign Justice O'Connor's opinion.[17] Justices O'Connor, Rehnquist, White, and Kennedy also believed that general societal discrimination had to be remedied through race-neutral means rather than through the use of racial classifications[18]—a proposition with which Justice Scalia would also appear to agree.[19] Four justices—Justices O'Connor, Rehnquist, White, and Scalia—believed that the *Fullilove* set-aside was distinguishable from the Richmond plan because § 5 of the Fourteenth Amendment gave Congress the power to use remedial race-conscious classifications that the states did not possess.[20]

Although Justice Stevens signed those portions of Justice O'Connor's opinion that constituted the majority opinion of the Court, Justice Stevens did differ from the four other justices in the majority in significant respects. Unlike the majority, he did not believe that racial classifications were constitutionally limited to ameliorating past discrimination. Rather, he believed that racial classifications would be constitutional as long as they served a legitimate public purpose, including the provision of some prospective public benefit.[21] In addition, Justice Stevens did not believe that the standard-of-review issue was particularly important, arguing that the Court should instead analyze the characteristics of the advantaged and disadvantaged classes that might justify disparate treatment.[22]

Justice Kennedy signed the majority opinion but wrote a brief concurrence rejecting the argument that Congress possessed special powers under § 5 that permitted it to use racial classifications that would be unconstitutional if utilized by the states.[23] Justice Scalia, who did not sign the majority opinion, argued that racial classifications could be justified only where necessary to eliminate the state's own maintenance of an unconstitutional racial classification, such as the use of race-conscious remedies to desegregate previously segregated schools.[24]

Justice Marshall dissented in an opinion signed by Justices Brennan and Blackmun arguing that the Richmond set-aside plan was indistinguishable from the set-aside upheld by the Court in *Fullilove*.[25] Justice Marshall argued that the Richmond City Council's findings of past discrimination were adequate to permit the use of racial classifications because they were based upon testimony before the city council, were supported by overwhelming statistical evidence, and were further supported by the same congressional findings that were relied upon to uphold the *Fullilove* plan.[26] Justice Marshall also argued that intermediate scrutiny was appropriate for benign racial classifications. He believed that the Richmond plan satisfied such scrutiny because the state had a substantial interest in both remedying past discrimination and avoiding the use of state funds to reinforce the continuing effects of such discrimination, and because the set-aside was narrowly tailored to advance those interests without unduly burdening innocent whites.[27] Justice Marshall argued finally that it was ironic to read the Fourteenth Amendment, which had been enacted to guard against state abuses, in a way that limited the power of the states to *remedy* their own prior discrimination. He also emphasized that the majority's restrictions on the use of race-conscious affirmative action would have the effect of invalidating the many state and local affirmative action plans that had been adopted in reliance on the Court's decision upholding *Fullilove*.[28] Justice Blackmun, in a separate dissent signed by Justice Brennan, further stressed the irony entailed in having the United States Supreme Court invalidate an affirmative action plan that had been adopted by the "cradle of the Old Confederacy."[29]

2. Metro Broadcasting *(1990)*

In 1990, the Court issued its second majority affirmative action decision. In *Metro Broadcasting v. FCC*,[30] the Court upheld two minority preference plans that had been adopted by the FCC for the award of radio and television broadcast licenses. The first plan awarded enhancements for minority ownership in comparative licensing proceedings that enabled some minority applicants to obtain licenses even though they scored lower than nonminority applicants with respect to the other factors that are considered in making licensing determinations. This plan was adopted in order to increase broadcast diversity by increasing the number of minority-owned stations in the nation. The second plan permitted licenses held by broadcasters whose qualifications for continued ownership had been called into question to be transferred voluntarily to minority broadcast companies at discounted "distress sale" prices. This plan was adopted in order to help minority broadcasters overcome the obstacles to financing that had historically precluded minorities from acquiring broadcast licenses.[31]

Five justices—Justices Brennan, White, Marshall, Blackmun, and Stevens—voted to uphold the FCC plans in a majority opinion written by Justice Brennan. Justice Brennan treated the FCC plans as having been mandated by Congress, and cited *Fullilove* for the proposition that benign racial classifications adopted by Congress were entitled to appropriate deference in light of the powers granted Congress under the commerce clause, the spending clause, and § 5 of the Fourteenth Amendment, as well as the institutional competence of Congress operating as a national legislature.[32] Justice Brennan then went on to hold that such classifications are subject to intermediate scrutiny requiring them to be upheld if they "serve important governmental objectives and are substantially related to achievement of those objectives."[33] Justice Brennan distinguished the *Croson* strict-scrutiny requirement as inapplicable to congressional classifications, citing the portion of Justice O'Connor's *Croson* opinion that emphasized the special powers granted Congress under § 5 of the Fourteenth Amendment.[34]

Although Congress had made findings of past discrimination in the broadcast industry, the constitutionality of the FCC plans did not depend upon the adequacy of those plans as a remedy for past discrimination.[35] Justice Brennan's opinion held that the FCC plans satisfied intermediate scrutiny because they were designed to advance a substantial governmental interest in promoting broadcast diversity, and they were substantially related to that interest.[36] Justice Brennan emphasized that he was not simply deferring to Congress or the FCC on a question of constitutional law, but noted that the expertise of Congress and the FCC was sufficient to establish an empirical nexus between minority ownership and broadcast diversity that was adequate to withstand constitutional scrutiny.[37] He rejected the suggestion that the plans were the product of mere racial stereotyping, citing empirical evidence to support the nexus between ownership and diversity.[38] Justice Brennan also found that the plans were narrowly drafted; that they had been adopted only after the failure of less restrictive alternatives; that they were subject to constant reevaluation by Congress and the FCC; and that administrative and judicial review would ensure their proper application in individual cases.[39] Finally, the plans did not impose impermissible burdens on nonminorities because they interfered only with future expectations and applied only to a limited number of licenses.[40] Justice Brennan asserted that the plans did not constitute quotas or set-asides.[41]

Justice Stevens wrote a brief concurring opinion stating that the Court was correct to focus on future benefits rather than remedial justifications in scrutinizing affirmative action plans.[42] He reaffirmed his view, first expressed in *Fullilove*, that racial classifications should be upheld only in those rare circumstances in which the reasons for the classifications are "clearly identified and unquestionably legitimate."[43] In addition, language in Justice Stevens's opinion suggests that he believes mere rational-basis scrutiny to be sufficient for affirmative action programs.[44]

Four justices—Justices O'Connor, Rehnquist, Scalia, and Kennedy—dissented in an opinion written by Justice O'Connor.[45] Justice O'Connor first emphasized that the equal protection clause embodied a constitutional guarantee that citizens would be treated by their government as individuals and not merely as members of racial groups. As a result, strict scrutiny of racial classifications was required in order to honor that guarantee and to ensure that citizens were not made the victims of racial stereotypes and stigmas.[46] Justice O'Connor rejected Justice Brennan's purported distinction of *Croson*, arguing that because the equal protection component of the Fifth Amendment is coextensive with the equal protection clause of the Fourteenth Amendment, both congressional and state racial classification must be equally subject to strict scrutiny.[47] She then distinguished *Fullilove* on three grounds: *Fullilove* was a case that turned on Congress's exercise of its special power to act with respect to the states under § 5 of the Fourteenth Amendment, whereas the FCC affirmative action plans did not entail any exercise of regulation respecting the states; *Fullilove* was limited to congressional classifications designed to remedy past discrimination, whereas the FCC plans were implemented in order to promote diversity; and *Fullilove* required a higher standard of review than the intermediate scrutiny that the majority used to uphold the FCC plans.[48] Justice O'Connor argued that reduced scrutiny for benign racial classifications was insupportable both because it was difficult to distinguish benign from malevolent classifications, and because the constitutional right to be treated as an individual rather than a member of a group made racial classifications inherently non-benign.[49] Justice O'Connor then stressed that the dispute over the proper standard of review was important and was not a mere lawyers' quibble over words.[50]

Justice O'Connor argued that the FCC plans could not survive strict scrutiny because they did not serve a compelling state interest and they were not narrowly tailored. The only state interest that had in the past been viewed as sufficiently compelling for equal protection scrutiny was the interest in remedying the effects of past discrimination, but the FCC plan was not implemented in order to remedy the effects of past discrimination. Rather, the FCC plan was designed to promote broadcast diversity, which is not a compelling state interest. The goal of promoting diversity—like the goals of providing role models, promoting racial balance, and remedying the effects of general societal discrimination that were found to be constitutionally inadequate in *Croson* and *Wygant*—is amorphous and has no logical stopping point. Moreover, the goal of promoting broadcast diversity poses the risk that the government will become actively involved in determining which ideas and viewpoints will be presented to the public in a way that presents First Amendment problems.[51]

According to Justice O'Connor, the FCC plans were not narrowly tailored because they promoted racial stereotyping by presuming that people think in ways that are associated with their race, thereby once again violating the constitutional right that citizens have to be treated as individuals rather than members of groups.[52] As a result, the FCC plans were both overinclusive and underinclusive because they used race as a proxy for viewpoint-diversity objectives that could have been better pursued in a race-neutral manner.[53] Although there might be some relationship between station ownership and broadcast viewpoint, there is not enough evidence of such a nexus to survive even intermediate scrutiny. The FCC programs are not supported by evidence of a nexus between ownership and diversity but ultimately rest on nothing more than the D.C. Circuit's assumption that such a nexus exists.[54] Finally, Justice O'Connor argued that the FCC plans were impermissibly burdensome on nonminorities because of the great monetary value of the broadcast licenses that they were precluded from receiving. This was especially true with respect to the FCC's distress sale policy because it amounted to the most rigid quota that there can be—a 100 percent minority set-aside.[55]

Justice Kennedy wrote a separate concurrence, signed by Justice Scalia, equating the absence of strict scrutiny in the majority's *Metro Broadcasting* decision with the Court's 1896 decision in *Plessy v. Ferguson*,[56] arguing that in both decisions the Court simply deferred to the legislature with respect to the reasonableness of racial classifications.[57] Justice Kennedy thought that *Metro Broadcasting* was also similar to *Plessy* in its fallacious belief that a court is able to distinguish between benign and malevolent acts of discrimination, or to determine accurately who was and was not a minority. Justice Kennedy quoted provisions from the law of Hitler's Third Reich and from South African law to emphasize his point.[58] Finally, Justice Kennedy feared the racial stigmatization that he thought would be produced by the majority's decision.[59]

3. Northeastern Florida *(1993)*

The Supreme Court's 1993 decision in *Northeastern Fla. Chapter of the Associated Gen. Contractors of Am. v. City of Jacksonville*[60] did not directly involve the merits of affirmative action, but rather involved the issue of standing to challenge affirmative action programs. In *Northeastern Florida*, the Court upheld the standing of a nonminority construction trade association to challenge a minority set-aside. The set-aside was a municipal program adopted by the city of Jacksonville, Florida, in 1984, which reserved 10 percent of the city's construction funds for minority, and women contractors.[61] The plan was originally modeled on the federal set-aside program upheld by the Supreme Court in *Fullilove*.[62] However, the Jacksonville City Council modified the plan during the course of the *Northeastern Florida* litigation, after the Supreme Court had issued its decision invalidating the Richmond set-aside plan in *Croson*. The modified Jacksonville plan attempted to comply with the Court's post-*Croson* affirmative action requirements by narrowing the scope of the program to encompass only blacks and women—against whom there was evidence of past discrimination—and by replacing the 10 percent set-aside with a more flexible range of 5–16 percent guidelines.[63]

The original Jacksonville plan resembled the Richmond plan so closely that the district court invalidated it on the basis of *Croson*.[64] However, the court of appeals reversed the district court decision on the grounds that the plaintiff trade association lacked standing to sue under the Supreme Court's stringent redressability rules because the plaintiff had not demonstrated that "but for the program, any [trade association] member would have bid successfully for any of [the set-aside] contracts."[65] The court of appeals cited *Warth v. Seldin*[66] for the proposition that a plaintiff seeking to challenge a government program as discriminatory had to "plead standing through 'specific, concrete facts'" showing that the plaintiff's injury was likely to be redressed by a favorable decision on the merits.[67] *Warth* was a case in which the Supreme Court denied standing to minority home seekers and to builders of low- and moderate-income housing who had attempted to challenge zoning practices alleged to be racially restrictive. The Supreme Court held that the plaintiffs lacked standing because the low-and moderate-income housing that they desired might not be built even if the allegedly restrictive zoning practices were invalidated.[68] The *Warth* redressability holding was reinforced by two subsequent environmental decisions that the Supreme Court handed down in *Lujan v. Defenders of Wildlife*[69] and *Lujan v. National Wildlife Federation*,[70] which held that plaintiffs would no longer be granted standing to maintain general challenges to governmental programs unless the programs injured them in particularized ways that were both highly imminent and highly redressable.[71] The *Lujan* decisions seemed to indicate that, as a matter of Article III constitutional law, a contractor would typically lack standing to maintain a facial challenge to a set-aside program because no one would typically know which nonminority bids would have been accepted in the absence of the challenged set-aside program.[72] As a result, it was unlikely that any particular nonminority contractor could satisfy the redressability requirement of standing by proving that it would have been awarded any particular contract if the minority set-aside program were invalidated.

The Supreme Court reversed the court of appeals and upheld the standing of the trade association in a majority opinion joined by seven members of the Court—Justices Rehnquist, White, Stevens, Scalia, Kennedy, Souter, and Thomas. Justice Thomas wrote the majority opinion, which stated that normal redressability rules did not preclude standing in *Northeastern Florida* because in an equal protection case, the race-based denial of the opportunity to bid on a construction project constituted an injury sufficient for standing even though the bid might not ultimately be accepted.[73] Justice Thomas did not fully elaborate his reason for concluding that Fourteenth Amendment equal protection claims were exempt from the new regime of standing stringency that had been imposed by the two *Lujan* cases, or why equal protection claims were to be treated differently than the environmental claims at issue in the *Lujan* cases. Justice Thomas did recognize that the grant of standing to white contractors in *Northeastern Florida* was in "some tension" with the denial of standing to the minority home seekers and home builders in *Warth*.[74] His basis for distinguishing *Northeastern Florida* from *Warth* was that in *Northeastern Florida* the plaintiffs were completely barred from bidding on the set-aside construction projects, while in *Warth* the plaintiffs were permitted to apply for zoning variances.[75] Justice Thomas did not explain why the ability to apply for zoning variances was material in *Warth* in light of the plaintiffs' allegation that such applications would automatically be denied under the racially restrictive zoning policy that the plaintiffs were challenging.[76]

Justice Thomas's opinion also rejected the argument that the case had been rendered moot by the city council's modification of the Jacksonville set-aside plan in order to comply with *Croson*, stating that the city's voluntary cessation of the challenged practice did not serve as a basis for mootness.[77] Justice Thomas noted that even though the city had modified its set-aside program in the wake of *Croson*, the modified program still contained a racial preference.[78] Therefore, in order to prevent the city from evading adjudication of its continuing desire to utilize a racial set-aside program, it was necessary to apply the "well-settled" voluntary cessation exception to the doctrine of mootness and to adjudicate the merits of the plaintiffs' equal protection claim.[79]

Justice O'Connor, joined by Justice Blackmun, dissented on the ground that the case had become moot when the city made its *Croson*-inspired modifications to the plan.[80] Justice O'Connor's dissenting opinion emphasized that the voluntary cessation exception to the doctrine of mootness was fashioned for cases in which a defendant ceased a challenged action with the intent of reinstituting that action once the lawsuit challenging it had been dismissed. Because the Jacksonville plan had been modified in order to *comply* with *Croson* rather than to circumvent it, there was no reason to believe that the initial plan would ever be reinstituted. As a result, the case should be dismissed as moot because the statute that the plaintiffs challenged no longer existed.[81] Although the modified statute did remain in effect, the constitutionality of that statute had never been challenged by the plaintiffs. The 5–16 percent guidelines in the modified plan presented a controversy substantially different from that presented by the 10 percent set-aside contained in the original plan. Moreover, because the guidelines were only one of five parts of the modified plan, it was not clear how—or even whether—those guidelines would ever be implemented.[82]

As a matter of substantive affirmative action law, *Northeastern Florida* added little in the way of doctrinal development. What it did add, however, was an indication of the vigor with which the 1993 Court wished to pursue its confinement of affirmative action. In order to uphold the district court's invalidation of the Jacksonville set-aside, the Supreme Court arguably had to strain traditional justiciability concepts of standing and mootness. Depending on how one views the case, the plan that the Court granted the plaintiffs standing to challenge had been either repealed or not yet used. Although the Court did not discuss the issue, the intricacies of the modified plan, which were heavily dependent upon the factual contexts in which the plan would be applied,[83] may also have rendered the legal issues not yet "fit for review" under traditional ripeness rules.[84] Because the Supreme Court decision permitted the plaintiff to maintain its legal challenge to the Jacksonville affirmative action program, *Northeastern Florida* is designated a decision that frustrates rather than facilitates affirmative action in the Affirmative Action Voting Chart included on pages 162–63.

4. Adarand *(1995)*

In the 1995 case of *Adarand Constructors v. Pena*,[85] the Supreme Court for the first time seemingly invalidated a purely federal affirmative action program through the application of strict scrutiny. The program, established by the Small Business Act[86] and the Surface Transportation Act,[87] provided financial incentives for general contractors to hire subcontractors who were socially and economically disadvantaged, by giving general contractors a bonus equal to 10 percent of the value of any subcontracts that they awarded to disadvantaged subcontractors. The feature of the program that raised constitutional difficulties was the inclusion in the statutes of a presumption that racial minorities were socially and economically disadvantaged.[88] Because the statutory presumption was rebuttable, individuals who were not members of enumerated minority groups could prove that they were nevertheless disadvantaged, and third parties such as disappointed bidders could prove that particular minority group members were not disadvantaged. In *Adarand*, the low bidder on a guardrail subcontract for a Colorado highway construction project was denied the contract in favor of the second-lowest bidder, who was Latino.[89] The nonminority low bidder sued to invalidate the program, arguing that the statutory presumption of minority disadvantage violated the equal protection clause. The district court and the court of appeals rejected the claim, upholding the program after the intermediate scrutiny that was then applied to congressional programs under *Metro Broadcasting*.[90]

Although the essence of the *Adarand* challenge in the lower courts concerned only the power of an agency to exceed congressional affirmative action goals without specific findings of past discrimination,[91] the Supreme Court used the case as an opportunity to announce a new standard of strict scrutiny for congressionally authorized affirmative action programs. Justice O'Connor wrote a majority opinion for five members of the Court—Justices O'Connor, Rehnquist, Scalia, Kennedy, and Thomas.[92] Her opinion first held that the plaintiff had standing to challenge the statutory presumption of minority disadvantage, citing *Northeastern Florida* for the proposition that the plaintiff need not demonstrate that it would have been awarded the contract in the absence of the challenged program.[93] Justice O'Connor then went on to reaffirm that the due process clause of the Fifth Amendment, which applies to the federal government, contained an equal protection component that was coextensive with the equal protection clause of the Fourteenth Amendment, which applies to the states.[94]

After tracing the Court's affirmative action precedents, Justice O'Connor found that they established "three general propositions with respect to governmental racial classifications."[95] First, the precedents established the principle of *skepticism*, meaning that racial classifications had to be subjected to strict scrutiny. Second, they established the principle of *consistency*, meaning that the equal protection guarantee of the Constitution extended to the white majority as well as to racial minorities. Accordingly, the strict-scrutiny standard of review governed *all* racial classifications, whether benign or invidious, and whether the benefits and burdens fell on whites or racial minorities. Third, the precedents established the principle of *congruence*, meaning that the requisite strict-scrutiny standard applied equally to state classifications under the Fourteenth Amendment and federal classifications under the Fifth Amendment.[96] Justice O'Connor then noted that the intermediate scrutiny the Court applied to benign congressional affirmative action programs under *Metro Broadcasting* was inconsistent with these principles, and announced that *Metro Broadcasting* was overruled to the extent that it was inconsistent with the Court's holding that strict scrutiny governed all racial classifications.[97] She also announced that *Fullilove* would also have to be considered overruled if it were read to be inconsistent with a unitary standard of review.[98]

Justice O'Connor described strict scrutiny as a standard that could be satisfied only by "narrowly tailored measures that further compelling governmental interests." She also noted that the purpose of strict scrutiny was to enable the Court to distinguish between benign and invidious uses of race—a distinction that can be difficult to make because affirmative action programs sometimes stigmatize the intended beneficiaries of those programs.[99] In a portion of her opinion joined only by Justice Kennedy, Justice O'Connor argued that the decision to overrule *Metro Broadcasting* was not inconsistent with the doctrine of *stare decisis* because the decision was too recent to have generated much reliance, and because the application of two different standards of review to affirmative action cases had been "consistently criticized by commentators."[100] She also denied that her own opinion in *Adarand* was inconsistent with her earlier opinion in *Croson*, which relied on the special powers of Congress under § 5 of the Fourteenth Amendment to distinguish the *Fullilove* decision upholding a federal set-aside program similar to the state program invalidated in *Croson*.[101]

Finally, Justice O'Connor asserted that debate about the proper standard of review was more than a mere "lawyers' quibble over words."[102] Although the Supreme Court had not upheld a racial classification since the now-discredited 1944 decision in *Korematsu v. United States*,[103] which upheld the infamous World War II Japanese exclusion order, Justice O'Connor stated, "we wish to dispel the notion that strict scrutiny is 'strict in theory, but fatal in fact,'"[104] thereby suggesting that some governmental justifications for race-based affirmative action programs might be able to survive strict scrutiny. Moreover, her opinion suggested that every member of the Supreme Court had viewed the federal affirmative action plan upheld by the Court in *United States v. Paradise* as sufficient to survive strict scrutiny.[105] The majority opinion then remanded the case to the district court for application of the proper strict scrutiny standard of review.[106]

Justice Scalia wrote an opinion concurring in part and concurring in the judgment, except insofar as the majority opinion was inconsistent with the views expressed in his own opinion.[107] Justice Scalia believed that the government could never have a compelling interest in using a race-conscious remedy for prior discrimination. Although individual victims of discrimination could be made whole, the Constitution did not recognize group-based remedies, because the concept of a creditor or a debtor race was alien to the Constitution's focus on the individual. Even benign race-conscious remedies would reinforce the way of thinking that produced slavery and racial hatred. Justice Scalia concluded that it was "unlikely, if not impossible" that the *Adarand* affirmative action program could survive this understanding of strict scrutiny on remand.[108]

Justice Thomas also concurred in part and concurred in the judgment.[109] He stressed that strict scrutiny should apply to all government classifications because there was a moral and constitutional equivalence between racial classifications designed to subjugate a race and those designed to benefit a race. He emphasized that there was no "paternalism exception" to the equal protection clause, and asserted that government cannot make people equal. Justice Thomas also asserted that benign discrimination stamped racial minorities with a badge of inferiority; that it fostered minority dependence; and that it engendered attitudes of either superiority or resentment in whites.[110]

Justice Stevens wrote a dissenting opinion that was joined by Justice Ginsburg.[111] Justice Stevens challenged the majority's conception of *skepticism* by noting that specification of a uniform standard of review would not necessarily provide for uniform resolution of the cases to which that standard of review was applied.[112] He challenged the majority's conception of *consistency* by noting that it failed to recognize the important distinction between burdens imposed on racial minorities in order to perpetuate a caste system, and benefits designed to foster equality by eradicating racial subordination.[113] He accused the majority of "disregard[ing] the difference between a 'No Trespassing' sign and a welcome mat."[114] Although the distinction between benign and invidious discrimination could sometimes be difficult to ascertain, it was no more difficult than the distinction that courts were required to make under *Washington v. Davis*[115] between intentional discrimination and discriminatory effect.[116] Justice Stevens noted that the majority's notion of consistency was difficult to square with its decision to apply strict scrutiny to benign racial classifications while applying intermediate scrutiny to benign gender classifications. This had the anomalous result of making it more difficult to remedy racial discrimination than to remedy gender discrimination under the Fourteenth Amendment, even though the primary purpose of the equal protection clause had been to end discrimination against former black slaves.[117] Justice Stevens also argued that the majority's conception of consistency obscured the essential distinction between decisions that the majority makes to burden racial minorities and the decision that the majority makes to burden itself in order to provide benefits to a disadvantaged minority group.[118]

Justice Stevens challenged the majority's conception of *congruence* by noting that it failed to take account of significant differences between congressional and noncongressional affirmative action programs that had been identified repeatedly and consistently in the Court's prior opinions, including the majority opinion in *Metro Broadcasting*, several opinions in *Fullilove*, and the opinions of Justices Scalia and O'Connor in *Croson*.[119] Congressional affirmative action plans were entitled to greater deference than state and local plans because Congress was granted special powers under § 5 of the Fourteenth Amendment to remedy racial discrimination that states and municipalities did not possess, so that Congress could serve as the primary defender of the racial minority interests that some states had historically proven unwilling to protect; the smaller size of state legislatures made it more likely that they would be captured by oppressive factions than that Congress would be so captured; and state legislative actions could impose externalities on nonresidents who were not represented in the state legislature in a way that was not true of congressional actions.[120] Justice Stevens asserted that the majority's conception of congruity ignored the purposeful incongruity that was fundamental in our governmental system.[121]

Justice Stevens argued that the majority's decision to overrule *Metro Broadcasting* and possibly *Fullilove* was inconsistent with the doctrine of *stare decisis*.[122] *Fullilove*, *Metro Broadcasting*, and *Adarand* were the only three Supreme Court cases that considered the constitutionality of federal affirmative action programs. Because *Fullilove* and *Metro Broadcasting* accorded special deference to congressional affirmative action programs, and because *Croson* relied on that deference in distinguishing *Fullilove*, the majority opinion in *Adarand* upset settled expectations when it changed the status quo by announcing that congressional programs were no longer entitled to special deference.[123] *Adarand*, however, did not overrule the portion of *Metro Broadcasting* holding that prospective diversity could serve as a legitimate justification for race-based affirmative action, because *Adarand* overruled *Metro Broadcasting* only insofar as it was "inconsistent" with the *Adarand* application of strict scrutiny to all racial classifications, and recognition of the legitimacy of prospective diversity is not inconsistent with that holding.[124] Justice Stevens characterized as disingenuous the majority's suggestion that *Adarand* might necessitate the overruling of *Fullilove*. Rather, the *Adarand* majority purported to adopt the strict scrutiny standard of review favored by Justice Powell in *Bakke*, and Justice Powell found that standard of review to have been satisfied in *Fullilove*. Once again, overruling *Fullilove* could not fairly be characterized as restoring previously settled law.[125] If the *Fullilove* program was able to survive strict scrutiny, then the *Adarand* plan should survive strict scrutiny as well because the *Adarand* plan was less objectionable than the *Fullilove* plan. This is because, unlike the *Fullilove* plan, the *Adarand* plan contained only a rebuttable presumption of minority disadvantage; a contractor's status as disadvantaged was subject to periodic review; the *Adarand* plan did not impose numerical quotas; and the *Adarand* plan was preceded by extensive congressional deliberations.[126]

Justice Souter wrote a dissenting opinion that was joined by Justices Ginsburg and Breyer.[127] Justice Souter argued that the issue presented by the *Adarand* case in the lower courts, and the primary issue on which certiorari was granted, was whether the Fourteenth Amendment required specific findings of past discrimination under *Croson* because the specific goals of the *Adarand* preference were specified by a federal agency rather than by Congress itself.[128] He also argued that the congressional findings of past construction-industry discrimination that were made in *Fullilove* controlled the outcome in *Adarand* under the doctrine of *stare decisis*, because those findings had not been challenged by the plaintiff.[129] With respect to the standard-of-review issue, Justice Souter argued that the three-tiered scrutiny structure for equal protection claims was best understood as elaborating a single standard of reasonableness under the relevant circumstances.[130] Because the majority had emphasized that strict scrutiny was no longer to be viewed as fatal scrutiny, the circumstance of congressional authorization for an affirmative action program remained a relevant circumstance, and the power of Congress under § 5 of the Fourteenth Amendment to remedy discrimination remained as broad as it was prior to *Adarand*.[131] Justice Souter finally argued that nothing in the majority opinion undermined the "long-accepted" view that the Constitution was not limited to the mere prohibition of prospective discrimination. It also permitted the use of racial classifications to eliminate the continuing effects of past discrimination when reasonable, temporary catch-up measures could be employed for this purpose, and the concomitant burden imposed on innocent whites did not make those measures unconstitutional.[132]

Justice Ginsburg also wrote a dissenting opinion, which was joined by Justice Breyer.[133] Justice Ginsburg chose to emphasize the areas of agreement that existed among the various opinions in *Adarand*.[134] She noted broad agreement about both the history of racial discrimination and the continuing existence of racial discrimination in the United States, and about the authority of Congress to counteract the lingering effects of past discrimination. She illustrated the scope of continuing discrimination through reference to various studies showing the magnitude of present racial discrimination in areas including consumer sales, rental housing, mortgage lending, and contracting.[135] Justice Ginsburg then suggested that the strict scrutiny that the *Adarand* majority had adopted would remain fatal for invidious discrimination that burdened racial minorities, but would permit benign efforts to "hasten the day when 'we are just one race.'"[136] She argued that the majority correctly realized that affirmative action programs should be carefully scrutinized to ensure that they were not malign programs masquerading as benign ones; to ensure that the beneficiaries were not harmed by catch-up mechanisms; and to ensure that once-preferred groups were not unduly harmed. However, such scrutiny should not result in the invalidation of the *Adarand* program.[137] Justice Ginsburg concluded that, because of the attention that the political branches were paying to the affirmative action issue, there was no need for Supreme Court intervention in *Adarand*.[138]

The Supreme Court's four majority affirmative action opinions were not receptive to the concept of affirmative action. Of the three programs that the Court considered on the merits, the Court invalidated the two programs at issue in *Croson* and *Adarand*, and initially upheld the program in *Metro Broadcasting* only subsequently to overrule *Metro Broadcasting* in *Adarand*. In *Northeastern Florida*, the Court granted the plaintiff nonobvious standing to maintain a challenge to the fourth program that it considered. The two transition cases of *Croson* and *Metro Broadcasting* initially established a dual standard of review for affirmative action, under which state and local programs were subject to presumptively fatal strict scrutiny, while congressional programs were subject to more permissive intermediate scrutiny. *Adarand* abandoned this dual standard of review in favor of a unitary standard of strict scrutiny that applied to all racial classifications, including federal, state, and local affirmative action programs. *Adarand*, however, did state that the strict scrutiny standard it was adopting should no longer be considered presumptively fatal scrutiny. The resistance that the

Supreme Court had shown to racial affirmative action in *Adarand* continued in the Court's post-*Adarand* actions on petitions for certiorari.

5. Post-Adarand *Actions on Certiorari*

Between 1995 and 1997, in the wake of its 1995 *Adarand* decision, the Supreme Court took actions on four petitions for certiorari that seemed to reflect and advance the Supreme Court's distaste for racial affirmative action. In 1995, the Supreme Court denied certiorari in *Podberesky v. Kirwan*,[139] declining to review a Fourth Circuit decision holding unconstitutional a state college scholarship program for black students. In 1996, the court denied certiorari in *Hopwood v. Texas*,[140] declining to review a Fifth Circuit decision invalidating a racial affirmative action admissions program adopted by the University of Texas School of Law. In 1997, the Supreme Court granted but subsequently dismissed a writ of certiorari in *Taxman v. Piscataway Township Board of Education*[141] to review a decision of the Third Circuit holding that a public high school violated Title VII when it chose to retain a black teacher and lay off a white teacher of equal seniority and qualifications in order to promote faculty diversity. Later in 1997, the Supreme Court denied certiorari in *Coalition for Economic Equity v. Wilson*,[142] declining to review a decision of the Ninth Circuit upholding the constitutionality of the California Proposition 209 ban on race and gender affirmative action. Supreme Court denials of certiorari have no formal precedential value. Nevertheless, grants of certiorari are statistically more likely to result in a Supreme Court reversal than a Supreme Court affirmance, and denials of certiorari are often interpreted to signify some degree of Supreme Court acquiescence in the lower court decisions that the Supreme Court declines to review.[143]

i. *Podberesky* (1995)

In 1995, the Supreme Court denied certiorari in *Podberesky v. Kirwan*,[144] thereby leaving in place a Fourth Circuit decision that held unconstitutional a University of Maryland scholarship program for black students. The University of Maryland historically maintained racially segregated schools. As part of its protracted effort to dismantle the vestiges of its former discriminatory system, and to come into compliance with Title VI of the Civil Rights Act of 1964, the university ultimately adopted a scholarship program designed to attract highly qualified black students.[145] By 1994, the University of Maryland maintained two merit-based scholarship programs for its students. The Francis Scott Key program was open to all students, and the Benjamin Banneker program was open only to black students. Daniel Podberesky, a Latino student who satisfied the academic criteria for the Banneker program but not for the Key program, filed suit challenging the constitutionality of the racial restriction on eligibility for the Banneker program.[146] In 1991, the United States District Court for the District of Maryland, in an opinion by Judge Motz, upheld the constitutionality of the Banneker scholarship program on cross motions for summary judgment.[147] In 1992, that decision was reversed by the United States Court of Appeals for the Fourth Circuit, and remanded for findings concerning the need for such a program to eliminate the continuing effects of past discrimination, in an opinion by Judge Restani, joined by Judges Widener and Hamilton.[148] In 1993, after remand and additional discovery, the district court made specific findings and again upheld the Banneker scholarship program on cross motions for summary judgment.[149] In 1994, the Fourth Circuit again reversed, holding the racial restriction in the Banneker program unconstitutional, in an opinion by Judge Widener, joined by Judges Wilkins and Hamilton.[150]

The 1994 Fourth Circuit decision held that the Banneker scholarship program was subject to strict scrutiny under the equal protection clause of the Fourteenth Amendment as an overt racial classification, and that the program did not survive strict scrutiny.[151] The Court cited *Croson* and *Wygant* for the proposition that the program could not be upheld unless the university demonstrated a "strong basis in evidence for its conclusion that remedial action [is] necessary" and established that the program was "narrowly tailored to meet the remedial goal" of the program.[152] Although the Fourth Circuit's earlier remand had been for the purpose of permitting district court findings concerning the need for the Banneker program, the district court had accorded too much deference to the university's own findings of need for the program, and had failed to engage in the searching inquiry demanded by strict scrutiny.[153]

The Fourth Circuit reversed the district court's grant of summary judgment for the university, rejecting each of the four continuing effects of past discrimination that the district court identified as adequate to justify the Banneker program. First, the fact that the university had a poor reputation in the black community resulting from its history of segregation could not be sufficient to justify a race-conscious remedy. If it were, then race-conscious remedies would be permissible as long as people continued to be aware of an institution's segregated past.[154] Second, present perceptions of the university's hostile climate to black students, documented by surveys, focus groups, school newspaper articles, and student self-segregation, was not sufficient to justify a race-conscious remedy. That hostile climate resulted not from the university's past segregation but from general societal discrimination, which under *Croson* and *Wygant* was not a permissible basis for a race-conscious remedy.[155]

The Fourth Circuit rejected the district court's third and fourth justifications for the Banneker program on the grounds that they could not properly have been relied on at the summary judgment stage of the litigation. The district court's third justification, that disproportionately low retention and graduation rates for black students was a lingering effect of the university's past discrimination, tacitly resolved a factual dispute between the university and the plaintiff concerning whether the disadvantage suffered by black students actually resulted from the university's past discrimination or rather resulted from economic factors. The existence of this factual dispute precluded the district court from properly relying on low retention and graduation rates to justify the program at the summary judgment stage. The district court's fourth justification, that the present underrepresentation of black students in the university student body resulted from the university's past discrimination, rested on an unresolved factual dispute. In order to determine whether black students were actually underrepresented in the student body, the court first needed to determine the size of the relevant applicant pool. This, in turn, required the court to determine the minimum criteria for admission to the University of Maryland, but there was again a factual dispute concerning the minimum admissions criteria, which could not properly be resolved on cross motions for summary judgment. As a result, the district court erred when it entered summary judgment for the university on the grounds that the Banneker program was necessary to remedy the continuing effects of the university's past discrimination.[156]

The Fourth Circuit also held that the district court had erred when it denied the plaintiff's motion for summary judgment. Even if factual disputes concerning retention, graduation, and underrepresentation of black students at the University of Maryland were resolved in favor of the university, the Banneker program would still be unconstitutional. That was because the Banneker program did not constitute a narrowly tailored remedy for past discrimination. The program served objectives different from the objectives that it was claimed to serve, and there were potential race-neutral alternatives that might be able to remedy the problems of past discrimination.[157] The Banneker program was not narrowly tailored because scholarships were awarded to high-achieving black students even though high achievers are not the students against whom the university discriminated in the past. (The Fourth Circuit did not explain why past segregation of high-achieving black students was not relevant.)[158] The program also awarded scholarships to black students who were not Maryland residents, but this was not a narrowly tailored remedy for past discrimination against black students who *were* Maryland residents.[159] The Banneker program was designed to remedy the underrepresentation of black students at the University of Maryland, but subtle factors—such as a black student's preference for predominantly black schools—might have contributed to such underrepresentation. As a result, the university might have overstated the degree of underrepresentation attributable to past discrimination, thereby causing a remedy directed at such underrepresentation to be excessive rather than narrowly tailored.[160] To the extent that the university was attempting to provide role models for other black students, *Wygant* rejected the use of role models as a justification for race-conscious remedies.[161] Moreover, a remedy designed to correct for underrepresentation resembled a remedy designed to promote racial balance, and the use of race-conscious remedies to promote racial balance was prohibited under *Croson*.[162] Finally, the Banneker program was not narrowly tailored to remedy the problem of black student attrition, because burdens attributable to off-campus housing and off-campus jobs were a significant factor in student attrition after the freshman year. As a result, the provision of on-campus housing and on-campus jobs might serve as a race-neutral alternative to the Banneker scholarship program.[163] Because the Banneker program was not narrowly tailored, the Fourth Circuit reversed and remanded with instructions for the district court to enter summary judgment in favor of the plaintiff.[164]

In March 1995, petitions for certiorari seeking Supreme Court review of the Fourth Circuit decision were filed by the University of Maryland and by individual supporters of the Banneker scholarship program who had participated in the case below.[165] The petitions for certiorari emphasized the one-hundred-year history of racial segregation at the University of Maryland; the many years of resistance to desegregation that followed; the continued existence of racially identified schools in the state university system; the unsuccessful prior efforts to attract blacks to the university; the small size of the scholarship program at issue; the fact that the program was part of the university's response to the United States Department of Education's findings of discrimination; and the fact that the program did not have an adverse effect on the admission of any student. The petitions sought review of whether the Banneker program violated the Fourteenth Amendment; whether it was authorized under the Supreme Court's decision in *Bakke*; whether the Fourth Circuit had been excessively technical in its evidentiary analysis; and whether the Fourth Circuit had improperly granted summary judgment for the plaintiff despite the admitted existence of disputes about material facts.[166] Without comment, the Supreme Court denied the petitions for certiorari on May 22, 1995.[167]

ii. *Hopwood* (1996)

In 1996, the Supreme Court denied certiorari in *Hopwood v. Texas*,[168] thereby leaving in place a Fifth Circuit decision holding unconstitutional an affirmative action program for minority students at the University of Texas School of Law. The denial of certiorari was notable because of the breadth of the Fifth Circuit decision, which held succinctly that the University of Texas "may not use race as a factor in law school admissions."[169] Moreover, the decision appeared to reject Justice Powell's frequently cited opinion in *Regents of the University of California v. Bakke*[170] by holding that race could not be taken into account even for the purpose of promoting diversity in the student body.[171]

In the early 1990s, the University of Texas School of Law utilized a racial affirmative action program to increase the admission of black and Mexican American students. The goal of the program was to admit an entering class that contained 5 percent black and 10 percent Mexican American students. The affirmative action program gave a preference to these two minority groups over whites and other nonpreferred minorities by admitting minority students in these two groups even though they had lower grade point averages and Law School Admission Test (LSAT) scores than other applicants. The admissions process also used separate procedures, a separate admissions subcommittee, and a separate waiting list for students in these two minority groups.[172]

Four white students who were denied admission to the 1992 entering class, even though they had higher grades and test scores than some admitted minority students, filed suit against the state university challenging the constitutionality of the law school's affirmative action program. The students sought injunctive relief, compensatory damages, and punitive damages.[173] In 1994, the United States District Court for the Western District of Texas, in an opinion by Judge Sparks, upheld that part of the Texas affirmative action program that gave a "plus" to minority students in the evaluation of grades and LSAT scores, but held unconstitutional the law school's use of separate procedures that permitted minority applicants to be admitted without ever being compared to white students. The district court issued a declaratory judgment, but denied injunctive relief and damages after the law school voluntarily agreed to abandon its separate admissions process for preferred minority students.[174] In 1996, the United States Court of Appeals for the Fifth Circuit reversed and remanded in a majority opinion by Judge Smith, joined by Judge DeMoss and concurred in specially by Judge Wiener, holding the entire Texas affirmative action program unconstitutional.[175]

The Fifth Circuit majority opinion began by asserting that the goal of the equal protection clause was to render the issue of race irrelevant in government decision making. The Fifth Circuit then held that the law school affirmative action program was subject to strict scrutiny because it made explicit use of racial classifications, and that strict scrutiny would apply even if the program were characterized as benign in nature. As a result, the Texas affirmative action program could be upheld only if it were shown to serve a compelling governmental interest and to be narrowly tailored to the achievement of that objective. The Fifth Circuit then rejected the district court conclusion that the racial preference in the Texas program was able to survive strict scrutiny as a narrowly tailored means of promoting student diversity and of remedying past discrimination at the law school and in other parts of the Texas educational system.[176]

The Fifth Circuit recognized that Justice Powell's influential opinion in *Bakke* permitted race to be used as a "plus" factor in promoting diversity in an educational context—as long as race was not used as a quota that precluded the interracial comparison of applicants—because the promotion of student diversity constituted a compelling state interest.[177] Nevertheless, the Fifth Circuit concluded that "any consideration of race or ethnicity by the law school for the purpose of achieving a diverse student body is not a compelling interest under the Fourteenth Amendment."[178] The Fifth Circuit thought that Justice Powell's opinion in *Bakke* was not binding precedent; Justice Powell was speaking only for himself in *Bakke*. Moreover, language from subsequent Supreme Court opinions in *Adarand* and *Croson* suggested that only the need to remedy past discrimination—and not the desire to promote diversity—could constitute a compelling state interest for equal protection purposes.[179] The Fifth Circuit thought that the use of race

in pursuit of diversity was more likely to foster than to eliminate governmental use of race, thereby treating minorities as a group rather than as individuals. Accordingly, the Fifth Circuit held that "the use of ethnic diversity simply to achieve racial heterogeneity, even as part of the consideration
of a number of factors, is unconstitutional."[180] The Fifth Circuit opinion
stated that universities could consider nonracial diversity factors such as
musical or athletic ability, home state, relationship to alumni, or economic
and social background, even if those factors correlated with race. But universities could not use race as a proxy for diversity factors because such use
of race entailed impermissible stereotyping. The Court also stated that
racial classifications stigmatize minorities in ways that can cause feelings of
inferiority, even if the classifications are purportedly benign in nature.[181]

The Fifth Circuit rejected the district court finding that the Texas affirmative action program was justified as a means of eliminating the present
effects of past discrimination in the Texas educational system, even though
Supreme Court precedents *did* recognize a state's interest in eliminating the
present effects of past discrimination as a compelling state interest. The
Fifth Circuit cited *Wygant* and *Croson* for the proposition that a racial classification could be used only as a remedy for past discrimination by the entity
using the classification, and could not be used as a remedy for general societal discrimination.[182] The district court concluded that past discrimination
in the Texas state primary and secondary educational systems could justify a
law school affirmative action program because such discrimination had affected the educational attainment and attitudes of the minority students
who applied for admission to the law school. However, in so doing the district court had improperly sought to remedy general societal discrimination.
Moreover, even if the state—which controlled the Texas educational system—were the appropriate unit for analysis, the state had not made the particularized findings of past discrimination and remedial need that were required to permit the law school affirmative action program to stand. Similarly, the Fifth Circuit rejected the claim that past discrimination by the
University of Texas as a whole could justify the law school affirmative action
program. The University of Texas was also too expansive an entity to be
scrutinized for past discrimination, and the law school was a functionally
separate unit operating within the university. Accordingly, only continuing
effects of past law school discrimination could be considered in evaluating
the law school affirmative action program.[183]

The law school had a history of *de jure* discrimination in denying admission to blacks, although Mexican Americans were never formally excluded

on the basis of race. The district court identified three present effects of past discrimination by the law school that it deemed sufficient to justify the law school affirmative action program. The district court found that the law school had a lingering reputation in the minority community as a "white" institution; that minority students were underrepresented in the student body; and that the law school was perceived as hostile to minorities. In rejecting these findings, the Fifth Circuit cited *Podberesky v. Kirwan* for the proposition that minority perceptions of the law school as "white," and as hostile to minorities, could not support a racial classification.[184] Mere knowledge of past discrimination was not enough to constitute a present effect of such discrimination. Rather, because the law school had long ago ceased its official discrimination, any lingering perceptions of hostility felt by the minority community had to be the result of current societal discrimination and not past discrimination by the law school.[185] The Texas affirmative action program was even less justifiable than the *Podberesky* program because the Texas program encompassed Mexican Americans who were never formally discriminated against by the law school. In addition, even if reputation in the minority community were deemed relevant, reputation could not justify the law school affirmative action program because the law school program assists only students who had chosen to apply to the law school despite the law school's reputation. In fact, the law school program could compound the hostile-environment problem by stigmatizing minority students as less qualified than other students.[186]

The Fifth Circuit also rejected the claim that minority underrepresentation in the law school student body was a result of past discrimination. The district court found that past discrimination in Texas primary and secondary education reduced the educational attainment of minority students, but that finding was inapposite. Again, it was the law school rather than the State of Texas that was the proper unit of analysis for equal protection purposes. Moreover, even if the state had contributed to formulation of the law school program as part of state negotiations with the Department of Education—negotiations intended to bring the state into compliance with the equality provisions of Title VI—the law school program would still have to satisfy the very same constitutional standards under the equal protection clause.[187] The Fifth Circuit also rejected the district court effort to distinguish *Croson* by arguing that race-conscious remedies were more permissible in an educational context than in an employment context. The Fifth Circuit concluded that the constitutional standards were the same in both contexts.[188] Because the law school program did not further a compelling state interest, the Fifth Circuit found no need to consider the arguments that the program was too broad to satisfy the narrow-tailoring requirement of strict scrutiny.[189]

The Fifth Circuit remanded with instructions for the district court to reconsider the appropriate injunctive and compensatory damage relief in light of the Fifth Circuit opinion. The Fifth Circuit did, however, state that punitive damages were inappropriate on the current state of the record because law school officials had behaved in good faith with respect to a difficult issue of law.[190] The Fifth Circuit also reiterated an earlier decision upholding the district court's denial of a motion to intervene filed by two University of Texas black student groups who supported the law school affirmative action program.[191]

Judge Wiener wrote an opinion concurring specially.[192] He agreed with the panel opinion that the law school affirmative action program could not be justified as a means for promoting student diversity, or as a remedy for the present effects of past discrimination. However, he was unwilling to agree that a state interest in promoting diversity could never constitute a compelling state interest.[193] Judge Wiener argued that the Supreme Court had never rejected Justice Powell's *Bakke* view that diversity could constitute a compelling state interest, and if that view were to be rejected, it should be rejected by the Supreme Court rather than by a three-judge court of appeals panel.[194] Despite the panel's contrary suggestion, *Adarand* did not hold that diversity could never constitute a compelling state interest; *Adarand* did not arise in a public, graduate educational context; and *Adarand* stressed that it was not sounding the death knell for racial affirmative action.[195] In order to avoid the unnecessary resolution of this constitutional issue—in a nonclass action affecting only four individuals who challenged only the Texas program as it existed in 1992—Judge Wiener preferred to reject the law school's diversity justification on the grounds that it was not narrowly tailored.[196] He found that the law school's effective use of quotas for blacks and Mexican Americans did not comport with Justice Powell's notion of diversity in *Bakke* because it ignored other racial groups and other diversity factors that were not related to race. As a result, the program was not narrowly tailored enough to satisfy the demands of strict scrutiny.[197] Judge Wiener also detected a Catch-22 tension in the law school's argument that its racial classification was narrow enough to constitute a necessary remedy for past discrimination, yet broad enough to promote meaningful diversity.[198] Finally, Judge Wiener disapproved of the panel's "commentary" on remedy, arguing that consideration of remedy should be left to the district court in the first instance on remand.[199]

In April 1996, the state of Texas filed a petition for certiorari, seeking Supreme Court review of the Fifth Circuit decision in *Hopwood*.[200] The Texas petition asked the Supreme Court to review, *inter alia*, the issue of whether *Bakke* should be abandoned by prohibiting state schools from considering race among the other factors that they consider in order to achieve diverse student bodies, and whether the Texas affirmative action program was a permissible remedy for the continuing effects of past *de jure* discrimination practiced in the state educational systems.[201] In addition to being signed by the Texas attorney general, the petition for certiorari was also signed by noted law professors including Laurence Tribe, Randall Kennedy, Charles Allan Wright, and Samuel Issacharoff.[202] On July 1, 1996, the Supreme Court denied the petition for certiorari.[203] Justices Ginsburg and Souter issued a statement accompanying the denial of certiorari. The statement asserted that the issue of whether race could be used as a factor in college admissions decisions was an issue of great national importance. However, Justices Ginsburg and Souter concluded that *Hopwood* did not properly present that issue because the 1992 program used by the University of Texas School of Law was no longer in use, thereby eliminating the continued existence of any genuine controversy about that program.[204]

iii. *Piscataway* (1997)

In 1997, the Supreme Court first granted, and then dismissed, a petition for certiorari in *Taxman v. Piscataway Township Board of Education* (*Piscataway*).[205] In *Piscataway*, the lower courts held that a school board affirmative action policy giving a layoff preference to a minority high school teacher over an equally qualified white teacher in order to promote faculty diversity violated Title VII of the Civil Rights Act of 1964.[206] Because the case arose under Title VII rather than the equal protection clause, the case had a potential effect on all voluntary affirmative action programs arising in an employment context, whether those programs involved public or private employers. Public employers, however, would still remain subject to constitutional restrictions on affirmative action even if Title VII did not prohibit the affirmative action programs at issue. After the Supreme Court granted certiorari in *Piscataway*, the parties settled the case, with the school board agreeing to pay damages to the laid-off white teacher. The settlement was urged by a coalition of prominent national civil rights groups who feared that a Supreme Court affirmance might have broad precedential effects that would prohibit most voluntary affirmative action based on race or gender.[207] As a result, the Supreme Court dismissed the writ of certiorari prior to argument. Accordingly, the Supreme Court never addressed the merits of the *Piscataway* case.[208]

In 1975, the Board of Education of the Township of Piscataway, New Jersey, adopted an affirmative action policy for the public schools designed to promote equal opportunity and prohibit discrimination by attracting minority students, teachers, and staff. The policy, which encompassed teacher hiring and layoffs, provided that "[i]n all cases, the most qualified candidate will be recommended for appointment. However, when candidates appear to be of equal qualification, candidates meeting the criteria of the affirmative action program will be recommended."[209] The phrase "candidates meeting the criteria of the affirmative action program" included blacks and other race, gender, and national-origin groups identified as minorities by the New Jersey State Department of Education. The parties stipulated that the program was designed to promote diversity, and not as a remedy for prior discrimination or underrepresentation of minorities in the school system. In fact, the percentage of black teachers during the relevant time period exceeded the population percentage of blacks in the available workforce.[210]

In 1989, the school board decided to lay off one teacher in the Business Education Department of Piscataway High School. Layoff decisions were made by seniority, but the two teachers in the department with the lowest seniority both began teaching on the same day, nine years earlier. The board also determined that the two teachers had equal qualifications. One of the teachers was Sharon Taxman, who is white, and the other was Debra Williams, who is black. In the past, ties in seniority had been broken through random selection procedures, but this time the board elected to invoke its affirmative action policy to break the tie. The board decided to lay off Taxman and retain Williams because Williams was the only black teacher in the Business Education Department.[211]

Taxman then filed a charge of employment discrimination with the United States Equal Employment Opportunity Commission. After unsuccessful attempts at conciliation, the United States filed suit against the board in the United States District Court for the District of New Jersey, alleging a violation of the employment discrimination provisions of Title VII. Taxman intervened as a plaintiff alleging a violation of Title VII and of the

New Jersey Law Against Discrimination. On cross motions for summary judgment concerning the issue of liability, the district court issued an opinion by Judge Barry. Her opinion granted summary judgment for the United States and Taxman under both statutes, and ordered a trial on the issue of damages. By the time of trial, Taxman had been rehired, so the district court declined to order reinstatement, and it denied Taxman's claim for punitive damages. The district court, however, did award Taxman $134,014.62 in compensatory damages for back pay, fringe benefits, and interest, and it ordered reinstatement of full seniority for Taxman. A jury also awarded Taxman an additional $10,000 for emotional suffering under the New Jersey statute.[212]

The school board appealed the district court's entry of summary judgment against it on the issue of liability, and Taxman cross-appealed the district court's denial of her claim for punitive damages. While the appeal was pending in the United States Court of Appeals for the Third Circuit, the United States changed sides in the litigation and requested leave to file a brief *amicus curiae* urging reversal of the district court decision. The Third Circuit denied this request but did permit the United States to withdraw as a party, leaving Taxman and the board as the only parties to the appeal.[213] The case was initially argued before a three-judge panel of the Third Circuit on November 29, 1995, and then reargued before the Third Circuit en banc on May 14, 1996.[214] On August 8, 1996, the en banc Third Circuit affirmed the district court decision in an opinion by Judge Mansmann,[215] accompanied by one concurrence and four dissenting opinions filed by the four dissenting judges.[216]

Judge Mansmann's majority opinion for the en banc Third Circuit held in pertinent part that the *Piscataway* affirmative action plan violated Title VII. Although the literal language of Title VII seemed to prohibit racial classifications in employment, the Supreme Court's 1979 decision in *United Steelworkers of America v. Weber* established that voluntary affirmative action plans in the employment context were permissible under Title VII as long as they (1) mirrored the purposes of Title VII; and (2) did not unnecessarily trammel the interests of nonminority employees.[217] The Supreme Court's 1987 decision in *Johnson v. Transportation Agency* applied *Weber* in a public employment context to permit affirmative action programs that were designed to remedy a manifest imbalance or underrepresentation of women or minorities in traditionally segregated job categories, where the programs did not terminate the jobs of existing employees.[218] Judge Mansmann's Third Circuit opinion found that Congress had dual purposes in enacting Title VII. Congress wished to end employment discrimination, thereby guaranteeing equal employment opportunity in the workplace, and Congress wished to remedy the segregation and minority underrepresentation that had been caused by past discrimination. Therefore, an affirmative action plan could not be said to mirror the purposes of Title VII, and thereby satisfy the first prong of the *Weber* test, unless it had a remedial purpose, as did the programs at issue in *Weber* and *Johnson v. Transportation Agency*. The *Piscataway* affirmative action policy did not satisfy this first prong of the *Weber* test because it did not have a remedial purpose.[219]

The Third Circuit concluded that the purpose of the *Piscataway* affirmative action policy was to promote faculty diversity, but the goal of diversity was not sufficient to avoid liability under Title VII. This was true even after the 1972 amendments to Title VII, which extended the statute's coverage to public and private educational institutions.[220] The Third Circuit also rejected the argument that because the goal of faculty diversity was permissible under the equal protection clause it should also be permissible under Title VII. The Court held that Title VII could be violated by a discriminatory practice that did not violate the equal protection clause.[221] Moreover, even if Title VII did incorporate equal protection standards, *Wygant v. Jackson Board of Education* now suggested that only remedial purposes could justify racial classifications under the equal protection clause.[222] The Third Circuit refused to infer from several cases sympathetic to diversity in an educational context that diversity ought to be a permissible objective under Title VII. The Court asserted that those educational cases were really cases involving remedies for past discrimination.[223] The Court also rejected the claim that *Regents of the University of California v. Bakke* and *Metro Broadcasting v. FCC* supported recognition of diversity as a permissible goal under Title VII.[224] The Court simply stated that *Bakke* was different from *Piscataway*, noting in a footnote that the Fifth Circuit decision in *Hopwood v. Texas* had declined to view Justice Powell's diversity opinion in *Bakke* as binding.[225] The diversity holding of *Metro Broadcasting* was inapposite because that portion of *Metro Broadcasting* had been overruled by *Adarand Constructors v. Pena*.[226] The Third Circuit also declined to follow language contained in Justice O'Connor's *Wygant* concurrence and Justice Stevens's concurrence in *Johnson v. Transportation Agency*, which suggested that diversity could be an appropriate affirmative action objective.[227]

The Third Circuit emphasized that, by stipulation of the parties, the *Piscataway* affirmative action policy was not designed to remedy past discrimination or underrepresentation in the Piscataway school system. Because the policy was intended only to promote diversity, it could not satisfy the first prong of the *Weber* test.[228] The Third Circuit also held that the *Piscataway* policy failed to satisfy the second prong of the *Weber* test, which required that an affirmative action plan not "unnecessarily trammel" nonminority interests.[229] The *Piscataway* policy had an "utter lack of definition and structure" because it failed to define racial diversity or to determine what degree of racial diversity in the Piscataway schools was appropriate.[230] The affirmative action programs that the Supreme Court had upheld under Title VII incorporated objectives and benchmarks that made it possible to limit the scope of those affirmative action programs. The *Piscataway* affirmative action policy, however, had no such limiting goals or standards, and was governed only by the whim of the school board. Moreover, the *Piscataway* policy was not limited in duration, as were the plans upheld in *Weber* and *Johnson v. Transportation Agency*.[231] Finally, the actual job loss that was entailed in layoffs imposed too heavy a burden on nonminorities to be permissible under the second prong of the *Weber* test.[232]

The Third Circuit affirmed the district court finding of liability under the New Jersey Law Against Discrimination, holding that the New Jersey statute incorporated the same analysis used under Title VII.[233] The Third Circuit also upheld the district court award of full back-pay damages, even though Taxman would have had only a 50 percent chance of avoiding a layoff even in the absence of the *Piscataway* affirmative action policy. The court reasoned that the board should pay Taxman her entire back salary because, by hypothesis, the board could not prove by a preponderance of the evidence that Taxman would have lost this salary under a random layoff selection process.[234] The Third Circuit also affirmed the district court award of prejudgment interest to Taxman, as well as the district court's denial of punitive damages.[235] The Third Circuit opinion concluded by emphasizing the desirability of diversity in an educational context, but reiterated the court's belief that Title VII did not permit the nonremedial use of racial classifications.[236]

Judge Stapleton wrote a concurring opinion. He agreed that the *Piscataway* affirmative action policy violated Title VII due to its lack of a remedial purpose. As a result, however, he believed that there was no need to consider whether the program unnecessarily trammeled the interests of nonminorities under the second prong of *Weber*, and did not therefore join that portion of the majority opinion.[237]

Four Third Circuit judges dissented from the en banc decision in *Piscataway*, and each wrote a dissenting opinion. Chief Judge Sloviter dissented in an opinion joined by Judges Lewis and McKee.[238] In her opinion, Judge Sloviter stated that the *Piscataway* case was not really an "affirmative action" case at all in the divisive sense of the term because the *Piscataway* policy did not give a preference to someone deemed "less qualified" over someone deemed "more qualified."[239] Judge Sloviter viewed the issue presented in the *Piscataway* case as whether Title VII *required* the school board to choose between equally qualified teachers on the basis of chance—something that would be "expected at one of the State's gaming tables"—or whether Title VII *permitted* the board to take diversity considerations into account in choosing between those teachers. The legal issue was presented clearly: the two teachers were equally qualified, and the school board's policy was voluntary. Moreover, even though the school board was a public entity, the *Piscataway* case did not involve the stringent constitutional standards that applied under the equal protection clause, but only the less-demanding standards applicable under Title VII. Accordingly, the *Piscataway* policy had to be analyzed the same way that such a policy would be analyzed if adopted by a private school.[240]

Judge Sloviter stressed that the Piscataway school board did not consider diversity in selecting Taxman rather than Williams to be laid off until after it had first considered seniority, work performance, certifications, evaluations, teaching ability, and volunteerism, and had found the two teachers to be equally qualified along all of those dimensions. Only then did the board consider the educational benefits of faculty diversity, and it chose to retain Williams in order to avoid having no minority teachers at all in the Business Education Department.[241]

Judge Sloviter argued that the majority's reading of Title VII as precluding consideration of diversity factors was an "anomalous result" not compelled by any Supreme Court decision. In fact, *Weber* and *Johnson v. Transportation Agency*—the two Supreme Court cases that had interpreted Title VII without the added scrutiny imposed by the equal protection clause—upheld affirmative action plans that gave a determinative preference to race or gender. *Weber* and *Johnson v. Transportation Agency* were significant for their holding that the literal language of Title VII should not be read to preclude race and gender affirmative action—not, as the majority read them, for the burdens that they impose on affirmative action efforts. The fact that the affirmative action plans at issue in *Weber* and *Johnson v. Transportation Agency* had remedial purposes did not mean that *only* remedial purposes were adequate to avoid Title VII liability. In fact, the opinions in those cases cautioned that they should not be read to establish the outer boundaries of voluntary affirmative action.[242]

Judge Sloviter agreed that Title VII was intended to permit remedies for past discrimination, but it was also intended to eliminate social forces and patterns of segregation that were potential causes of continuing or future discrimination.[243] The 1972 amendments to Title VII recognized the connection between racial homogeneity in schools and attitudes that lead to discrimination. Moreover, the Supreme Court often recognized the benefits of diversity as a strategy for reducing future discrimination, especially in an educational context.[244] Judge Sloviter found it ironic that the majority would find efforts to combat discrimination through diversity to violate Title VII, which had been enacted to eliminate racial injustice.[245] The Supreme Court had held Title VII standards to be less demanding than equal protection clause standards, and ultimately it should be the Supreme Court rather than a court of appeals to reject the benefits of diversity.[246]

Judge Sloviter recognized that layoffs imposed a heavy burden on affected employees. However, because Taxman had only a 50 percent chance of avoiding a layoff, she did not have a "legitimate and firmly rooted expectation" of continued employment.[247] As in *Johnson v. Transportation Agency*, which upheld an affirmative action plan imposing a burden on one of six employees who met the qualifications for the job at issue, Taxman's qualifications similarly placed her in a tie for the teaching job at issue. And just as the plaintiff in *Johnson v. Transportation Agency* remained eligible for later promotion to the job at issue, Taxman remained eligible for rehiring and in fact did regain her job.[248] Judge Sloviter argued that the majority's reliance on *Wygant* was misplaced because *Wygant* applied the narrow-tailoring, *equal protection* standard to find that an affirmative action plan requiring the layoff of an employee with *greater* seniority than a minority employee was unconstitutional. *Wygant* therefore involved a legal standard different from the more permissive Title VII standard, and in *Piscataway*, both employees had *equal* seniority. Moreover, in *Wygant*, only three members of the Supreme Court subscribed to the view that layoffs could never be justified in an affirmative action program.[249] Judge Sloviter believed that the majority similarly misread *Weber* and *Johnson v. Transportation Agency* in suggesting that those cases required an affirmative action plan to be temporary in nature.[250] Neither of those cases held that a plan must just be temporary. Rather, they discussed duration as a factor that was relevant to a plan's effort to minimize burdens on other employees. Here, the *Piscataway* policy *did* take actions to minimize the impact on other employees: it was discretionary rather than mandatory; it had been applied to a layoff decision only once in twenty years; by its terms it could be invoked only when there was a tie in the qualifications of candidates who were of different races, in a department that was not already diverse; and the plan was a flexible plan rather than a rigid plan relying on specific numerical goals.[251] Judge Sloviter stated that it was not the province of the court to intrude into educational decisions concerning the value of diversity. As *Weber* had noted, it was ironic to read Title VII as negating the civil rights goals that gave birth to the statute.[252] Accordingly, she believed that Title VII *permitted* educational officials to consider diversity factors in making layoff decisions rather than *requiring* those decisions to be made by lottery.[253] Judge Sloviter also concluded that if Taxman were entitled to damages, she was entitled only to receive 50 percent of her lost back pay because she had only a 50 percent chance of avoiding the layoff that caused her to lose that back pay.[254]

Judge Scirica dissented in an opinion joined by Judge Sloviter.[255] As Justice Powell's opinion had explained in *Bakke*, the educational context raised special concerns that made diversity particularly desirable. Accordingly, Title VII did not preclude consideration of diversity concerns for a policy as narrow as the *Piscataway* affirmative action policy.[256]

Judge Lewis also dissented in an opinion joined by Judge McKee.[257] Judge Lewis feared the impact that the majority's decision would have on private efforts to eliminate the vestiges of discrimination. For example, the majority opinion would seem to require a law firm forced to chose between laying off a white associate or the only black associate that the firm had ever hired by flipping a coin rather than by making a considered business judgment about what would best serve the interests of the firm. Similarly, a college trying to decide whether to give its one tenure slot to a white candidate or an equally qualified Latino candidate would have to flip a coin rather than consider what would best serve the interests of the school. Judge Lewis did not believe that Title VII required a coin toss in such circumstances.[258]

Judge McKee also wrote a dissenting opinion, which was joined by Judges Sloviter and Lewis.[259] Judge McKee believed that the purpose of Title VII, as explained in the legislative history of the statute, was to move the country closer to an integrated society and away from its separate-but-equal legacy. The Piscataway school board applied an affirmative action policy in a way that was designed to advance that objective. The majority's interpretation of Title VII came full circle and used the statute to undermine the very purpose for which the statute had been enacted. Supreme Court precedents did not require this outcome, and Title VII should have been read to permit consideration of diversity under the facts of the *Piscataway* case.[260]

On October 31, 1996, the school board filed a petition for certiorari, seeking Supreme Court review of the Third Circuit decision in *Piscataway*.[261] The petition asked the Supreme Court to consider whether Title VII permitted employers to take race into account for purposes other than remedying past discrimination; whether fostering faculty diversity in a high school was a permissible purpose; whether a layoff was invariably an unacceptable burden to impose on a nonminority employee; and whether an award of full back pay was proper for an employee who had only a 50 percent chance of avoiding a layoff.[262]

On January 21, 1997, while the petition for certiorari was still pending, the Supreme Court invited the solicitor general to file a brief in the case expressing the views of the United States.[263] The position of the United States had fluctuated at previous stages of the litigation. In September 1991—during the Bush Administration—the United States had originally filed suit on behalf of Taxman in the district court. However, in September 1994—during the Clinton Administration and after the district court decision in favor of Taxman—the United States switched sides and withdrew from the case while it was on appeal in the Third Circuit.[264] On June 6, 1997—after being invited to participate in Supreme Court proceedings—the United States changed course yet again, urging the Supreme Court to deny certiorari and to let the Third Circuit decision stand.[265] On June 27, 1997, the Supreme Court granted certiorari over the objection of the United States.[266] On August 22, 1997, the United States filed a brief *amicus curiae* asking the Supreme Court to issue a narrow ruling in favor of Taxman, but arguing that there were some circumstances in which Title VII did permit employers to take race into account for nonremedial purposes. The brief cited four examples of such circumstances: the selection of police to infiltrate a racially homogeneous gang; the selection of police in a context of racial unrest; the need for an integrated workforce to address racial tensions in prisons; and the need for a diverse faculty to combat student stereotypes and promote mutual understanding and respect.[267]

In November 1997, the school board settled with Taxman after being urged to do so by a coalition of prominent national civil rights groups. Under the terms of the settlement, the board agreed to pay Taxman $433,500 in back pay, interest, and legal fees. The civil rights groups agreed to assist the school board by raising $308,500 of that amount. The reason that the civil rights groups wished to have the case settled was that they feared the issuance of a broad, adverse Supreme Court decision that would undermine the future of affirmative action.[268] As a result of the settlement, the Supreme Court dismissed the writ of certiorari, and never addressed the merits of the *Piscataway* case.[269]

iv. *Coalition for Economic Equity* (1997)

In a second 1997 decision, the Supreme Court denied certiorari in *Coalition for Economic Equity v. Wilson*,[270] thereby leaving in place a Ninth Circuit decision upholding the constitutionality of the California anti-affirmative-action measure popularly known as "Proposition 209." Formally entitled the "California Civil Rights Initiative," Proposition 209 was adopted as a ballot initiative by the California electorate in the November 5, 1996, general election.[271] Proposition 209 amended the California Constitution so that it generally prohibited race- and gender-based affirmative action by California state agencies in the areas of public employment, education, and contracting.[272] Proposition 209 attracted national attention because of the political controversy that has long surrounded affirmative action, and because of the impact that the ultimate constitutional fate of Proposition 209 could have on similar proposals to eliminate affirmative action—proposals that have been under consideration by Congress and by other states.[273]

On November 6, 1996—the day after Proposition 209 was adopted—a coalition representing the interests of women and racial minorities who opposed Proposition 209 filed suit in the United States District Court for the Northern District of California, mounting a facial challenge to the anti-affirmative-action provisions of Proposition 209 on equal protection and federal preemption grounds. On December 23, 1996, after having certified a plaintiff class and issuing a temporary restraining order, the district court, in an opinion by Judge Henderson, issued a preliminary injunction preventing implementation of Proposition 209 pending a trial on the merits.[274] In issuing the preliminary injunction, the district court found as a matter of fact that women and minority members of the plaintiff class would suffer irreparable injury from Proposition 209's invalidation of race and gender preferences,[275] and concluded as a matter of law that Proposition 209 was likely to be held unconstitutional after trial.[276] The district court believed that Proposition 209 would be held unconstitutional because its preference prohibition discriminated against women and minorities. By amending the

California Constitution to prohibit race and gender preferences while permitting all other types of preferences—such as preferences based on age, disability, or veteran status—Proposition 209 singled out race and gender for the imposition of special political burdens.[277]

The district court found that proponents of race and gender preferences could advance their political interests only at the statewide level by amending the California Constitution, while proponents of all other preferences could advance their interests at any level of government through the ordinary political process.[278] Proposition 209 therefore restructured the California political process in a way that seemed to violate the equal protection clause of the Fourteenth Amendment under *Hunter v. Erickson*[279] and *Washington v. Seattle School District No. 1.*[280] In *Hunter*, the Supreme Court had invalidated an Akron, Ohio, City Charter amendment that effectively precluded the city council from adopting fair housing ordinances without approval by a majority of Akron voters. The charter amendment violated the equal protection clause by making it more difficult to secure the enactment of fair housing laws that minorities tend to favor than it was to secure the enactment of laws regulating any other aspects of real estate transactions.[281] In *Seattle*, the Supreme Court used similar reasoning to invalidate a statewide ballot initiative that effectively precluded local school boards from adopting busing plans to facilitate school desegregation.[282] Doctrinally, the district court held first that Proposition 209 constituted a race- and gender-based classification,[283] and second that it restructured the political process in a way that could not survive heightened equal protection scrutiny.[284] The district court also found it likely that Proposition 209 was preempted by Title VII, which favored voluntary affirmative action.[285]

On April 8, 1997, the United States Court of Appeals for the Ninth Circuit unanimously vacated the district court preliminary injunction and upheld the legality of Proposition 209, in an opinion written by Judge O'Scannlain and joined by Judges Leavy and Kleinfeld.[286] The court first held that it was appropriate to reach the merits of the challenge to Proposition 209, even though the state courts had not yet applied the newly adopted ballot initiative, because there was little dispute that Proposition 209 would invalidate race and gender preferences.[287] The Ninth Circuit went on to state that it was reviewing the district court preliminary injunction under an "abuse of discretion" standard, but that it would review the district court's legal determinations de novo. The Ninth Circuit then considered whether the district court determination that the plaintiffs were likely to prevail on the merits was based on "an erroneous legal premise" as a matter of "conventional" equal protection analysis, or as a matter of "political structure" equal protection analysis.[288]

The Ninth Circuit held that "[a]s a matter of 'conventional' equal protection analysis, there is simply no doubt that Proposition 209 is constitutional."[289] The equal protection clause prohibited discrimination on the basis of race and gender, and it prohibited race and gender classifications regardless of the race or gender of those benefited or burdened. Proposition 209 could not therefore violate the equal protection clause because it merely restated this same equal protection prohibition on discrimination.[290] In rejecting the claim that Proposition 209 itself constituted a race and gender classification, the Ninth Circuit asserted, "If merely stating this alleged equal protection violation does not suffice to refute it, the central tenet of the Equal Protection Clause teeters on the brink of incoherence."[291] Although Proposition 209 treated race and gender classifications differently than other legislative classifications, such differential treatment was permissible because the equal protection clause itself treated race and gender classifications differently than other classifications by deeming them presumptively unconstitutional and by subjecting them to heightened scrutiny.[292] Accordingly, the Ninth Circuit concluded that "Proposition 209's ban on race and gender preferences, as a matter of law and logic, does not violate the Equal Protection Clause in any conventional sense."[293]

The Ninth Circuit also held that, as a matter of "political structure" analysis, Proposition 209 did not restructure the California political process in a way that violated the equal protection clause under *Hunter* and *Seattle*.[294] Although the court was skeptical of the claim that women and minorities, who together constitute a majority of the state electorate, could restructure the political process in a way that violated their own equal protection rights,[295] the court chose to root its political-structure holding in the belief that Proposition 209 did not discriminate on the basis of race, but rather addressed race-related matters in a neutral fashion.[296] The Ninth Circuit found that Proposition 209 was not controlled by *Hunter* and *Seattle*, but rather was controlled by *Crawford v. Board of Education of the City of Los Angeles*,[297] a case in which the Supreme Court upheld the constitutionality of a California constitutional amendment that precluded state courts from ordering busing as a remedy for *de facto* school segregation.[298] *Crawford* found that the equal protection clause did not prohibit the mere repeal of a desegregation or antidiscrimination law. Unlike the measures at issue in *Hunter* and *Seattle*, which removed particular matters of minority concern to remote levels of government, Proposition 209 removed *all* race and gender preferences to a remote level of government—*i.e.* to the state initiative process.[299] Moreover, Proposition 209 did not violate the equal protection clause because Proposition 209 was not discriminatory. It did not impose political burdens on the ability of women and minorities to secure equal treatment, but only on the ability of women and minorities to secure preferences. And that burden was a burden imposed by the equal protection clause itself, through its application of heightened scrutiny to race and gender classifications.[300] The court stressed that "[t]he Fourteenth Amendment, lest we lose sight of the forest for the trees, does not require what it barely permits."[301] Because Proposition 209 was neutral rather than discriminatory, the district court had relied on an erroneous legal premise when it found a likelihood that Proposition 209 would violate the equal protection clause.[302]

The Ninth Circuit also found that the district court had erroneously concluded that Proposition 209 was likely preempted by Title VII under the supremacy clause of the Constitution. The district court, deferring to the Equal Employment Opportunity Commission interpretation of Title VII, found that Proposition 209 was inconsistent with the statutory policy of favoring voluntary affirmative action. However, the Ninth Circuit disagreed because Title VII did not expressly preempt laws prohibiting race and gender preferences, and because Title VII was not inconsistent with the antidiscrimination purpose of Proposition 209.[303] The Ninth Circuit concluded that the district court preliminary injunction should not have been issued because, as a matter of law, Proposition 209 did not violate the Constitution.[304]

After the Ninth Circuit panel upheld the constitutionality of Proposition 209, the plaintiffs filed a petition with the full Ninth Circuit requesting rehearing en banc, but the Ninth Circuit denied that petition on August 21, 1997.[305] Four judges dissented from the denial of rehearing en banc, and one additional judge filed a comment on the denial. Judge Schroeder wrote a dissenting opinion that was joined by Judges Pregerson, Norris, and Tashima.[306] She argued that en banc review was warranted for two reasons. First, the case was "extraordinarily important" because the panel decision permitting the state to prohibit the use of narrowly tailored remedies that served compelling interests "put equal protection law in a state of turmoil." Second, the panel decision was contrary to controlling Supreme Court precedent prohibiting states from restructuring the political process in order to disadvantage minorities.[307] The panel decision treated Proposition 209 as if it were a mere repeal of past remedies that were not constitutionally required, but Proposition 209 also restructured the political process to bar future remedies in a way that was prohibited by *Seattle*.[308] Judge Schroeder also disputed the panel's claim that Proposition 209 merely adopted equal protection standards because Proposition 209 barred remedies that were permissible under the equal protection clause.[309] Judge Schroeder believed that the purpose of judicial review was to check majoritarian excesses, and for that reason, the district court decision invalidating Proposition 209 should have been affirmed.[310]

Judge Norris also filed an opinion "respecting the denial of rehearing en banc," that was joined by Judges Schroeder, Pregerson, and Tashima.[311] Judge Norris believed that under the reasoning of *Hunter* and *Seattle*, Proposition 209 constituted a "racial classification" that was "discriminatory on its face," which could not be used to restructure the political process in a way that was intended to place special burdens on minorities.[312] Proposition 209 permitted most special interest groups to press for change at any level of the state political process, but race and gender special interests could secure political change only through a statewide initiative process with the onerous financial burdens that such a process entailed. The panel decision upholding Proposition 209 did not follow Supreme Court precedent.[313] The *Hunter-Seattle* political restructuring cases prohibit the imposition of political burdens on legislation that is beneficial to minorities. The panel, however, deemed those cases to be inapplicable because the panel distinguished between antidiscrimination laws and affirmative action programs. It viewed affirmative action programs as inherently discriminatory, even when they passed constitutional muster. That view reflected that panel's own subjective impressions about the desirability of affirmative action, but the panel was not authorized to inject its subjective preferences into the equal protection clause. Moreover, *Seattle* rejects the panel's suggested distinction between affirmative action and antidiscrimination measures by according the same constitutional protection to an affirmative action busing plan that *Hunter* accorded to an antidiscrimination housing measure. The panel's opposition to affirmative action might be relevant in a political debate, but it was not relevant to constitutional interpretation.[314]

Judge Norris also rejected the panel's other efforts to distinguish *Hunter* and *Seattle*. The panel's claim that the equal protection clause did not require tolerance of affirmative action was inapposite because the issue raised by Proposition 209 was not whether the equal protection clause required affirmative action but whether minorities could be precluded from seeking legislation that they desired on equal terms with others.[315] The panel suggestion that *Hunter* and *Seattle* did not apply to Proposition 209 because Proposition 209 neutrally applied at *every* level of the state political process rather than at only one level, as in *Seattle*, was also unsupportable. Neither *Hunter*, nor *Seattle*, nor common sense supported the conclusion that constitutional difficulties could be reduced by *expanding* the levels at which the state disadvantaged minorities.[316] The panel suggested that Proposition 209 did not pose constitutional difficulties because the majority needed no constitutional protection from discrimination, and women and minorities collectively made up a majority of the electorate. However, Judge Norris found no merit whatsoever in the panel's claim.[317] Similarly, the panel's suggestion that Proposition 209 was valid under *Crawford* because it constituted a mere repeal of existing affirmative action programs ignored the fact that Proposition 209 also prohibited the adoption of race and gender affirmative action programs in the future.[318] Judge Norris concluded that rule of law required federal judges to follow precedent, but the panel had improperly disregarded controlling Supreme Court precedent in the service of "conservative judicial activism."[319]

Judge Hawkins wrote an opinion "commenting on the denial of rehearing en banc."[320] He believed that the disagreement between the district court and the panel concerned the issue of how a lower court ought properly to treat a precedent that it predicted the Supreme Court would no longer follow. Judge Hawkins concluded that the *Hunter-Seattle* analysis offered by Judge Norris was a proper analysis of existing precedent, and that lower courts were obligated to follow that line of precedent rather than disregard that line of precedent based on a prediction that the Supreme Court would abandon it.[321]

On August 26, 1997, the Ninth Circuit panel denied a motion to stay the effectiveness of its decision pending Supreme Court action on a petition for certiorari, thereby permitting Proposition 209 to take effect on August 28, 1997.[322] On September 4, 1997, the Supreme Court denied a motion for an emergency stay, thereby permitting Proposition 209 to remain in effect while the Supreme Court considered whether to grant certiorari.[323]

On August 29, 1997, the plaintiffs filed a petition for certiorari seeking review of the Ninth Circuit decision upholding the legality of Proposition 209.[324] The petition asked the Supreme Court to review, *inter alia*, whether Proposition 209 violated the *Hunter* and *Seattle* prohibition on discriminatory restructuring of the political process where race and gender preferences were singled out for political burdens not imposed on the adoption of other types of preferences, and whether Proposition 209 was preempted by Title

VII.[325] The Supreme Court denied the petition for certiorari on November 3, 1997.[326]

The post-*Adarand* affirmative action decisions of the Supreme Court in ruling on petitions for certiorari seemed consistently skeptical about the value of affirmative action. The Supreme Court's denial of certiorari in *Podberesky*, *Hopwood*, and *Coalition for Economic Equity* permitted lower court decisions that were adverse to affirmative action to remain in place, even though each of those decisions rested on novel resolutions of legal issues that seem ultimately destined for Supreme Court resolution. The Supreme Court did grant certiorari to review a lower court decision that was adverse to affirmative action in *Piscataway*, but proponents of affirmative action seemed so afraid of the current Court's political opposition to affirmative action that they were unwilling to risk Supreme Court resolution of the novel legal issues that were presented in that case. Because the Supreme Court did not issue explanatory opinions in taking its actions on these four petitions for certiorari, nothing can be said with certainty about the Court's position on any of the underlying issues. But the anti-affirmative-action climate on the current Court seems unmistakable. The Supreme Court's general lack of receptivity to racial affirmative action, evidenced in *Adarand* and the Court's post-*Adarand* actions on petitions for certiorari, has also been largely replicated in the Supreme Court's voting rights cases.

4

The Voting Rights Cases

The Supreme Court has decided a series of cases relating to the Voting Rights Act of 1965[1] that can also be viewed as affirmative action cases because of the affirmative obligations that the act imposes on covered jurisdictions to prevent the abridgment of minority voting strength. Although the Fifteenth Amendment prohibits states from abridging the right to vote on account of race,[2] some states and political subdivisions have historically attempted to circumvent the Fifteenth Amendment guarantee through the use of racially correlated voting requirements and racially gerrymandered voting districts. When a racially discriminatory purpose *and* effect can be proved, intentional efforts to abridge minority voting rights violate the equal protection clause of the Fourteenth Amendment.[3] However, such discrimination also violates the Voting Rights Act of 1965, which Congress enacted pursuant to its enumerated power to enforce the Fifteenth Amendment.[4] As amended in 1982, § 2 of the Voting Rights Act prohibits voting practices, including the adoption of voter reapportionment or districting plans, that have the *effect* of *diluting* the voting strength of covered racial minorities.[5] In the 1986 decision of *Thornburg v. Gingles*[6] the Supreme Court interpreted the effect or "results" test of the 1982 amendments. The Court held that three threshold requirements had to be proved in order to establish that minority voting strength was diluted by a particular districting plan. First, a minority plaintiff had to prove that his or her minority group was "sufficiently large and geographically compact to constitute a majority" in the alternate voting district contended for. Second, the minority group had to be "politically cohesive." Third, it had to be the case that "the white majority votes sufficiently as a bloc to enable it . . . usually to defeat the minority's preferred candidate."[7] In addition, § 5 of the act provides that states or political subdivisions with a history or likely presence of voting discrimination cannot change their voting practices or requirements without prior approval by the attorney general of United States or the United States District Court for the District of Columbia.[8] Because race-conscious remedial reapportionment that is designed to comply with the Voting Rights Act also constitutes race-conscious affirmative action, Voting Rights Act remedies pose the risk of violating the Fourteenth Amendment equal protection rights of white voters. Accordingly, efforts by racial minorities to increase or preserve their voting strength are subject to both statutory constraints under the Voting Rights Act and constitutional constraints under the equal protection clause.[9]

1. Voting Rights Act

The Supreme Court has decided a series of recent statutory cases interpreting the amended Voting Rights Act of 1965[10] that affect the utility of the act as a device for protecting minority voting rights. The Voting Rights Act cases that have been decided since the Court's 1993 decision in *Shaw v. Reno* have acquired special significance because the Court has used those Voting Rights Act decisions in tandem with its *Shaw v. Reno* line of equal protection decisions to restructure the ways in which race-conscious affirmative action will be permitted in the voting rights context. In 1993, the Court issued two unanimous decisions—*Voinovich v. Quilter*[11] and *Growe v. Emison*[12]—reversing three-judge federal district courts in Voting Rights Act cases. *Voinovich* rejected a claim that minority voting strength had been diluted by "packing" minority voters into a small number of election districts,[13] and *Growe* rejected a claim that minority voting strength would be diluted *unless* minority voters were concentrated into a small number of districts in order to prevent the fragmentation of minority voters.[14] Then, in 1994, the Court decided two additional Voting Rights Act cases—*Holder v. Hall*[15] and *Johnson v. De Grandy*,[16]—limiting the scope of vote-dilution claims that could be maintained under the act. *Holder* held that § 2 of the Voting Rights Act did not permit a vote-dilution challenge to the single or multimember nature of a representational scheme,[17] and *De Grandy* rejected a vote-dilution claim where the number of pertinent minority voting districts was proportional to the minority's pertinent population percentage.[18]

In 1997, the Court decided three more Voting Rights Act cases—*Young v. Fordice*,[19] *Reno v. Bossier Parish School Board*,[20] and *City of Monroe v. United States*[21]—all of which concerned the standards for preclearance under the Voting Rights Act. *Young* held that preclearance was required for even minor changes in voting practices by covered jurisdictions where those changes were discretionary rather than ministerial;[22] *Bossier Parish* held that preclearance was governed by a nonretrogression standard rather than a vote-dilution standard;[23] and *City of Monroe* held that the attorney general had constructively precleared a voting practice on which the attorney general had never specifically focused.[24] In 1999, the Supreme Court issued another preclearance decision, in *Lopez v. Monterey County,*[25] which held that a covered jurisdiction was required to obtain preclearance for voting changes even when those changes were compelled by the law of a state that was not itself a covered jurisdiction.[26]

i. *Voinovich* (1993)

In *Voinovich v. Quilter*[27] Justice O'Connor wrote an opinion for a unanimous Court rejecting an "influence dilution" claim under the Voting Rights Act for failure to satisfy the *Gingles* requirement that the white majority be shown to vote as a bloc against minority-preferred candidates.[28] An Ohio redistricting plan, adopted by a state apportionment board, created a number of majority-minority voting districts—districts in which a majority of voters were members of a minority group. The plan was challenged on the grounds that it diluted black voting strength by "packing" black voters into a smaller number of districts in which they would constitute a majority (thereby facilitating the election of a smaller number of representatives) rather than by spreading them over a larger number of districts in which they would constitute substantial minorities (thereby allowing them to *influence* the election of a larger number of representatives). It is not clear that opposition to the plan was entirely racial. The plan appears to have been favored by the Republican majority on the Ohio apportionment board and opposed by the Democratic minority. However, because the plan virtually ensured the election of some minority representatives, it was also supported by the Ohio NAACP.[29] When the plan was challenged by black and white voters and politicians as a violation of the Voting Rights Act, a three-judge district court invalidated the plan. It held that, in the absence of a demonstrated need to remedy past discrimination, majority-minority districts were a per se violation of § 2 of the Voting Rights Act, and it appointed a special master to prepare a new redistricting plan.[30] The district court also held that, because the plan deviated from the principle of one-person, one-vote and intentionally neutralized minority voting strength in those 35 percent-minority districts from which minority candidates had repeatedly been elected in the past, the plan also violated the Fourteenth and Fifteenth Amendments of the Constitution.[31]

In reversing the district court, Justice O'Connor's opinion rejected the argument that the Voting Rights Act contained a per se prohibition on the nonremedial use of majority-minority districts. Although a federal *court* could not order the creation of a majority-minority district unless necessary to remedy a past violation of federal law, a state *legislature* could create such districts without violating the Voting Rights Act, as long as the creation of such districts did not have the effect of abridging the voting strength of a protected minority group.[32] Such a vote-dilution claim could not be established under the facts of *Voinovich* because white voters did not consistently vote as a bloc against minority candidates, as evidenced by the fact that crossover white voters had enabled blacks to elect black candidates in districts where black voters did not constitute a majority of the electorate.[33] Justice O'Connor expressly declined to address the question of whether the race-conscious creation of majority-minority districts might nevertheless violate the Fourteenth Amendment.[34]

ii. *Growe* (1993)

In *Growe v. Emison*,[35] the Supreme Court's other 1993 Voting Rights Act decision, the Court set aside a remedial reapportionment plan adopted by a three-judge district court, this time on the grounds that the plaintiffs had failed to satisfy the "political cohesiveness" requirement of *Gingles*.[36] Justice Scalia wrote an opinion for a unanimous Court holding that the district court plan was inconsistent with the comity-based doctrine of abstention,[37] and that it was not required by the Voting Rights Act.[38]

After the 1990 census, there was general agreement that population shifts had caused the Minnesota districting plans for state legislative and federal congressional elections to become unconstitutional in violation of the one-person, one-vote principle of the Fourteenth Amendment. As a result, reapportionment proceedings were commenced in state court, in the state legislature, and in federal court, but only the federal court proceeding encompassed a racial vote-dilution claim under § 2 of the Voting Rights Act. When the governor of Minnesota vetoed a reapportionment bill that had been passed by the Minnesota legislature, the Minnesota state court ordered the adoption of its own judicially formulated reapportionment plan.

However, the federal district court enjoined implementation of the state-court plan because the plan had not considered the Voting Rights Act claims that had been made in the federal action. The federal court then adopted a reapportionment plan that it had formulated, which included clear or "super" majority-minority districts designed to comply with the Voting Rights Act.[39]

Justice Scalia stated that the federal court should have deferred to the state court's ongoing reapportionment proceeding rather than adopting a reapportionment plan of its own, notwithstanding the fact that the state-court plan failed to encompass Voting Rights Act claims.[40] The reason that the federal district court had given for invalidating the state-court reapportionment plan was that it did not contain supermajority-minority districts, which the district court deemed to be required by the Voting Rights Act. Justice Scalia, however, found that supermajority-minority districts were *not* required by the Voting Rights Act because the district court had not made the preliminary factual finding of racially cohesive, minority bloc voting that was necessary to trigger such a remedy for vote-dilution claims under the Voting Rights Act. In the absence of such bloc voting, minorities would not be able to ensure the election of their preferred candidate even in a supermajority-minority district.[41]

iii. *Holder* (1994)

In 1994, the Supreme Court decided two more Voting Rights Act cases, in which it rejected voting rights challenges on nonconstitutional grounds. In *Holder v. Hall,*[42] the Court held that § 2 of the Voting Rights Act did not permit a challenge to the single- or multimember character of a representative governmental system.[43] The voters of Bleckley County, Georgia, had chosen by referendum to retain their single-commissioner form of government rather than adopt a multimember system authorized by state law. No black had ever been elected county commissioner under the single-member system, but the 20 percent black voting population would have been able to elect one of five commissioners under the rejected multimember system.[44] Black voters challenged the referendum as constituting intentional discrimination prohibited by the Fourteenth and Fifteenth Amendments, as well as vote dilution prohibited by § 2 of the Voting Rights Act. The district court rejected all three claims, but the Court of Appeals for the Eleventh Circuit reversed and accepted the statutory vote-dilution claim without reaching the constitutional claims.[45]

The Supreme Court reversed the court of appeals decision in a plurality opinion written by Justice Kennedy and joined by Justices Rehnquist and O'Connor.[46] The opinion stated that the size of a governing body was not subject to a § 2 vote-dilution challenge because there was no standard size for governing bodies that could be used as a benchmark against which to test the validity of the Bleckley County single-commissioner system. Vote dilution implied a deviation from some objective baseline, because in the absence of a baseline it was not possible to conclude that minority voting strength had been "diluted."[47] The Georgia state legislature had authorized the adoption of five-member county commissions; five-member commissions were the most common form of government in the state; and Bleckley County itself had adopted a five-member system for the election of school board members. Nevertheless, Justice Kennedy found that a five-member commission could not serve as a baseline for assessing vote dilution in Bleckley County because Bleckley County itself had never utilized a five-member commission.[48] In a portion of the opinion joined only by Chief Justice Rehnquist, Justice Kennedy rejected the argument that the size of a governing body must be subject to a vote-dilution challenge under § 2 because the Court had already held a change in the size of a governing body to be subject the preclearance provisions of § 5. Justice Kennedy distinguished § 2 from § 5 challenges. He reasoned that, because § 5 actions applied only where there was a *change* in voting qualifications or procedures, the old qualification or procedure could be used to establish a baseline against which any dilution entailed in the new qualification or procedure could be assessed.[49]

Justice O'Connor wrote a concurring opinion in which she agreed with the importance of finding an objective baseline in vote-dilution cases, and agreed that no baseline could ever be found in a § 2 case challenging the size of a governing body.[50] Justice O'Connor, however, disagreed with Justice Kennedy's conclusion that § 2 and § 5 were not coterminous. She asserted that the nearly identical operative language of the two sections, and the fact that the Court had already recognized § 5 actions to encompass challenges to the size of a governing body, meant that as a threshold matter § 2 could also encompass vote-dilution challenges to the size of a governmental body. The problem was that, in addition to ensuring satisfaction of the threshold requirement, a court would have to "choose an objectively reasonable alternative [size] for the dilution comparison."[51] This could never be done because there were many alternative size governing systems that a county might conceivably adopt. Moreover, the fact that a five-member commission was the norm for the state of Georgia was inconsequential, because too many § 2 vote-dilution challenges would be possible if mere deviation from the state norm were sufficient to establish a vote-dilution claim.[52]

Justice Thomas wrote a lengthy opinion concurring in the judgment, joined by Justice Scalia, which argued that as a matter of statutory construction, § 2 of the Voting Rights Act did not encompass vote-dilution claims at all.[53] Arguing for a strict textual interpretation, Justice Thomas asserted that the language of § 2, which applies to a "voting qualification or prerequisite to voting or standard, practice or procedure," did not include electoral mechanisms alleged to dilute minority voting strength. Rather, the statutory language was limited to "state enactments that limit citizens' access to the ballot," such as the literacy tests to which the statute was originally addressed.[54] In addition, the Court's efforts to read § 2 as encompassing vote-dilution claims not only had proved unworkable but had produced federal court remedies that imprudently segregated voters by race.[55] Justice Thomas also noted that the elusive baseline problem entailed in reading the Voting Rights Act to encompass vote-dilution claims would implicate the federal judiciary in a quest for the most appropriate political theory of representative democracy—something that politically unaccountable judges are poorly equipped to undertake.[56] Justice Thomas argued that his limited reading of the Voting Rights Act emanated from the plain meaning of the statutory language because neither racial gerrymandering nor discriminatory sizing of governing bodies constituted a "'standard, practice, or procedure' . . . *with respect to voting*."[57] He concluded his opinion by rejecting the argument that the legislative history supported a vote-dilution interpretation of the act—adopting Justice Scalia's now-famous aversion to legislative history[58]—and by rejecting the claim that *stare decisis* required deference to prior Supreme Court interpretations of the act as extending to vote-dilution claims.[59]

Justice Blackmun wrote a dissenting opinion, joined by Justices Stevens, Souter, and Ginsburg, which argued that the size of a governing body was a "standard, practice or procedure" encompassed by the Voting Rights Act, and that size was subject to vote-dilution challenges under the act.[60] In concluding that the act encompassed governmental size as a "standard, practice or procedure," Justice Blackmun relied on "[n]early 30 years of precedent" establishing that the remedial provisions of the act should be given "'the broadest possible scope'";[61] on a series of Supreme Court precedents construing the act to encompass a wide variety of election- and voting-related practices;[62] and on Supreme Court precedents treating the size of a governing body as within the § 5 preclearance provisions of the act.[63] He also argued that the 1982 amendments to the act constituted congressional ratification of this expansive coverage, and he noted that five members of the *Holder* Court agreed that the act encompassed challenges to the size of a governing body.[64] In concluding that the size of a governing body was subject to vote-dilution challenges, Justice Blackmun argued that, under the facts of *Holder*, the rejected five-member Bleckley County Commission constituted a reasonable alternative that could be used as a benchmark for determining vote-dilution claims because it was specifically authorized by the state legislature, was the most common governmental system in the state, and was the system that Bleckley County had adopted for its school board.[65] He also argued that the requirements of objective reasonableness, through reference to "history, custom, or practice," would eliminate specious size challenges based upon mere mathematical abstractions.[66] Finally, Justice Blackmun stressed that the purposes of the Voting Rights Act would not be adequately served if it were read only to prohibit blatant voting discrimination while permitting more subtle evasions.[67]

Justice Ginsburg also wrote a brief dissent.[68] She conceded that there was an inherent tension in the Voting Rights Act between the desire to prevent vote dilution and the desire to avoid a right to proportional representation for minority voters. For her, however, this was a common sort of tension in congressional legislation because the give-and-take of the legislative process often failed to reconcile conflicting goals.[69] She argued that it was the job of the federal judiciary to reach a proper accommodation of such competing policy objectives.[70]

Justice Stevens also wrote a dissenting opinion, which was joined by Justices Blackmun, Souter, and Ginsburg.[71] Justice Stevens argued that the original enactment of the Voting Rights Act in 1965, as well as the amendments to that act in 1970, 1975, and 1982, all constituted unambiguous congressional ratification of the Supreme Court's prior decisions under the Fifteenth Amendment, and under earlier versions of the Voting Rights Act itself, to provide a remedy for vote-dilution claims.[72] Justice Stevens also termed the suggestion by Justice Thomas that the act be reinterpreted to preclude vote-dilution challenges a "radical" proposal that was inconsistent with the doctrine of *stare decisis* because it would entail overruling a large number of settled Supreme Court precedents. Even though vote-dilution challenges might require the Court to consider difficult questions of political theory, that was an appropriate function for the federal judiciary.[73]

iv. *Johnson v. De Grandy* (1994)

The second Voting Rights Act case that the Supreme Court decided in 1994 was *Johnson v. De Grandy*.[74] In *De Grandy*, Latino and black plaintiffs, as well as the United States attorney general, challenged a 1992 Florida state legislative reapportionment plan under § 2 of the Voting Rights Act for failing to take adequate account of population shifts reflected in the 1990 census and thereby fragmenting cohesive minority communities in a way that diluted minority voting strength. The district court found a history of voting discrimination, as well as a level of racial bloc voting sufficient to establish a § 2 violation, and ordered the creation of two additional majority-Latino voting districts for House elections. Although it also found that an additional majority-black district could have been created for Senate elections, it did not order this remedy because it found that the additional Senate district could be created only by further diluting Latino voting strength, thereby making remedies for black and Latino vote dilution mutually exclusive.[75] The Supreme Court unanimously reversed.[76]

Justice Souter wrote a majority opinion for the Court in *De Grandy*, the bulk of which was joined by a total of seven justices—Justices Souter, Rehnquist, Blackmun, Stevens, O'Connor, Kennedy, and Ginsburg.[77] Justice Souter argued that even though the district court had found the three *Gingles* factors to be satisfied—minority compactness and numerousness, minority cohesion or bloc voting, and majority bloc voting—when the totality of circumstances was considered, no § 2 violation could be established. This was because the number of majority-minority districts for both minorities in the pertinent county roughly corresponded to each minority's percentage of the voting population in the county. Such substantial proportionality, while not alone dispositive, nevertheless showed that minority votes had not been impermissibly diluted.[78] Justice Souter went on to note that although § 2 of the Voting Rights Act explicitly disclaimed the creation of any right to proportional representation for individual minorities, this disclaimer focused merely on the outcome of particular elections; it did not make population proportionality irrelevant to § 2, which focuses on equality of *opportunity* and not on equality of *success* by minority political candidates at the polls.[79] The error that the district court had made was to assume that § 2 of the Voting Rights Act compelled an apportionment scheme that incorporated the maximum number of majority-minority voting districts possible, without regard to population proportionality.[80] Justice Souter added, however, that the existence of population proportionality did not automatically preclude the existence of a § 2 violation, because states could still adopt subtle methods of voting discrimination even within a universe of population proportionality.[81]

Justice O'Connor wrote a concurring opinion emphasizing that in § 2 vote-dilution cases, population proportionality was always relevant in establishing a baseline against which dilution claims could be assessed. However, population proportionality was never dispositive. What was most important was careful consideration of the totality of circumstances.[82]

Justice Kennedy wrote an opinion concurring in part and concurring in the judgment.[83] Although he agreed with the result that the majority reached, he disagreed with the majority's willingness to consider population proportionality as a permissible factor in determining the existence of a § 2 vote-dilution violation. Justice Kennedy viewed the majority's concession that population proportionality was relevant to a vote-dilution claim as an incentive for states to engage in race-conscious districting in order to approximate population proportionality, and for the attorney general to assess population proportionality in making preclearance determinations under § 5 of the act. Such race consciousness was inconsistent with the race-neutral, color-blind objectives of the equal protection guarantee, and might well be unconstitutional under the Fourteenth and Fifteenth Amendments. However, Justice Kennedy was willing to concur in the result reached by the majority because those constitutional issues had not been presented to the Court.[84]

Justice Thomas dissented in an opinion, joined by Justice Scalia. His opinion reiterated the view he initially expressed in *Holder v. Hall*, that § 2 of the Voting Rights Act did not encompass vote-dilution claims.[85]

v. *Young* (1997)

In 1997, the Supreme Court decided three preclearance cases concerning the legal standards that govern attorney general preclearance under § 5 of the Voting Rights Act. The first was *Young v. Fordice*,[86] in which the Court held that preclearance was required for even subtle changes in voter registration procedures where there was a danger that minority voting rights would be abridged.[87] The change in voting procedures at issue in *Young* resulted from the enactment by Congress of the National Voter Registration Act of 1993, which required certain changes in Mississippi voting procedures to be implemented by January 1, 1995. The purpose of this statute was to simplify voter registration for federal elections by allowing registration on driver's license applications, at "public assistance" offices, and in other convenient ways. The statute was also designed to make it more difficult for states to purge registered voters from the rolls because they had not voted in recent elections.[88]

Prior to enactment of the National Voter Registration Act, Mississippi had utilized a unitary voter registration system for both state and federal elections. After enactment, Mississippi voting officials proposed a new streamlined registration procedure to comply with the statute, and provisionally applied the new procedures to both state and federal elections while awaiting final approval of the plan by the Mississippi legislature. Mississippi was subject to a preclearance requirement under § 5 of the Voting Rights Act, and the United States attorney general precleared the provisional plan on February 1, 1995. However, the Mississippi legislature ultimately failed to adopt the streamlined federal registration procedures for state elections, and continued to rely on the older, more cumbersome registration procedures for state elections. Under its new bifurcated plan, Mississippi was the only state in the country to have different registration procedures for state and federal elections. As a result, voters who had been registered under the streamlined provisional plan were registered for only federal and not state elections. The United States attorney general took the position that her earlier preclearance of the provisional unitary plan did not apply to the final bifurcated plan. Then, in consolidated suits, the United States and four Mississippi voters challenged the new bifurcated plan on the grounds that it had never received § 5 preclearance. A three-judge federal district court rejected the challenge and entered summary judgment for the state. The district court held that the attorney general's February 1, 1995, preclearance of the provisional plan was adequate for the federal registration changes, and that no preclearance was needed for the state's continuation of its old registration procedures for state elections. On appeal, the Supreme Court reversed.[89]

Justice Breyer wrote an opinion for a unanimous Supreme Court, holding that the bifurcated Mississippi registration plan had never been precleared, as was required by § 5 of the Voting Rights Act. Justice Breyer agreed with the three-judge court that the provisional unitary plan had never been "in force or effect" within the meaning of the Voting Rights Act in a way that established it as the baseline against which the new bifurcated plan had to be measured for § 5 retrogression purposes.[90] Nevertheless, Justice Breyer concluded that the new bifurcated plan required § 5 preclearance because it deviated in significant ways from the old unitary plan that did serve as the applicable baseline. Justice Breyer emphasized that even minor changes in voting procedures required § 5 preclearance, and that this was true even when changes were made in an effort to comply with federal law, "so long as those changes reflect policy choices made by state or local officials."[91] Moreover, preclearance was required regardless of whether a change initially appeared to be neutral, or to favor or disfavor a covered minority.[92] Although the National Voter Registration Act imposed highly specific obligations on states, the statute left enough policymaking discretion in the hands of implementing state officials to warrant application of the § 5 preclearance requirement. For example, state officials retained the discretion not to tell registrants using the new streamlined procedure that they would be registered for federal but not state elections.[93] Justice Breyer rejected Mississippi's contention that the attorney general had precleared the state's new dual registration system when she approved the provisional system on February 1, 1995, finding that the attorney general had assumed that she was approving a unitary rather than a dual registration system.[94] Justice Breyer also rejected the state's claim that Mississippi's retention of its old registration system for state elections did not trigger the need for § 5 preclearance. Although § 5 did not apply to changes mandated by federal law, and although retention of a prior state system did not alone trigger § 5, the discretionary aspects surrounding the state's administration of the National Voter Registration Act for federal elections were sufficient to trigger the need for § 5 preclearance. This was especially true in a context suggesting that the dual registration system might have been adopted for discriminatory purposes.[95] The Court then remanded, instructing the district court to enjoin further use of Mississippi's dual registration system prior to preclearance.[96]

vi. *Bossier Parish* (1997)

The Supreme Court's second 1997 preclearance case was *Reno v. Bossier Parish School Board*.[97] In *Bossier Parish*, the Court held that even if a districting plan violated the § 2 antidilution provision of the Voting Rights Act, the plan could not be denied § 5 preclearance for that reason alone. Preclearance could be denied under § 5 only if the plan was retrogressive, meaning that the plan had either the intent or effect of giving a protected minority group less voting strength than the group had possessed prior to adoption of the challenged plan.[98] However, the Court also held that vote dilution prohibited by § 2 could nevertheless be relevant in a § 5 preclearance inquiry, to the extent that it constituted evidence of retrogressive intent.[99]

After the 1990 census, the School Board of Bossier Parish, Louisiana, decided to redraw its election districts in order to equalize the population distribution. The board was covered by the § 5 preclearance requirements of the Voting Rights Act because of its past discriminatory voting practices. Therefore, in an effort to secure preclearance, the board adopted the same twelve-single-member-district reapportionment plan that the attorney general had previously approved for the Bossier Parish Police Jury, the parish's primary governing body. Neither the pre-1990 school board apportionment scheme nor the new school board plan based on the approved police jury plan contained any majority-minority districts. As a result, the parties stipulated that the new school board plan was not retrogressive insofar as it maintained rather than reduced the existing number of majority-minority districts. Although the attorney general had precleared the police jury plan despite its lack of majority-minority districts, the attorney general refused to preclear the new school board plan. This was because after the police jury plan had been precleared, the NAACP had proposed an alternate school board plan containing two majority-black districts that the school board had rejected. The attorney general stated that the board's rejection of the NAACP plan constituted vote dilution that violated § 2 of Voting Rights Act, and invoked a Justice Department regulation authorizing the attorney general to deny preclearance under § 5 when necessary to prevent a violation of § 2. The school board then filed an action seeking preclearance from a three-judge district court for the District of Columbia. The three-judge court disagreed with the attorney general and precleared the school board plan, stating that § 5 did not permit a denial of preclearance on the basis of a § 2 violation.[100] The Supreme Court affirmed this aspect of the district court decision.[101]

Justice O'Connor wrote a majority opinion in *Bossier Parish* that was signed in relevant part by seven members of the Court—Justices O'Connor, Rehnquist, Scalia, Kennedy, Thomas, Ginsburg, and Breyer.[102] Justice O'Connor's opinion cited *Holder v. Hall* for the proposition that § 2 and § 5 were designed to combat different evils, and accordingly imposed different duties on the states.[103] Section 5 preclearance was designed to prevent states from circumventing the protections of the Voting Rights Act by replacing a discriminatory voting practice that had been invalidated by the courts with a second discriminatory practice that would remain in effect until it too was eventually invalidated. Section 5 preclearance, therefore, shifted both the burden of proof and the burden of inertia to covered states wishing to change their voting practices.[104] Because the goal of § 5 was simply to freeze election procedures, § 5 preclearance was required only if a plan by design or effect "would lead to a retrogression in the position of racial minorities with respect to their effective exercise of the electoral franchise."[105] A plan that did not decrease minority voting strength could not therefore be denied preclearance on retrogressive-effect grounds.[106] Unlike § 5, § 2 was designed to serve the broader purpose of eradicating voting practices engaged in by *any* state—whether covered by § 5 or not—if those practices diluted minority voting strength under the *Thornburg v. Gingles* standards, by making it harder for minority voters than for other members of the electorate to elect candidates of their choice.[107]

Justice O'Connor concluded that, because § 5 focused on retrogression, § 2 vote dilution could not justify a denial of § 5 preclearance in the absence of such retrogression. If § 5 authorized a denial of preclearance for a § 2 violation, states would have to litigate the § 2 validity of their voting practice changes before implementing them, which would impose excessive federalism costs.[108] Justice O'Connor did concede that even a nonretrogressive voting change would warrant denial of § 5 preclearance if the change was unconstitutional, but that did not make § 2 and § 5 coterminous. Justice O'Connor emphasized that a vote-dilution *effect* prohibited by § 2 did not amount to a violation of the discriminatory *intent* standard of the Constitution because Congress intended the § 2 prohibition to be broader than the constitutional prohibition on discrimination under the equal protection clause.[109] Justice O'Connor also rejected the argument that the Court should defer to a Justice Department regulation requiring the denial of § 5 preclearance even in the absence of retrogression when necessary to prevent a clear § 2 violation. She asserted that, despite some contrary language in the legislative history, and despite the deference that was normally owed the attorney general's interpretation of the Voting Rights Act, the Justice Department regulation at issue here did not comport with the intent of Congress in adopting the Voting Rights Act.[110] Justice O'Connor also rejected the argument that § 2 violations ought to be cognizable in § 5 proceedings for reasons of judicial economy and sound equitable discretion, again asserting that the Voting Rights Act precluded such a collapse of the two distinct standards.[111]

Justice O'Connor's majority opinion finally vacated a portion of the district court decision that viewed § 2 violations as completely irrelevant to a § 5 preclearance inquiry. Although § 5 focused on retrogression rather than

§ 2 vote dilution as the basis for a denial of preclearance, § 2 vote dilution *was* relevant to a § 5 inquiry into whether a voting plan had been adopted with intent to retrogress. If a plan had a dilutive *effect*, that effect was evidence of retrogressive *intent*. Although mere § 2 dilutive effect could not alone establish § 5 retrogressive intent without once again collapsing the distinction between the two standards, § 2 dilutive effect could be taken into consideration as evidence that was relevant to retrogressive intent.[112] Justice O'Connor's opinion explicitly reserved the question of whether a § 5 intent inquiry could ever encompass any issue other than retrogressive intent.[113]

Justice Thomas wrote a concurring opinion reiterating his *Holder v. Hall* view that § 2 should not be read to permit vote-dilution challenges,[114] anticipating that § 2 problems would be exacerbated in § 5 retrogression inquiries.[115] Justice Thomas argued that any reapportionment change could be characterized as retrogressive for § 5 purposes. A change reducing the number of majority-minority districts could be viewed as retrogressive because it reduced minority voting strength, but a change *increasing* the number of majority-minority districts could also be viewed as retrogressive because it reduced minority influence in surrounding voting districts that would otherwise have had more minority voters. The indeterminacy inherent in the concept of vote dilution, therefore, gave the attorney general and the federal courts the power to displace political judgments of the states concerning what best served minority interests.[116] Justice Thomas also disagreed with Justice O'Connor's suggestion that Justice Department regulations concerning preclearance were "normally" entitled to deference.[117] He argued that the primary route for § 5 preclearance was through the United States District Court for the District of Columbia, with attorney general preclearance serving as merely an alternative mechanism for preclearance. If the district court were required to defer to the attorney general's preclearance standards, such deference would undermine the independence of the district court.[118]

Justice Breyer wrote an opinion concurring in part and concurring in the judgment that was joined by Justice Ginsburg.[119] Justice Breyer addressed the issue expressly reserved in Justice O'Connor's majority opinion, arguing that the § 5 purpose inquiry should not be limited to mere intent to retrogress, but should include the intent to engage in unconstitutional vote dilution as well.[120] Because Justice Breyer joined the bulk of the majority opinion, he presumably agreed that a § 2 vote-dilutive *effect* was beyond the scope of a § 5 preclearance inquiry. However, he believed that the *intent* to engage in vote dilution—which was unconstitutional under present

Fourteenth and Fifteenth Amendment standards—should also be encompassed within the scope of § 5, even if the resulting plan was not retrogressive. Justice Breyer argued that if a covered jurisdiction choosing between two nonretrogressive districting plans rejected a plan creating one or two majority-minority districts in favor of a plan creating no majority-minority districts, and did so for the purpose of diluting minority voting strength, such a purpose would both be unconstitutional and constitute grounds for denying preclearance under § 5. Justice Breyer further argued that the Court's recent Fourteenth Amendment voting rights decisions in *Shaw v. Hunt* and *Miller v. Johnson* were consistent with this understanding.[121]

Justice Stevens wrote an opinion dissenting in part and concurring in part, which was joined by Justice Souter.[122] Although Justice Stevens concurred in the decision remanding the case to the district court, he dissented from the majority's holding that § 5 did not permit a denial of preclearance to be based upon § 2 vote dilution.[123] Justice Stevens first emphasized that the majority was willing to assume that the Bossier Parish School Board plan, although nonretrogressive, was nevertheless discriminatory in violation of § 2—an assumption that was borne out in the record, as emphasized by the dissenting district judge.[124] Justice Stevens then argued that discriminatory vote dilution under § 2 was a sufficient basis for a denial of preclearance under § 5. The § 2 prohibition on vote dilution applied to every state in the country, and the party challenging a voting practice had the burden of proving that the practice was discriminatory. However, § 5 provided an additional safeguard in states with a history of circumventing federal efforts to end voting discrimination. In those states, § 5 required preclearance of voting practices *before* they could take effect, and it imposed the burden of proving compliance with the act on the covered jurisdictions. Accordingly, Congress intended § 5 preclearance to enhance federal protections in districts with a history of discrimination; it did not intend to make § 2 discrimination inapplicable to preclearance in such jurisdictions.[125]

Justice Stevens also argued that the text of § 5 and the applicable Supreme Court precedents were consistent with his reading of § 5. Moreover, the legislative history of the 1982 amendments to the Voting Rights Act, as well as other postenactment legislative history, indicated that Congress intended preclearance to be denied for § 2 violations. As a result, Justice Stevens believed that the majority should have deferred to the attorney general's interpretation of § 5, which was contained in the Justice Department regulations.[126] Finally, Justice Stevens agreed with Justice Breyer that the Court should have held that the § 5 intent inquiry encompassed more than mere intent to retrogress. If a jurisdiction responded to increases in minority population by repeatedly redrawing district lines in order to maintain the status quo with respect to minority voting strength, such gerrymandering would certainly constitute intentional discrimination under § 5 even though it did not constitute intent to retrogress. Therefore, judicial economy would be increased by making that holding clear, so that the district court could apply the proper legal standard on remand.[127]

The Supreme Court granted review a second time in the *Bossier Parish* case during its 1998–99 Term, to consider further the degree to which the attorney general was authorized to withhold preclearance under the discriminatory purpose standard of § 5, even in the absence of a retrogressive intent, where the attorney general believed that a proposed plan was unconstitutionally discriminatory. After the case was argued, the Court declined to issue a decision, setting the case for reargument during the 1999–2000 Term. On reargument, the parties were directed to file supplemental briefs on the issue of whether "the purpose prong of § 5 of the Voting Rights Act of 1965 extend[s] to a discriminatory but non-retrogressive purpose," and if so, whether the government or the covered jurisdiction bears the burden of proof on that issue.[128]

vii. *City of Monroe* (1997)

The Supreme Court's third 1997 preclearance case was *City of Monroe v. United States*,[129] in which the Court found that the attorney general had constructively precleared a municipal voting change that adversely affected minority voters. Prior to enactment of the Voting Rights Act of 1965, the city of Monroe, Georgia, had a practice of using plurality rather than majority voting for its mayoral elections. However, this practice was not incorporated into the Monroe City Charter, which was silent on the issue of whether a majority or plurality of the vote was required for victory in mayoral elections. In 1966, the Georgia state legislature amended the Monroe City Charter to require majority voting in municipal elections. Although Georgia's history of voting discrimination made this change subject to § 5 preclearance under the Voting Rights Act, neither the state of Georgia nor the city of Monroe sought preclearance of the change. In 1968, the Georgia legislature adopted a new election code, applicable to Monroe and all other Georgia municipalities, providing for plurality elections in jurisdictions where a municipal charter provided for such elections, but providing a default majority rule for all other jurisdictions. Georgia obtained § 5 preclearance from the attorney general for this 1968 change. In 1971, the Georgia legislature again amended the Monroe City Charter to provide for majority mayoral elections, and again the change was not submitted for § 5 preclearance. Finally, in 1990, the Georgia legislature amended the Monroe City Charter yet again, carrying forward the majority-vote requirement. This time, Monroe did seek preclearance from the attorney general, but preclearance was denied. In 1994, the attorney general filed suit against Monroe to enjoin the city's use of the unprecleared majority voting system, and to require Monroe to return to its earlier plurality voting system. A three-judge district court granted the government's motion for summary judgment and issued the requested injunction, but the Supreme Court reversed.[130] Although the Supreme Court majority did not discuss the matter, Justice Breyer's dissent points out that a change from plurality to majority voting adversely affects minorities by increasing the voting strength that minorities must possess to elect the candidates of their choice.[131]

The Supreme Court upheld Monroe's use of majority voting in a per curiam opinion joined by six members of the Court—Justices Rehnquist, Stevens, O'Connor, Kennedy, Thomas, and Ginsburg.[132] The opinion held that the attorney general had precleared majority voting in Monroe when the attorney general precleared the 1968 state election code. The election code deferred to plurality voting in municipalities whose charters provided for plurality voting, but Monroe had never had a charter that provided for plurality voting. In fact, all of its charters since 1966 (which provided for majority voting) were invalid as a matter of federal law because they had never received § 5 preclearance. As a result, the 1968 election code default rule governed, and that rule required majority voting in Monroe.[133]

The per curiam opinion went on to assert that the three-judge district court had improperly read the Supreme Court's earlier decision in *City of Rome v. United States* to preclude a finding of preclearance based on the 1968 election code. Although *City of Rome* had held that preclearance of the 1968 election code did not constitute preclearance of a change from plurality to majority voting in Rome, Georgia, the change from plurality to majority voting in Monroe, Georgia, was distinguishable. In Monroe, the initial plurality-vote regime had been a matter of practice—not a matter addressed in the city charter, as it had been in Rome. Accordingly, the precleared 1968 default rule applied to the voting change in Monroe, even though it did not apply to the change in Rome. In *City of Monroe*, unlike *City of Rome*, the 1968 election code gave the attorney general "an adequate opportunity to determine the purpose of the [default-rule] electoral changes and whether they will adversely affect minority voting."[134]

Justice Scalia did not join the per curiam opinion, but he concurred in the judgment.[135] He thought that the 1968 election code rule deferring to existing municipal charters did not give the attorney general adequate notice that the 1968 code would result in any voting changes. However, Justice Scalia believed that the 1968 election code default rule providing for majority voting *was* adequate to give the attorney general notice that at least some jurisdictions would be required to switch to majority voting as a result of the code's enactment. Although the attorney general could not know which jurisdictions would be required to change practices without knowing the content of each municipal charter, Justice Scalia thought that the attorney general should bear the burden of making further inquiries if the attorney general did not wish to preclear such changes. States should not be required to shoulder the burden of submitting a city-by-city breakdown of consequences each time they adopt statewide statutes that affect voting.[136]

Justice Souter dissented in an opinion that was joined by Justice Breyer.[137] Justice Souter noted that in *City of Rome*, the Supreme Court rejected the argument that preclearance of the 1968 code also constituted preclearance of the city's change from plurality to majority voting. The Court there held that the 1968 statewide statute did not notify the attorney general "in some unambiguous and recordable manner" of changes that would occur in particular municipalities, and did not therefore afford the attorney general an adequate opportunity to determine whether the electoral changes would adversely affect minority voting.[138] In *City of Monroe*, as in *City of Rome*, the 1968 statute again failed to provide the attorney general adequate notice of the consequences that the statewide election code would have in particular jurisdictions. The fact that Monroe's prior plurality voting was achieved through practice rather than through a charter provision was not relevant to the attorney general's need for adequate notice of voting changes. The language of § 5 applied to a voting "practice" or "procedure" as well as to a formal voting "standard." Moreover, because both Monroe and Rome had failed to disclose their prior voting practices to the attorney general—something that could have been accomplished by submitting their 1966 charter amendments for preclearance—the attorney general had never been given sufficient notice of those prior practices to warrant a finding that preclearance of the 1968 statute also constituted preclearance of the undisclosed prior practices.[139]

Justice Breyer also wrote a dissenting opinion, which was joined by Justice Souter.[140] Justice Breyer began by emphasizing the similarities between *City of Monroe* and *City of Rome*. In both cases, the municipalities changed from a plurality to a majority voting system. In both cases the change was made in 1966. In both cases the change was not precleared. And in both cases the municipalities argued that the attorney general's subsequent preclearance of the 1968 statewide election statute also constituted preclearance of the prior change to a majority voting system.[141] Justice Breyer believed that the Supreme Court's rejection of the 1968 preclearance argument in *City of Rome* also applied in *City of Monroe*. In *City of Rome*, the Supreme Court held that the state's preclearance submission of the 1968 statute did not constitute submission of the 1966 electoral change because it did not put the attorney general on notice of the effect that the 1968 statue would have in the more than five hundred towns and cities in Georgia. The *City of Rome* Court also noted that Georgia had not submitted the pertinent municipal charter when seeking preclearance of its 1968 statute. Justice Breyer believed that this same reasoning precluded a finding that the 1968 preclearance applied to Monroe's 1966 electoral change.[142]

Although the majority believed that *City of Monroe* was distinguishable from *City of Rome* because the Monroe plurality voting practice had not been included in a city charter, Justice Breyer found that difference to be irrelevant. In both cases, the attorney general was equally unlikely to have known about the voting change, and in both cases the attorney general was equally unlikely to have intended approval of the change when preclearing the 1968 statewide statute. This was particularly true because the majority-vote change may have been precisely the type of discriminatory voting change that the Voting Rights Act was intended to prevent.[143] Justice Breyer viewed *City of Rome* as having accepted the attorney general's argument that the 1968 preclearance applied to the statewide statute on its face, but not to the statute as it would be applied to each of Georgia's several hundred municipalities.[144] Justice Breyer also disagreed with Justice Scalia's suggestion that the attorney general should have borne the burden of ascertaining how the 1968 statewide statute would affect particular municipalities, arguing that Supreme Court precedents established that ambiguities in preclearance submissions were to be resolved against the submitting jurisdiction.[145]

viii. *Lopez* (1999)

In 1999, the Supreme Court further elaborated on the preclearance provision of the Voting Rights Act in *Lopez v. Monterey County*.[146] *Lopez* held that preclearance was required for nondiscretionary voting changes implemented by a covered jurisdiction, even when those changes were mandated by a noncovered jurisdiction.[147] Monterey County, California, was a "covered jurisdiction" under the Voting Rights Act because its previous use of literacy tests for voting suggested the likelihood of voting discrimination. However, the state of California was not a covered jurisdiction. Between 1972 and 1987, a series of county ordinances and state laws reduced the number of judicial election districts in Monterey County from nine to one. Although one of those state law changes had been precleared by the attorney general under § 5 of the Voting Rights Act, none of the other changes had been submitted for preclearance.[148] In 1991, a group of Latino voters residing in Monterey County filed suit, asserting that the consolidation of nine voting districts into one—which had a retrogressive effect on Latino voting strength—was invalid because it had not been precleared under § 5. During the course of litigation and negotiations that followed, a three-judge district court ordered an election under an interim plan. However, the Supreme Court reversed because the interim plan had not been precleared under § 5.[149] On remand, the district court granted the state's motion to dismiss, finding that the consolidation of voting districts was ultimately traceable to a mandatory state law rather than to the discretion of county officials. As a result, § 5 did not require preclearance because California was not a covered jurisdiction under the Voting Rights Act. The Supreme Court again reversed in an 8–1 decision.[150]

Justice O'Connor wrote a majority opinion that was signed by six members of the Court—Justices O'Connor, Stevens, Scalia, Souter, Ginsburg, and Breyer.[151] Justice O'Connor's opinion held that the language of § 5, which applies to any covered jurisdiction that "seek[s] to administer" a voting change, applied to a covered county's actions in *administering* a nondiscretionary voting change required by state law. Justice O'Connor noted that the Supreme Court had treated other "partially covered" states as subject to § 5 when they imposed voting changes on covered counties, highlighting the court's decision in *United Jewish Organizations v. Carey* as a case in which § 5 applied to voting changes that the noncovered state of New York made to a covered New York county. She also stressed that the attorney general had viewed § 5 as applicable to partially covered jurisdictions, and that this interpretation was entitled to deference in light of the central role that the attorney general plays in implementing § 5.[152] Justice O'Connor then rejected the claim that federalism concerns precluded the application of § 5 to noncovered jurisdictions, emphasizing that the Voting Rights Act authorized preclearance when necessary to prevent voting changes that would produce a discriminatory *effect*. In addition, the act was adopted under the special congressional powers granted by the Fifteenth Amendment, which itself reduced state policymaking autonomy in the area of voting.[153] Finally, Justice O'Connor's opinion rejected the claim that preclearance was required only when officials in a covered jurisdiction exercised discretion in formulating a voting change. Although preclearance was not required when local officials implemented changes required by Congress or by a federal court, those exceptions were narrow ones that did not give rise to a general exception for nondiscretionary changes.[154]

Justice Kennedy wrote an opinion concurring in the judgment that was joined by Chief Justice Rehnquist.[155] Justice Kennedy stated that he would not reach the issue of whether the preclearance requirement applied when the covered jurisdiction had not exercised some discretion in making a voting change. In light of the constitutional concerns addressed in Justice Thomas's dissent, and the Supreme Court precedents excusing preclearance for nondiscretionary voting changes mandated by Congress or a federal court, the issue of whether the § 5 "seeks[s] to administer" language contemplates the exercise of discretion was better left unresolved. However, under the facts of *Lopez*, Justice Kennedy believed that the county *had* exercised discretion in consolidating its judicial election districts. Although the consolidation was required by state law, the state law was enacted at the request of the county. Accordingly, Justice Kennedy believed that § 5 preclearance was required.[156]

Justice Thomas wrote a dissenting opinion, arguing that constitutional considerations required a reading of the § 5 preclearance requirement that was limited to policy choices made by a covered jurisdiction.[157] He believed that the "seek[s] to administer" language of § 5 was better interpreted to refer to the exercise of discretion than to the nondiscretionary implementation of voting changes mandated by a superior authority. The purpose of § 5 was to guard against policy choices made by the perpetrators of voting discrimination. Moreover, the record did not support the conclusion that the state colluded with the county in ordering the consolidation of judicial voting districts.[158] Justice Thomas also favored his reading of § 5 because he thought that it avoided federalism-based constitutional difficulties. Supreme Court precedents had read the Fifteenth Amendment to authorize § 5 preclearance—despite the ensuing interference with the ability of states to implement their voting policies—because of the need to provide a remedy for prior voting discrimination. However, there is no prior discrimination to be remedied with respect to noncovered jurisdictions. Accordingly, the federalism difficulties entailed in § 5 interference with the voting policies of noncovered states is substantial. Those difficulties, therefore, ought to be avoided by reading the § 5 preclearance requirement to apply only where the policymaking discretion of a covered jurisdiction suggests the danger of voting discrimination.[159]

The Supreme Court's eight statutory cases decided under the Voting Rights Act since 1993, when the Court increased its voting rights activity with the issuance of its decision in *Shaw v. Reno*,[160] have tended to limit the scope of the act as a device for increasing minority voting strength. *Voinovich* and *Growe* rejected § 2 claims of minority vote dilution through both the packing and dispersal of minority voters. *Holder* refused to permit a § 2 vote-dilution challenge to the single- versus multimember structure of a representation scheme, and *De Grandy* rejected a § 2 vote-dilution claim where the number of minority voting districts was proportional to the minority population. In *Young*, the Court held that § 5 preclearance was required for even minor discretionary voting changes. However, *Bossier Parish* held that attorney general withholding of preclearance was governed by the § 5 nonretrogression standard rather than the § 2 vote-dilution standard, and *City of Monroe* found constructive preclearance of a voting change on which the attorney general had never focused. Nevertheless, in *Lopez* the Court did require preclearance of voting changes in a covered jurisdiction, even when those changes were mandated by a noncovered state. These Voting Rights Act decisions were issued in a new doctrinal climate that had been created by the Court's constitutional decision in *Shaw v. Reno*.

2. Shaw v. Reno *(1993)*

In addition to the statutory cases that the Supreme Court has decided under the Voting Rights Act, the Court has decided a series of cases concerning the constitutionality of race-conscious Voting Rights Act remedies. The first constitutional Voting Rights Act case was the previously discussed 1977 plurality decision in *United Jewish Organizations v. Carey*,[161] in which the Supreme Court upheld the constitutionality of a race-conscious New York districting scheme that was adopted to comply with the Voting Rights Act.[162] The Court's first majority opinion in a constitutional Voting Rights Act case was its 1993 decision in *Shaw v. Reno*,[163] which came to be the basis for a new legal cause of action. In *Shaw v. Reno* the Court held 5–4 that a North Carolina voter reapportionment plan, designed to comply with the Voting Rights Act by increasing minority voting strength, was subject to strict scrutiny under the equal protection clause.[164] The case was decided at a time when *Croson* and *Metro Broadcasting* had established a dual standard of review, applying strict scrutiny to state and local affirmative action plans, and intermediate scrutiny to congressional plans.[165] The North Carolina plan for reapportioning the state's congressional districts initially contained one district in which racial minorities constituted a majority of the general population. However, the plan was subject to § 5 preclearance under the Voting Rights Act, and the attorney general disapproved the plan on the grounds that the state's population patterns permitted a second majority-minority district to be created. The North Carolina legislature then revised the plan by adding a second majority-minority district, and the attorney general approved the revised plan. However, the second district was very oddly shaped, thereby suggesting that it had been drawn with the intent of enhancing minority voting strength. As a result, five white North Carolina voters challenged the constitutionality of the reapportionment plan under the equal protection clause of the Fourteenth Amendment.[166]

The Supreme Court majority opinion, which subjected the challenged reapportionment plan to strict scrutiny, was written by Justice O'Connor for five members of the Court—Justices O'Connor, Rehnquist, Scalia, Kennedy, and Thomas. Justice O'Connor's opinion emphasized that race-conscious reapportionment, while not always unconstitutional, *was* inconsistent with the ideal of a "'color-blind' Constitution," thereby making strict scrutiny appropriate.[167] Because the equal protection clause prohibits intentional discrimination, a bizarrely shaped voting district that ignored the factors of compactness, contiguity, and respect for political subdivisions became highly suspect when it turned out to include primarily voters of one race.[168] Justice O'Connor conceded that legislatures can be *aware* of race when they draw voting district lines.[169] However, she found that racial gerrymandering as conspicuous as that in *Shaw v. Reno* was unconstitutional. It bore "an uncomfortable resemblance to political apartheid" because it reinforced the stereotypical view that members of racial groups think alike and share the same political interests, as well as the view that it is permissible for elected officials to represent only some and not all of their constituents. Accordingly, racial gerrymandering could exacerbate the very racial bloc voting that it was designed to counteract.[170]

Justice O'Connor offered a distinction between *Shaw v. Reno* and earlier vote-dilution cases in which the Court had read the Fourteenth Amendment to impose a fairly high standard of proof with respect to both discriminatory purpose and *effect* in order to establish a discrimination claim.[171] Although the dissenters argued that the white plaintiffs in *Shaw v. Reno* would not be able to satisfy the effect prong of this standard because of the substantial voting power that they retained even under the modified reapportionment plan, Justice O'Connor argued that the prior vote-dilution cases were inapposite. The prior cases concerned plans that merely entailed claims of a racially motivated reduction in minority voting strength; they did not concern plans that *classified* voters on the basis of race.[172] Justice O'Connor also offered a distinction between *Shaw v. Reno* and *United Jewish Organizations v. Carey*[173]—the factually similar affirmative action case in which race-conscious redistricting was found to be constitutionally permissible under the equal protection clause as a remedy for past voting discrimination. She argued that *United Jewish Organizations* was distinguishable because it did not address a voting district whose shape was "so irrational on its face that it immediately offend[ed] principles of racial equality."[174]

Justice O'Connor also rejected the argument that the "benign" nature of the reapportionment plan at issue in *Shaw v. Reno* made relaxed scrutiny appropriate. She reasoned that strict scrutiny was still necessary to determine whether the plan was *really* benign. Moreover, mere acceptability of a reapportionment plan under § 5 of the Voting Rights Act did not preclude the possibility of an equal protection violation because a state might choose to do more under the approval provisions of § 5 than was statutorily required under the antiabridgment provisions of § 2.[175] Justice O'Connor expressly declined to consider whether an affirmative action reapportionment plan that was required under § 2 of the Voting Rights Act could nevertheless violate the equal protection clause of the Fourteenth Amendment. In addition, she expressly declined to decide whether the presence of past discrimination sufficient to trigger § 5 of the Voting Rights Act was adequate evidence of past discrimination to make the race-conscious creation of majority-minority voting districts a constitutionally acceptable remedy.[176]

Justice White—the author of the *United Jewish Organizations* opinion that upheld the constitutionality of a race-conscious reapportionment plan adopted to comply with the Voting Rights Act—dissented in an opinion joined by Justices Blackmun and Stevens.[177] He argued that white voters could not plausibly argue that a reapportionment plan adopted by the white majority violated the equal protection rights of the very white majority that had adopted it.[178] As prior vote-dilution cases had recognized, race consciousness was inevitable in reapportionment decisions, and the presence of race consciousness was not alone sufficient to establish an equal protection violation.[179] In order to establish such a violation, the white plaintiffs would have to show not only discriminatory intent but a substantial discriminatory *effect* as well, by demonstrating that the political process was not "equally open" to whites,[180] or that whites "had less opportunity" than racial minorities "to participate in the political process and to elect legislators of their choice."[181]

Justice White further asserted that *United Jewish Organizations* was controlling, and that it established that remedial reapportionment under the Voting Rights Act failed to constitute the type of discriminatory intent required for an equal protection violation.[182] In addition, the only discriminatory effect of the *Shaw v. Reno* reapportionment plan that was not also present in *United Jewish Organizations* was an oddly shaped voting district, which Justice White found to be legally inconsequential.[183] Finally, Justice White argued that even if strict scrutiny were appropriate, compliance with the attorney general's recommendations under § 5 of the Voting Rights Act was sufficiently compelling and narrowly tailored to satisfy strict scrutiny. Moreover, affirmative action reapportionment was distinguishable from other types of affirmative action in that it constituted an effort to *equalize* treatment rather than to give minorities *preferential* treatment.[184]

Justice Blackmun also wrote a brief dissent. Like Justice White, he objected to the creation of a new constitutional injury in reapportionment cases based solely on the conscious use of race, where there was no significant discriminatory effect in terms of minimized voting strength or denied access to the political process. Justice Blackmun also emphasized that Justice O'Connor's majority opinion had chosen to abandon settled law and to create this new constitutional claim in a challenge made by *white* voters after North Carolina had sent its first post-Reconstruction black representatives to Congress.[185]

Justice Stevens wrote a dissent emphasizing three points. First, despite the contrary inference that might be drawn from Justice O'Connor's opinion, the Constitution does not require compactness or contiguity in the establishment of voting districts. Second, although gerrymandering is unconstitutional when used to undermine minority voting strength, it is not unconstitutional when used to benefit minorities by increasing their voting strength. Third, the fact that the minority being benefited is defined by race does not, as Justice O'Connor argued, establish an equal protection violation; it would be perverse to hold that racial minorities were precluded from receiving the benefits of affirmative action by the very equal protection clause that was enacted to protect racial minorities.[186] Justice Stevens further pointed out that Justice O'Connor's distaste for stereotyped assumptions about the homogeneity of racial minority political interests was inconsistent with the *requirement* that minorities establish such homogeneity in order to establish a vote-dilution claim under the Voting Rights Act.[187]

Justice Souter also dissented, on the grounds that Justice O'Connor had created an unwarranted new cause of action. He stressed that voting-rights claims had historically been treated differently than other discrimination claims for equal protection purposes because race consciousness was inevitable in reapportionment plans, and because no particularized injury to any individual—as opposed to a group—resulted from the adoption of a reapportionment plan.[188] Given that only a substantial reduction in group voting power can establish the validity of a vote-dilution claim, in the absence of such a reduction, Justice Souter saw no point in applying strict scrutiny to a reapportionment plan.[189] Moreover, he viewed Justice O'Connor's application of strict scrutiny based solely upon the presence of a bizarrely shaped voting district as advancing only the government's interests in compactness and contiguity, but those interests were not constitutionally compelled.[190]

3. Hays *(1995)*

In 1995, the Supreme Court issued a majority opinion in *United States v. Hays*,[191] denying standing to white voters who sought to challenge a redistricting plan for a voting district in which they themselves did not reside. Louisiana was required to modify its districting scheme after it lost one congressional seat in the 1990 census. Prior experience with the United States attorney general concerning state school board election districts had caused state officials to conclude that no redistricting plan would secure preclearance under § 5 of the Voting Rights Act unless the plan created two majority-minority voting districts. As a result, the Louisiana legislature adopted a redistricting plan containing two majority-minority districts, and the plan was approved by the attorney general.[192] The plan was then challenged by four white plaintiffs who resided in District 4, an oddly shaped district that was one of the two majority-minority districts created by the plan. The plaintiffs alleged that the redistricting plan violated their equal protection rights, but a three-judge federal district court initially rejected their claim. However, after the Supreme Court issued its decision in *Shaw v. Reno*, the district court reversed itself and held the plan unconstitutional. The district court focused almost exclusively on the shape of District 4. While that decision was on appeal to the Supreme Court, Louisiana modified its redistricting plan so that District 4 remained a majority-minority district but had a shape that was less unusual. Under the modified plan, the plaintiffs resided in District 5, which was not a majority-minority district.[193] The Supreme Court vacated the district court's initial judgment and remanded for consideration of the modified Louisiana plan. On remand, the district court again invalidated the Louisiana redistricting plan as unconstitutional under *Shaw v. Reno*. The state of Louisiana, and the United States as a defendant-intervenor, appealed to the Supreme Court.[194]

Justice O'Connor's majority opinion reversing the district court was joined by seven members of the Supreme Court—Justices O'Connor, Rehnquist, Scalia, Kennedy, Souter, Thomas, and Breyer. Justice O'Connor first stated that the Supreme Court had an obligation to address the issue of standing, even though the district court had not addressed the issue under the most recent version of the Louisiana districting plan, because standing "'was perhaps the most important of [the jurisdictional] doctrines.'"[195] She emphasized that the injury requirement of standing was jurisdictional in nature; that a generalized grievance was not sufficient to establish standing; and that a plaintiff had the burden of proving facts adequate to establish standing. Because the rule against generalized grievances applied with as much force in the equal protection context as in any other context, it was not true that all voters in a state had standing to challenge that state's districting scheme.[196] Justice O'Connor then cited *Shaw v. Reno* for the proposition that racial classifications can injure voters by stigmatizing them or by generating "representational harms" that result when an official elected from an obviously gerrymandered district neglects the interests of his or her entire constituency in favor of the interests of the group for whom the district was gerrymandered. She deemed such injuries difficult to establish by voters who did not actually live in the racially gerrymandered district being challenged.[197]

Justice O'Connor's opinion then held that the plaintiffs in *Hays* had failed to demonstrate that *they* had suffered any injury as a result of the Louisiana redistricting plan. Mere legislative awareness of race in drawing district lines was not sufficient to establish a legally cognizable injury.[198] The plaintiffs argued that District 5—the District in which they *did* reside under the modified Louisiana plan—was a "segregated" voting district to which they had been assigned on the basis of their race. However, Justice O'Connor found that the record did not demonstrate that the Louisiana legislature intended District 5 to have any particular racial composition. The fact that the racial composition of District 5 might have been different if District 4 had been drawn in a different manner was not enough to establish a cognizable injury under the Fourteenth Amendment. The racial composition of a voting district, without more evidence of discrimination, had never been held to violate the Constitution.[199] Even though the plaintiffs claimed that they had challenged the entire redistricting plan—not just the portions of the plan that concerned District 4— Justice O'Connor found that claim to be irrelevant. The fact that the plan *affected* all Louisiana voters did not give all voters in the state standing to sue. Only those voters able to establish a direct personal injury in the form of a denial of equal treatment had standing.[200] Justice O'Connor distinguished *Powers v. Ohio*,[201] a case holding that individual jurors have a right not to be excluded from particular juries on account of race, by emphasizing that a juror excluded from a jury on racial grounds *does* suffer a personal race-based harm.[202] Justice O'Connor did, however, conclude her opinion by rejecting the suggestion that a cognizable injury under *Shaw v. Reno* could consist only of demonstrable vote dilution.[203]

Justice Ginsburg concurred in the result without opinion, but did not join Justice O'Connor's opinion.[204] Justice Breyer, joined by Justice Souter, concurred in Justice O'Connor's opinion to the extent that it concerned voters who did not reside in the district that they challenged.[205] Justice Stevens wrote an opinion concurring in the judgment denying standing to the plaintiffs, because the plaintiffs had not demonstrated that their votes had been substantially diluted by the Louisiana redistricting plan. To Justice Stevens, it did not matter for standing purposes whether the plaintiffs resided in the election district that they were challenging.[206] *Hays* is designated a case that facilitates rather than frustrates affirmative action in the Affirmative Action Voting Chart included on pages 162–63, because the Supreme Court decision in *Hays* denied standing to challengers of an affirmative action redistricting plan.[207]

4. Miller *(1995)*

Also in 1995, the Supreme Court issued a majority opinion in *Miller v. Johnson*[208] holding unconstitutional a redistricting plan that had been adopted by the Georgia legislature in order to comply with the Voting Rights Act. *Miller* was decided a few weeks after *Adarand,* and was therefore governed by the unitary standard of strict scrutiny that replaced the dual standards imposed by *Croson* and *Metro Broadcasting.*[209] Like the districting plan at issue in *Shaw v. Reno,* the congressional districting plan in *Miller* was designed to secure preclearance from the attorney general under § 5 of the Voting Rights Act. When Georgia obtained an additional congressional seat after the 1990 census, the state legislature initially submitted to the attorney general a reapportionment plan that increased the number of majority-black voting districts in the state from one to two. The attorney general denied preclearance of that initial plan, and then of a second reapportionment plan on the grounds that it was possible to create three majority-black districts in the state rather than two. The Georgia legislature then submitted a third plan, containing three majority-black election districts, to which the attorney general granted preclearance under § 5 of the Voting Rights Act. Black members of Congress were elected from each of these three districts in 1992, but five white voters residing in one of the districts filed suit alleging that the reapportionment plan was unconstitutional. A three-judge federal district court then held that the plan violated the equal protection clause of the Fourteenth Amendment.[210]

The Supreme Court affirmed the district court's invalidation of the Georgia districting plan in a majority opinion written by Justice Kennedy and signed by the same five justices who made up the majority in *Shaw v. Reno* and *Adarand*—Justices Kennedy, Rehnquist, O'Connor, Scalia, and Thomas.[211] Justice Kennedy's opinion first held that the plaintiffs had standing to challenge the reapportionment plan under *Hays* because they were residents of the voting district alleged to have been unconstitutionally apportioned.[212] The opinion then held that, under *Shaw v. Reno,* a bizarrely shaped voting district was not necessary to establish that the district lines had been unconstitutionally drawn.[213] Justice Kennedy stated that the claim recognized in *Shaw v. Reno* was "analytically distinct" from a vote-dilution claim.[214] A vote-dilution claim alleges that a state has adopted a particular voting plan in order "to minimize or cancel out the voting potential of racial or ethnic minorities,"[215] whereas a *Shaw v. Reno*-type racial gerrymandering claim alleges that a state has assigned a voter to a particular district because of the voter's race.[216] Just as a state may not segregate citizens in public facilities such as schools and parks, a state may not segregate citizens in voting districts. Race-based assignment to voting districts deprives citizens of their right to be treated as individuals rather than stereotyped as members of a particular racial group. It also demeans citizens by perpetuating the view that members of a particular race "think alike, share the same political interests, and will prefer the same candidates at the polls."[217] Even remedial classifications pose the danger of racial balkanization that "threatens to carry us further from the goal of a political system in which race no longer matters."[218] As a result, the equal protection claim recognized in *Shaw v. Reno* does not require a threshold showing that a voting district is bizarrely shaped in order to be unconstitutional. Shape is relevant only because it is circumstantial evidence of racial motivation, but other evidence can also be relied on to establish race-based districting.[219] Justice Kennedy rejected the claim that districting by definition involves racial considerations, characterizing the argument as entailing the very stereotypical assumptions about race that the equal protection clause forbids. He also rejected the claim that *United Jewish Organizations* had upheld the constitutionality of race-conscious districting, arguing that the "highly fractured decision" in *United Jewish Organizations* was a vote-dilution decision that did not govern a *Shaw v. Reno*-type voter-separation claim.[220] He added that, to the extent *United Jewish Organizations* could be interpreted as applying anything less than strict scrutiny to a *Shaw v. Reno*–type claim, it should not be deemed controlling.[221]

Justice Kennedy then noted that districting is a vital local function over which state legislatures must have discretion to make political judgments and to balance competing interests. Accordingly, the good faith of a state legislature is to be presumed unless a threshold showing of impropriety can be made. It is not improper for a state legislature simply to be aware of racial demographics. Rather, the necessary threshold showing requires a challenger to prove that race was the "predominant factor" motivating the legislature's districting decisions because "the legislature subordinated traditional race-neutral districting principles, including but not limited to compactness, contiguity, respect for political subdivisions or communities defined by actual shared interests, to racial considerations."[222] Under the facts of *Miller*, the district court finding that race was the predominant factor motivating enactment of the Georgia districting scheme had to be affirmed because it was not clearly erroneous. The shape and racial demographics of the challenged district, combined with evidence that the state legislature had complied with the attorney general's desire to maximize the number of minority-black districts in order to obtain preclearance under § 5 of the Voting Rights Act, supported the district court finding. Moreover, the Georgia attorney general stated that the state could not create a third majority-black voting district without abandoning reasonable standards of compactness and contiguity.[223] Although traditional districting principles permit a state to recognize shared communities of interest, race could not be deemed to constitute a shared community of interests without violating the very equal protection prohibition on racial stereotyping that was at issue.[224] As a result, the Georgia redistricting plan could not be upheld unless it survived strict scrutiny.[225]

Justice Kennedy's opinion cited *Shaw v. Reno* for the proposition that, in order to survive strict scrutiny, the districting plan had to be narrowly tailored to achieve a compelling state interest.[226] Although "[t]here is a 'significant state interest in eradicating the effects of past racial discrimination,'"[227] the Georgia legislature was not trying to remedy past discrimination. Rather, it was trying to satisfy the attorney general's preclearance demands by maximizing the number of majority-minority districts in the state, and compliance with the attorney general's preclearance demands was not alone sufficient to constitute a compelling state interest.[228] Under the doctrine of judicial review established in *Marbury v. Madison*,[229] strict scrutiny did not permit judicial deference to executive uses of racial classifications or to executive interpretations of the Voting Rights Act.[230] Properly interpreted, the Voting Rights Act did not require the creation of a third majority-black district in Georgia. The first two plans submitted to the attorney general were ameliorative plans that increased the number of minority-black districts in Georgia from one to two. As a result, those plans could not transgress the nonretrogression principle of § 5 unless they were somehow shown to be so discriminatory that they violated the Constitution. Georgia's initial decision to create two rather than three majority-black districts was not unconstitutional because it was motivated by a desire to adhere to traditional districting principles, rather than by a desire to dilute minority voting strength.[231] The nonretrogression principle of § 5 of the Voting Rights Act was designed merely to prevent states from undoing gains that had recently been made by minority voters. Section 5 did not encompass the policy of maximizing minority voting strength that was embodied in the attorney general's interpretation of the statute. The attorney general's interpretation of § 5 posed constitutional difficulties under the Fourteenth Amendment that there is no indication Congress intended.[232]

Justice O'Connor wrote a brief concurring opinion. She emphasized that the threshold standard adopted by the majority for establishing a *Shaw v. Reno*–type racial gerrymandering claim was a high one that would be difficult to satisfy. In order to show that the legislature subordinated traditional race-neutral districting principles to racial considerations, a plaintiff had to make the same showing that would be required to invalidate a districting plan that had been drawn to favor any other ethnic group. The majority's standard did not treat legislative efforts to benefit blacks less favorably than efforts to benefit other ethnic groups. That would be an ironic result because the Fourteenth Amendment was adopted in order to end legal discrimination against blacks.[233] Justice O'Connor also emphasized that the majority's standard did not "throw into doubt the vast majority of the Nation's 435 congressional districts," even though race may have been considered along with customary districting principles in creating those districts.[234] Justice O'Connor concluded that the majority's threshold standard would help achieve the basic objective of *Shaw v. Reno*, which was to permit judicial review of extreme instances of gerrymandering.[235]

Justice Stevens dissented on the grounds that the plaintiffs in *Miller*, like the plaintiffs in *Hays*, lacked standing because they had not suffered any legally cognizable injury.[236] The majority distinguished a *Shaw v. Reno* racial gerrymandering claim from a vote-dilution claim, so the harm to the white plaintiffs could not be an increased likelihood that their preferred candidate would lose.[237] The concept of "representational harm" invoked in *Shaw v. Reno* was similarly unavailing. Representational harm is harm to white voters that results when the black majority in a gerrymandered district elects a representative who discounts the interests of the white minority in that district. However, there is no reason to believe that such discounting will occur unless one assumes that minority voters will think alike, vote alike, and share the same political interests—the very same assumption that the *Miller* majority found so "offensive and demeaning" as to be unconstitutional.[238]

Justice Stevens argued that the majority's assertion that white voters suffer the same type of injury that blacks suffer when they are excluded from public facilities also fails. Segregation *excluded* blacks from the benefits of public facilities, but in *Miller* the plaintiffs are protesting the *inclusion* of blacks in the challenged district. In addition, segregation frustrated the public interest in diversity and racial tolerance, but the *Miller* districting plan promotes diversity and tolerance by increasing the likely number of black representatives who will participate in legislative debates.[239] Justice Stevens then cited *Allen v. Wright*[240]—a case in which the Supreme Court denied black plaintiffs standing to challenge federal tax benefits for segregated schools—to illustrate the anomalous proposition that efforts to promote racial integration had now become more vulnerable to judicial challenge than efforts to perpetuate racial bias.[241] According to Justice Stevens, districting plans that disadvantage a politically weak minority group should be held to violate the equal protection clause, but districting plans that *favor* politically weak groups should not be held unconstitutional. Moreover, racial groups were entitled to neither more nor less protection from gerrymandering than other groups, but the majority's decision to treat racial groups differently than other groups of voters was itself an invidious racial classification.[242]

Justice Ginsburg wrote a dissenting opinion that was joined by the four *Shaw v. Reno* dissenters—Justices Ginsburg, Stevens, Souter, and Breyer.[243] Justice Ginsburg began by stating that all members of the Court agreed on several things: federalism and limited judicial competence argue against judicial intervention in state districting decisions; there has been a long history of voting discrimination against blacks in the United States—by states including Georgia—that is now redressable under the equal protection clause and the Voting Rights Act; state legislatures must consider race as a factor in drawing district lines in order to comply with the Voting Rights Act; and state legislatures are permitted to recognize communities of shared interests, including racial communities.[244]

Prior to *Shaw v. Reno*, the equal protection clause had been used in the voting context only to enforce the one-person, one-vote principle, and to prevent dilution of a minority group's voting strength. *Shaw v. Reno* recognized a third basis for equal protection challenge, which could be maintained when a voting district's extreme irregularity suggested that race was virtually the only districting principle that had been considered.[245] The *Miller* record did not show that race had similarly supplanted traditional districting practices. The challenged district was not bizarrely shaped; it did not disregard political subdivision boundaries; and it respected the districting principle of accommodating incumbents.[246] Although the attorney general pressured the Georgia legislature to maximize the number of majority-minority districts in the state, the plan that the legislature adopted differed from the plan favored by the attorney general in ways that show consideration of factors other than race.[247] The plan also recognized the shared political interests of the black population in the challenged district, which is a traditional districting principle whose validity the majority deems appropriate.[248]

Justice Ginsburg argued that *Miller* was controlled by *United Jewish Organizations*, which upheld a redistricting plan under the equal protection clause despite its consideration of race as a factor in districting. Although the majority attempted to distinguish *United Jewish Organizations* as a vote-dilution case, the plaintiffs made no vote-dilution claim in that case, but rather made a racial gerrymandering claim much like that involved in *Shaw v. Reno*.[249] The majority's objection that the Georgia districting plan treated individuals as members of a group rather than as individuals ignored the fact that apportionment plans by their very nature assemble voters into groups rather than treating them as individuals who are assigned to voting districts based on merit or achievement. Districting Irish or Italian voters together had never been viewed as a constitutional infirmity, and black voters should not be dissimilarly treated. Such dissimilar treatment in the name of equal protection would shut out the very minority that the equal protection clause was adopted to protect.[250]

In a portion of Justice Ginsburg's opinion that was joined by Justices Stevens and Breyer, but not Justice Souter, Justice Ginsburg criticized the majority for applying the same strict-scrutiny standard to plans that enhance minority voting strength as it applies to plans that dilute minority voting strength. Because a history of discrimination has left racial minorities with less political power than that possessed by the majority, the majority does not need the same degree of judicial protection as racial minorities. The majority is able to protect itself adequately through the political process.[251] In a final portion of her opinion—once again joined by Justices Stevens, Souter, and Breyer—Justice Ginsburg noted that the majority's departure from the bizarre-configuration standard of *Shaw v. Reno* would promote uncertainty about a state's obligation under the Voting Rights Act and the equal protection clause in a way that would inappropriately enlarge the judicial role in the apportionment process.[252]

5. DeWitt *(1995)*

In *DeWitt v. Wilson*[253]—also decided in 1995, on the same day as *Hays* and *Miller*—the Supreme Court summarily affirmed a three-judge district court decision upholding the use of race in a California redistricting plan, on the grounds that race had not been a predominant factor in the formulation of that plan.[254] Although the Supreme Court did not write an opinion in *DeWitt*,[255] and although summary affirmances have less precedential value than decisions affirmed after plenary review,[256] the Supreme Court's summary affirmance in *DeWitt* may nevertheless have been significant. It constituted the first time that the Supreme Court had upheld the constitutionality of a majority-minority redistricting plan since the Court began invalidating such plans in its 1993 *Shaw v. Reno* decision. *DeWitt*, therefore, seems to establish that it is actually possible—as opposed to theoretically possible—for majority-minority voting districts to withstand constitutional challenge, even in the view of the post–*Shaw v. Reno* Supreme Court. *De-Witt* also provides an example of a situation in which the Court was willing to forgo strict equal protection scrutiny of a redistricting plan because race was a factor, but not the *predominant* factor, in drawing district lines.[257]

In 1991, California governor Pete Wilson vetoed a new reapportionment plan for state and federal elections that had been adopted by the California legislature in response to the 1990 census. The California Supreme Court then appointed three special masters to develop a substitute redistricting plan, which the California Supreme Court approved in 1992.[258] The approved redistricting plan was designed to comply with federal law—including the § 2 antidilution and the § 5 preclearance requirements of the Voting Rights Act—as well as with traditional districting principles imposed by the California Constitution and California Supreme Court precedent.[259] The plan attempted to maximize the number of majority-minority voting districts for geographically compact minority groups in order to increase the likelihood of attorney general preclearance under § 5 of the Voting Rights Act.[260] However, in 1993, two California voters challenged the plan in federal court, asserting *inter alia* that the conscious consideration of race in drawing district lines violated the equal protection clause of the United States Constitution under *Shaw v. Reno.*[261] A three-judge federal district court rejected the challenge on cross motions for summary judgment, and upheld the redistricting plan.[262] The three-judge court decision was issued after the Supreme Court decision in *Shaw v. Reno*, but before the Supreme Court decisions in *Miller v. Johnson,*[263] *Shaw v. Hunt*[264] and *Bush v. Vera.*[265] Then, the United States Supreme Court summarily affirmed the three-judge court decision without opinion.[266] The Supreme Court's summary affirmance occurred after the *Miller, Shaw v. Hunt,* and *Bush* decisions.

The three-judge court distinguished *DeWitt* from *Shaw v. Reno* by emphasizing the degree to which the *DeWitt* redistricting plan incorporated traditional districting principles that were mandated by California law.[267] The court read *Shaw v. Reno* to invalidate districts that "'rationally cannot be understood as anything other than an effort to separate voters into different districts on the basis of race.'"[268] The California redistricting plan did not "fit within the narrow holding" of *Shaw v. Reno* because it "emphasized geographical compactness" and "created majority-minority districts in a manner that was consistent with traditional redistricting principles, not based solely on race, and not involving extremely irregular district boundaries."[269] The court found that the California plan involved a question expressly left open by *Shaw v. Reno*, where the Supreme Court stated, "'[W]e express no view as to whether the intentional creation of majority-minority districts, without more, always gives rise to an equal protection claim.'"[270] Because the California plan considered political boundaries, population equality, contiguity, geographic integrity, community of interest, and compactness, as well as race, the district court found that there was no equal protection violation. The court cited *United Jewish Organizations* for the proposition that proper use of race-conscious majority-minority districting was constitutionally permissible.[271] The court also noted that the special masters who designed the plan had specifically refused to create certain proposed districts because of their irregular shapes. The court concluded that the California plan did not result from "racial gerrymandering," but rather resulted from "a thoughtful and fair example of applying traditional redistricting principles, while being conscious of race."[272] The district court held that strict scrutiny was not required, but that even if it were, the California plan would survive strict scrutiny because it had been narrowly tailored to meet the compelling state interest of complying with the Voting Rights Act. The court noted the federalism-based need to defer to the primary role of the state in making reapportionment decisions, and held that the California plan was constitutionally valid unless the Voting Rights Act itself was unconstitutional in its authorization of majority-minority districts.[273]

Because the Supreme Court's affirmance of the three-judge district court decision was a summary affirmance issued without opinion,[274] it is clear that the Supreme Court endorsed the district court outcome. However, it is not clear whether the Supreme Court endorsed the district court reasoning.[275] The precedential value of *DeWitt* is therefore uncertain. This is particularly true because many of the arguments made by the district court in *DeWitt*'s assertion that race was not the *predominant* factor in the redistricting plan at issue are similar to the rejected arguments made by the dissenters in *Bush, Shaw v. Hunt, Miller,* and *Shaw v. Reno*.[276] Accordingly, it is difficult to know how much significance to attribute to the Supreme

Court's summary affirmance in *DeWitt*, but the fact that the Court unanimously chose to uphold at least one redistricting plan in the midst of a series of decisions invalidating other redistricting plans is at least noteworthy.

6. Shaw v. Hunt (1996)

In 1996, the Supreme Court issued a second decision in the *Shaw* litigation, after the case had been remanded for application of the strict-scrutiny standard of review that the Court had ordered in its 1993 *Shaw v. Reno* decision.[277] After remand, under the name *Shaw v. Hunt*[278] the Supreme Court issued a majority opinion holding that the North Carolina redistricting plan that was at issue in the case could not survive strict scrutiny.[279] In allocating the additional congressional seat that North Carolina received after the 1990 census, the state legislature had adopted a redistricting plan that increased from one to two the number of majority-minority election districts in the state. The legislature had done this in order to secure preclearance of the State's redistricting plan by the United States attorney general under § 5 of the Voting Rights Act. In *Shaw v. Reno*, the Supreme Court had responded to the bizarre shape of the state's second majority-minority district by instructing the district court on remand to determine whether race was the factor that had motivated creation of this district and, if so, whether such racially motivated redistricting satisfied strict scrutiny. After a six-day trial, the district court concluded that race *had* motivated creation of the second majority-minority district, but that the redistricting plan satisfied strict scrutiny because it was a narrowly tailored effort to advance the state's compelling interest in complying with the Voting Rights Act.[280]

The Supreme Court reversed in a majority opinion that was written by Chief Justice Rehnquist and joined by the same five justices who constituted the majority in *Shaw v. Reno*, *Adarand*, and *Miller*—Justices Rehnquist, O'Connor, Scalia, Kennedy, and Thomas.[281] Justice Rehnquist's opinion first held that, of the five plaintiffs who had challenged the redistricting scheme, only the two who actually lived in the challenged majority-minority district had standing under *Hays*.[282] Justice Rehnquist next cited *Shaw v. Reno* and *Adarand* for the proposition that racially motivated districting was constitutionally suspect even if it was benign in nature.[283] His opinion then held that the district court's finding of racial motivation was supported by both circumstantial and direct evidence sufficient to establish race as the "predominant" factor in creating the challenged district within the meaning of the *Miller* standard that the Court had adopted subsequent to the remand *Shaw v. Reno*.[284] Justice Rehnquist emphasized that, even though creation of the majority-minority district was motivated in part by the traditional districting principles of separating urban and rural districts and of protecting incumbents, those principles had nevertheless been subordinated to race.[285] Justice Rehnquist then cited *Miller* for the proposition that strict scrutiny required the North Carolina districting plan to be narrowly tailored to advance a compelling state interest.[286]

North Carolina advanced three interests in support of its redistricting plan, but Justice Rehnquist's opinion held that none of these interests was compelling.[287] The state first argued that its interest in remedying the effects of past or present racial discrimination was a compelling state interest. Justice Rehnquist responded that such an interest could rise to the level of a compelling state interest, but only if the past discrimination was identified with specificity—it could not be mere general societal discrimination—and the past discrimination had a strong evidentiary basis.[288] Justice Rehnquist did not determine whether these requirements were satisfied by the North Carolina redistricting plan, however, because he accepted as not clearly erroneous the district court's finding that the desire to remedy North Carolina's history of prior voting discrimination was not the factor that motivated a majority of North Carolina legislators to vote for the plan.[289]

The second interest that the state asserted as compelling was its interest in complying with § 5 of the Voting Rights Act. Like Justice Kennedy's opinion in *Miller*, Justice Rehnquist's opinion in *Shaw v. Hunt* left open the question of whether compliance with the Voting Rights Act could ever constitute a compelling state interest.[290] In *Shaw v. Hunt*, as in *Miller*, § 5 of the Voting Rights Act did not require creation of the second majority-minority district that the attorney general had pressured the North Carolina legislature to adopt as a condition on obtaining preclearance. The single majority-minority district that North Carolina had initially proposed to the attorney general would have been sufficient to comply with § 5. This is because the state's initial preference for one rather than two majority-minority districts was intended to give effect to traditional districting principles, including a desire to keep voting precincts and counties whole, while optimizing minority voting strength. And the state's initial preference for a single majority-minority district was not a pretextual act of racial discrimination sufficient to constitute an equal protection violation. As the Court recognized in *Miller*, the attorney general's desire to create as many majority-minority districts as possible did not stem from a proper interpretation of the Voting Rights Act.[291]

The third interest that the state asserted as compelling was its interest in avoiding liability for vote-dilution claims under § 2 of the Voting Rights Act.[292] Justice Rehnquist's opinion assumed for the sake of argument that the state's interest in avoiding a violation of § 2 constituted a compelling state interest. Even so, the state's creation of a second majority-minority district was not a narrowly tailored means of remedying that assumed § 2 violation. In fact, the state's plan would not remedy a § 2 violation at all. In order to establish liability for vote dilution under § 2, one of the things that *Thornburg v. Gingles* required a minority group to demonstrate was that the group was "geographically compact."[293] Due to the bizarre shape of the challenged district in *Shaw v. Hunt*, the district could not reasonably be said to contain a geographically compact population of any race.[294] The state argued that once a § 2 violation was found to exist in the state, that violation could be remedied by creating a majority-minority voting district anywhere in the state.[295] However, Justice Rehnquist rejected this argument, stating that it misconceived the nature of a vote-dilution claim. The claim belonged not to the disadvantaged minority group as a whole, but rather to the individual minority voters whose votes had been diluted. Creating a majority-minority district in some part of the state other than the part in which those minority voters resided would do nothing to remedy their vote-dilution claim. Because the second majority-minority district contained in the North Carolina redistricting plan could not remedy a § 2 violation, it was not a narrowly tailored effort to advance a compelling state interest.[296]

Justice Stevens wrote a dissenting opinion, joined in part by Justices Ginsburg and Breyer, that faulted the majority for failing to distinguish majority efforts to increase minority participation in the electoral process from majority efforts to oppress minorities.[297] In an initial portion of the opinion not joined by any other justices, Justice Stevens reiterated his view, first expressed in *Miller* and *Hays*, that the *Shaw v. Reno* cause of action was misguided because it did not rest on any cognizable injury.[298] In the remaining portions of the opinion, which were joined by Justices Ginsburg and Breyer, Justice Stevens argued that strict scrutiny should not have been applied to the North Carolina redistricting plan, but that even if it were applied, the plan was able to satisfy the requirements of strict scrutiny.[299]

In the portion of the opinion written for himself alone, Justice Stevens stressed the uncertain nature of the injury that serves as the basis of a *Shaw v. Reno* racial gerrymandering claim. He argued that this uncertain nature had enabled plaintiffs who were unhappy with the North Carolina districting scheme for partisan political reasons, rather than racial reasons, to second-guess the districting scheme in federal court. Justice Stevens noted that the plaintiff intervenors in *Shaw v. Hunt* were Republicans who had in a previous suit unsuccessfully challenged the North Carolina plan as an unconstitutional political gerrymander. The Republican Party had earlier proposed plans to create two majority-minority districts in a way that would have increased Republican voting strength, but chose to oppose the present plan that increased Democratic voting strength. Justice Stevens argued that this demonstrated that the *Shaw v. Reno* racial gerrymandering cause of action would inevitably be used to mask political gerrymandering claims.[300]

Justice Stevens argued that even those plaintiffs who may genuinely have been concerned with the use of race in districting failed to allege any injury that was adequate to serve as a basis for standing. Those plaintiffs did not claim that they had been shut out of the electoral process, or that their votes had been diluted on account of race. Although *Shaw v. Reno* recognized a cause of action for plaintiffs who had been separated from other plaintiffs on the grounds of race, the North Carolina plan did not separate voters by race but, rather, required the plaintiffs to *share* a district with voters of a different race. The plaintiffs were, therefore, complaining of racial integration, not racial segregation.[301] The plaintiffs argued that the redistricting plan essentially labeled voting districts by race, just as water fountains had been labeled by race in the segregated South. But here there was no injurious consequence to that labeling because any voter of any race was free to live in any voting district. Justice Stevens cited *Reynolds v. Sims*[302] and *Palmer v. Thompson*[303] for the proposition that an equal protection clause violation requires not merely discriminatory intent but some discriminatory effect as well. Any generalized harm resulting from the state's race-conscious districting would affect blacks and whites equally rather than discriminatorily stamping one race with a badge of inferiority. It was geography—not race—that determined whether North Carolina voters were assigned to voting districts in a race-conscious or race-neutral manner.[304]

Justice Stevens asserted that the *Shaw v. Reno* cause of action did not implicate equal protection concerns because it did not rest on any race-based differential treatment. Rather, the *Shaw v. Reno* cause of action rested on some unarticulated substantive due process right to color-blind districting itself. That meant that the *Shaw v. Reno* cause of action could not flow from the equal protection precedents on which the majority relied. Moreover, because it is unclear whether race-conscious districting will ultimately promote or frustrate racial harmony, the legislature was entitled to more deference than it is accorded under the strict scrutiny that is applied in a genuine equal protection case. By way of analogy, Justice Stevens suggested that the federal government could require individuals to disclose their race on census forms, even though doing so indicated that the government deemed race to be a relevant social classification. If the government imposed such a disclosure requirement only on citizens living in particular geographic areas, residents of those areas would have standing to challenge the discriminatory imposition of the requirement, but their claim would not trigger strict scrutiny of the requirement because the requirement would entail only geographic rather than racial discrimination.[305]

Justice Stevens disputed the majority's application of *Hays* to grant standing to those plaintiffs in *Shaw v. Hunt* who resided in a challenged majority-minority voting district but not to the plaintiffs who resided in other districts. If the injury relevant to a *Shaw v. Reno* racial gerrymandering claim is the representational injury that results when an elected representative neglects the interests of constituents who are not members of the majority-minority race, there is no particular reason to believe that this injury correlates with residence in the majority-minority district. Only a stereotypical assumption about the type of representation that a politician elected by minority voters was likely to accord could establish such a correlation. The plaintiffs introduced no evidence of actual representational harm. If the injury relevant to a *Shaw v. Reno* claim is stigmatic harm that results from race-based districting, it should not matter whether a plaintiff lives in a gerrymandered district or not. All voters in the state would be equally stigmatized by the message of "balkanization" that racial gerrymandering supposedly conveys. Moreover, there is no reason to believe that voters who live in a gerrymandered district that is highly integrated are specially stigmatized by that fact with the type of badge of inferiority that was found unacceptable in *Brown v. Board of Education*.[306]

In the portions of his opinion that were joined by Justices Ginsburg and Breyer, Justice Stevens argued that the majority was wrong to conclude that the North Carolina redistricting plan triggered strict scrutiny, but that even if it did, the plan satisfied the requirements of strict scrutiny.[307] Justice Stevens argued that the district court had utilized the wrong legal standard in electing to apply strict scrutiny to the redistricting plan. It had applied strict scrutiny because it deemed race to have been a "substantial" or "motivating" factor in the decision to create two majority-minority districts, but under the Supreme Court's subsequent decision in *Miller*, strict scrutiny was triggered only if race was the "predominant" consideration in adopting a redistricting plan. Accordingly, Justice Stevens believed that the case should have been remanded to the district court for application of the proper legal standard, rather than have the Supreme Court itself apply that standard in the first instance, because the district court was more familiar with the record and with local dynamics.[308]

Justice Stevens argued that, if the Supreme Court were itself to determine whether strict scrutiny applied to the North Carolina redistricting plan, it should conclude that strict scrutiny did not apply because race was not the predominant factor in the state's adoption of the plan. Under *Shaw v. Reno, Miller,* and the Court's other voting rights precedents, a state is permitted to take race into account as long as the state does not subordinate traditional, race-neutral districting principles to a racial goal.[309] Although the majority believed that strict scrutiny was justified by the state's admission that it desired to create two majority-minority voting districts and by the geographically noncompact shape of the challenged district, neither was adequate to trigger strict scrutiny. The state's admission was simply that the state complied with its interpretation of federal law contained in the Voting Rights Act, and that it attempted to create two black districts that each contained communities of shared interest.[310] The shape of the challenged district complied with the race-neutral requirements of the North Carolina Constitution, which requires voting districts to be contiguous but not to be compact.[311]

Justice Stevens added that the fact that North Carolina adopted a bizarrely shaped district, rather than the more-regular majority-minority district proposed by the attorney general for preclearance under the Voting Rights Act, indicated that the state was responding to factors other than race. Racial considerations would have been fully addressed under the rejected attorney general proposal.[312] Moreover, irregular shape might be relevant under a mapmaker's elevated perspective on an election district, but is hardly relevant to the manner in which a district is experienced by district voters who live on the ground, as illustrated by the lack of representation-related complaints lodged by voters who live in irregularly shaped states such as Massachusetts and Hawaii.[313] Justice Stevens argued that the record demonstrated that the North Carolina plan reflected two race-neutral districting criteria: protecting incumbents and separating rural from urban voters.[314] The desire to protect Democratic incumbents was evident from the Democratic legislature's rejection of Republican proposals to create two majority-minority districts drawn in ways that would have increased

Republican voting strength. And the desire to separate rural from urban voters is what accounted for the irregular shape of the challenged district, which despite its irregular shape, was located entirely within a region of the state that was defined by a community of actual shared interests. The shape of the challenged district should therefore have been disregarded in light of evidence that race-neutral districting considerations were dispositive.[315] Justice Stevens also argued that, if strict scrutiny were to be applied even to those majority-minority districts that were drawn in a way that respected traditional race-neutral districting considerations, no state would ever be able to create the majority-minority districts required to comply with the Voting Rights Act.[316]

Justice Stevens asserted that the North Carolina goal of avoiding costly federal litigation and complying with the Voting Rights Act was not the type of invidious discrimination that should trigger strict scrutiny, but if strict scrutiny were to be applied, the North Carolina plan satisfied strict scrutiny. He identified three state interests that were sufficiently "compelling" to satisfy the strict-scrutiny standard. First, the desire to increase black representation in Congress was a legitimate effort to remedy "the sorry history of race relations in North Carolina." Second, the desire of a state covered under § 5 preclearance requirements to avoid litigation with the attorney general was a compelling state interest, even if the attorney general's reading of the Voting Rights Act did not ultimately prove to be accepted by the Supreme Court. This was particularly true where, unlike *Miller*, the state made its own independent determination of the requirements of the Voting Rights Act, and where that determination was found by the district court to have been reasonable. Third, the state's desire to avoid private litigation alleging vote-dilution liability under § 2 of the Voting Rights Act was a compelling state interest, especially where a § 2 claim was as substantial as the claim that could have been asserted under the facts of *Shaw v. Hunt*.[317]

Justice Stevens pointed out that the majority had assumed for the sake of argument that a state's desire to avoid vote-dilution liability under § 2 of the Voting Rights Act could constitute a compelling state interest, but the majority concluded that creation of the challenged majority-minority district was not a narrowly tailored means of advancing that interest because the challenged district did not "remedy" any § 2 violation. Justice Stevens argued that this view ignored the fact that creation of the challenged district, even if not ultimately required by the Voting Rights Act, would nevertheless prevent a § 2 vote-dilution suit from being successfully maintained. In ad-

action claims at issue.[75] The more consistent voting pattern exhibited by Justice Stevens since 1990 may have come from a desire on the part of Justice Stevens to distance himself from the conservative voting bloc that has emerged on the present Court. In addition to Justice Stevens, the other three justices who make up the present Court's liberal bloc on affirmative action—Justices Souter,[76] Ginsburg,[77] and Breyer[78]—have voted to uphold each affirmative action program that they considered in a constitutional case. Although Justices Stevens and Souter always vote together in constitutional cases, they tend not to sign each other's opinions.[79] In sum, the present Supreme Court contains a solid five-justice conservative majority that has opposed affirmative action on constitutional grounds with an extremely high degree of consistency, and a four-justice liberal minority that has rejected constitutional challenges to affirmative action with an extremely high degree of consistency.

ii. Affirmative Action Voting Chart

The voting chart on pages 162–63 shows how individual Supreme Court justices voted in the significant affirmative action cases to which the Court gave plenary consideration.

2. Issues

Although the Supreme Court has addressed the issue of racial affirmative action in thirty-two cases,[80] it has had great difficulty determining when affirmative action programs are constitutionally and statutorily permissible. Those thirty-two cases have, however, discussed three sets of issues that appear relevant to the lawfulness of affirmative action. First, the Court has focused most heavily on the standard of review that is to be applied to affirmative action programs; whether the standard of review varies with the federal or local nature of the affirmative action program in question; and whether the strict-scrutiny standard that it now applies to all racial affirmative action programs can ever be satisfied. Second, the Court has debated what justifications are adequate for affirmative action; what findings are necessary in connection with those justifications; and whether set-asides and quotas constitute permissible means of pursuing the otherwise permissible goals of an affirmative action program. Third, the Court has discussed the levels of stigmatization and racial stereotyping entailed in a program, as

Affirmative Action Voting Chart

JUSTICES

CASES	OUTCOME	DOUGLAS	BRENNAN	STEWART	WHITE	MARSHALL	BURGER	BLACKMUN	POWELL	REHNQUIST	STEVENS	O'CONNOR	SCALIA	KENNEDY	SOUTER	THOMAS	GINSBURG	BREYER
14th Amendment—Merits																		
United Jewish Orgs. (1977)	+		+	+	+	o	−	+	+	+	+							
Bakke (1978)	−		+	−	+	+	−	+	−	−	−							
Fullilove (1980)	+		+	−	+	+	+	+	+	−	−							
Wygant (1986)	−		+		−	+	−	+	−	−	+	−						
Sheet Metal Workers (1986)	+		+		−	+	−	+	+	−	+	−						
Paradise (1987)	+		+		−	+		+	+	−	+	−	−					
Croson (1989)	−		+		−	+		+		−	−	−	−	−				
Metro Broadcasting (1990)	+		+		+	+		+		−	+	−	−	−				
Shaw v. Reno (1993)	−				+			+		−	+	−	−	−	+	−		
Adarand (1995)	−									−	+	−	−	−	+	−	+	+
Miller (1995)	−									−	+	−	−	−	+	−	+	+
Shaw v. Hunt (1996)	−									−	+	−	−	−	+	−	+	+
Bush (1996)	−									−	+	−	−	−	+	−	+	+
Abrams (1997)	−									−	+	−	−	−	+	−	+	+
Lawyer (1997)	+									−	+	+	−	−	+	−	+	+
Hunt v. Cromartie (1999)	+									+	+	+	+	+	+	+	+	+
14th Amendment—Justiciability																		
DeFunis (1974)	+	−	?	+	?	?	+	+	+	+								
Northeastern Florida (1993)	−				−			+		−	−	+	−	−	−	−		
Hays (1995)	+									+	+	+	+	+	+	+	+	+

	JUSTICES																	
CASES	OUTCOME	DOUGLAS	BRENNAN	STEWART	WHITE	MARSHALL	BURGER	BLACKMUN	POWELL	REHNQUIST	STEVENS	O'CONNOR	SCALIA	KENNEDY	SOUTER	THOMAS	GINSBURG	BREYER
Title VII																		
Weber (1979)	+		+	+	+	+	−	+	o	−	o							
Stotts (1984)	−		+		−	+	−	+	−	−	−	−						
Firefighters v. Cleveland (1986)	+		+		−	+	−	+	+	−	+	+						
Johnson v. Trans. Agency (1987)	+		+		−	+		+	+	−	+	+	−					
Voting Rights Act																		
Voinovich (1993)	−				−			−		−	−	−	−	−	−	−		
Growe (1993)	−				−			−		−	−	−	−	−	−	−		
Holder (1994)	−							+		−	+	−	−	−	+	−	+	
De Grandy (1994)	−							−		−	−	−	−	−	−	−	−	
Young (1997)	+									+	+	+	+	+	+	+	+	+
Bossier Parish (1997)	−									−	+	−	−	−	+	−	−	−
City of Monroe (1997)	−									−	−	−	−	−	+	−	−	+
Lopez (1999)	+									+	+	+	+	+	+	−	+	+
Census Act																		
Dept. of Commerce (1999)	−									−	+	−	−	−	+	−	+	+

(+) Favored minority claim; (–) Disfavored minority claim; (?) Indeterminate; (o) Did not participate
No symbol indicates that justice was not on Court when case was decided.
Justices named in **bold** are presently on Court.

well as the burden that a program imposes on innocent whites. The magnitude of permissible burdens may vary with whether an affirmative action plan is public or private, and with whether it is voluntary or court-ordered. The Court's decision in *Adarand* nominally resolved some, but not all, of these issues. Then a series of decisions concerning the constitutionality of race-conscious districting undertaken to comply with the Voting Rights Act, and statistical sampling under the Census Act, raised an additional set of issues concerning the role that race will be permitted to play in the process of electoral politics. Now, the doctrinally nebulous nature of all the legal issues that have arisen in the context of racial affirmative action has made any resolution of those issues seem tentative and highly subject to the Court's personnel at particular points in time.

i. Standard of Review

The issue that has captured most of the Court's attention in its affirmative action cases has been the appropriate standard of review. Because racial affirmative action programs employ race-based classifications to make resource allocation decisions, they are arguably subject to strict judicial scrutiny under *Korematsu v. United States*,[81] which holds that racial classifications are "immediately suspect" and subjects them to "the most rigid scrutiny."[82] The legal test traditionally applied under the strict-scrutiny standard is that, in order to be valid, the racial classification under review must advance a compelling state interest, and must be narrowly tailored or even "necessary" to the advancement of that interest.[83] However, application of this strict-scrutiny test to affirmative action classifications is controversial. To the extent that affirmative action programs are benign rather than invidious in nature—to the extent that they are intended to *promote* rather than undermine equality by neutralizing the effects of prior discrimination—affirmative action classifications should arguably be exempt from the strict scrutiny to which racial classifications that burden racial minorities are subject. The reason that the standard-of-review issue has received so much attention is that the standard-of-review issue may well be dispositive in affirmative action cases. Since the Supreme Court issued its *Korematsu* decision in 1944, no racial classification has withstood strict scrutiny by the Supreme Court.[84]

The Court began considering the affirmative action issue in 1974,[85] but was unable to achieve majority agreement on an appropriate standard of review until its 1989 decision in *City of Richmond v. J.A. Croson Co.*[86] In an opinion by Justice O'Connor, the Court held that strict scrutiny applied to a municipal affirmative action program that set aside 30 percent of the municipality's government contracting funds for minority construction contractors.[87] Four justices believed that it was inappropriate to apply strict scrutiny to benign affirmative action programs.[88] Justice O'Connor limited her opinion to state and local affirmative action programs because a 1980 Supreme Court decision in the case of *Fullilove v. Klutznick*[89] had previously upheld the constitutionality of a virtually identical federal set-aside program.[90] Justice O'Connor's *Croson* opinion distinguished *Fullilove* on the grounds that Congress possessed special powers under section 5 of the Fourteenth Amendment, that state and local legislatures did not possess, to remedy racial discrimination.[91]

Notwithstanding *Croson*, the Court's 1990 decision in *Metro Broadcasting v. FCC*[92] upheld the constitutionality of two FCC minority preference plans that had been designed to increase broadcast diversity.[93] One plan gave a preference to minority-owned broadcasters in the award of FCC broadcast licenses, and the other plan provided certain tax advantages to marginal licensees who sold their stations to minority-owned broadcasters.[94] *Metro Broadcasting* held that only intermediate scrutiny applied to federal affirmative action programs—or more specifically, to affirmative action plans authorized by Congress in the exercise of its power to remedy discrimination under section 5 of the Fourteenth Amendment.[95] Intermediate scrutiny is typically viewed as requiring that a classification be *substantially* related to an *important* governmental interest,[96] rather than *necessary* to advance a *compelling* state interest, as is required under strict scrutiny.[97] Justice Brennan's majority opinion distinguished *Croson* as involving a local rather than a congressional affirmative action program[98]—just as Justice O'Connor's *Croson* opinion had invoked that factor as a basis for distinguishing *Fullilove*.[99] Realistically, the justices seem simply to have been voting in accordance with their political views about affirmative action.[100] Only Justice White—who has often favored federal regulation under circumstances in which he disfavored analogous state regulation—appears actually to have believed that the distinction between congressional and local affirmative action programs was important.[101] Justice White was one of the swing votes in the *Croson* and *Metro Broadcasting* cases. The other swing vote was Justice Stevens,[102] who tended to focus on the presence or absence of legislative findings of prospective benefit in determining the validity of an affirmative action plan.[103]

Adarand overruled *Metro Broadcasting* and established a single strict-scrutiny standard of review for all affirmative action programs, whether congressional or local in nature.[104] Justice O'Connor wrote a majority opinion for the present Court's conservative voting bloc—Justices O'Connor, Rehnquist, Scalia, Kennedy, and Thomas—that simply extended the reasoning that Justice O'Connor had adopted in *Croson*.[105] Although this seems at least superficially to have settled the standard-of-review issue, four justices dissented in *Adarand*, arguing that congressional affirmative action plans are entitled to greater deference than local plans. The four dissenters in *Adarand* were the members of the present Court's liberal voting bloc—Justices Stevens, Souter, Ginsburg, and Breyer.[106] Ironically, now that *Metro Broadcasting* has been overruled, the four dissenters may have *actually* come to believe in the importance of a distinction between federal and local affirmative action programs.

In addition to the fact that four justices dissented from the strict-scrutiny holding of *Adarand*, the *Adarand* decision has left it unclear whether the strict scrutiny that the majority envisions is fatal scrutiny. All nine of the justices who participated in the *Adarand* decision appear formally to view strict scrutiny as permitting some forms of affirmative action. Justice O'Connor's majority opinion—joined by Justices Rehnquist, Scalia, Kennedy, and Thomas—expressly states that strict scrutiny is not "fatal in fact,"[107] but is intended merely to insure that affirmative action programs are benign rather than invidious.[108] Justice O'Connor reiterated this point in *Missouri v. Jenkins*,[109] a school desegregation case that was decided the same day as *Adarand*.[110] In addition, Justice Stevens pointed out that the majority purported to adopt the concept of strict scrutiny articulated by Justice Powell in *Regents of the University of California v. Bakke*[111]—a case invalidating a racial preference in a medical school admissions program[112]—which Justice Powell found to have been satisfied in *Fullilove*.[113] Justice Souter believed that the affirmative action program at issue in *Adarand* was adequate to survive the majority's strict scrutiny on remand.[114] Justice Ginsburg believed that strict scrutiny was fatal for invidious racial classifications, but not for benign classifications in affirmative action programs.[115] Justice Breyer joined the dissents of both Justices Souter and Ginsburg.[116]

Although the five justices in the *Adarand* majority signed Justice O'Connor's majority opinion stating that strict scrutiny was not necessarily fatal scrutiny, there is some reason to be skeptical about the degree of commitment that those five justices have to this principle. Justice Scalia seems to have rejected the suggestion that an affirmative action program could ever survive strict scrutiny. He expressly limited the degree to which he was joining the majority opinion by including the unusual proviso that he was willing to "join the opinion of the Court . . . except insofar as it may be inconsistent with" the views expressed in his concurrence.[117] His concurrence goes on to assert that the desire to remedy the effects of past discrimination could never constitute a compelling governmental interest.[118] In addition, Justice Scalia has in the past favored limiting affirmative action to the actual victims of discrimination.[119] This limitation does not seem to recognize the legitimacy of race-based affirmative action at all, but rather applies the "race neutral" principle that the state can compensate the victims of the state's own prior misconduct.[120] Justice Kennedy has also been receptive to the actual-victim limitation,[121] and Chief Justice Rehnquist has endorsed this limitation in Title VII cases.[122] Justice Thomas forcefully asserted in *Adarand* that all racial classifications were immoral, whether invidious or benign, terming affirmative action "racial paternalism."[123] However, in *Missouri v. Jenkins,*[124] which was decided the same day as *Adarand,* Justice Thomas expressed a certain fondness for historically black schools.[125] This might cause him to view strict scrutiny as less than fatal if necessary to permit the voluntary maintenance of historically black schools in black neighborhoods.[126]

It may turn out that after *Adarand,* strict scrutiny will remain "fatal in fact" because a majority of the Court will never find an affirmative action program adequate to meet the strict-scrutiny standards that are theoretically capable of being satisfied. This would be consistent with the history of the Court's equal protection jurisprudence since *Korematsu,* and it would satisfy the draconian pronouncements of Justices Scalia and Thomas. Because the program at issue in *Adarand* is a mild one, ultimately consisting of only a rebuttable presumption that minority contractors are disadvantaged, the fate of *Adarand* on remand may be telling. After remand, the district court entered summary judgment for the plaintiff, holding that the *Adarand* affirmative action plan did not survive strict scrutiny because it was not narrowly tailored. The court of appeals then vacated the district court decision, finding that the case had become moot.[127] Nevertheless, the district court invalidation of the *Adarand* presumption may be an indication that the Supreme Court's *Adarand* holding is indeed sweeping, and that Justice O'Connor is mistaken in her assertion that strict scrutiny will not always be fatal scrutiny.

Justice O'Connor—like all of the other justices in the *Adarand* majority—has never voted to uphold an affirmative action program after strict scrutiny in a constitutional case.[128] However, assuming that Justice O'Connor is sincere in her assertion that strict scrutiny is not fatal scrutiny, her vote plus the votes of the four *Adarand* dissenters may provide a bare majority to uphold at least some affirmative action programs. In fact, it may be that the *Adarand* majority's conception of strict scrutiny will turn out to be the functional equivalent of *Metro Broadcasting*'s intermediate scrutiny, and that the ultimate significance of *Adarand* will be more rhetorical than substantive. It may also turn out that in practice the Court will give more deference to Congress than it gives to state and local legislatures, thereby ironically preserving the operative distinction between *Croson* and *Metro Broadcasting* that *Adarand* nominally overruled.[129] Because *Adarand* was a 5–4 decision, resolution of this issue may remain tentative, shifting with subsequent Supreme Court appointments.

ii. Justifications, Findings, and Quotas

If *Adarand* is ultimately interpreted to permit some affirmative action programs to survive strict scrutiny, it remains unclear what justifications for affirmative action the Court will recognize as legitimate. In the past, the Court has distinguished between two types of justifications and has treated them differently. The Court held in *Croson* that when strict scrutiny applies, permissible affirmative action is limited to that which is necessary to remedy particularized acts of past discrimination, and is not available merely to remedy the effects of general societal discrimination that has caused the underrepresentation of racial minorities in particular occupations or social roles.[130] However, in *Metro Broadcasting*, the Court held that the pursuit of prospective diversity was a permissible goal for a congressional affirmative action program.[131] The prospective-diversity justification upheld in *Metro Broadcasting* is very similar to the general-societal-discrimination justification that the Court rejected in *Croson*, in that it de-emphasizes the importance of particularized acts of past discrimination and permits affirmative action addressed to the underrepresentation of minorities in particular aspects of the culture. But, *Metro Broadcasting* was decided under the relatively more tolerant standard of intermediate scrutiny[132] that the Court expressly rejected in *Adarand*.[133]

Adarand notwithstanding, it is uncertain how meaningful the general-societal-discrimination restriction will prove to be. It is likely that the four dissenters in *Adarand* would permit an affirmative action plan that they found otherwise acceptable to be justified on the grounds that it sought to remedy general societal discrimination. Justice Stevens voted to uphold the FCC prospective diversity plan in *Metro Broadcasting*,[134] and he has often stated his preference for prospective benefit over identifiable past discrimination as a justification for affirmative action.[135] Justice Ginsburg joined the opinion of Justice Stevens, expressing this preference in *Adarand*.[136] The tone of Justice Souter's dissenting opinion in *Adarand* suggests receptivity to prospective benefit as a justification for affirmative action in its emphasis on the need to eliminate forces that "skew the operation of public systems" and its insistence that the prospectively oriented *Fullilove* decision controlled the affirmative action program at issue in *Adarand*.[137] Note, however, that Justice Souter also described his concerns as being relevant to the provision of a remedy for past discrimination.[138] Justice Breyer may also be receptive to the prospective benefit justification for affirmative action, as evidenced by his decision to join Justice Souter's dissent, which Justice Ginsburg also joined.[139]

In addition to the *Adarand* dissenters, even Justice O'Connor—the author of the *Adarand* and *Croson* majority opinions, and of the primary *Metro Broadcasting* dissent—has in the past recognized the legitimacy of using prospective diversity as a justification for affirmative action in educational contexts.[140] However, Justice O'Connor also appears to believe that there is a distinction between the permissible promotion of prospective diversity and the impermissible effort to remedy general societal discrimination.[141] What this shows is not so much that Justice O'Connor may change her mind on the remedy-for-past-discrimination versus general-societal-discrimination issue, but that the issue is more rhetorical than substantive. An affirmative action program can be characterized as serving either justification without much difficulty. Accordingly, Justice O'Connor was able to characterize the *Fullilove* set-aside plan as a program that was designed to remedy past discrimination, while characterizing the seemingly indistinguishable *Croson* set-aside plan as a program that was designed to remedy general societal discrimination.[142] In thus characterizing these two programs, Justice O'Connor credited congressional findings of past discrimination that are notoriously cursory,[143] and disregarded the well-known history of past discrimination in Richmond, Virginia.[144]

Closely related to the issue of what goals constitute legitimate justifications for affirmative action is the issue of what findings are required for an affirmative action plan to be valid. If affirmative action is to be limited to the provision of narrow remedies for identifiable acts of prior discrimination, the Court must know both that there were such acts of prior discrimination and how widespread the prior discrimination was in order to ensure that a remedy is sufficiently narrow.[145] The Supreme Court has frequently addressed the need for formal findings of past discrimination, but the actual importance of formal findings is difficult to assess. In *Croson*, the Court relied heavily on both the absence of reliable findings of past discrimination and the absence of narrow tailoring in invalidating the Richmond set-aside plan.[146] Moreover, the *Metro Broadcasting* case stressed the presence of congressional findings in upholding the FCC affirmative action plans at issue in that case.[147] This suggests that the presence or absence of reliable findings may continue to be dispositive. However, the Court was unreceptive to the evidence of extensive congressional deliberations that was before it in *Adarand*,[148] but was quite deferential to the cursory congressional consideration that occurred in *Fullilove*.[149]

In addition, the findings whose existence the Court stressed so heavily in *Metro Broadcasting* as a basis for upholding the FCC broadcast-diversity affirmative action plans ultimately prove to be rather chimerical. The FCC affirmative action programs that Justice Brennan found to have been authorized by Congress in *Metro Broadcasting* were actually programs that had been developed by the FCC.[150] As political controversy concerning affirmative action increased during the Reagan Administration, Congress failed to enact pending legislation that would have codified the FCC programs. It was able only to adopt a series of appropriations riders that preserved the status quo while Congress continued to debate the affirmative action issue.[151] Judge Williams termed the appropriations riders "a kind of mental standstill" when *Metro Broadcasting* was before the court of appeals,[152] although Justice Brennan disagreed with this characterization in his *Metro Broadcasting* majority opinion.[153] Not only was the program more an FCC program than a program authorized by Congress in the exercise of its powers under section 5 of the Fourteenth Amendment, but the FCC program had ceased even to be supported by the FCC. During the Reagan Administration, the FCC shifted policy and wished to abandon the FCC affirmative action programs that had been implemented during the Carter Administration, citing doubts about the FCC's jurisdiction to engage in such affirmative action.[154] However, the United States Court of Appeals for the District of Columbia Circuit declined to cooperate with the Reagan FCC strategy for curtailing affirmative action, and held that the FCC did in fact possess the requisite jurisdiction.[155] Accordingly, the FCC programs can be deemed judicially authorized programs as readily as they can be deemed congressionally authorized programs. The FCC was opposed to them, and Congress lacked the votes needed to codify them. Only the D.C. Circuit favored them. Ultimately, the deference to Congress that Justice Brennan purported to be exhibiting in *Metro Broadcasting* may really have been deference to the D.C. Circuit. In any event, Congress has now repealed the FCC "distress sale" program,[156] and in the wake of the *Adarand* decision, the FCC has begun to substitute race-neutral disadvantaged-applicant programs for its minority preference programs.[157]

All of this suggests that findings are less relevant as an actual basis for decision than they are as a post-hoc justification for judicial outcomes that have been reached on other grounds. Justice Powell, who was the Court's strongest proponent of formal findings,[158] is no longer on the Court.[159] Moreover, Justice O'Connor—who wrote the majority opinions in *Adarand* and *Croson*, and the primary dissent in *Metro Broadcasting*—has in the past stated that formal findings are unnecessary.[160] Because the entities that adopt affirmative action programs in the wake of recent Supreme Court decisions will be on notice to buttress their programs with elaborate findings, the significance of findings in future cases may well dissipate. In this regard, the elaborate congressional deliberations that were before the Court in *Adarand* may well have been a reaction to the *Croson* decision,[161] but those findings were seemingly insufficient to save the constitutionality of the *Adarand* affirmative action plan.[162]

Assuming that some remedial affirmative action programs will be upheld if they are accompanied by adequate findings of particularized past discrimination, the degree to which the Court will permit the use of racial quotas remains another unresolved issue. "Quota" has, of course, become the pejorative term of choice for political opponents of affirmative action. For example, conservative Republicans successfully opposed President Clinton's selection of Lani Guinier to be assistant attorney general in charge of the Civil Rights Division of the Department of Justice by dubbing her a "Quota Queen" in light of her support for cumulative voting as a means of increasing minority voting strength.[163] In addition to conservative political opposition to the concept of quotas, quotas have proved to be judicially unpopular as well. In his *Adarand* dissent, Justice Stevens justified voting in favor of the *Adarand* preference despite voting against the *Fullilove* set-aside on the grounds that *Fullilove* involved a numerical quota whereas *Adarand* did not.[164] The *Croson* Court viewed quotas as undesirable because they treat citizens as mere members of a group rather than as individuals.[165] Further, even the *Metro Broadcasting* majority felt compelled to assert that the preferences and set-asides that it was upholding did not constitute quotas.[166] Justices Brennan and Marshall have also attempted to recast the Court's general opposition to quotas as opposition to "quota[s] in the invidious sense of a ceiling" that is imposed on minority participation.[167] Although Justice Scalia did not sign the four-justice plurality portion of Justice O'Connor's *Croson* opinion that opposed quotas, his opposition to racial quotas is subsumed in his general opposition to affirmative action.[168]

Notwithstanding the Court's stated aversion to quotas, the Court has been willing to uphold racial quotas on several occasions. The Court upheld the "distress sale" program in *Metro Broadcasting*, which the dissent characterized as a rigid quota and a 100 percent set-aside,[169] although the majority rejected that characterization.[170] In addition, the Court upheld quotas in *Paradise*,[171] *Sheet Metal Workers*,[172] and *Fullilove*.[173] The Court also upheld the percentage targets used as the basis for the reapportionment plan in *United Jewish Organizations*.[174] It may be that *United Jewish Organizations* was tacitly overruled in *Miller*, which reached the opposite result under very similar facts. But whether this seems true or not depends upon how seriously one takes Justice Kennedy's efforts in *Miller* to distinguish *United Jewish Organizations*.[175] And despite the Court's contrary assurances, the "distress sale" set-aside that the Court upheld in *Metro Broadcasting* appears to have been a quota in every meaningful sense of the term.[176]

The Supreme Court's sometime aversion to quotas is traceable to Justice Powell's opinion in *Regents of the University of California v. Bakke*,[177] where the Court invalidated a 16 percent minority preference in a medical school admissions program, but nevertheless upheld the use of race as a permissible basis for affirmative action in appropriate cases.[178] Justice Powell opposed rigid quotas but approved of the consideration of race as a factor, favorably citing the Harvard College admissions criteria.[179] Presumably, such opposition to quotas is based upon their mechanistic inflexibility and their potential to generate divisive resentment, both of which may decrease as the consideration of race becomes less visible. Nevertheless, both proponents and targets of affirmative action may well secretly favor quotas because they are administratively convenient. Quotas clearly convey the degree of minority representation that is appropriate in particular circumstances, and they provide a safe harbor from potential liability for racial discrimination. However, quotas also constitute a blatant admission that race is an important social category, thereby belying the aspirational claim that the United States is a color-blind nation. Once again, characterization of an affirmative action program as involving a disfavored quota or a permissible guideline that treats race as a factor is likely to be determined by how a justice otherwise feels about the desirability of the particular affirmative action program at issue.

iii. Stigmas, Stereotypes, and Burdens

The question of whether an affirmative action plan stigmatizes or stereotypes either its intended beneficiaries or the innocent whites who are forced to bear the burden of the plan is a question that the Supreme Court discusses in virtually all of its affirmative action decisions.[180] Nevertheless, this too appears to be an issue that is of rhetorical rather than operative importance. The general stigmatization argument is that affirmative action will ultimately backfire: it will brand the intended beneficiaries of an affirmative action plan as inferior because of their inability to compete successfully on the merits; and it will fuel latent racial tensions as innocent whites come to resent having to bear the burdens of affirmative action. A version of this argument was first articulated by Justice Douglas in *DeFunis v. Odegaard*,[181] and then reasserted by Justice Brennan in *United Jewish Organizations v. Carey*,[182] and by Justice Powell in *Bakke*.[183] However, the argument has not been asserted in a case in which it appears to have been dispositive. For example, Justice O'Connor referred to—but the Court did not rely upon—the general stigmatization argument in her opinion invalidating the Richmond set-aside plan in *Croson*.[184] She also unsuccessfully asserted the general stigmatization argument in her dissent from the Court's opinion upholding the FCC plans in *Metro Broadcasting*.[185] Moreover, Justice Stevens—who is sensitive to the stigmatization argument—chose not to accept that argument as a basis for invalidating the preferential teacher layoff plan in *Wygant*.[186] In *Adarand*, Justice O'Connor argued that strict scrutiny was necessary to distinguish legitimate affirmative action programs from illegitimate racial stereotyping, but she did not place any particular stress on the danger of stigmatization.[187] To the extent that stigmatization is deemed to be synonymous with racial stereotyping, the *Metro Broadcasting* Court's acceptance of both the proffered broadcast diversity rationale and the asserted nexus that exists between station ownership and broadcast diversity seems to have constituted acceptance of a relatively high degree of racial stereotyping.[188]

In theory, an affirmative action plan can also be invalidated because of the manner in which it stigmatizes whites.[189] The argument appears to be that, to the extent that affirmative action is used to remedy the effects of past discrimination, affirmative action stigmatize whites by charging them with having engaged in past racial discrimination.[190] Sometimes, the issue of stigmatization or stereotyping that adversely affects whites seems to be conflated with the issue of burden on whites.[191] Again, however, no plan has actually been found invalid because of the imposition of such a stigma. In *United Jewish Organizations,* the reapportionment plan at issue benefited black voters by diluting the voting strength of white Hasidic Jews. Although that plan presented perhaps the strongest case for invalidating an affirmative action plan because of the stigma that it imposed on whites, the Court nevertheless chose to uphold the plan.[192]

The degree of burden that an affirmative action plan places on innocent whites is likely to be a significant factor. The Court almost always discusses the burden imposed on innocent whites by an affirmative action plan that it is reviewing[193]—although the majority opinion in *Croson* curiously did not contain any explicit discussion of the burden imposed on innocent whites.[194] *Metro Broadcasting* upheld a plan that interfered only with the prospective expectations of innocent whites and did not burden whites with any change in the status quo,[195] while *Wygant* invalidated a plan that called for the layoff of white teachers rather than minority teachers with less seniority. In fact, four of the five justices who voted to invalidate the *Wygant* plan focused on the burden that the plan imposed on white teachers.[196] The distinction between frustrated expectations and reduction of the status quo may not ultimately have much meaning.[197] Nevertheless, some justices have treated the distinction as outcome-determinative, and have stressed their opposition to the use of layoffs—as opposed to prospective hiring goals—in affirmative action plans.[198] Among currently sitting justices, Chief Justice Rehnquist has viewed the distinction as dispositive,[199] and Justice O'Connor has endorsed the distinction without endorsing its dispositive character.[200] In addition, the Court's Title VII affirmative action cases indicate that the Court is quite attentive to both the nature and scope of the burden imposed upon innocent whites, including whether the burden is voluntarily assumed or court-imposed.[201]

It is unclear whether the Court will ultimately prove more receptive to voluntary or court-ordered affirmative action plans. The Court's Title VII cases state that, for statutory purposes, voluntary affirmative action plans can be implemented free from restrictions that would apply to court-ordered plans.[202] The issue is most likely to be relevant with respect to the burden borne by innocent whites. If a burden has been voluntarily assumed, it may be acceptable without evidence of prior discrimination or narrow tailoring even though a court could not have imposed that burden as part of a remedial order in the absence of such a voluntary assumption.[203]

The voluntary affirmative action issue is directly related to the often-imposed requirement that the affirmative action plan be justifiable as a remedy for past discrimination. If it turns out that acceptable affirmative action in particular contexts is limited to plans that seek to remedy the effects of past discrimination,[204] evidence of past discrimination may be required before voluntary affirmative action is permitted. This view was rejected by the Court in *United Steelworkers of America v. Weber*,[205] which permitted voluntary affirmative action plans even in the absence of a showing of prior unlawful discrimination.[206] Nevertheless, the holding of *Weber* is rather fragile. Four justices—Justices Rehnquist, White, O'Connor, and Scalia—have expressed the view that *Weber* was incorrectly decided, and that voluntary affirmative action should not be permitted in the absence of grounds for court-ordered affirmative action.[207] In addition, Justices Kennedy and Thomas, who were not on the Court when *Weber* was decided, have almost never voted in favor of an affirmative action program.[208] This creates a five-justice majority—consisting of Justices Rehnquist, O'Connor, Scalia, Kennedy, and Thomas—who may be willing to disallow the voluntary affirmative action that the Supreme Court authorized in *Weber*. Moreover, these conservative-bloc justices are the same five justices who comprised the majority in *Adarand*,[209] and their willingness to overrule *Metro Broadcasting*[210] indicates that they may also be willing to overrule *Weber*.[211]

It may be that *Adarand* itself renders unconstitutional any reading of Title VII that does not insist on demonstrable prior discrimination as a prerequisite to voluntary affirmative action. The financial incentive at issue in *Adarand* encouraged private parties to consider race in the selection of subcontractors.[212] If such official encouragement of private race consciousness in the absence of a demonstrated need to remedy prior discrimination violates the equal protection clause in the *Adarand* bidding context,[213] it may be that the similar official encouragement to engage in race-conscious employment decisions in order to avoid a potential Title VII violation would also violate the equal protection clause—at least in the absence of a showing that such race consciousness was a narrowly tailored remedy for past discrimination. This is an issue that the Supreme Court did not address in *Weber*.[214] In addition, to the extent that *Weber* was rooted in the belief that affirmative action is subject to less demanding scrutiny because of its benign nature,[215] *Weber* seems to be in direct conflict with the *Adarand* holding that the benign nature of affirmative action does not provide immunity from strict scrutiny.[216]

Finally, it is interesting to note that the Court first flirted with and then rejected the notion that no race-conscious burden could *ever* be imposed upon innocent whites unless necessary to provide a remedy to an actual victim of discrimination.[217] An actual-victim limitation would constitute a rejection of the concept of affirmative action. It would rely solely on tort-type remedies to compensate victims of discrimination, without any effort to overcome the limitations of the tort system in dealing with widespread undifferentiated injuries.[218] Nevertheless, the current Court appears to contain at least two justices who approve of the actual-victim limitation—Justices Rehnquist and Scalia.[219] In addition, up to three other justices— Justices O'Connor, Kennedy, and Thomas—may come to adopt the actual-victim view, as evidenced by the fact that they almost always vote against affirmative action.[220]

iv. Doctrinal Effect of *Adarand*

Justice O'Connor's majority opinion in *Adarand* makes it clear that strict scrutiny now applies to all race-based affirmative action programs, whether federal, state, or local.[221] It is less clear, however, whether the *Adarand* escalation from intermediate to strict scrutiny for congressional programs—and the analogous *Croson* escalation for state and local programs[222]—will have any significant doctrinal effect. As has been discussed,[223] if strict scrutiny remains "fatal in fact," this escalated scrutiny will indeed prove to be significant in those cases to which it applies. It will be outcome-determinative, and affirmative action initiatives such as the *Metro Broadcasting* preference and the *Fullilove* set-aside will no longer be constitutional. However, Justice O'Connor's assurance that strict scrutiny is no longer fatal scrutiny,[224] raises the possibility that at least five members of the present Court will vote to uphold some affirmative action programs under *Adarand*'s new strict scrutiny standard.[225] Regardless of what strict-scrutiny comes to mean, however, it is likely that many existing affirmative action programs can be restructured so that they will remain constitutionally permissible even after *Adarand* and *Croson*.

The strict scrutiny that the Supreme Court invoked in *Adarand* and *Croson* applies only to affirmative action programs that intentionally utilize racial classifications to advance their objectives.[226] This is because under *Washington v. Davis*,[227] the equal protection clause prohibits only intentional discrimination. It does not prohibit the use of race-neutral classifications that have an unintended racially disparate impact.[228] Typically, pre-*Adarand* affirmative action programs contained explicit racial preferences, thereby providing strong evidence of intentional discrimination within the meaning of *Washington v. Davis*.[229] However, if those programs are restructured in a way that accords preferential treatment to individuals on the basis of social or economic disadvantage, without explicit reference to race, those programs should not be subject to heightened scrutiny under the equal protection clause because they will not utilize racial classifications.

Restructuring a race-based affirmative action program to be a disadvantage-based program will inevitably have a racially disparate impact. This is because racial minorities are disproportionately represented among those who suffer social and economic disadvantage.[230] Although restructured programs are likely to have a racially disparate impact, it is also likely that in absolute terms many such programs will provide more benefits to whites than to racial minorities. In *Personnel Administrator v. Feeney,*[231] the Supreme Court held that mere knowledge of such disparate impact was not sufficient to establish the type of intentional discrimination that *Washington v. Davis* demands to trigger strict scrutiny under the equal protection clause.[232] *Feeney* held that the intent necessary for an equal protection violation was "because of" actuating intent, not merely "in spite of" tolerance of a known consequence.[233] It would seem to follow, therefore, that a restructured affirmative action plan that was genuinely intended to aid those who are socially or economically disadvantaged would be constitutional despite any racially disparate impact that it might have, while a plan that was drafted in race-neutral terms relating to "disadvantage," but was really intended to aid minorities because of their race, would not be constitutional. Most intentional efforts to aid racial minorities stem from the disproportionate levels of disadvantage being suffered by racial minorities. Accordingly, it seems that most affirmative action plans can honestly be described as plans that rest on an intent that is constitutionally permissible under *Washington v. Davis* and *Feeney.* Indeed, it seems that the long history of disadvantage suffered by racial minorities in the United States is central to what it means to *be* a racial minority in the United States. It is what accounts for the cultural significance of race, and it is what makes skin color different from eye color or hair color. As a result, it is not clear that the contending conceptions of intent that arguably lie beneath a disparate-impact classification are metaphysically different in the context of race. It seems reasonably clear, however, that most affirmative action programs could be recast as programs that are designed to assist disadvantaged individuals. Similar issues, concerning the distinction between impermissible racial gerrymandering and permissible political gerrymandering of voting district lines, are implicated in the Court's Voting Rights Act cases.[234]

Affirmative action is sometimes criticized as benefiting those racial minorities who are successful rather than those racial minorities who are disadvantaged. At any given level of socioeconomic accomplishment, however, it seems clear that racial minorities are disadvantaged relative to whites at that same level of accomplishment.[235] Accordingly, this objection to affirmative action seems to confuse affirmative action programs with subsistence income-redistribution programs. If affirmative action is viewed as a remedy for racial discrimination, it would not seem to matter whether the beneficiaries of an affirmative action program are indigent or wealthy.

Title VII poses a special problem for affirmative action plans that are restructured to be race-neutral. In *Griggs v. Duke Power*,[236] the Supreme Court held that Title VII—unlike the equal protection clause—*does* prohibit the use of classifications that have a racially disparate impact. As a result, it might be that a restructured, race-neutral affirmative action program that did not violate the equal protection clause of the Constitution would nevertheless violate Title VII. However, it may be that such a result will ultimately be deemed unsound.

The Supreme Court held, in *United Steelworkers of America v. Weber*,[237] that race-conscious affirmative action programs do not necessarily violate Title VII.[238] It would seem to follow, therefore, that race-neutral affirmative action programs with a racially disparate impact would also be valid under Title VII. The problem is the that the reasoning of *Weber* is in tension with the reasoning of *Adarand*. In *Weber*, the Court concluded that the benign nature of affirmative action was a sufficient justification for the racially disparate impact of an affirmative action program that did not excessively burden whites.[239] As has been discussed,[240] it may be that the *Weber* reading of Title VII does not survive *Adarand*, precisely because the present Court no longer views the distinction between benign and invidious discrimination to be dispositive. However, it seems likely that Title VII will be construed to permit affirmative action programs that are permissible under the equal protection clause.

To the extent that affirmative action programs are congressional programs, such as the programs at issue in *Adarand*, *Metro Broadcasting*, and *Fullilove*, they may be deemed valid under Title VII because it is difficult to conclude that Congress intended Title VII to invalidate its own programs. To the extent that state and local programs mirror congressional programs—in the way that the *Croson* set-aside mirrored the *Fullilove* set-aside—it is similarly difficult to conclude that Congress intended Title VII to invalidate those programs, precisely because of their similarity to the congressional programs. To the extent that affirmative action programs are private, voluntary programs to which the equal protection clause does not apply, the *Weber* Court's finding that Congress did not intend Title VII to preclude such programs would still seem to be controlling. If the Supreme Court did not interpret Title VII in these ways, Congress could amend the statute, in a way that it cannot amend the equal protection clause, to permit the desired degree of affirmative action. It is only if the Supreme Court is willing to hold that a *Weber*-type reading of Title VII that allows benign affirmative action is itself a violation of the equal protection clause that restructured programs would be invalid. However, this would be a peculiar contortion of the equal protection clause. The Supreme Court would be substituting a disparate impact standard in the context of affirmative action for the *Washington v. Davis* intentional discrimination standard on which it insisted in the context of invidious discrimination. It would be curious if the constitutional standard applied to a discrimination remedy were held to be more demanding than the standard applied to the discrimination itself. However, it is true that the present Supreme Court's insistence on strict scrutiny in *Adarand* does require that affirmative action be narrowly tailored to advance a compelling state interest, even though the prior discrimination that affirmative action is intended to remedy was broad-based, categorical discrimination that was based solely on race.

The uncertainty that surrounds Justice O'Connor's new strict scrutiny makes it difficult to predict what the doctrinal effect of *Adarand* will ultimately be. If strict scrutiny results in the unsalvageable invalidation of affirmative action programs that were valid prior to *Adarand*, the doctrinal effect of the decision will have been significant. However, if *Adarand* strict scrutiny turns out to be largely a replication of pre-*Adarand* intermediate scrutiny,[241] or if pre-*Adarand* affirmative action programs can be salvaged by restructuring them as race-neutral programs, the doctrinal effect of the case will prove to be negligible. Regardless of the doctrinal effect that *Adarand* ultimately turns out to have, the case has already had a significant rhetorical effect. *Adarand* signifies a political alignment of the Supreme Court with the increasingly conservative mood of the nation concerning the issue of affirmative action.[242] Whether this constitutes appropriate or inappropriate conduct on the part of the Supreme Court is infinitely debatable, but as a realist matter, Supreme Court conduct of this sort does seem to be largely inevitable.[243]

v. Redistricting

In recent years, most of the Supreme Court's affirmative action cases have involved redistricting. Seven of the eight constitutional affirmative action cases that the Supreme Court has decided since 1993 concerned the validity of redistricting plans containing majority-minority, or substantial-minority voting districts.[244] In a series of 5–4 rulings, the Court's conservative-bloc justices—Justices Rehnquist, O'Connor, Scalia, Kennedy, and Thomas—have invalidated or applied strict scrutiny to the majority-minority districting plans at issue in five of the seven cases.[245] Moreover, the two districting plans that the Court upheld were plans that eliminated rather than added any new majority-minority districts.[246] Although the rulings of the current Court have been largely consistent in the redistricting context, the underlying cause of action that permits white voters to challenge majority-minority districts has been supported by only a bare majority of the Court. In addition, it is difficult to know when the existence of a majority-minority district will trigger strict scrutiny, or whether any such districts will ever be able to survive strict scrutiny.

The legal cause of action for racial gerrymandering, which permits white voters to challenge the creation of majority-minority districts even in the absence of any vote-dilution claim, was first recognized by the Supreme Court in *Shaw v. Reno*.[247] Justice O'Connor's majority opinion held that strict scrutiny applied to majority-minority voting districts whose shapes were bizarre enough to suggest that those districts had been drawn for racial purposes.[248] Justice O'Connor distinguished earlier cases that had upheld the constitutionality of race-conscious districting—particularly *United Jewish Organizations v. Carey*[249]—on the grounds that those cases did not classify voters according to race or contain voting districts that were bizarrely shaped.[250] Justice Kennedy's majority opinion in *Miller* for the five conservative-bloc justices refined the *Shaw v. Reno* racial gerrymandering cause of action. Justice Kennedy emphasized that the *Shaw v. Reno* cause of action was not based on the same danger of vote dilution that was involved in *United Jewish Organizations*, but rather was a cause of action recognizing that individual voters had a right not to be assigned to voting districts on the basis of their race, just as they had a right not to be assigned to public schools or parks on the basis of their race. Race-based districting deprived voters of their right to be treated as individuals rather than stereotyped as members of a racial group that possessed homogeneous political views.[251] The Court's final refinement to the racial gerrymandering cause of action came in *United States v. Hays*.[252] The opinion of Justice O'Connor in *Hays*—this time writing for a seven-justice majority comprised of Justices O'Connor, Rehnquist, Scalia, Kennedy, Souter, Thomas, and Breyer—held that white voters lacked standing to challenge the constitutionality of majority-minority districts unless they themselves resided in the districts that they were challenging.[253] According to *Shaw v. Reno*, *Miller*, and *Hays*, the theory underlying the racial gerrymandering cause of action is that race-conscious districting reinforces racial stereotypes and incites racial hostility,[254] and that white voters will either be stigmatized or forced to suffer representational harms if they reside in a majority-minority district, because the officials elected from that district may ignore the interests of their white constituents.[255]

Although the five conservative-bloc justices favored the creation of a cause of action for racial gerrymandering, the creation of that cause of action was opposed by the four liberal-bloc justices—Justices Stevens, Souter, Ginsburg, and Breyer. Justice Stevens joined the dissenting opinion of Justice White in *Shaw v. Reno*, which argued that white voters could not plausibly be injured by a redistricting plan that the white majority had itself chosen to adopt, and that white voters could not plausibly argue that the effect of such a plan was to give whites less overall voting strength than it gave to minorities.[256] Justice Stevens also wrote a dissenting opinion of his own that stressed the irony of using the Fourteenth Amendment to *preclude* remedies for prior racial discrimination in voting when the whole point of the Fourteenth Amendment was to *provide* remedies for prior racial discrimination.[257] Justice Steven wrote a dissenting opinion in *Miller*, arguing that whites were not injured by the creation of majority-minority districts.[258] He thought that the representational injury on which the *Shaw v. Reno* racial gerrymandering cause of action was based suffered from internal inconsistency. The view that white voters would not be adequately represented by officials elected from majority-minority districts made the very same stereotyped assumptions about racial homogeneity that the *Miller* majority found to be unconstitutionally "offensive and demeaning."[259] Justice Stevens further argued that race-conscious districting was different from race-conscious assignment of individuals to schools or parks, because race-conscious districting was intended to *include* minorities in the political process rather than to *exclude* minorities from segregated facilities.[260] In *Shaw v. Hunt*, Justice Stevens claimed that white voters who complained about the creation of majority-minority districts were not really complaining about voter segregation but about the integration of minorities into the political process.[261] In *Bush*, Justice Stevens reiterated his view that the *Shaw v. Reno* cause of action was misconceived, claiming that it threatened more significant harms than it prevented.[262] He also argued that the cause of action imposing stringent requirements on the validity of majority-minority districts was discriminatory because it did not impose equally stringent requirements on the validity of majority-white districts.[263]

Justice Souter wrote an opinion in *Shaw v. Reno* dissenting from the creation of a racial gerrymandering cause of action, arguing that race consciousness was inevitable in the districting process, and that whites were not injured in any particularized way by the existence of majority-minority districts.[264] He also argued that the Constitution did not require voting districts to have nonbizarre shapes.[265] In *Bush*, Justice Souter argued that any abstract representational harms that resulted from voting districts in which one race constituted a majority were harms that were shared by all races, not just whites.[266] Justice Souter ultimately concluded that *Shaw v. Reno* should be overruled.[267]

Justices Ginsburg and Breyer also opposed the creation of a racial gerrymandering cause of action. In *Miller*, Justice Ginsburg wrote a dissenting opinion that was joined by Justice Breyer—as well as by Justices Stevens and Souter—that questioned the coherence of the *Shaw v. Reno* cause of action.[268] Justice Ginsburg contested the relevance of the majority's claim that race-conscious districting improperly treated voters as members of a racial group rather than as individuals, because the whole point of a districting plan was to aggregate voters by groups. Individual considerations such as merit or achievement were simply not relevant to districting decisions, and there was no reason to treat racial minorities any differently than other voters who are routinely assigned to particular voting districts because of their ethnic group membership.[269] Justice Breyer wrote a dissenting opinion in *Abrams* concluding that the Constitution did not embody a cause of action for racial gerrymandering.[270]

The *Shaw v. Reno* cause of action for race-based assignment to a voting district currently has the support of five Supreme Court justices, and is vigorously opposed by four justices. Because each justice seems to be firmly committed to his or her position on the desirability of such a cause of action, it is unlikely that any justice will shift positions on this issue. However, the fact that the cause of action is supported by only a bare majority of the Court suggests that a single Supreme Court appointment could change the position of the overall Court on this issue. Assuming that the racial gerrymandering cause of action remains viable, the existence of such a cause of action still raises questions about the proper standard of review, and whether majority-minority districts will be able to survive that standard of review.

The standard of review that applies to redistricting cases is not always clear. Although *Adarand* seemingly simplified matters by adopting a unitary standard of strict scrutiny for all racial classifications, *Adarand* did not provide a test for determining what constitutes a racial classification. In *Shaw v. Reno*,[271] the Supreme Court held that race-conscious districting plans *sometimes*—but not *always*—constitute racial classifications that are subject to strict scrutiny under the equal protection clause.[272] Justice O'Connor's opinion for the five-justice, conservative-bloc majority in *Shaw v. Reno* seemed to suggest that strict scrutiny would be triggered in the voting rights context when voting districts were so bizarrely shaped that their shapes could be explained only on the grounds of race.[273] However, that reading of *Shaw v. Reno* was rejected in *Miller v. Johnson*[274]—a case decided only a few weeks after *Adarand*.[275] Justice Kennedy's opinion for the same five-justice, conservative-bloc majority in *Miller* stated that strict scrutiny could be triggered even if a voting district was not bizarrely shaped. Under *Miller*, the test for determining whether a districting plan constitutes a racial classification that triggers strict scrutiny is whether race was the "predominant factor" in the formulation of the plan, thereby indicating that "the legislature subordinated traditional race-neutral districting principles . . . to racial considerations."[276]

Where race is one of many factors considered in the formulation of a districting plan, it is difficult to know what it means for race to be the "predominant factor," especially after *Miller*'s admonition that the shape of a voting district is not dispositive. *Miller* seems designed to reflect a distinction first articulated in *Washington v. Davis*[277] and *Personnel Administrator v. Feeney*[278] between impermissible discriminatory intent on the one hand and permissible awareness of disparate impact on the other.[279] *Miller* prohibits legislatures from being overly motivated by racial considerations in making districting decisions, but it permits legislatures to be "aware" of race when making those decisions.[280] However, even Justice Kennedy's opinion in *Miller* recognized that such a distinction is difficult to apply in the voting rights context[281]—an observation that has also been made by the four liberal-bloc justices.[282] Justice Kennedy's subsequent concurring opinion in *Bush* indicates that he believes that strict scrutiny should always be applied when a majority-minority district is intentionally created[283]—a view that seems to be shared by Justices Scalia and Thomas,[284] but not by Justice O'Connor.[285]

The facts of the decided cases fail to provide much guidance. Although *Miller* held that the districting plan at issue in the *Miller* case itself was subject to strict scrutiny, on the same day that *Miller* was decided, the Supreme Court summarily affirmed a lower court decision in *DeWitt v. Wilson,*[286] holding that race had not been the "predominant factor" in formulating the *DeWitt* plan. The two cases produced different outcomes, but the redistricting plans in each case seemed very similar. Both the *Miller* and *DeWitt* plans resulted from the same preclearance pressure exerted by the United States Department of Justice on state districting authorities to maximize the number of majority-minority voting districts created by the redistricting plans at issue.[287] Considered together, *Miller* and *DeWitt* may stand for the proposition that the Supreme Court will simply defer to trial court findings of fact concerning whether race was the "predominant factor" in fashioning a districting plan. In *Miller,* the district court had found that race was the "overriding, predominant force," and in *DeWitt* the district court had found that race had not predominated over traditional districting principles.[288] There is language in *Lawyer v. Department of Justice,*[289] *Miller,*[290] and *Abrams v. Johnson*[291] suggesting that such district court findings of fact should not be set aside unless they are clearly erroneous. However, this rule of deference to district court findings provides little guidance to the district courts themselves—or to litigants—concerning the meaning of the *Miller* "predominant factor" test. Note also that the Supreme Court has not always deferred to district court conclusions of law. In *Shaw v. Reno*[292] and *Shaw v. Hunt,*[293] the Court reversed legal determinations that had been made by the three-judge district court in order to invalidate majority-minority voting districts that the district court had upheld. More recently, the Court in *Hunt v. Cromartie* reversed a district court ruling invalidating a redistricting plan. The Supreme Court found that factual disputes precluded the entry of summary judgment, even though the district court had found that "the uncontroverted material facts" established that the challenged voting district had been racially gerrymandered.[294]

Justice O'Connor wrote a concurring opinion in *Miller* stressing that the threshold showing required to satisfy the "predominant factor" test ought to be a high one. She deemed this necessary to ensure that most existing congressional districts would remain constitutionally valid even though race had been taken into account in drawing the district lines that created those districts. Justice O'Connor has stated that strict scrutiny should be triggered in the voting rights context only in extreme cases.[295] The views of Justice O'Connor on this issue are important because she was the author of the *Shaw v. Reno* opinion that first created the racial gerrymandering cause of action,[296] and because her vote is necessary to maintain the five-justice, conservative-bloc majority that presently exists for the Supreme Court's racial gerrymandering cause of action.[297] However, despite her statement that strict scrutiny should be reserved for extreme districting cases,[298] Justice O'Connor has voted against the districting plans at issue in six of the seven constitutional districting cases to which the Court has given plenary consideration.[299] Moreover, the Court as a whole has ruled against the districting plans at issue in five of those seven cases.[300] This suggests that whatever the *Miller* "predominate factor" test for triggering strict scrutiny may mean as a nominal matter, as a realist matter it means that most affirmative action districting plans containing majority-minority districts are now likely to be subject to strict scrutiny if challenged on equal protection grounds.

Assuming that strict scrutiny is deemed to apply to a districting plan, it is still necessary to determine whether that plan can survive strict scrutiny. As a realist matter, the answer is probably that districting plans found to have been predominantly motivated by racial considerations will be held unconstitutional. Again, this is because no racial classification has withstood strict equal protection scrutiny since *Korematsu*.[301] But the *Adarand* insistence that strict scrutiny is no longer to be deemed fatal scrutiny may again be relevant as well.[302] One question that naturally arises is whether a state's desire to comply with the Voting Rights Act can constitute a compelling state interest for purposes of strict scrutiny. The five justices in the conservative voting bloc have recognized this to be an issue, but have repeatedly declined to resolve that issue—first in *Shaw v. Reno*,[303] then in *Miller*,[304] then in *Shaw v. Hunt*,[305] and then again in *Abrams*.[306] *Shaw v. Hunt*, however, suggests that these five justices may ultimately be reluctant to view compliance with the Voting Rights Act as a compelling state interest.

After the Supreme Court remand in *Shaw v. Reno*, the three-judge district court once again considered the constitutionality of the North Carolina redistricting plan at issue—this time under the name *Shaw v. Hunt*. The district court found that race had motivated the creation of the contested majority-minority district, but that the redistricting plan satisfied strict scrutiny because the plan was a narrowly tailored effort to comply with the § 5 preclearance and § 2 antidilution provisions of the Voting Rights Act.[307] Nevertheless, the five-justice, conservative-bloc majority rejected this conclusion and reversed, holding that the desire to comply with the Voting Rights Act did not satisfy strict scrutiny under the facts of *Shaw v. Hunt*.[308] The five conservative-bloc justices also rejected similar Voting Rights Act claims in *Abrams*,[309] *Bush*,[310] and *Miller*,[311] where the Supreme Court affirmed lower court decisions invalidating or rejecting majority-minority districts that had been adopted in an effort to comply with the Voting Rights Act. Note that even in *DeWitt*—a case in which the conservative bloc voted summarily to affirm a district court decision upholding a redistricting plan—the conservative bloc did not conclude that the plan satisfied strict scrutiny. Rather, it acquiesced in the district court decision that strict scrutiny was not triggered under the facts of *DeWitt*.[312] Similarly, in *Hunt v. Cromartie* and *Lawyer*—the two cases in which the Court upheld redistricting plans after the elimination of majority-minority districts—the Court never considered the plans to be predominately motivated by race, and therefore did not apply strict scrutiny.[313]

It may be that compliance with the § 5 preclearance and § 2 antidilution provision of the Voting Rights Act will ultimately be treated differently with respect to their compelling-state-interest status. Justice Kennedy's majority opinion in *Miller*—which was joined by all five conservative-bloc justices—went so far as to state that if the § 5 preclearance provision of the Voting Rights Act incorporated the attorney general's policy of maximizing the number of majority-minority voting districts, then the Voting Rights Act itself would pose constitutional difficulties under the equal protection clause.[314] *Miller*, therefore, suggests that the five conservative-bloc justices are unwilling to view compliance with the attorney general's interpretation of § 5 preclearance requirements as a compelling state interest.[315]

The constitutional status of the § 2 antidilution provision of the act is less clear. Chief Justice Rehnquist has not spoken directly to this issue, except to assume without deciding that compliance with § 2 could constitute a compelling state interest[316]—an assumption that he has made always in the process of voting against the majority-minority district at issue.[317] In *Bush*, Justices Thomas and Scalia seemed unwilling to tolerate any active consideration of race in the districting context, arguing that the intentional creation of a majority-minority district should always trigger strict scrutiny.[318] This suggests that Justices Scalia and Thomas—who have never voted to uphold an affirmative action plan as constitutional after strict scrutiny[319]—would not consider compliance with § 2 to constitute a compelling state interest. They might even vote to hold § 2 of the Voting Rights

Act unconstitutional if § 2 were read to require the creation of majority-minority districts.

The nominal positions of Justices O'Connor and Kennedy have been less extreme. In *Bush,* Justice O'Connor—the author of the majority opinions in both *Adarand*[320] and *Shaw v. Reno*[321]—stated that a state's desire to comply with the antidilution provisions of § 2 of the Voting Rights Act *can* constitute a compelling state interest for strict-scrutiny purposes,[322] as long as the consideration given to race does not become "predominant."[323] This seems consistent with Justice O'Connor's stated view in *Adarand* that strict scrutiny is not necessarily fatal.[324] However, it remains true that Justice O'Connor has never voted to uphold the constitutionality of an affirmative action plan of any sort after strict scrutiny.[325] It is also true that Justice O'Connor sometimes modifies her views over time about what it takes to satisfy strict scrutiny. In *Wygant v. Jackson Board of Education,*[326] Justice O'Connor rejected the need for formal findings to satisfy strict scrutiny, and viewed the state interest in racial diversity as potentially compelling.[327] Three years later, however, in *City of Richmond v. J.R. Croson,*[328] she appears to have adopted the view that *very* formal findings are required to survive strict scrutiny, and that affirmative action can be used only to provide a narrowly tailored remedy for past discrimination.[329] The following year, in *Metro Broadcasting v. FCC,*[330] Justice O'Connor wrote a dissenting opinion that distinguished even more forcefully between constitutionally permissible remedies for past discrimination and constitutionally impermissible efforts to promote diversity.[331]

Similarly, Justice Kennedy wrote a concurring opinion in *Bush* stating that strict scrutiny always applied to race-conscious districting, but strict scrutiny permitted a state to take race-conscious districting actions that were *required* to prevent vote dilution under § 2 of the Voting Rights Act— although he did not believe that strict scrutiny permitted a state to enhance minority voting strength in ways that were not required by the act.[332] Nevertheless, the overall thrust of Justice Kennedy's concurrence in *Bush* was to narrow rather than expand the range of cases in which race could be considered in making districting decisions.[333] And like Justice O'Connor, Justice Kennedy has never voted to uphold the constitutionality of an affirmative action plan of any sort after strict scrutiny.[334]

The four justices in the liberal bloc seem to believe that compliance with either § 2 or § 5 of the Voting Rights Act can constitute a compelling state interest. This is evidenced by the willingness of those justices to affirm the district court decision in *Shaw v. Hunt*, which upheld the North Carolina redistricting plan at issue after remand in *Shaw v. Reno*. In *Shaw v. Hunt*, Justices Stevens, Ginsburg, and Breyer did not believe that strict scrutiny was triggered by the North Carolina plan,[335] but if it were, they believed that the state's interest in complying with §§ 2 and 5 of the Voting Rights Act constituted a compelling state interest sufficient to satisfy strict scrutiny.[336] In *Bush*—decided the same day as *Shaw v. Hunt*—Justice Stevens wrote a dissenting opinion stating that compliance with the Voting Rights Act constituted a compelling state interest.[337] Justice Souter also wrote a dissenting opinion joined by Justices Ginsburg and Breyer, indicating that he too believed that compliance with the Voting Rights Act constituted a compelling state interest.[338]

In the final analysis, the current Supreme Court appears to have five justices—Justices Rehnquist, O'Connor, Scalia, Kennedy, and Thomas—who are unlikely to view compliance with the Voting Rights Act as a compelling state interest for purposes of strict scrutiny. Two of those justices—Justices O'Connor and Kennedy—recognize the possibility that compliance with § 2 of the Voting Rights Act could in theory constitute a compelling state interest, but they have never actually voted to uphold an affirmative action program on that ground. Four additional justices—Justices Stevens, Souter, Ginsburg, and Breyer—are likely to view a state's interest in complying with either § 2 or § 5 of the Voting Rights Act as constituting a compelling state interest. The uncertain views of Justices O'Connor and Kennedy are likely to be dispositive with respect to the ultimate constitutional status of § 2.

The Supreme Court's Census Act decision in 1999 was reminiscent of its Voting Rights Act cases. In *Department of Commerce* the five-justice conservative bloc issued another 5–4 ruling that nullified an effort by the Clinton Administration to increase minority voting strength—this time by using statistical sampling techniques to reduce the census undercount of minority voters.[339] In holding that the Census Act precluded the use of statistical sampling for purposes of congressional apportionment, the five conservative-bloc justices interpreted the Census Act as an impediment to increased minority political strength in much the same way that they had interpreted the Voting Rights Act. However, the Court may be growing tired of voting rights cases. In addition to *Department of Commerce*, seven of the eight constitutional affirmative action cases that the Court has decided since 1993 have been redistricting cases.[340] Moreover, some of the challenged redistricting plans have been before the Court two or even three times in the six-year period between 1993 and 1999.[341]

The Supreme Court's Voting Rights Act cases grew out of the 1990 Census, after the Court created a racial redistricting cause of action in *Shaw v. Reno*. It is now time to conduct the 2000 census, and a similar flood of litigation is likely to follow if the Court does not narrow or clarify the scope of its *Shaw v. Reno* cause of action. The Court's most recent voting rights decision—*Hunt v. Cromartie*—suggests that the Court may be considering a way to domesticate *Shaw v. Reno*. Although racial gerrymandering is unconstitutional, language in *Hunt v. Cromartie* suggests that it may be constitutionally permissible to use race as a proxy for party affiliation in the process of political gerrymandering. And political gerrymandering appears largely to be permissible under the Constitution.[342] If the Court were to follow that route, most of the racial gerrymandering that is now suspect under *Shaw v. Reno* could be restructured by state legislatures—or reinterpreted by courts—to constitute permissible political gerrymandering. Although such a strategy might allow the Supreme Court to withdraw gracefully from the racial redistricting business, it would do so at a doctrinal cost. The essence of the current Supreme Court's opposition to affirmative action seems to lie in the Court's aversion to the use of racial stereotypes as a proxy for other traits.[343] However, the use of race as a proxy for party affiliation would seem to fly directly in the face of the Supreme Court's stated justification for invalidating racial affirmative action.

3. Conclusion

The law of affirmative action now appears to be rather straightforward. Racial affirmative action now appears simply to be unconstitutional. The Supreme Court has never explicitly so held, but it has implicitly so insinuated. After fifteen years of inconclusive plurality decisions issued between 1974 and 1989—decisions that were often sympathetic to the concept of racial affirmative action—the Supreme Court has issued ten years of majority opinions since 1989 that have almost always disapproved of affirmative action. The present Court contains a stable five-justice majority that consistently votes against affirmative action, and an equally stable four-justice minority that consistently votes in favor of affirmative action. These judicial voting blocs seem to reflect a current division in popular support for affirmative action, and the Court's bare-majority opposition to affirmative action seems to reflect the view that majoritarian patience with affirmative action has now run its course. Although the Court has articulated affirmative action doctrine in a manner that leaves open the theoretical possibility that some racial affirmative action programs will still be able to withstand constitutional scrutiny, it is realistically unlikely that any meaningful affirmative action programs will be upheld by the Supreme Court in the absence of a political realignment produced by new Supreme Court appointments.

Doctrinally, the Supreme Court has now adopted a unitary standard of review for all racial affirmative action programs. In *Adarand*, the Court held 5–4 that all race-conscious affirmative action is subject to strict scrutiny under the equal protection clause of the Constitution,[344] expressly declining to distinguish between benign and invidious racial classifications.[345] This has allowed the Supreme Court to invalidate affirmative action programs on the grounds that they are unfair to the white majority, even when the white majority has made a political decision to impose affirmative action burdens on itself. Although the *Adarand* Court emphasized that strict scrutiny was not to be confused with fatal scrutiny,[346] the Supreme Court has not upheld a racial classification after strict scrutiny since its 1944 wartime decision in *Korematsu*,[347] and no justice in the *Adarand* majority has ever voted to uphold a racial classification after strict scrutiny.[348]

Because strict scrutiny applies to all racial affirmative action, the constitutionality of an affirmative action program can be upheld only if the program is shown to constitute a narrowly tailored means of advancing a compelling state interest.[349] *Croson* suggests that only the need to remedy very particularized acts of official discrimination can constitute a compelling state interest, and that neither the desire to remedy general societal discrimination nor the desire to promote racial diversity is a constitutionally legitimate objective.[350] In fact, the constitutional standard is so demanding that the well-known history of racial discrimination in Richmond, Virginia, was not sufficient to establish the showing of past discrimination demanded by *Croson*.[351] The narrow-tailoring requirement of strict scrutiny is also very stringent, insisting on a high correlation between identified acts of past discrimination and affirmative action remedies.[352] As a result, something as seemingly incontestable as a rebuttable presumption that racial minorities have been economically and socially disadvantaged in the United States was not sufficiently correlated with particularized acts of past discrimination to survive strict scrutiny in *Adarand*.[353] Although the Court has nominally rejected the argument that race-conscious remedies should be limited to the actual victims of discrimination,[354] the demands of the narrow-tailoring requirement have begun to approach the stringency of an actual-victim limitation.

Although the Supreme Court has insisted on the application of strict scrutiny to all racial classifications in the normal affirmative action context, it has chosen to permit substantial amounts of race-conscious decision making in the redistricting context. *Shaw v. Reno* created a cause of action permitting white voters to maintain challenges to the constitutionality of majority-minority voting districts even in the absence of any claim of vote dilution.[355] The theory behind this cause of action is that it is simply wrong to assign someone to a voting district based upon that person's race.[356] However, because the consideration of race in the districting process has always been commonplace, the Supreme Court was forced in *Miller v. Johnson* to limit the reach of its new racial gerrymandering cause of action to extreme cases in which race has become the "predominant factor" motivating a districting decision.[357] Where race is not the "predominant factor," but is simply considered along with other districting factors, the districting decision is deemed not to rest on the use of a racial classification, and is therefore not subject to strict scrutiny.[358] Thus far, the Supreme Court has used the new racial gerrymandering cause of action only to invalidate majority-minority voting districts, and never to invalidate a majority-white voting district. And the Court has used the new racial gerrymandering cause of action to invalidate majority-minority districts even when the United States attorney general has determined that the creation of those districts was necessary to comply with the Voting Rights Act.[359] Ironically, the burden imposed on the federal judiciary by redistricting cases may ultimately cause the Court to begin upholding challenged districts on the grounds that race is permissibly being used as a proxy for party affiliation,[360] even though such use of race as a proxy seems inconsistent with the Court's stated basis for opposing affirmative action.[361]

The doctrinal rules governing affirmative action appear to have grown out of political considerations. Most of the constitutional affirmative action cases resolved by the present Supreme Court have been resolved by 5–4 decisions.[362] A five-justice conservative voting bloc—consisting of Justices Rehnquist, O'Connor, Scalia, Kennedy, and Thomas—consistently votes against affirmative action programs, and a four-justice liberal voting bloc—consisting of Justices Stevens, Souter, Ginsburg, and Breyer—consistently votes in favor of affirmative action.[363] The stability of these voting blocs, and their high correlation with the general political views of the justices who comprise them, suggest that the Supreme Court's law of affirmative action is heavily influenced by the politics of affirmative action. Although the law of affirmative action seems stable today, it could all change dramatically tomorrow with even a single new Supreme Court appointment.

We live in a political culture where the Supreme Court is now routinely asked to join in the formulation of social policy. As a result, the Supreme Court often ends up substituting its views of affirmative action for the views of the political branches. This happens each time the Supreme Court invalidates an affirmative action program that one of the political branches has chosen to adopt. The countermajoritarian dangers of such a situation are obvious. The Supreme Court is not elected; it is not representative; and it is not politically accountable in any traditional sense. If the Supreme Court is truly "reading the Constitution," rather than asserting judicial policy preferences when it rules on the constitutionality of affirmative action, the countermajoritarian dangers seem minimal. But these days, no one really believes that the Court is simply "reading the Constitution." The policy-making discretion of the Court is both too vast and too obvious to permit any indulgence in that view. Why then do we tolerate Supreme Court participation in our affirmative action policy-making endeavors?

If we thought that the Supreme Court had some relative institutional advantage over the political branches of government in the formulation of affirmative action policy, such Supreme Court involvement might make sense. But after voyeuristically viewing the details of the Supreme Court's involvement with affirmative action over a twenty-five-year period—after "experiencing" the Court's decision-making processes through a "thick description" of the Court's judicial behavior—no relative institutional advantage is apparent. At best, the Supreme Court decision-making process seems to replicate political decision-making. On both sides of the issue political alliances are struck; voting blocs are formed; arguments are made for their strategic value; principles are invoked for their rhetorical resonance rather than their substantive content; and no one seems particularly troubled by disingenuousness or inconsistency. It is difficult to see why anyone would think that our social policy-making processes are improved by the involvement of an institution that behaves in the way that the Supreme Court has behaved with respect to the issue of affirmative action. It is difficult to see why the Court does not simply step aside and defer to political resolutions of the affirmative action debate. However, the Court has shown little inclination to step aside. And we have shown little inclination to ask it to do so. To me, this is all quite puzzling.

There may be invidious reasons for the Supreme Court's tenacious involvement in the affirmative action debate. But that is another story.

Notes

1. Numerous commentators have written about race relations in the United States. To facilitate the process of locating full citations, while complying with the conventions of legal citation, secondary sources to which this book makes multiple references have been collected in this footnote. In addition, all sources cited in this book are listed in the bibliography. The secondary sources to which the book makes multiple references are *Affirmative Action Settlement; Excerpts From Statement By School Board Lawyer On Lawsuit's Settlement*, N.Y. TIMES, Nov. 22, 1997, at B4; Barry Bearak, *Affirmative Action Settlement: The Reaction; Settlement Ends High Court Case On Preferences: Rights Groups Ducked A Fight, Opponents Say*, N.Y. TIMES, Nov. 22, 1997, at A1; ALEXANDER BICKEL, THE MORALITY OF CONSENT (1975); Joan Biskupic, *Rights Groups Pay To Settle Bias Case; High Court Affirmative Action Ruling Avoided*, WASH. POST, Nov. 22, 1997, at A1; JOHN HART ELY, DEMOCRACY AND DISTRUST: A THEORY OF JUDICIAL REVIEW (1980); *Employment Discrimination—Race: Clinton Administration Switches Stance On Use Of Race As Factor In Teacher's Layoff*, 66 U.S.L.W. 2134 (Sept. 9, 1977); RICHARD H. FALLON ET AL., HART AND WECHSLER'S THE FEDERAL COURTS AND THE FEDERAL SYSTEM (4th ed. 1996); Howard Fineman, *Race And Rage: Affirmative Action: Republicans Hope It Will Drive A Wedge Between Liberal Democrats And White Swing Voters*, NEWSWEEK, Apr. 3, 1995, at 23; ERIC FONER, RECONSTRUCTION: AMERICA'S UN-FINISHED REVOLUTION (1988); CLIFFORD GEERTZ, *The Thick Description: Toward An Interpretive Theory Of Culture, in* THE INTERPRETATION OF CULTURES: SELECTED ESSAYS 3 (1973); Abby Goodnough, *Affirmative Action Settlement: The Decision; Prospect Of A Costly Loss Led Board To Drop Case*, N.Y. TIMES, Nov. 22, 1997, at B4; Linda Greenhouse, *Affirmative Action Settlement: The Overview; Settlement Ends High Court Case On Preferences: Tactical Retreat*, N.Y. TIMES, Nov. 22, 1997, at A1 [hereinafter cited as "*Affirmative Action Settlement; The Overview*"]; Linda Green-house, *By 5–4, Justices Cast Doubts On U.S. Programs That Give Preferences Based Upon Race: Debate Is Fueled: Rigorous Criteria Set For Court's Approval Of Such Pro-grams*, N.Y. TIMES, June 13, 1995, at A1 [hereinafter cited as "*Justices Cast Doubts*"]; GERALD GUNTHER & KATHLEEN M. SULLIVAN, CONSTITUTIONAL LAW (13th ed. 1997); John F. Harris, *For Clinton, A Challenge Of Balance*, WASH. POST, June 14,

1995, at A1; A. Leon Higginbotham, In the Matter of Color: Race and the American Legal Process (1978); Steven A. Holmes, *A Dilemma Led To A Deal Over Hiring Tied To Race*, N.Y. Times, Nov. 23, 1997, § 1, at 37; Charles R. Lawrence, *The Id, The Ego, And Equal Protection: Reckoning With Unconscious Racism*, 39 Stan. L. Rev. 317 (1987); Nicholas Lemann, *Taking Affirmative Action Apart*, N.Y. Times, June 11, 1995, § 6 (Magazine), at 36; Richard H. Pildes and Richard G. Niemi, *Expressive Harms, "Bizarre Districts," And Voting Rights: Evaluating Election-District Appearances After* Shaw v. Reno, 92 Mich. L. Rev. 483 (1993); Eric Schnapper, *Affirmative Action And The Legislative History Of The Fourteenth Amendment*, 71 Va. L. Rev. 753 (1985); Girardeau A. Spann, *Color-Coded Standing*, 80 Cornell L. Rev. 1422 (1995) [hereinafter cited as "*Color-Coded Standing*"]; Girardeau A. Spann, *Proposition 209*, 47 Duke L.J. 187 (1997) [hereinafter cited as "*Proposition 209*"]; Girardeau A. Spann, Race Against the Court: The Supreme Court And Minorities In Contemporary America (1993) [hereinafter cited as "Race Against the Court"]; Robert L. Stern et al., Supreme Court Practice (7th ed. 1993); Geoffrey R. Stone et al., Constitutional Law (3d ed. 1996); *The Supreme Court, 1977 Term*, 92 Harv. L. Rev. 57 (1978); *The Supreme Court, 1979 Term*, 94 Harv. L. Rev. 75 (1980); Abigail Thernstrom, *A Class Backwards Idea: Why Affirmative Action For The Needy Won't Work*, Wash. Post, June 11, 1995, at C1; Laurence H. Tribe, American Constitutional Law (2d ed. 1988); Eugene Volokh, *The California Civil Rights Initiative: An Interpretive Guide*, 44 UCLA L. Rev. 1335 (1997).

2. Dred Scott v. Sandford, 60 U.S. (19 How.) 393 (1857).

3. Plessy v. Ferguson, 163 U.S. 537 (1896).

4. Brown v. Board of Educ., 347 U.S. 483 (1954) (*Brown I*) (invalidating separate-but-equal public schools), 349 U.S. 294 (1955) (*Brown II*) (ordering dismantling of segregated school systems "with all deliberate speed").

5. DeFunis v. Odegaard, 416 U.S. 312 (1974).

6. *See* Geertz, *supra* chapter 1, note 1, at 10–13, 29–30 (discussing elusiveness of objectivity in anthropology, but resisting submission to total subjectivity).

7. *See id.* at 5–10 (building upon Gilbert Ryle's concept of "thick description").

8. *See* Geertz, *supra* chapter 1, note 1, at 24–28 (discussing theory). For an application of the thick-description technique in a legal context see Lawrence Rosen, The Anthropology Of Justice: Law As Culture In Islamic Society (1989).

9. *See, e.g.,* Spann, Race Against the Court, *supra* chapter 1, note 1(suggesting that the Supreme Court acts not as a countermajoritarian institution but as a veiled majoritarian institution that functions to perpetuate the subordination of racial minorities).

10. *See* Schnapper, *supra* chapter 1, note 1, at 754–83 (discussing legislative history of race-conscious Reconstruction enactments designed to benefit blacks); *see also* Regents of the Univ. of Cal. v. Bakke, 438 U.S. 265, 397–98 (1978) (opinion

of Marshall, J.) (discussing Reconstruction programs intended to benefit blacks); *see generally* FONER, *supra* chapter 1, note 1.

11. *See, e.g.,* Schnapper, *supra* chapter 1, note 1, at 754–83 (discussing race-conscious programs designed to benefit blacks); *see generally* FONER, *supra* chapter 1, note 1(same).

12. Brown v. Board of Educ., 347 U.S. 483 (1954) (*Brown I*) (invalidating separate-but-equal public schools), 349 U.S. 294 (1955) (*Brown II*) (ordering dismantling of segregated school systems "with all deliberate speed").

13. *See Brown I,* 347 U.S. 483 (1954) (invalidating separate-but-equal public schools).

14. *See* Exec. Order No. 10,925, 3 C.F.R. 448, 449–50 (1959–1963) (emphasis added), *reprinted in* 1961 U.S.C.C.A.N. 1274, 1276 (1961), *quoted in* Volokh, *supra* chapter 1, note 1, at 1347 n.33; *see also* Middleton v. City of Flint, 92 F.3d 396, 404 n.6 (6th Cir. 1996) (discussing evolution in use of term "affirmative action"); Lemann, *supra* chapter 1, note 1, at 40, 42 (discussing origin of "affirmative action" concept).

15. *See* Lemann, *supra* chapter 1, note 1, at 39–40, 42 (discussing growth of controversy over affirmative action).

16. *See, e.g.,* Fineman, *supra* chapter 1, note 1, at 25 (reporting that Jesse Jackson has protested threatened retreat from national commitment to affirmative action); Harris, *supra* chapter 1, note 1, at A6 (reporting that Jesse Jackson threatens rebellion if Clinton withdraws support of affirmative action).

17. See B. Drummond Ayres, Jr., *University Regents in California Battle Over Affirmative Action,* N.Y. TIMES, July 21, 1995, at A1; William Booth, *U. of Calif. Ends Racial Preferences: Pioneer in Diversity Adopts Stance Urged by Gov. Pete Wilson,* WASH. POST, July 21, 1995, at A1.

18. California Proposition 209, the "California Civil Rights Initiative," which was adopted in the November 5, 1996, general election, amends the California Constitution to prohibit the use of affirmative action preferences that entail any consideration of race, gender, ethnicity, or national origin in state hiring, contracting, or education. Proposition 209 is discussed in chapter 3, part 5, section iv. *See also* Fineman, *supra* chapter 1, note 1, at 24; Greenhouse, *Justices Cast Doubts, supra* chapter 1, note 1, at D25; Harris, *supra* chapter 1, note 1, at A1; Lemann, *supra* chapter 1, note 1, at 39; Spann, *Proposition 209, supra* chapter 1, note 1; Thernstrom, *supra* Chapter 1, note 1, at C1.

Washington Initiative 200, which was adopted by the voters of Washington State as a state law on November 3, 1998, similarly bans "preferential treatment" for women and minorities in the award of public contracts, jobs, and university admissions. *See* Ethan Bronner, *U. of Washington Will End Race-Conscious Admissions,* N.Y. TIMES, Nov. 7, 1998, at A12; Tom Brune, *Now that I-200 Is Law, What's Next?—UW Alters Admission Policy,* SEATTLE TIMES, Nov. 5, 1998, at A1; Heath

Foster, *Affirmative Action Rules Tossed Out By State Voters*, SEATTLE POST-INTELLI-GENCER, Nov. 4, 1998, at A1; Rene Sanchez, *Washington's New Affirmative Action Question: How to End It*, WASH. POST, Nov. 13, 1998, at A2; Mike Tharp, *Copying California: A New Battleground for Affirmative Action in the Pacific Northwest*, U.S. NEWS & WORLD REPORT, Nov. 9, 1998, at 34; *Vagueness of I-200 Could Limit Damage (Editorial)*, SEATTLE TIMES, Nov. 5, 1998, at B8.

19. *See* Kevin Merida, *Senate Rejects Gramm Bid to Bar Affirmative Action Set-Asides*, WASH. POST, July 21, 1995, at A13 (describing legislative efforts by Phil Gramm and Bob Dole to reduce affirmative action); Lemann, *supra* chapter 1, note 1, at 62 (discussing repeal of FCC minority "distress sale" tax certificate program); Thernstrom, *supra* chapter 1, note 1, at C1 (describing bill introduced by Rep. Canady to end preferences in federal programs).

20. Republican presidential candidates for 1996, including Pat Buchanan, Pete Wilson, Phil Gramm, and Bob Dole, made opposition to affirmative action essential components of their campaign strategies. *See* Fineman, *supra* chapter 1, note 1, at 24–25; Greenhouse, *Justices Cast Doubts*, *supra* chapter 1, note 1, at D25; Harris, *supra* chapter 1, note 1, at A6; Lemann, *supra* chapter 1, note 1, at 39, 54; Thernstrom, *supra* chapter 1, note 1, at C1. As governor of California in 1991, Pete Wilson vetoed legislation that encouraged the University of California to strive for ethnic diversity in admissions, and in 1995, as part of his presidential campaign, he issued an executive order abolishing some of California's existing affirmative action programs. *See* Lemann, *supra* chapter 1, note 1, at 39.

21. President Clinton's response to anti-affirmative-action sentiment by Republicans and right-wing Democrats was to order an "urgent, intensive" review of the federal government's affirmative action programs. *See* Fineman, *supra* chapter 1, note 1, at 25; Lemann, *supra* chapter 1, note 1, at 39; Thernstrom, *supra* chapter 1, note 1, at C1.

22. *See* John F. Harris, *Clinton Avows Support For Affirmative Action: 'Mend It, but Don't End It,' President Says in Speech*, WASH. POST, July 20, 1995, at A10; Todd S. Purdum, *President Shows Fervent Support For Goals of Affirmative Action*, N.Y. TIMES, July 20, 1995, at A1.

23. *See, e.g.*, Michael Kinsley, *The Spoils Of Victimhood: The Case Against The Case Against Affirmative Action*, NEW YORKER, Mar. 27, 1995, at 62 (favoring continued racial affirmative action).

24. *See* DeNeen L. Brown, *Gray in the Debate on Color: Many See Both Sides of Affirmative Action*, WASH. POST, June 5, 1995, at A1 (surveying attitudes on affirmative action); Greenhouse, *Justices Cast Doubts*, *supra* chapter 1, note 1, at D25 (reporting that affirmative action is the subject of vigorous debate in Congress and states); Harris, *supra* chapter 1, note 1, at A7 (describing popular ambivalence about affirmative action); Louis Harris, *Affirmative Action and the Voter*, N.Y. TIMES, July 31, 1995, at A13 (stating that Republicans are exploiting confusion among voters

between affirmative action, which voters favor, and preferences, which voters do not favor); Lemann, *supra* chapter 1, note 1, at 39–43, 52–54 (same).

25. *See* Loving v. Virginia, 388 U.S. 1 (1967) (invalidating state statute prohibiting racial intermarriage).

26. *See* Brown v. Board of Educ., 347 U.S. 483 (1954) (*Brown I*) (invalidating separate-but-equal public schools); 349 U.S. 294 (1955) (*Brown II*) (ordering dismantling of segregated school systems "with all deliberate speed").

27. *See* Plessy v. Ferguson, 163 U.S. 537 (1896) (upholding racially segregated public facilities under separate-but-equal doctrine).

28. *See* Dred Scott v. Sandford, 60 U.S. (19 How.) 393 (1857) (holding blacks not citizens within meaning of Constitution and invalidating congressional restrictions on slavery contained in Missouri Compromise).

29. The equal protection clause of the Constitution provides that "[n]o State shall . . . deny to any person within its jurisdiction the equal protection of the laws." U.S. CONST. amend XIV, § 1.

30. The federal statute that speaks most directly to the issue of affirmative action is Title VII of the Civil Rights Act of 1964, which prohibits, *inter alia,* discrimination in employment on the basis of race. *See* Pub. L. No. 88–352, 78 Stat. 241, 243 (1964) (codified as amended at 42 U.S.C. §§ 2000e to 2000e-17 (1994)).

31. The Voting Rights Act of 1965, as amended in 1982, is designed to prevent and remedy racial discrimination in voting. *See* Pub. L. No. 89-110, 79 Stat. 445 (codified as amended at 42 U.S.C. § 1973c (1994)).

32. *See* U.S. CONST. amend. XIII (abolishing slavery).

33. *See* U.S. CONST. amend. XIV (granting blacks citizenship with due process and equal protection rights).

34. *See* U.S. CONST. amend. XV (granting blacks right to vote).

35. *See, e.g.,* Owen Fiss, *Groups and the Equal Protection Clause,* 5 J. PHIL. & PUB. AFF. 107, 147–70 (1976) (arguing that equal protection clause should prevent groups from occupying position of subordination for extended period of time); *see also* Ruth Colker, *Anti-Subordination Above All: Sex, Race and Equal Protection,* 61 N.Y.U. L. REV. 1003, 1005–16 (1986) (arguing that equal protection clause should prevent groups from occupying subordinate status because of lack of power in society as whole); *cf.* Kathleen M. Sullivan, *Comment: Sins of Discrimination: Last Term's Affirmative Action Cases,* 100 HARV. L. REV. 78, 91–98 (1986) (arguing that affirmative action is better justified as prospective effort at corrective justice than as a retrospective effort at retributive justice directed against those who are guilty of past discrimination).

36. *See, e.g.,* Wygant v. Jackson Bd. of Educ., 476 U.S. 267, 273 (1986) (opinion of Powell, J.) ("This Court has 'consistently repudiated "[d]istinctions between citizens solely because of their ancestry" as being "odious to a free people whose institutions are founded upon the doctrine of equality"'" (citing Loving v. Virginia,

388 U.S. 1, 11 (1967), quoting Hirabayashi v. United States, 320 U.S. 81, 100 (1943)); Regents of the Univ. of Cal. v. Bakke, 438 U.S. 265, 355 (1978) (Brennan, J., concurring in judgment in part and dissenting in part) (race is irrelevant classification).

37. *See, e.g.,* Adarand Constructors v. Pena, 515 U.S. 200, 271–76 (1995) (Ginsburg, J., dissenting) (discussing lingering effects of past discrimination); *cf. id.* at 236 (majority opinion of O'Connor, J.) (same).

38. *See, e.g., Bakke,* 438 U.S. at 291 (opinion of Powell, J.) (discussing slavery origins of Fourteenth Amendment); *id.* at 326 (Brennan, J., concurring in judgment in part and dissenting in part) (same); *id.* at 387–90 (opinion of Marshall, J.) (same); *see generally* HIGGINBOTHAM, *supra* chapter 1, note 1(discussing laws regulating slavery).

39. *See, e.g., Adarand,* 515 U.S. at 272 (Ginsburg, J., dissenting) (discussing *Plessy* endorsement of official segregation); *Bakke,* 438 U.S. at 390–94 (opinion of Marshall, J.) (same).

40. *See* United States v. Carolene Prods., 304 U.S. 144, 153 n.4 (1938) (positing Supreme Court duty to protect "discrete and insular" minorities); *see generally* ELY, *supra* chapter 1, note 1, at 155–60 (discussing representation-reinforcement theory of judicial review as means of protecting racial minorities).

41. Dred Scott v. Sandford, 60 U.S. (19 How.) 393 (1857).

42. The Slaughter-House Cases, 83 U.S. (16 Wall.) 36 (1873). *The Slaughter-House Cases* entailed a narrow construction of the Thirteenth and Fourteenth Amendments that was based on federalism concerns. *See generally* STONE ET AL., *supra* chapter 1, note 1, at 508–09 (discussing *Slaughter-House Cases*).

43. Subsequent Supreme Court decisions adopted limiting interpretations of Reconstruction statutes and amendments that were more racially motivated. *See, e.g.,* United States v. Harris, 106 U.S. 629 (1882) (Ku Klux Klan Act of 1871 did not permit prosecution of white lynch mob because Fourteenth Amendment did not reach private conduct); United States v. Cruikshank, 92 U.S. 542 (1875) (criminal conspiracy provisions of Enforcement Act of 1870 did not permit prosecution for lynching blacks who were not engaged in act of petitioning federal government as required by Fourteenth Amendment); United States v. Reese, 92 U.S. 214 (1875) (criminal prosecution under Enforcement Act of 1870 against election officials for refusing to permit blacks to vote could not be maintained because act was not expressly limited to racially motivated election interference as required under Fifteenth Amendment). *See generally* STONE ET AL., *supra* chapter 1, note 1, at 508–12 (discussing limiting effect of Supreme Court Reconstruction decisions on Reconstruction statutes and amendments).

44. The Civil Rights Cases, 109 U.S. 3 (1883) (invalidating Civil Rights Act of 1866 on federalism grounds); *see generally* STONE ET AL., *supra* chapter 1, note 1, at 510–12 (discussing *Civil Rights Cases*).

45. Plessy v. Ferguson, 163 U.S. 537 (1896).

46. In fact, contrary to popular understanding, *Plessy* did not actually impose a requirement that separate facilities be equal. *See* STONE ET AL., *supra* chapter 1, note 1, at 516 (arguing that separate schools did not have to be equal).

47. Korematsu v. United States, 323 U.S. 214 (1944).

48. *See Brown I*, 347 U.S. 483 (1954) (invalidating separate-but-equal public schools).

49. *See Brown II*, 349 U.S. 294 (1955) (ordering dismantling of segregated school systems "with all deliberate speed").

50. *See* Milliken v. Bradley, 418 U.S. 717 (1974) (refusing to order interdistrict school desegregation remedies that included white suburban students necessary for meaningful desegregation of inner-city schools); San Antonio Independent School District v. Rodriguez, 411 U.S. 1 (1973) (upholding constitutionality of property tax-based public school financing despite drastic discrepancies in funds allocated to white and minority schools). *See generally* SPANN, RACE AGAINST THE COURT, *supra* chapter 1, note 1, at 73–82 (discussing Supreme Court failure to desegregate northern schools); *id.* at 109, 116 (discussing Supreme Court tolerance of racially disproportionate school funding and consequent inferiority of minority schools).

51. Professor Lawrence has emphasized the unconscious nature of much contemporary racial discrimination. *See* Lawrence, *supra* chapter 1, note 1, at 317–44.

52. *See* SPANN, RACE AGAINST THE COURT, *supra* chapter 1, note 1, at 120–22 (discussing underrepresentation of racial minorities in allocation of societal resources); *cf.* Spann, *Proposition 209*, *supra* chapter 1, note 1, at 238–41 (citing commentators documenting continuing discrimination against minorities).

53. *See* SPANN, RACE AGAINST THE COURT, *supra* chapter 1, note 1, at 120–22 (discussing lower levels of health and safety to which racial minorities are vulnerable).

54. *See, e.g.,* Fullilove v. Klutznick, 448 U.S. 448, 473–74 (1980) (opinion of Burger, C.J.) (Constitution permits remedies to prevent perpetuation of past discrimination); *Bakke*, 438 U.S. at 326–27, 336, 355–73 (Brennan, J., concurring in judgment in part and dissenting in part) (race neutrality is aspirational rather than literal goal; race-conscious remedies for past discrimination are constitutional); *id.* at 395–402 (opinion of Marshall, J.) (same).

55. *See, e.g., Adarand*, 515 U.S. at 262 (Stevens, J., dissenting) (affirmative action will permit minorities to "graduate" into status where they can compete on equal terms); *Fullilove*, 448 U.S. at 485–89 (opinion of Burger, C.J.) (Constitution permits affirmative action no broader than necessary to achieve legitimate remedial goals); *id.* at 507–08 (Powell, J., concurring) (Constitution does not permit Congress to enact bare racial preference); *Bakke*, 438 U.S. at 400–02 (opinion of Marshall, J.) (affirmative action needed for minorities to achieve equality).

56. *See, e.g., Adarand*, 515 U.S. at 214 (majority opinion of O'Connor, J.) ("The Court observed—correctly—that 'distinctions between citizens solely because of their ancestry are by their very nature odious to a free people whose

institutions are founded upon the doctrine of equality,' and that 'racial discriminations are in most circumstances irrelevant and therefore prohibited.'"); *id.* at 239 (Scalia, J., concurring in part and concurring in judgment) (government cannot have compelling interest in racial classifications, even to compensate for past discrimination); *id.* at 240–41 (Thomas, J., concurring in part and concurring in judgment) (racial distinctions are immoral and unconstitutional); City of Richmond v. J.A. Croson Co., 488 U.S. 469, 518 (1989) (Kennedy, J., concurring in part and concurring in judgment) ("The moral imperative of racial neutrality is the driving force of the Equal Protection Clause"); *id.* at 521 (Scalia, J., concurring in judgment) ("'discrimination on the basis of race is illegal, immoral, unconstitutional, inherently wrong, and destructive of democratic society,'" quoting BICKEL, *supra* chapter 1, note 1, at 133).

57. *See supra*, text accompanying and following chapter 1, note 37 (discussing history of racial discrimination).

58. *See id.*(discussing Supreme Court involvement in history of racial discrimination).

59. *See Adarand*, 515 U.S. at 236 (vigilant strict scrutiny necessary to prevent recurrence of racial discrimination such as that wrongly tolerated in *Korematsu*).

60. *See, e.g., id.* at 224, 225–27 (right to be free from racial discrimination is individual rather than group right) (citing *Bakke*, 438 U.S. at 299 (opinion of Powell, J., citing Shelley v. Kraemer, 334 U.S. 1, 22 (1948)); *Metro Broadcasting v. FCC*, 497 U.S. 547, 602, 609–10 (1990) (O'Connor, J., dissenting) (same); *Croson*, 488 U.S. at 493–94 (opinion of O'Connor, J.) (same).

61. *See, e.g., Croson*, 488 U.S. at 518–19 (Kennedy, J., concurring in judgment) (rule limiting racial preferences to what is necessary to compensate actual victims of discrimination is appealing); *id.* at 524–25 (Scalia, J., concurring in judgment) (state can use racial classifications only to compensate actual victims of state's own discrimination); *cf.* Local 93, Int'l Ass'n of Firefighters v. Cleveland, 478 U.S. 501, 535–45 (1986) (Rehnquist, J., dissenting) (Title VII remedies that override seniority must be limited to actual victims of discrimination); Local 28, Sheet Metal Workers Int'l Ass'n v. EEOC, 478 U.S. 421, 500 (1986) (Rehnquist, J., dissenting) (same); Firefighters Local Union No. 1784 v. Stotts, 467 U.S. 561, 578–83 (1984) (same).

62. *See, e.g., Adarand*, 515 U.S. at 229 (overly broad race-based remedies will foster resentment and delay time when race will become truly irrelevant factor); *id.* at 239 (Scalia, J., concurring in part and concurring in judgment) (race-based remedies designed to "make up" for past discrimination reinforce racial discrimination); *id.* at 240–41 (Thomas, J., concurring in part and concurring in judgment) (racial discrimination is immoral and unconstitutional whether invidious or benign); *Croson*, 488 U.S. at 524–28 (racial remedies going beyond what is necessary to benefit actual victims of discrimination reinforce and perpetuate discrimination).

63. *See, e.g., Bakke*, 438 U.S. at 298–99 (opinion of Powell, J.) (affirmative ac-

tion can harm intended beneficiaries through stigmatization); *cf. id.* 438 U.S. at 358–62 (opinion of Brennan, J.) (same); United Jewish Orgs. v. Carey, 430 U.S. 144, 172–74 (1977) (Brennan, J., concurring in part) (same); DeFunis v. Odegaard, 416 U.S. 312, 340–41 (1974) (Douglas, J., dissenting) (same).

64. *See Brown I*, 347 U.S. at 483 (overruling separate-but-equal doctrine of *Plessy*).

65. *See, e.g., Metro Broadcasting,* 497 U.S. at 612–17, 621–23, 630–31 (O'Connor, J., dissenting) (objecting to over- and underinclusiveness of remedies that do not narrowly compensate for past discrimination as impermissibly burdening innocent whites); *Wygant v. Jackson Bd. of Educ.,* 476 U.S. 267, 279–84 1986 (opinion of Powell, J.) (opposing layoffs as impermissible burden on innocent whites); *id.* at 294–95 (White, J., concurring in judgment) (opposing layoffs of innocent whites to benefit minorities who were not actual victims of discrimination); *Bakke*, 438 U.S. at 294–99 (opinion of Powell, J.) (opposing racial preferences that impermissibly burden innocent whites); *cf. Firefighters v. Cleveland,* 478 U.S. at 535–45 (Rehnquist, J., dissenting) (Title VII remedies that override seniority must be limited to actual victims of discrimination); *Sheet Metal Workers,* 478 U.S. at 500 (Rehnquist, J., dissenting) (same); *Stotts*, 467 U.S. at 578–83 (same).

66. *See, e.g., Metro Broadcasting,* 497 U.S. at 603–04 (O'Connor, J., dissenting) (danger of racial classifications is that they contribute to racial hostility and reinforce stereotypes in way that stigmatizes beneficiaries); *Croson*, 488 U.S. at 493–94 (opinion of O'Connor, J.) (same); *Bakke*, 438 U.S. at 298–99 (opinion of Powell, J.) (same); *cf. Wygant*, 476 U.S. at 313–19 (Stevens, J., dissenting) (recognizing but rejecting stigmatization and hostility arguments); *cf. United Jewish Orgs.* 430 U.S. at 172–74 (Brennan, J., concurring in part) (same).

67. *See, e.g., Adarand* 515 U.S. at 229 (overly broad race-based remedies will foster resentment and delay time when race will become truly irrelevant factor); *id.* at 239 (Scalia, J., concurring in part and concurring in judgment) (race-based remedies designed to "make up" for past discrimination reinforce racial discrimination); *Croson*, 488 U.S. at 524–28 (racial remedies going beyond what is necessary to benefit actual victims of discrimination reinforce and perpetuate discrimination).

68. *See, e.g., Croson*, 488 U.S. at 507–08 (opinion of O'Connor, J.) (quotas reflect stereotyped thinking about racial minorities); *id.* at 526–27 (Scalia, J., concurring in judgment) (quotas derogate human dignity and individuality (citing BICKEL, *supra* chapter 1, note 1, at 133)); *Bakke*, 438 U.S. at 272–75, 315–19 (opinion of Powell, J.) (permitting consideration of race but opposing quotas).

69. *See* ALDOUS HUXLEY, BRAVE NEW WORLD (1932).

70. *Cf. Adarand*, 515 U.S. at 205–10 (describing affirmative action program encouraging award of construction contracts to minority subcontractors rather than to low bidders able to perform them most cheaply); *Croson*, 488 U.S. at 477–86 (describing minority set-aside program requiring award of construction contracts to minority subcontractors rather than to low bidders able to perform them most

cheaply); *Wygant,* 476 U.S. at 270–73 (opinion of Powell, J.) (describing affirmative action program requiring layoffs of more-experienced teachers in order to retain less-experienced minority teachers).

71. *Cf. Bakke,* 438 U.S. at 272–81 (opinion of Powell, J.) (describing affirmative action program reserving medical school seats for disadvantaged minority applicants rather than making them available for better-qualified white applicants).

72. *Cf.* Miller v. Johnson, 515 U.S. 900, 905–10 (1995) (describing voter districting scheme intended to elect minority candidates rather than best candidates); Shaw v. Reno, 509 U.S. 630, 634–39 (1993) (same).

73. This is the view that animated California's Proposition 209 anti-affirmative-action initiative. *See* Lemann, *supra* chapter 1, note 1, at 40; Spann, *Proposition 209,* *supra* chapter 1, note 1, at 201–07 (discussing California anti-affirmative-action initiative).

74. *See supra,* text accompanying chapter 1, notes 15–31 (discussing affirmative action controversy).

NOTES TO CHAPTER 2

1. The statutory and constitutional standards adopted by the Supreme Court to govern invidious discrimination do not always coincide. Title VI of the Civil Rights Act of 1964, Pub. L. 88–352, 78 Stat. 241, 252 (codified as amended at 42 U.S.C. §§ 2000d, *et seq.* (1994)), which generally prohibits discrimination in federally funded programs, seems to mirror the antidiscrimination provisions of the equal protection clause. *See* Guardians Ass'n v. Civil Serv. Comm'n of the City of N.Y., 463 U.S. 582, 610–11 (1983) (Powell, J., concurring in judgment) (arguing that Title VI antidiscrimination provision is coextensive with antidiscrimination provision of equal protection clause); *id.* at 612–13 (O'Connor, J., concurring in judgment) (same); *id.* at 639–42 (Stevens, J., dissenting) (same); *Bakke,* 438 U.S. 265, 287 (1978) (opinion of Powell, J.) (same); *id.* at 324–26, 352 (opinion of Brennan, J., concurring in judgment in part and dissenting in part, joined by White, Marshall, & Blackmun, JJ.) (same); *see also* Podberesky v. Kirwan, 764 F. Supp. 364, 371–77 (D. Md. 1991) (same). However, Title VII of the Civil Rights Act of 1964, Pub. L. No. 88-352, 78 Stat. 241, 253 (codified as amended at 42 U.S.C. §§ 2000e to 2000e-17 (1994)), which generally prohibits discrimination in employment, is typically viewed as containing a prohibition on discriminatory effects that is broader than the equal protection prohibition on discriminatory intent. *Compare* Griggs v. Duke Power, 401 U.S. 424, 429–30 (1971) (adopting effects standard for Title VII), *with* Washington v. Davis, 426 U.S. 229, 238–48 (1976) (adopting intent standard for equal protection clause). The manner in which those differences should affect the validity of affirmative action programs, as opposed to acts of invidious discrimination, is unclear. *See, e.g.,* United Steelworkers of Am. v. Weber, 443 U.S. 193, 206 n.6 (1979) (Title VII permits more affirmative action than does the equal

protection clause); *but see* Johnson v. Transportation Agency, 480 U.S. 616, 664, 669 (1987) (Scalia, J., dissenting) (accusing majority of improperly construing Title VII of Civil Rights Act of 1964 to permit affirmative action by public employer that Constitution prohibits); *see also* Taxman v. Board of Educ. of the Township of Piscataway, 91 F.3d 1547, 1559–60 (3d Cir. 1996) (arguing that Title VII imposes more stringent limitations on affirmative action than does the equal protection clause); *but see id.* at 1567–68, 1570–71 (Sloviter, C.J., dissenting) (arguing that Title VII permits more affirmative action than does the equal protection clause).

2. Brown v. Board of Educ., 347 U.S. 483 (1954) (*Brown I*) (declaring maintenance of segregated public schools unconstitutional); 349 U.S. 294 (1955) (*Brown II*) (requiring constitutional violation recognized in *Brown I* to be remedied through school desegregation "with all deliberate speed").

3. Plessy v. Ferguson, 163 U.S. 537 (1896).

4. *See Brown I*, 347 U.S. at 499 (citing Korematsu v. United States, 323 U.S. 214, 216 (1944)). *Plessy* never actually required equality in racially separate facilities. *See* STONE ET AL., *supra* chapter 1, note 1, at 516. Nevertheless, *Plessy* has come to stand for the proposition that separate facilities do not violate the Constitution as long as the facilities are equal. *See Brown I*, 347 U.S. at 488.

5. Many of the affirmative action decisions analyzed below, which preceded adoption of the Court's current position on affirmative action, are summarized and discussed in GUNTHER & SULLIVAN, *supra* chapter 1, note 1, at 793–814; STONE ET AL., *supra* chapter 1, note 1, at 648–52; TRIBE, *supra* Chapter One, note 1, at 1521–44.

6. *See Brown II*, 349 U.S. at 301 (requiring desegregation with "all deliberate speed").

7. *See, e.g.,* United States v. Montgomery County Bd. of Educ., 395 U.S. 225, 235–36 (1969); Green v. County School Bd., 391 U.S. 430, 439 (1968); Griffin v. School Bd., 377 U.S. 218, 233–34 (1964) (all holding that desegregation remedies had to be effective).

8. Swann v. Charlotte-Mecklenburg Bd. of Educ., 402 U.S. 1 (1971).

9. *See id.* at 27–28 (authorizing race-conscious remedies).

10. *See id.* at 16–18, 22–25 (endorsing population proportionality to achieve racial balance).

11. North Carolina State Bd. of Educ. v. Swann, 402 U.S. 43 (1971).

12. *See id.* at 45–46 (invalidating color-blind pupil assignment). Later cases authorized the use of racial classifications as a remedy for statutory employment-discrimination violations, thereby permitting the use of racial classifications even in the absence of a constitutional violation. *See, e.g.,* International Bhd. of Teamsters v. United States, 431 U.S. 324 (1977); Franks v. Bowman Transp. Co., 424 U.S. 747 (1976). For a fuller discussion of cases related to the use of racial classifications as a remedy for unlawful discrimination see GUNTHER & SULLIVAN, *supra* chapter 1, note 1, at 793–814; STONE ET AL., *supra* chapter 1, note 1, at 648–52.

13. *See* SPANN, RACE AGAINST THE COURT, *supra* chapter 1, note 1, at 78–79 (arguing that Supreme Court lost its desegregation resolve as desegregation effort moved north and lost popular political support).

14. Keys v. School District No. 1, Denver, Colorado, 413 U.S. 189 (1973).

15. *See id.* at 198–205, 208–09 (citing Swann v. Charlotte-Mecklenburg Bd. of Educ., 402 U.S. 1, 17–18 (1971)) (court-ordered desegregation limited to remedies for *de jure* segregation).

16. Milliken v. Bradley, 418 U.S. 717 (1974).

17. *See id.* at 722–36, 744–47 (court-ordered desegregation not permitted to remedy *de facto* segregation).

18. *See* SPANN, RACE AGAINST THE COURT, *supra* chapter 1, note 1, at 79 (noting that *Milliken* was first Supreme Court invalidation of school desegregation program in twenty years since *Brown I*).

19. *See id.* at 78, 111 (arguing that exclusion of white suburban students from desegregation plans precluded possibility of meaningful desegregation).

20. *See id.* at 78–79 (suggesting that Supreme Court decisions reflected loss of public support for school desegregation).

21. The Court's first majority "affirmative action" opinion was issued in the Court's 1989 decision in City of Richmond v. J.A. Croson Co., 488 U.S. 469 (1989). *Croson* is discussed in chapter 3, part 1.

22. DeFunis v. Odegaard, 416 U.S. 312 (1974).

23. *See id.* at 319–20 (finding controversy to be moot).

24. *See id.* at 314–16, 320 (vacating decision of Supreme Court of Washington as moot, even though controversy was not moot under state law).

25. *See id.* at 348 (Brennan, J., dissenting, joined by Douglas, White, & Marshall, JJ.).

26. *See id.* at 348–50 (arguing that controversy was not moot).

27. *See id.* at 333–34 (Douglas, J., dissenting). Justice Douglas favored vacating the state supreme court decision and remanding for trial, arguing that the record before the Court was not adequate to permit the requisite scrutiny. *See id.* at 335–36.

28. *See id.* at 340–41, 343; *see also* Lemann, *supra* chapter 1, note 1, at 36 (describing ambivalence of Justice Douglas concerning issue of affirmative action).

29. *See* United States v. Munsingwear, 340 U.S. 36, 39–41 (1950) (holding that vacation by appellate court of lower court decision and remand with direction to dismiss nullify lower court decisions).

30. United Jewish Orgs. v. Carey, 430 U.S. 144 (1977).

31. *See id.* at 147–55 (opinion of White, J.).

32. *See id.* at 155–62 (opinion of White, J., joined by Stevens, Brennan, & Blackmun, JJ.).

33. *See id.* at 165–68 (opinion of White, J., joined by Stevens & Rehnquist, JJ.).

34. *See id.* at 179–80 (Stewart, J., concurring in judgment). Washington v. Davis, 426 U.S. 229, 238–48 (1976), held that the Fourteenth Amendment prohibited only intentional discrimination and not facially neutral classifications that had a racially disparate impact.

35. *See United Jewish Orgs.,* 430 U.S. at 171–79 (Brennan, J., concurring in part). Brennan chose not to consider whether the plan would have been valid in the absence of such authorization. *See id.* at 170–71.

36. *See id.* at 180–87 (Burger, J., dissenting).

37. *See DeFunis v. Odegaard,* 416 U.S. 312, 319–20 (1974) (majority agreeing to dismiss as moot, arguably to avoid troublesome decision on the merits).

38. *See United Jewish Orgs.,* 430 U.S. at 155–62 (opinion of White J., joined by Stevens, Brennan, & Blackmun, JJ.); *id.* at 165–68 (opinion of White, J., joined by Stevens & Rehnquist, JJ.); *id.* at 179–80 (Stewart, J., concurring in judgment, joined by Powell, J.); *cf. id.* at 180–87 (Burger, C.J., dissenting). Note, however, that Chief Justice Burger had authored opinions permitting the use of race-conscious plans, *see, e.g.,* Swann v. Charlotte-Mecklenburg Bd. of Educ., 402 U.S. 1, 27–28 (1971) (school desegregation); *cf.* North Carolina State Bd. of Educ. v. Swann, 402 U.S. 43, 45–46 (1971) (invalidating state prohibition on race-based pupil assignments), as he would later do again in Fullilove v. Klutznick, 448 U.S. 448 (1980) (opinion of Burger, C.J., upholding race-conscious congressional set-aside). Although Justice Douglas had expressed opposition to explicit racial classifications in *DeFunis,* 416 U.S. at 333–34 (Douglas J., dissenting), by the time *United Jewish Orgs.* was decided, Justice Stevens had replaced Justice Douglas on the Supreme Court. Justice Marshall did not participate in *United Jewish Orgs.,* but he would acquiesce in the use of race-conscious affirmative action when he first addressed the issue in Regents of the Univ. of Cal. v. Bakke, 438 U.S. 265, 387–402 (1978) (opinion of Marshall, J.).

39. *See DeFunis,* 416 U.S. at 340–41 (Douglas, J., dissenting). Although Justice Douglas voted to invalidate the Davis affirmative action plan, he indicated that he would approve of a plan that appeared to be race neutral but had the effect of benefiting minorities at the expense of whites. *See id.* at 343.

40. *See United Jewish Orgs.,* 430 U.S. at 171–79 (Brennan, J., concurring in part). Justice Brennan noted that both minorities and politically powerless whites could be adversely affected by awakening society's latent race consciousness, *see id.,* thereby evidencing some degree of sympathy with Justice Douglas's preference for color blindness.

41. *See id.* at 165 (opinion of White, J.).

42. *See id.* at 180–87 (Burger, J., dissenting).

43. *See id.* at 155–62 (opinion of White, J., joined by Stevens, Brennan, & Blackmun, JJ.); *id.* at 171–79 (Brennan, J., concurring in part). Note that the reapportionment plan at issue in *United Jewish Orgs.* was adopted by the state of New York in order to comply with the congressional Voting Rights Act of 1965, *see id.* at

147–55, thereby making it amenable to characterization as either a state or a federal remedy.

44. *See id.* at 179–80 (advocating application of *Washington v. Davis* intentional-discrimination standard).

45. In the affirmative action context, the intent standard may be deceptively simply. For example, it is unclear whether intent should properly modify motive, or knowledge of likely consequences, or tolerance of ignorance of consequences. *Cf.* Personnel Adm'r v. Feeney, 442 U.S. 256, 278–80 (1979) (discussing meaning of intent for equal protection purposes). Moreover, it is not clear that the intent inquiry ultimately has any useful content. *See* David A. Strauss, *Discriminatory Intent and the Taming of* Brown, 56 U. CHI. L. REV. 935 (1989) (arguing that intent inquiry is ultimately meaningless). Or it may be that subjecting benign racial classifications to the relatively permissive intent test of Washington v. Davis, 426 U.S. 229, 238–48 (1976), would require the Court to uphold an unacceptably high number of affirmative action plans. The same concerns that caused the Court to adopt the intent standard in Washington v. Davis itself may have caused the Court to find the standard unacceptable for judging the validity of affirmative action. Ultimately, the Supreme Court did choose to apply strict scrutiny to affirmative action programs using facial race-based classifications in Adarand Constructors v. Pena, 515 U.S. 200 (1995), and the Court chose *not* to inquire into the benign or invidious intent with which such classifications were used prior to invoking strict scrutiny. *Adarand* is discussed in chapter 3, part 4.

46. Regents of the Univ. of Cal. v. Bakke, 438 U.S. 265 (1978).

47. *See id.* at 272–75 (opinion of Powell, J.).

48. *See* Title VI of The Civil Rights Act of 1964, Pub. L. 88–352, 78 Stat. 241, 252 (codified as amended at 42 U.S.C. §§ 2000d, *et seq.* (1994)).

49. *See Bakke,* 438 U.S. at 411–21 (Stevens, J., concurring in judgment in part and dissenting in part, joined by Burger, Stewart, & Rehnquist, JJ.). These four justices would have sidestepped the constitutional issue yet again, finding that it was not properly before the Court. *See id.* at 411–12.

50. *See id.* at 305–20 (opinion of Powell, J.). Because Justice Powell found the Title VI prohibition to be coextensive with that of the equal protection clause, he found it necessary to reach the constitutional issue. *See id.* at 281–87.

51. *See id.* at 355–62 (opinion of Brennan, J., concurring in judgment in part and dissenting in part, joined by White, Marshall, & Blackmun, JJ.). The Brennan plurality adopted the intermediate scrutiny used in previous gender discrimination cases, which required that the subject classification serve an important governmental objective and that it be substantially related to the achievement of that objective. Justice Brennan stated that intermediate rather than rational-basis scrutiny was necessary to guard against the danger that an ostensibly benign classification might be misused, causing effects similar to invidious discrimination. *See id.* at 358–61.

52. *See id.* at 325, 362–69. Brennan seems to have equated the findings require-ment with the requirement that there be an "articulated purpose of remedying the effects of past societal discrimination." *See id.*

53. *See id.* at 324–26. Because, like Justice Powell, these four justices found the scope of the Title VI prohibition to be coextensive with the equal protection clause, they deemed it necessary to reach the constitutional issue. *See id.* Justice White be-lieved that Title VI gave no cause of action to private litigants to enforce its funding restrictions. *See id.* at 379–87 (opinion of White, J.).

54. *See id.* at 287–320 (opinion of Powell, J.).

55. Note, however, that while Chief Justice Burger had evidenced hostility to the general concept of remedial racial classifications in *United Jewish Orgs., see supra* text accompanying chapter 2, notes 36–42, Justices Stevens, Stewart, and Rehnquist had yet to address the racial preference issue.

56. *See, e.g.,* Miller v. Johnson, 515 U.S. 900, 904 (1995) (citing opinion of Powell, J., in *Bakke* as authoritative); Adarand Constructors v. Pena, 515 U.S. 200, 218, 224–25 (same); City of Richmond v. J.A. Croson Co., 488 U.S. 469 493–94, 496–98 (1989) (plurality opinion of O'Connor, J.) (same).

57. *See Bakke,* 438 U.S. at 287–91 (opinion of Powell, J.). The test traditionally required under the strict scrutiny standard is that the classification under review ad-vance a compelling state interest and that it be narrowly tailored to the advance-ment of that interest. *See* Loving v. Virginia, 388 U.S. 1, 11 (1967); *cf.* Korematsu v. United States, 323 U.S. 214, 216 (1944).

58. *See Bakke,* 438 U.S. at 294–99 (opinion of Powell, J.).

59. *See id.* at 265.

60. *See id.* at 307–10. Justice Powell also stated that a university, whose mission was to educate students, lacked the institutional competence to make such findings. *See id.* 309–10. In this regard, Justice Powell seems to have contemplated a much more stringent findings requirement than that contemplated by the Brennan plural-ity. *Cf. id.* at 362–69 (Brennan, J., concurring in judgment in part and dissenting in part). *See The Supreme Court, 1977 Term, supra* chapter 1, note 1, at 137–39.

61. *See Bakke,* 438 U.S. at 310–11 (opinion of Powell, J.).

62. *See id.* at 311–20. Justice Powell pointed to the Harvard College admissions program as an example of a plan that was constitutionally acceptable in this regard. *See id.* at 316–17.

63. The Fourth and Fifth Circuits appear to have rejected Justice Powell's views in Podberesky v. Kirwin, 38 F. 3d 147 (4th Cir. 1994), *cert. denied,* 514 U.S. 1128 (1995), and Hopwood v. Texas, 78 F. 3d 932 (5th Cir. 1996), *cert. denied,* 518 U.S. 1033 (1996). *See infra,* text accompanying chapter 3, notes 166 & 171 (discussing treatment of *Bakke* in *Podberesky* and *Hopwood*). *Podberesky* and *Hopwood* are dis-cussed in chapter 3, part 5, sections i & ii respectively.

64. *See Bakke,* 438 U.S. at 387–402 (opinion of Marshall, J.).

65. *See id.* at 402–08 (opinion of Blackmun, J.).

66. *See id.* at 324–26 (Brennan J., concurring in judgment in part and dissenting in part, joined by White, Marshall, & Blackmun, JJ.).

67. *See id.* at 287–91 (opinion of Powell, J.).

68. *See id.* at 307–10 (insisting on formal findings).

69. *See id.* at 311–20 (insisting on treatment of people as individuals rather than members of racial group).

70. *See id.* at 387–402 (opinion of Marshall, J.).

71. Fullilove v. Klutznick, 448 U.S. 448 (1980).

72. *See* Public Works Employment Act of 1977, Pub. L. 95–28, 91 Stat. 116 (codified as amended at 42 U.S.C. § 6701 *et seq.* (1994)).

73. *See Fullilove*, 448 U.S. at 453–54, 468–72 (opinion of Burger, C.J.). The act defined minorities to be United States citizens who were "Negroes, Spanish-speaking, Orientals, Indians, Eskimos, and Aleuts." *See id.* at 454.

74. *See id.* at 492. Because the constitutionality of a congressional enactment was involved, the Court's constitutional analysis occurred under the equal protection component of the Fifth Amendment due process clause rather than the equal protection clause of the Fourteenth Amendment. *See id.* at 480.

75. *See id.* at 472–84 (specifying congressional powers permitting creation of affirmative action program).

76. *See id.* at 484–85 (permitting burdens on innocent nonminority contractors).

77. *See id.* at 485–89 (rejecting claims of overinclusiveness and underinclusiveness). The opinion also stressed that the program was a pilot program limited in scope and duration. *See id.* at 489.

78. *See id.* at 495–99 (Powell, J. concurring, stressing need for strict scrutiny and findings).

79. *See id.* at 517 (Marshall, J., concurring in judgment, joined by Brennan & Blackmun, JJ.).

80. *See id.* at 517–21 (favoring intermediate scrutiny).

81. *See id.* at 521 (quoting *Bakke*, 438 U.S. at 375 (opinion of Brennan, J., stressing that quotas were not invidious ceilings)).

82. *See id.* at 519–21 (no danger of racial stigmatization).

83. *See id.* at 522–27 (Stewart J., dissenting, joined by Rehnquist, J.) (citing Plessy v. Ferguson, 163 U.S. 537 (1896)).

84. *See id.* at 527–30 (Stewart, J., dissenting). Justice Stewart also expressed the fear that the program would reinforce common racial stereotypes, and make race rather than merit a relevant criterion. *See id.* at 531–32.

85. *See id.* at 537, 548 (Stevens, J., dissenting).

86. *See id.* at 550–51 (implying that strict scrutiny was appropriate).

87. *See id.* at 537–48 (program was not narrow enough).

88. *See id.* at 541–42 (impermissible effort to give minorities "a piece of the action").

89. *See id.* at 545, 548–54 (danger of resentment and stereotyping).

90. *See id.* at 539 (program created spoils system for minorities).

91. *See id.* at 482–84 (opinion of Burger, C.J., joined by White & Powell, JJ.); *id.* at 517–19 (Marshall, J., concurring in judgment, joined by Brennan & Blackmun, JJ.); *id.* at 548 (Stevens, J., dissenting). This observation is made in *The Supreme Court, 1979 Term, supra* chapter 1, note 1, at 128.

92. Three members of the Court thought that the quota component of the set-aside program defeated the constitutional narrowness requirement, *see Fullilove*, 448 U.S. at 530 n.12 (Stewart, J., dissenting, joined by Rehnquist, J.); *id.* at 535–36, 540, 549 n.25, 552 n.30 (Stevens J., dissenting), but Justice Stevens's opposition was based on procedural rather than substantive grounds. *See id.* at 552.

93. *See id.* at 537 (Stewart, J., dissenting, joined by Rehnquist, J.). Justice Stewart attempted to distinguish *United Jewish Orgs.* simply by asserting that the redistricting plan at issue there did not discriminate on the basis of race. *See id.* at 524–25 n.3. Although this offered distinction is puzzling, Justice Stewart's opinion can perhaps be best understood as finding that the burden imposed on white voters in *United Jewish Orgs.* was minor because it did not affect whites individually but only as a group.

94. *See, e.g., Fullilove*, 448 U.S. at 519–21 (Marshall, J., concurring in judgment); *Bakke*, 438 U.S. at 294–99 (opinion of Powell, J.); *United Jewish Orgs.*, 430 U.S. at 165–68 (opinion of White, J.); *id.* at 172–74 (opinion of Brennan, J.); *DeFunis*, 416 U.S. at 343 (Douglas, J., dissenting). *Cf. The Supreme Court, 1979 Term, supra* chapter 1, note 1, at 128.

95. *See Bakke*, 438 U.S. at 311 (opinion of Powell, J.).

96. *See Fullilove*, 448 U.S. at 526 (Stewart J., dissenting, joined by Rehnquist, J.). *Cf. The Supreme Court, 1979 Term, supra* chapter 1, note 1, at 129. Note that the position of Justices Stewart and Rehnquist in this regard in *Fullilove* is consistent with their effort to distinguish *United Jewish Orgs.* as a case that disadvantaged white voters as a group but not as individuals. *See Fullilove*, 448 U.S. at 524 n.3 (Stewart, J., dissenting).

97. *See id.* at 520 n.4 (Marshall, J., concurring in judgment). This point is made in *The Supreme Court, 1979 Term, supra,* chapter 1, note 1, at 132.

98. *See Fullilove*, 448 U.S. at 464–67, 476–79 (opinion of Burger, C.J.); *id.* at 520 (Marshall, J., concurring in judgment). This point too is made in *The Supreme Court, 1979 Term, supra* chapter 1, note 1, at 132–33.

99. *See Fullilove*, 448 U.S. at 527–30 (Stewart, J., dissenting).

100. *See id.* at 472–84 (opinion of Berger, C.J.).

101. The Court had upheld congressional plans in *United Jewish Orgs.* and *Fullilove* while permitting state plans to be invalidated in *DeFunis* and *Bakke*.

102. Wygant v. Jackson Bd. of Educ., 476 U.S. 267 (1986).

103. *See id.* at 270–73 (opinion of Powell, J., describing facts of case).

104. *See id.* at 297–99 (Marshall, J., dissenting, describing racial tensions and other pressures imposed on school board to integrate faculty).

105. *See id.* at 273–74 (opinion of Powell, J., joined by Burger, Rehnquist, & O'Connor, JJ.).

106. *See id.* at 274–76 (plan did not survive strict scrutiny).

107. *See id.* at 277–78 (no findings of past discrimination and no need for remand).

108. *See id.* at 269, 279–84 (opinion of Powell, J., joined by Burger & Rehnquist, JJ., arguing that layoffs imposed too heavy a burden on innocent whites).

109. *See id.* at 283 n.12 (citing Franks v. Bowman Transp. Co., 424 U.S. 747 (1976), for proposition that competitive seniority could be used for provision of make-whole relief to identifiable victims of prior discrimination).

110. *See Wygant,* 476 U.S. at 284 (O'Connor, J., concurring).

111. *See id.* at 293–94 (remand was not necessary because plan pursued improper goals).

112. *Compare id.* at 287–88 (arguing that lack of formal administrative findings of past discrimination by school board was due to settlement of earlier discrimination proceedings) *with id.* at 277–78 (opinion of Powell, J.) (emphasizing lack of trial court findings of past discrimination by school board).

113. *See id.* at 286–93 (opinion of O'Connor, J., diversity could constitute compelling governmental interest).

114. *See id.* at 288 n.* (distinguishing diversity from role model justification).

115. *See id.* at 294–95 (White, J., concurring in judgment, arguing that layoffs were an impermissible burden to impose on innocent whites).

116. Firefighters Local Union No. 1784 v. Stotts, 467 U.S. 561, 576–83 (1984).

117. *Stotts* is discussed in chapter 2, part 5, section ii.

118. *See Wygant,* 476 U.S. at 301–03 (Marshall, J., dissenting, joined by Brennan & Blackmun, JJ.).

119. *See id.* at 303–06 (state had compelling interest in maintaining faculty integration).

120. *See id.* at 306–10 (plan was narrowly tailored).

121. *See id.* at 310–11 (plan did not impose impermissible burden on whites).

122. *See id.* at 296, 312 (advocating remand for any findings that were necessary).

123. *See id.* at 313 (Stevens, J., dissenting, appearing to apply minimal scrutiny and focusing on prospective benefit of plan).

124. *See id.* at 313–17 (faculty-diversity and role-model justifications were constitutionally sufficient).

125. *See id.* at 317–18 (plan was procedurally adequate and did not impose impermissible burden on whites). The views of Justice Stevens in Fullilove v. Klutznick, 448 U.S. 448, 537, 548 (1980), are discussed in chapter 2, part 3.

126. Local 28, Sheet Metal Workers Int'l Ass'n v. EEOC, 478 U.S. 421 (1986).

127. *See id.* at 426–40 (describing case).

128. *See id.* at 440–44 (majority opinion).

129. *See id.* at 422, 444–81, 482–83 (opinion of Brennan, J., joined by Marshall, Blackmun, & Stevens, JJ.).

130. *See id.* at 444–79 (discussing Title VII).

131. *See id.* at 444–70 (Title VII does not prohibit remedial use of race-conscious measures).

132. Firefighters Local Union No 1784 v. Stotts, 467 U.S. 561 (1984). *Stotts* is discussed in chapter 2, part 5, section ii.

133. *See Sheet Metal Workers,* 421 U.S. at 471–75 (opinion of Brennan, J., distinguishing *Stotts*).

134. *See id.* at 475–79 (discussing need for affirmative action remedies).

135. *See id.* at 479–81 (discussing equal protection claim).

136. *See id.* at 480 (discussing constitutional standard for benign racial classifications).

137. *See id.* at 480–81 (applying constitutional standard).

138. *See id.* at 481 (marginal impact on white employees).

139. *See id.* at 482–83 (race-conscious remedies not limited to actual victims of discrimination).

140. *See id.* at 483–89 (Powell, J., concurring in part and concurring in judgment).

141. *See id.* at 484 (discussing *Stotts*).

142. *See id.* at 484–89 (applying strict scrutiny).

143. *See id.* at 488 (no direct burden imposed on white employees).

144. *See id.* at 489 (O'Connor, J., concurring in part and dissenting in part, objecting to use of quotas and arguing that Title VII typically limits racial preferences to actual victims of discrimination); *id.* at 499 (White, J., dissenting, arguing that district court remedy was inequitable and therefore not authorized by Title VII); *id.* at 500 (Rehnquist, J., dissenting, joined by Burger, C.J., arguing that Title VII remedies are limited to actual victims of discrimination).

145. *See id.* at 489 (O'Connor, J., concurring in part and dissenting in part).

146. *See id.* at 489–90 (rejecting distinction between make-whole and affirmative action remedies).

147. *See id.* at 490–98 (hiring goals constituted impermissible racial quotas).

148. *See id.* at 499 (remedial fund also constituted racial quota).

149. *See id.* at 499 (White, J., dissenting, arguing that Title VII sometimes permits race-conscious remedies for nonvictims).

150. *See id.* at 499–500 (hiring goals constituted inequitable racial quota).

151. *See id.* at 500 (Rehnquist, J., dissenting, joined by Burger, C.J., arguing that Title VII remedies are limited to actual victims of discrimination).

152. United States v. Paradise, 480 U.S. 149 (1987).

153. *See id.* at 154 (quoting NAACP v. Allen, 340 F. Supp. 703, 705 (M.D. Ala. 1972)).

154. *See id.* at 153–66 (opinion of Brennan, J., discussing facts and procedural history of case).

155. *See id.* at 152, 165–66 (enumerating votes of justices and affirming Court of Appeals by plurality decision).

156. *See id.* at 166–86 (opinion of Brennan, J., joined by Marshall, Blackmun, & Powell, JJ.).

157. *See id.* at 166–67 (district court order satisfied even strict scrutiny).

158. *See id.* at 167–71 (district court order advanced compelling government interest in remedying past discrimination).

159. *See id.* at 170 n.20, 178 (rejecting argument that district court sought to impose racial balance on department).

160. *See id.* at 171–79 (district court order was narrowly tailored).

161. *See id.* at 179–82 (25 percent promotion goal and one-to-one promotion ratio were constitutionally permissible).

162. *See id.* at 182–83 (one-for-one promotion quota did not impermissibly burden whites).

163. *See id.* at 183–85 (district court equitable discretion was entitled to deference).

164. *See id.* at 186–89 (Powell J., concurring, emphasizing narrowness and limited burden of district court order).

165. *See id.* at 187 n.2 (stressing need for strict scrutiny, and distinguishing school desegregation cases).

166. *See id.* at 187 (listing five factors relevant to narrow-tailoring requirement).

167. *See id.* at 186–89 (applying strict scrutiny to judicial remedies).

168. *See id.* at 189–95 (Stevens, J., concurring in judgment).

169. Swann v. Charlotte-Mecklenburg Bd. of Educ., 402 U.S. 1 (1971).

170. *See Paradise*, 480 U.S. at 189–90 (Stevens, J., concurring in judgment, objecting to application of strict scrutiny).

171. *See* id. at 193–94 (favoring broader remedial discretion for courts than for other state actors); *see also* TRIBE, *supra* chapter 1, note 1, at 1544 n.119 (endorsing views of Justice Stevens in *Paradise*).

172. *See Paradise*, 480 U.S. at 196 (White, J., dissenting).

173. *See id.* at 196–201. (O'Connor, J., dissenting, joined by Rehnquist & Scalia, JJ.).

174. *See id.* at 196–99 (50 percent promotion quota was not narrowly tailored).

175. *See id.* at 199–201 (district court should have used nonracial alternatives).

176. *See* Wygant v. Jackson Bd. of Educ., 476 U.S. 267, 273–78 (1986). (opinion of Powell, J., joined by Burger, Rehnquist, & O'Connor, JJ.).

177. *See id.* at 279–84 (opinion of Powell, J., joined by Burger & Rehnquist, JJ.).

178. *See id.* at 286–93 (O'Connor, J., concurring).

179. *See id.* at 313–17 (Stevens, J., dissenting).

180. *See Sheet Metal Workers,* 478 U.S. 421 (1986).

181. *See Paradise,* 480 U.S. 149 (1987).

182. *See id.* at 196–201 (O'Connor, J., dissenting, joined by Rehnquist & Scalia, JJ.). Technically, Justice Rehnquist replaced Justice Burger as chief justice, and Justice Scalia replaced Justice Rehnquist as an associate justice. *See* STONE ET AL., *supra* chapter 1, note 1, at cii–ciii.

183. *Compare Wygant,* 476 U.S. 267 (invalidating voluntary plan) *with Sheet Metal Workers,* 478 U.S. 421 (upholding constitutionality of court-ordered remedy for Title VII violation) and *Paradise,* 480 U.S. 149 (upholding constitutionality of court-ordered remedy for Fourteenth Amendment violation).

184. Local 28, Sheet Metal Workers Int'l Ass'n v. EEOC, 478 U.S. 421 (1986). The *Sheet Metal Workers* decision is discussed in chapter 2, part 4, section ii.

185. Title VII of the Civil Rights Act of 1964 prohibits discrimination in employment on the basis of race, color, religion, sex, or national origin. *See* Pub. L. No. 88-352, 78 Stat. 241, 253 (1964) (codified as amended at 42 U.S.C. §§ 2000e to 2000e–17 (1994)). Section 703(a) prohibits discrimination in hiring, discharges, compensation, terms, conditions, or privileges of employment. *See* 78 Stat. 255, as amended, 86 Stat. 109 (codified as amended at 42 U.S.C. § 2000e–2(a) (1994)). Section 703(d) prohibits discrimination in apprenticeship or other training programs. *See* 78 Stat. 256 (codified at 42 U.S.C. § 2000e–2(d) (1994)).

186. United Steelworkers of Am. v. Weber, 443 U.S. 193 (1979).

187. *See id.* at 195 (enumerating votes of justices); *id.* at 197–200 (describing plan); *id.* at 222–23, 246 (Rehnquist, J., dissenting, discussing motivation for affirmative action plan).

188. *See id.* at 200–08, 209 (majority opinion of Brennan, J., joined by Stewart, White, Marshall, & Blackmun, JJ., holding that Title VII permits voluntary affirmative action).

189. *See id.* at 208–09 (plan does not "unnecessarily trammel" interests of whites). The distinction between the apparently permissible use of target percentages as benchmarks to eliminate the effects of past discrimination and the impermissible use of racial quotas to maintain racial balance is not clear. *See* TRIBE, *supra* chapter 1, note 1, at 1530 n.35.

190. *Cf. Weber,* 443 U.S. at 208–09 (plan falls within area of discretion left by Title VII for voluntary affirmative action).

191. *See id.* at 209–16 (Blackmun, J., concurring, discussing arguable-violation limitation on voluntary affirmative action).

192. *See id.* at 212–16 (favoring some voluntary affirmative action remedies that extended beyond arguable-violation limitation).

193. *See id.* at 216 (Burger, C.J., dissenting); *id.* at 219 (Rehnquist, J., dissenting, joined by Burger, C.J.).

194. *See id.* at 216–19 (Burger, C.J., dissenting, arguing that Title VII does not permit race-conscious affirmative action).

195. *See id.* at 219–22 (Rehnquist, J., dissenting, joined by Burger, C.J., arguing that statutory language, legislative history, and Supreme Court precedents precluded race-conscious affirmative action).

196. *See id.* at 230–53 (discussing legislative history).

197. *See id.* at 195 (enumerating votes of justices).

198. Firefighters Local Union No. 1784 v. Stotts, 467 U.S. 561 (1984).

199. *See id.* at 564–65 (protecting nonminority seniority rights). For a more detailed discussion of the *Stotts* decision see Girardeau A. Spann, *Simple Justice*, 73 GEO. L.J. 1041 (1985).

200. *See Stotts*, 467 U.S. 561 at 565–68 (stating facts of case).

201. *See* Stotts v. Memphis Fire Dep't, 679 F.2d 541, 546 (6th Cir. 1982) (affirming district court injunction).

202. *See Stotts*, 467 U.S. at 564–65 (reversing lower courts).

203. *See id.* at 563 (listing votes of justices).

204. *See id.* at 590–92 (Stevens, J., concurring in judgment).

205. *See id.* 568–72 (majority opinion of White, J., holding that case was not moot).

206. *See* Spann, *supra* chapter 1, note 1, at 1046 n.30 and accompanying text (discussing alphabetical layoffs).

207. *See Stotts*, 467 U.S. at 572–76 (consent decree did not by its terms permit affirmative action to override seniority).

208. *See id.* at 576–83 (district court lacked authority to modify consent decree).

209. Teamsters v. United States, 431 U.S. 324, 367–71 (1977).

210. *See* Title VII, § 703(h), codified as amended at 42 U.S.C. § 2000e-2(h) (1994).

211. *See* Title VII, § 706(g), codified as amended at 42 U.S.C. § 2000e-5(g) (1994).

212. *See Stotts*, 467 U.S. at 576–83 (majority opinion of White, J., holding that minority firefighters could not displace nonminority firefighters with greater seniority).

213. *See id.* at 576–83 (limiting affirmative action to actual victims of discrimination).

214. *See id.* at 586–90 (O'Connor, J., concurring).

215. *See id.* at 583–86 (arguing that case was not moot because collateral effects would not be eliminated by vacating lower court judgments under United States v. Munsingwear, 340 U.S. 36, 39 (1950)).

216. *See id.* at 586–90 (affirmative action concerns could not override seniority concerns).

217. *See id.* at 590 (Stevens, J., concurring in judgment).

218. *See id.* at 590 (arguing that case was not moot).

219. *See id.* at 590–91 (Title VII was not relevant to validity of consent decree).

220. *See id.* at 591–92 (seniority could not be overridden by terms of, or modification of, consent decree).

221. *See id.* at 593 (Blackmun J., dissenting, joined by Brennan & Marshall, JJ.).

222. *See id.* at 593–601 (arguing that case was moot, and that lower court judgments should be vacated under United States v. Munsingwear, 340 U.S. 36, 39 (1950)).

223. *See id.* at 601–04 (abuse of discretion was proper standard for reviewing district court preliminary injunction).

224. *See id.* at 605–06 (district court did not require any layoffs).

225. *See id.* at 606–10 (terms of consent decree permitted district court order).

226. *See id.* at 610–20 (Title VII did not prohibit modification of consent decree).

227. Teamsters v. United States, 431 U.S. 324 (1977).

228. *See Stotts,* 467 U.S. at 616–20 (Blackmun, J., dissenting, arguing that Title VII did not preclude classwide, race-conscious affirmative action, citing *Teamsters,* 431 U.S. at 347–48, 364–71).

229. *See id.* at 576–83 (majority opinion) (limiting relief to actual victims of discrimination).

230. Local 28, Sheet Metal Workers Int'l Ass'n v. EEOC, 478 U.S. 421 (1986). *Sheet Metal Workers* is discussed in chapter 2, part 4, section ii.

231. *See id.* at 499 (White, J., dissenting, arguing that Title VII sometimes permits race-conscious remedies for nonvictims).

232. Local 28, Sheet Metal Workers Int'l Ass'n v. EEOC, 478 U.S. 421 (1986). *Sheet Metal Workers* is discussed in chapter 2, part 4, section ii.

233. Local 93, Int'l Ass'n of Firefighters v. Cleveland, 478 U.S. 501 (1986).

234. *See id.* at 504–15 (describing facts); *id.* at 514 n.6 (discussing position of United States in United Steelworkers of Am. v. Weber, 443 U.S. 193 (1979)).

235. *See Firefighters v. Cleveland,* 478 U.S. at 511–15 (describing procedural history).

236. *See id.* at 504 (majority opinion of Brennan, J., joined by Marshall, Blackmun, Powell, Stevens, & O'Connor, JJ.).

237. *See id.* at 515–30 (Title VII limitations do not apply to voluntary consent decrees).

238. *See id.* at 514 (quoting § 706(g) of Title VII, 78 Stat. 261, codified as amended at 42 U.S.C. § 2000e-5(g)) (1994).

239. Firefighters Local Union No. 1784 v. Stotts, 467 U.S. 561 (1984). *Stotts* is discussed in chapter 2, part 5, section ii.

240. *See Firefighters v. Cleveland,* 478 U.S. at 515 (noting *Sheet Metal Workers* rejection of actual-victim limitation); *see also supra* text accompanying chapter 2, note 139 (discussing *Sheet Metal Workers* rejection of actual-victim limitation).

241. *See id.* at 524–28 (distinguishing *Stotts* as case in which district court order itself violated Title VII).

242. *See id.* at 528–30 (union's consent was not needed for settlement).

243. *See id.* at 530 (O'Connor, J., concurring).

244. *See id.* at 530–31 (majority opinion did not preclude third-party challenges on remand).

245. *See id.* at 531 (White, J., dissenting).

246. *See id.* at 531–35 (arguing that Title VII prohibited even voluntary race-conscious remedies for nonvictims).

247. *See id.* at 535 (Rehnquist, J., dissenting, joined by Burger, C.J.).

248. *See id.* at 535–40 (arguing that voluntary remedies could not exceed scope of judicially imposed remedies).

249. *See id.* at 540–45 (arguing that race-conscious remedies were limited to actual victims of discrimination).

250. Johnson v. Transportation Agency, 480 U.S. 616 (1987).

251. *See id.* at 620–26 (describing affirmative action plan); *id.* at 635 n.13 (Court's analysis applied to race as well as gender).

252. *See id.* at 625–26 (describing challenge by male employee).

253. *See id.* at 619–21, 625–26 (discussing district court reliance on United Steelworkers of Am. v. Weber, 443 U.S. 193 (1979)).

254. *See Johnson v. Transportation Agency,* 480 U.S. at 619–21, 625–26 (describing procedural history).

255. *See id.* at 618 (enumerating votes of justices); *id.* at 627–28 n.6, 632 (majority opinion of Brennan, J., joined by Marshall, Blackmun, Powell, & Stevens, JJ., holding that Title VII imposes fewer restrictions on affirmative action than equal protection clause).

256. *See id.* at 626–30 (quoting *Weber,* 443 U.S. at 209, for proposition that conspicuous imbalance was sufficient predicate for affirmative action under Title VII).

257. *See id.* at 631–36 (plan was designed to remedy conspicuous imbalance).

258. *See id.* at 637–40 (plan did not impermissibly burden male employees).

259. *See id.* at 640–42 (agency plan facilitated Title VII policy favoring voluntary remedies for discrimination).

260. *See id.* at 642–47 (Stevens, J., concurring, asserting that arguable Title VII violation should not be predicate to permissible affirmative action).

261. *See id.* at 642–44 (discussing change in law made by Regents of the Univ. of Cal. v. Bakke, 438 U.S. 265 (1978), and United Steelworkers of Am. v. Weber, 443 U.S. 193 (1979)).

262. *See id.* at 644–46 (Title VII should not be construed to prohibit voluntary efforts to benefit minorities).

263. *See id.* at 646–47 (Title VII permits goals other than providing remedies for past violations).

264. *See id.* at 647 (O'Connor, J., concurring in judgment).

265. *See id.* at 647–53 (arguing that Title VII violation was necessary predicate for permissible affirmative action); *but cf. supra* chapter 2, note 113 and accompanying text (noting Justice O'Connor's willingness to recognize prospective diversity as compelling state interest in Wygant v. Jackson Bd. of Educ., 476 U.S. 267, 286–93 (1986) (O'Connor, J., concurring).

266. *See id.* at 650 (opposing requirement of formal findings).

267. *See id.* at 647–48 (arguing that *stare decisis* required adherence to *Weber* criteria for permissible affirmative action).

268. *See id.* at 653–57 (arguing that agency plan satisfied *Weber* standards).

269. *See id.* at 657 (White, J., dissenting, arguing that *Weber* should be overruled).

270. *See id.* (arguing that Title VII requires more than imbalance in workforce as predicate for affirmative action).

271. *See id.* at 657 (Scalia, J., dissenting, joined by Rehnquist, C.J., and joined in part by White, J.).

272. *See id.* at 657–58 (arguing that majority transformed Title VII from antidiscrimination into prodiscrimination statute).

273. *See id.* at 658–64 (arguing that plan did not remedy prior discrimination, and gender was dispositive factor).

274. *See id.* at 664–66, 669–70 (arguing that *Wygant* does not permit affirmative action to be used to remedy general societal discrimination, and Title VII should not be read to permit discrimination that Constitution prohibits).

275. *See id.* at 666–68 (arguing that majority ignored *Sheet Metal Workers* and *Weber*).

276. *See id.* at 669–75 (Scalia, J., dissenting, joined by Rehnquist, C.J., arguing that *Weber* was wrong when decided, and should not be extended to public employers).

277. *See id.* at 675–77 (arguing that majority opinion inverted meaning of Title VII).

278. *See id.* at 674–77 (offering Marxist interpretation of majority opinion).

279. *See Firefighters v. Cleveland,* 478 U.S. at 515–30; *Johnson v. Transportation Agency* 480 U.S. at 626–40 (five justices voting to uphold plans).

280. *Firefighters v. Cleveland,* 478 U.S. at 515–30 (five justices rejecting actual-victim limitation).

281. *See id.* at 524–28 (recognizing constructive consent).

282. *See id.* at 530–31 (O'Connor, J., concurring); *Johnson v. Transportation Agency,* 480 U.S. at 647 (O'Connor, J., concurring in judgment).

283. *See Johnson v. Transportation Agency,* 480 U.S. at 664–68 (Scalia, J., dissenting, joined by Rehnquist & White).

284. Taxman v. Piscataway Township Bd. of Educ., 91 F.3d 1547 (3d. Cir. 1996) (en banc), *cert. granted,* 117 S. Ct. 2506 (1997), *cert. dismissed,* 118 S. Ct. 595 (1997).

285. *See* Piscataway Township Bd. of Educ. v. Taxman, 118 S. Ct. 595 (1997) (dismissing certiorari).

286. *See Johnson v. Transportation Agency*, 480 U.S. at 618 (opinion of Brennan, J., for the Court, joined by Marshall, Blackmun, Powell, & Stevens, JJ.); *Paradise*, 480 U.S. at 153 (opinion of Brennan, J., joined by Marshall, Blackmun, & Powell JJ.); *Firefighters v. Cleveland*, 478 U.S. at 504 (opinion of Brennan, J., for the Court, joined by Marshall, Blackmun, Powell, Stevens, & O'Connor, JJ.); *Sheet Metal Workers*, 478 U.S. at 426 (opinion of Brennan, J., joined in full by Marshall, Blackmun, & Stevens, JJ.); *Wygant*, 476 U.S. at 295 (Marshall, J., dissenting, joined by Brennan & Blackmun, JJ.); *Fullilove*, 448 U.S. at 517 (Marshall, J., concurring in judgment, joined by Brennan & Blackmun, JJ.); *Weber*, 443 U.S. at 197 (opinion of Brennan, J., for the Court, joined by Stewart, White, Marshall, & Blackmun, JJ.); *id.* at 209 (Blackmun, J., concurring); *Bakke*, 438 U.S. at 324 (Brennan, J., concurring in judgment in part and dissenting in part, joined by White, Marshall, & Blackmun, JJ.); *id.* at 387 (opinion of Marshall, J.); *id.* at 402 (opinion of Blackmun, J.); *United Jewish Orgs.* 430 U.S. at 155 (opinion of White, J., joined by Stevens, Brennan, & Blackmun) (Justice Marshall did not participate).

287. Justice Burger voted to uphold only the *Fullilove* plan, *see Fullilove*, 448 U.S. at 492 (opinion of Burger, C.J.), and Justices Stewart and Rehnquist voted to uphold only the *United Jewish Orgs.* plan. *See United Jewish Orgs.*, 430 U.S. at 179–80 (Stewart, J., concurring in judgment); *id.* at 165–68 (opinion of White, J., joined by Stevens & Rehnquist, JJ.). Each of these justices voted only to uphold a plan that was traceable to the federal government.

288. Justice O'Connor voted to invalidate the affirmative action plans in *Paradise*, 480 U.S. at 196 (O'Connor, J., dissenting), *Sheet Metal Workers*, 478 U.S. at 489 (O'Connor, J., dissenting), and *Wygant*, 476 U.S. at 284 (O'Connor, J., dissenting). Justice O'Connor did vote to uphold affirmative action plans against Title VII challenges in *Johnson v. Transportation Agency* and *Firefighters v. Cleveland*. In *Johnson v. Transportation Agency*, however, she refused to sign the majority opinion upholding the plan because she believed that voluntary affirmative action plans were invalid if not preceded by a prima facie case of prior discrimination that was sufficient to establish a Title VII violation. *See Johnson v. Transportation Agency*, 480 U.S. at 647–53 (O'Connor, J., concurring). Moreover, in *Firefighters v. Cleveland* she noted that affirmative action consent decrees might still be held invalid on Fourteenth Amendment grounds in a suit filed by disadvantaged white workers. *See Firefighters v. Cleveland*, 478 U.S. at 530 (O'Connor, J., concurring). Justice O'Connor was not on the Court when *Weber* was decided, but she has stated that she believes *Weber*, which authorized voluntary affirmative action in the absence of an adjudication of past discrimination, to have been incorrectly decided. *See Johnson v. Transportation Agency*, 480 U.S. at 647–48. Nevertheless, Justice O'Connor stated that she would not overrule *Weber* for *stare decisis* reasons, *see id.* at 647–48.

Justice Scalia voted to invalidate the affirmative action plans in the two cases that he had then considered as a Supreme Court justice. *See Johnson v. Transportation Agency*, 480 U.S. at 657 (Scalia, J., dissenting in Title VII case); *Paradise*, 480 U.S. at 196 (O'Connor, J., dissenting in Fourteenth Amendment case, joined by Rehnquist & Scalia, JJ.). Like Justice O'Connor, Justice Scalia was not on the Court when *Weber* was decided, but he too has stated that he believes *Weber* to have been incorrectly decided. Unlike Justice O'Connor, Justice Scalia would disregard *stare decisis* considerations and overrule *Weber. See Johnson v. Transportation Agency*, 480 U.S. at 669–77 (Scalia, J., dissenting).

289. *See Wygant*, 476 U.S. at 313–16, 317–18 (Stevens, J., dissenting, voting to uphold plan as containing appropriate use of race-conscious classification and as procedurally adequate, distinguishing *Fullilove* plan as procedurally inadequate).

290. *See, e.g., id.* at 294–95 (White, J., concurring in judgment, arguing that layoffs are an impermissible burden to impose on innocent whites in order to benefit minorities who are not themselves the actual victims of discrimination); *Stotts*, 467 U.S. at 576–83 (majority opinion of White, J., holding that minority firefighters could not displace nonminority firefighters with greater seniority, and limiting affirmative action remedies to actual victims of discrimination).

291. Justice White voted to uphold the plans in *Fullilove*, 448 U.S. at 453 (opinion of Burger, C.J., joined by White & Powell, JJ.), and *United Jewish Orgs.*, 430 U.S. at 147 (opinion of White, J.). In constitutional cases, he voted to invalidate the plans in *Paradise*, 480 U.S. at 196 (White, J., dissenting), *Sheet Metal Workers*, 478 U.S. at 499 (White, J., dissenting, voting to invalidate plan on Title VII grounds), and *Wygant*, 476 U.S. at 294 (White, J., concurring in judgment). In Title VII cases, Justice White voted to invalidate the affirmative action plans in *Johnson v. Transportation Agency*, 480 U.S. at 657 (White, J., dissenting), *Firefighters v. Cleveland*, 478 U.S. at 531 (White, J., dissenting), and *Stotts*, 467 U.S. at 576–83 (majority opinion of White, J.,). The only plan not involving the federal government that Justice White voted to uphold was the preferential admissions plan in *Bakke*, 438 U.S. at 324 (Brennan, J., concurring in judgment in part and dissenting in part, joined by White, Marshall, & Blackmun, JJ.).

NOTES TO CHAPTER 3

1. *See* STONE ET AL., *supra* chapter 1, note 1, at ciii (table listing appointments of Chief Justice Rehnquist, and Justices O'Connor, Scalia, & Kennedy).

2. City of Richmond v. J.A. Croson Co., 488 U.S. 469 (1989).

3. *See id.* at 475 (majority opinion of O'Connor, J., joined by Rehnquist, White, Stevens, & Kennedy, JJ.); *id.* at 520 (Scalia, J., concurring in judgment).

4. *See id.* at 475–86, 498–508 (majority opinion of O'Connor, J., joined by Rehnquist, White, Stevens, & Kennedy, JJ.).

5. Metro Broadcasting v. FCC, 497 U.S. 547 (1990).

6. *See id.* at 551, 552 (majority opinion of Brennan, J., joined by White, Marshall, Blackmun, & Steven).

7. Although the Court did subsequently uphold the constitutionality of two redistricting plans in Hunt v. Cromartie, 119 S. Ct. 1545 (1999), and Lawyer v. Department of Justice, 117 S. Ct. 2186 (1997), it is difficult to view those plans as true affirmative action plans because they eliminated rather than added majority-minority voting districts. *See infra* chapter 5, note 246 and accompanying text (discussing *Hunt v. Cromartie* and *Lawyer*).

8. Northeastern Fla. Chapter of the Associated Gen. Contractors of Am. v. City of Jacksonville, 508 U.S. 656 (1993).

9. Adarand Constructors v. Pena, 515 U.S. 200 (1995).

10. *See id.* at 225–28 (overruling *Metro Broadcasting*).

11. The Voting Rights cases are discussed in chapter 4, and the Supreme Court actions on petitions for certiorari are discussed in chapter 3, part 5. Only two constitutional Voting Rights Act cases decided since *Metro Broadcasting* were arguably sympathetic to affirmative action, but it is difficult to view those as genuine affirmative action cases. *See supra* chapter 3, note 7.

12. City of Richmond v. J.A. Croson Co., 488 U.S. 469 (1989).

13. *See id.* at 475–86 (describing program).

14. *See id.* (describing procedural history).

15. *See id.* at 498–508 (majority opinion of O'Connor, J., joined by Rehnquist, White, Stevens, & Kennedy, JJ.).

16. *See id.* at 493–98 (opinion of O'Connor, J., joined by Rehnquist, White, & Kennedy, JJ.,). Justice Stevens did not believe that strict scrutiny was appropriate. *See id.* at 511 (Stevens, J., concurring in part and concurring in judgment).

17. *See id.* at 520. (Scalia, J., concurring in judgment). Justice Scalia did, however, state that he agreed with much of the majority opinion. *See id.*

18. *See id.* at 507–08. (opinion of O'Connor, J., joined by Rehnquist, White, & Kennedy, JJ.).

19. *See id.* at 520–28 (Scalia, J., concurring in judgment). Justice Scalia argued in favor of limiting race-conscious affirmative action to the elimination of the state's own maintenance of a racial classification. *See id.* Note that this is different from the more stringent view that racial classifications should be limited to the actual victims of discrimination—a view that was advanced and then apparently rejected in some of the Court's earlier cases involving Title VII. *Compare* Firefighters Local Union No. 1784 v. Stotts, 467 U.S. 561, 578–83 (1984) (Title VII remedies that override seniority must be limited to actual victims of discrimination) *with* Local 28, Sheet Metal Workers Int'l Ass'n v. EEOC, 478 U.S. 421, 482–83 (1986) (Justice Brennan stating that six members of Court agreed that both Title VII and equal protection clause permitted remedial racial classifications that benefited individuals who were not themselves actual victims of discrimination). Justice Scalia, however, has also expressed sympathy with the view that race-conscious remedies should be limited to

the actual victims of discrimination. *See* Johnson v. Transportation Agency, 480 U.S. 616, 666–68 (1987) (Scalia, J., dissenting). In addition, Justice Scalia favored overruling *Weber* because of its use of racial classifications to remedy racial imbalance. *See id.* at 672–77.

20. *See Croson*, 488 U.S. at 486–91 (opinion of O'Connor, J., joined by Rehnquist & White); *id.* at 520 (Scalia, J., concurring in judgment).

21. *See id.* at 511 n.1 (Stevens, J., concurring in part and concurring in judgment.)

22. *See id.* at 514–15 (minimizing importance of standard of review).

23. *See id.* at 518–20 (Kennedy, J., concurring in part and concurring in judgment).

24. *See id.* at 524–25 (Scalia, J., concurring in judgment). Although Justice Scalia believed that Congress possessed greater power by virtue of § 5 of the Fourteenth Amendment to remedy past discrimination than did the states, his acceptance of the *Fullilove* precedent was at best reluctant. *See id.* at 521–22.

25. *See id.* at 528 (Marshall, J., dissenting, joined by Brennan & Blackmun, JJ.).

26. *See id.* at 528–35, 539–48 (Marshall, J., dissenting, joined by Brennan & Blackmun, JJ.).

27. *See id.* at 535–51 (Richmond plan satisfied intermediate scrutiny).

28. *See id.* at 555–61 (finding irony in reading of Fourteenth Amendment that prohibited remedies for past discrimination).

29. *See id.* at 561–62 (Blackmun, J., dissenting, joined by Brennan, J.); *cf. id.* at 739 (Marshall, J., dissenting, joined by Brennan & Blackmun, JJ., emphasizing that Richmond was the capital of the Confederacy).

30. Metro Broadcasting v. FCC, 497 U.S. 547 (1990).

31. *See id.* at 552–63 (describing affirmative action plans).

32. *See id.* at 563 (Congress has special powers under § 5 of Fourteenth Amendment).

33. *See id.* at 564–65 (applying intermediate scrutiny, quoting Fullilove v. Klutznick, 448 U.S. 448, 519 (1980) (Marshall, J., concurring in judgment)).

34. *See id.* at 565 (citing and distinguishing *Croson*, 488 U.S. at 491 (opinion of O'Connor, J.)).

35. *See id.* at 566 (valid affirmative action plans not limited to providing remedy for past discrimination).

36. *See id.* at 566 (FCC plans advanced interest in promoting broadcast diversity).

37. *See id.* at 569. Justice Brennan relied upon a series of recent appropriations bills directed specifically at the issue of broadcast diversity and on extensive legislative history, including the legislative history of other related statutes. *See id.* at 572–79.

38. *See id.* at 579–83 (FCC plans did not rest on mere racial stereotypes).

39. *See id.* at 584–96 (FCC plans were narrowly tailored).

40. *See id.* at 596–600 (FCC plans did not impose impermissible burdens on nonminorities).

41. *See id.* at 599 (FCC plans did not constitute quotas or set-asides).

42. *See id.* at 601–02 (Stevens, J., concurring).

43. *See id.* at 601 (valid affirmative action plans should have goals that are clearly identified and unquestionably legitimate).

44. *See id.* at 601 (". . . the Court demonstrates that this case falls within the extremely narrow category of governmental decisions for which racial or ethnic heritage may provide a rational basis for differential treatment" [footnote omitted]).

45. *See id.* at 602 (O'Connor, J., dissenting, joined by Rehnquist, Scalia, & Kennedy, JJ.).

46. *See id.* at 602–06 (arguing that strict scrutiny is required to ensure that citizens are treated as individuals and not as mere members of a racial group).

47. *See id.* at 604–06 (arguing that federal and nonfederal affirmative action plans should be subject to same standard of review).

48. *See id.* at 606–09 (arguing that *Fullilove* was distinguishable).

49. *See id.* at 609–10 (arguing that reduced equal protection scrutiny was insupportable).

50. *See id.* at 610 (standard of review was not mere lawyers' quibble over words).

51. *See id.* at 610–17. Justice O'Connor also pointed out that the diversity rationale could result in discrimination *against* minorities if minority viewpoints were deemed to be overrepresented, thereby illustrating the difficulty inherent in distinguishing benign from malevolent racial classifications. *See id.* at 614–16.

52. *See id.* at 618–20 (arguing that FCC plans were not narrowly tailored).

53. *See id.* at 621–24 (arguing that FCC plans were both overinclusive and underinclusive).

54. *See id.* at 624–29. The FCC initially interpreted its enabling statute to preclude it from utilizing any racial or ethnic preferences in the award of broadcast licenses, and adopted a 1965 Policy Statement incorporating that interpretation. In 1973, however, the United States Court of Appeals for the District of Columbia rejected the agency's position on statutory grounds in *TV 9, Inc. v. FCC*, 495 F.2d 929 (D.C. Cir. 1973), assuming that diversity in station ownership would produce diversity in programming. The FCC then adopted a 1978 Policy Statement reflecting the D.C. Circuit's reading of the agency's statutory public interest obligation, and adopted the affirmative action plans at issue in *Metro Broadcasting*. Then, in the mid-1980s, the FCC responded to the increasingly restrictive affirmative action decisions issued by the Supreme Court by attempting to initiate an inquiry into the factual basis for the nexus between ownership and broadcast diversity that the D.C. Circuit had assumed to exist. Congress, however, passed a series of appropriations bills that precluded the FCC from conducting the contemplated investigation. *See Metro Broadcasting*, 497 U.S. at 576–79.

55. *See id.* at 630–31 (arguing that FCC plans were too burdensome on nonminorities).

56. Plessy v. Ferguson, 163 U.S. 537 (1896) (articulating separate-but-equal doctrine of constitutional law).

57. *See Metro Broadcasting,* 497 U.S. at 631–34 (Kennedy, J., dissenting, joined by Scalia, J.). Justice Kennedy believed that the FCC affirmative action plans could not properly be said to satisfy even the intermediate scrutiny that the majority purported to apply, thereby rendering the plans effectively subject to only minimal, reasonableness scrutiny. *See id.*

58. *See id.* at 632–35 (analogizing FCC plans to law of Third Reich and South Africa).

59. *See id.* at 635–38 (fearing racial stigmatization).

60. Northeastern Fla. Chapter of the Associated Gen. Contractors of Am. v. City of Jacksonville, 508 U.S. 656 (1993).

61. *See id.* at 658. "Minority" was defined to include individuals who were "black, Spanish-speaking, Oriental, Indian, Eskimo, Aleut, or handicapped." *See id.* These are roughly the same categories that Congress enumerated in the Public Works Employment Act of 1977 set-aside, which the Supreme Court upheld in *Fullilove. See supra* chapter 2, note 73 (listing minority categories upheld in *Fullilove*).

62. Not only the 10 percent minority set-aside concept but the specification of particular racial minority groups—including Aleuts, who are unlikely to be prevalent in Jacksonville—and the definition of minority corporate control that was utilized in the Jacksonville ordinance—including different percentages for publicly and privately owned businesses—were identical to those specified in the federal Public Works Employment Act of 1977, which the Supreme Court upheld in *Fullilove. See Fullilove,* 448 U.S. at 456–59. Because the law of affirmative action was very uncertain in 1984, when the Jacksonville ordinance was enacted, municipalities often copied the provisions of the federal statute that had been upheld in *Fullilove* in order to maximize the likelihood that their ordinances would also be found constitutional. *See, e.g.,* City of Richmond v. J.A. Croson Co., 488 U.S. 469, 477–80, 505–06 (1989) (discussing belief of city's legal counsel that plan would be constitutional under *Fullilove* decision); *id.* at 528–29 (Marshall, J., dissenting) (asserting that Richmond set-aside plan was patterned upon plan upheld in *Fullilove*).

63. *See Northeastern Fla.,* 508 U.S. at 660–61.

64. *See id.* at 660 (discussing district court invalidation of Jacksonville plan).

65. *See* Northeastern Fla. Chapter of the Associated Gen. Contractors of Am. v. City of Jacksonville, 951 F.2d 1217, 1218–19 (11th Cir. 1992).

66. Warth v. Seldin, 422 U.S. 490 (1975).

67. *See Northeastern Fla.,* 951 F.2d at 1219 (citing *Warth,* 422 U.S. 490 (1975)).

68. *See Warth*, 422 U.S. at 502–08.

69. Lujan v. Defenders of Wildlife, 504 U.S. 555 (1992).

70. Lujan v. National Wildlife Federation, 497 U.S. 871 (1990).

71. *See Lujan v. Defenders of Wildlife*, 504 U.S. at 555 (environmentalists with general, but not specific, future plans to view endangered species lack standing to enforce Endangered Species Act); *Lujan v. National Wildlife Federation*, 497 U.S. at 871 (recreational users of public lands lack standing to challenge general government decision to open public lands to increased mining, oil, and natural gas exploitation). *But cf.* United States v. Students Challenging Regulatory Agency Procedures (SCRAP), 412 U.S. 669 (1973) (case from earlier era granting standing for law students to maintain programmatic challenge to ICC rate increase alleged to have adverse environmental effects).

72. *See Lujan v. Defenders of Wildlife*, 504 U.S. at 562–78 (art. III injury requirement for standing not satisfied in absence of strong showing of specificity and redressability); *Lujan v. National Wildlife Federation*, 497 U.S. at 879–94 (general challenge to government programs not sufficiently particular, imminent, proximate, or redressable for standing)

73. *See Northeastern Fla.*, 508 U.S. at 663–68.

74. *See id.* at 668 (noting tension between *Warth* and line of cases on which standing was based in *Northeastern Fla.*).

75. *See id.* at 667–68 (distinguishing *Northeastern Fla.* from *Warth*).

76. *See id.* Justice Thomas also stated that standing had been denied in *Warth* because *Warth* did not involve any particular proposed construction project. *See id.* at 666–68. This turns out to be mistaken, however. *Warth* did involve at least one particular proposed construction project, which the Court simply disregarded after suggesting, without any basis in the record, that it might have become stale while the litigation was pending. *See Warth*, 422 U.S. at 514–17. Ironically, it is *Northeastern Fla.* that failed to involve any particular construction contract that had been denied the plaintiffs due to the challenged set-aside program. *See Northeastern Fla.*, 508 U.S. at 666–68. This point is developed more fully in Spann, *Color-Coded Standing*, supra chapter 1, note 1, at 1450 n.145, 1464 n.225 (1995), which argues that the Supreme Court's standing decisions are racially discriminatory when measured against the Supreme Court's own standards for discriminatory intent and discriminatory effect.

77. *See Northeastern Fla.*, 508 U.S. at 660–63 (rejecting claim that case had become moot).

78. *See id.* at 661–63 (modified program still contained racial preference).

79. *See id.* (applying voluntary cessation exception to mootness).

80. *See id.* at 669 (O'Connor, J., dissenting, joined by Blackmun, J.).

81. *See id.* at 673–78 (arguing that case was moot because voluntary cessation exception did not apply).

82. *See id.* at 669–75 (modified plan had not yet been implemented).

83. *See id.* at 660–61 (describing details and contingencies of modified plan).

84. *See* Abbott Laboratories v. Gardner, 387 U.S. 136, 148–56 (1967) (case not ripe for judicial review until legal issues become fit for review through elimination of factual contingencies). *Abbott Laboratories* also considered the hardship to the parties of withholding review as one of the factors that affected ripeness. *See id.* at 149–51. In *Northeastern Fla.*, it may be that little new hardship would result from delaying review until the legal issues were crystallized through further factual development because the modified affirmative action program precluded nonminority contractors from bidding on only 5–16 percent of the available construction contracts. *See Northeastern Fla.*, 508 U.S. at 660–61. This may not have significantly changed the status quo, under which those contractors had for the previous nine years been precluded form bidding on 10 percent of the available construction contracts. *See id.* at 658–59 (plan that Supreme Court reviewed in 1993 was originally enacted in 1984).

85. Adarand Constructors v. Pena, 515 U.S. 200 (1995).

86. The Small Business Act, Pub. L. No. 85-536, 72 Stat. 384 (codified as amended at 15 U.S.C. §§ 631–6201 (1994)).

87. The Surface Transportation and Uniform Relocation Assistance Act, Pub. L. No. 100-17, 100 Stat. 145 (codified as amended at 23 U.S.C. §§ 101–160 (1994)).

88. The Small Business Act stated that "[t]he contractor shall presume that socially and economically disadvantaged individuals include Black Americans, Hispanic Americans, Native Americans, Asian Pacific Americans, and other minorities, or any other individual found to be disadvantaged by the [Small Business] Administration pursuant to section 8(a) of the Small Business Act." *See Adarand*, 515 U.S. at 205 (quoting 15 U.S.C. §§ 637(d)(2), (3) (1994)). The Surface Transportation Act also adopted the Small Business Act presumption, and added a presumption that women were socially and economically disadvantaged. *See id.* at 208 (quoting § 106(c)(2)(B) of the act, 101 Stat. 146 (1987)).

89. *See id.* at 205–10 (1995) (describing operation of program in *Adarand*). The record did not indicate whether the Latino subcontractor was deemed disadvantaged because of the statutory presumption or because of direct evidence of social and economic disadvantage. *See id.* at 207–08, 238 (application of presumption unclear). Presumably, this is one of the issues that the district court was to resolve on remand. *See id.* at 238–39.

90. *See id.* at 210 (citing Adarand Constructors, Inc. v. Skinner, 790 F. Supp. 240 (D. Colo. 1992), *aff'd* 16 F.3d 1537, 1547 (10th Cir. 1995)).

91. *See id.* at 264–65 (Souter, J., dissenting) (describing issues considered by lower courts).

92. *See id.* at 202–03 (listing votes of justices). Justice Scalia joined Justice O'Connor's opinion "except insofar as it may be inconsistent with" his own concurrence. *See id.* at 239 (Scalia, J., concurring).

93. *See id.* at 210–12 (discussing standing, citing *Northeastern Fla.*, 508 U.S. at

666, 667). Although the record did not indicate whether the presumption had actually been applied in the *Adarand* case, *see supra* chapter 3, note 89, the Court did not discuss whether the plaintiff's standing was affected by this uncertainty. *See Adarand*, 515 U.S. at 210–12.

94. *See id.* at 213–18 (discussing equal protection component of Fifth Amendment due process clause). Unlike the Fourteenth Amendment, the Fifth Amendment does not contain an explicit equal protection clause. *Compare* U.S. CONST. amend. V *with* U.S. CONST. amend. XIV.

95. *See Adarand*, 515 U.S. at 218–23 (tracing precedents).

96. *See id.* at 223–24 (describing three principles).

97. *See id.* at 225–27 (overruling *Metro Broadcasting*).

98. *See id.* at 237 (arguably overruling *Fullilove*).

99. *See id.* at 227–28 (describing strict-scrutiny standard).

100. *See id.* at 231–36 (opinion of O'Connor, J., joined by Kennedy, J.) (discussing *stare decisis*). Justice O'Connor distinguished her vote not to overrule the right to abortion established by *Roe v. Wade*, 410 U.S. 113 (1973), in *Planned Parenthood of Southeastern Pa. v. Casey*, 505 U.S. 833 (1992), on the grounds that *Roe v. Wade* had generated two decades' worth of reliance. *See Adarand* 515 U.S. at 233 (distinguishing *Casey*).

101. *See id.* at 230–31 (denying inconsistency between *Croson* and *Adarand*).

102. *See id.* at 236 (quoting *Metro Broadcasting*, 497 U.S. at 610 (O'Connor, J., dissenting)) (standard of review not mere lawyers' quibble).

103. Korematsu v. United States, 323 U.S. 214 (1944).

104. *See Adarand*, 515 U.S. at 237 (quoting *Fullilove*, 448 U.S. at 519 (Marshall, J., concurring in judgment)) (strict scrutiny not fatal).

105. *See id.* at 237 (suggesting *Paradise* would survive strict scrutiny). Although the Supreme Court voted 5–4 to uphold the court-ordered affirmative action plan in *Paradise*, Justice O'Connor voted to invalidate it. *See Paradise*, 480 U.S. at 196–201 (O'Connor, J., dissenting).

106. *See id.* at 239 (remanding).

107. *See id.* at 239 (Scalia, J., concurring in part and concurring in judgment).

108. *See id.* at 239 (rejecting race-conscious remedies for past discrimination).

109. *See id.* at 240–41 (Thomas, J., concurring in part and concurring in judgment).

110. *See id.* (rejecting distinction between benign and invidious discrimination).

111. *See id.* at 242 (Stevens, J., dissenting, joined by Ginsburg, J.)

112. *See id.* at 242 (challenging majority conception of skepticism).

113. *See id.* at 243 (challenging majority conception of consistency). Justice Stevens argued that the government's motive in using a racial classification must surely be relevant to the majority's flexible standard of strict scrutiny, but he criticized the majority for using the "strict scrutiny" label for that standard because strict

scrutiny had previously been understood to mean fatal scrutiny. *See id.* at 243 n.1 (objecting to strict-scrutiny label).

114. *See id.* at 245 (noting difference between "No Trespassing" sign and welcome mat).

115. Washington v. Davis, 426 U.S. 229 (1976).

116. *See Adarand,* 515 U.S. at 246 (Stevens, J., dissenting) (distinction between benign and invidious discrimination is no more subtle than distinction between intentional discrimination and discriminatory effect).

117. *See id.* at 247 (majority standard makes it easier to remedy gender discrimination than racial discrimination).

118. *See id.* at 247–48 (majority decision to burden racial minorities different from majority decision to burden itself). In response to Justice Thomas's argument that affirmative action stigmatized racial minorities, Justice Stevens pointed out that the white plaintiff in *Adarand* did not have standing to make that argument, and that the minority beneficiaries of the *Adarand* affirmative action plan had not chosen to make that argument. He also emphasized that the stigmatization issue was one that could properly be left to the political branches because a legislature that was trying to benefit racial minorities could be expected to remedy affirmative action programs that did more harm than good. The fact that this was not true of legislative actions that were motivated by invidious intent provided yet another reason for distinguishing between benign and invidious racial classifications. *See id.* at 247–48 nn.5 & 6. Justice Stevens also noted that Justice Thomas's concern with the effect rather than the intent of a stigmatizing affirmative action program had a strong element of common sense, but was at odds with the Court's focus on intent under *Washington v. Davis,* 426 U.S. 229 (1976). *See Adarand,* 515 U.S. at 247 n.5.

119. *See id.* at 249–53 (challenging majority conception of congruence).

120. *See id.* at 249–55 (congressional affirmative action plans entitled to greater deference than noncongressional plans).

121. *See id.* at 255 (majority ignores purposeful incongruity in federal system).

122. *See id.* at 255–57 (majority opinion inconsistent with *stare decisis*).

123. *See id.* (*Adarand* upset settled expectations).

124. *See id.* at 257–58 (*Adarand* does not overrule prospective diversity holding of *Metro Broadcasting*).

125. *See id.* at 258 (*Adarand* does not overrule *Fullilove*). Justice Stevens also noted that Justice Burger's opinion in *Fullilove* stated that the federal statute there at issue would satisfy either intermediate or strict scrutiny. *See id.*

126. *See id.* at 259–64 (*Adarand* plan better able to survive strict scrutiny than *Fullilove* plan).

127. *See id.* at 264 (Souter, J., dissenting, joined by Ginsburg & Breyer, JJ.).

128. *See id.* at 264–65 (issue presented by *Adarand* concerned adequacy of findings of past discrimination). Cases like *Fullilove, Croson,* and *Metro Broadcasting* did not make clear the extent to which Congress could delegate its § 5 remedial powers

to federal agencies or to the states. The Supreme Court order granting certiorari did not specify the issues on which certiorari was granted. *See* Adarand Constructors v. Pena, 512 U.S. 1288 (1994) (granting certiorari).

129. *See Adarand*, 515 U.S. at 264–67 (Souter, J., dissenting) (*Fullilove* congressional findings control *Adarand*).

130. *See id.* at 268 (advocating reasonableness as unitary standard of scrutiny). In support of this proposition, Justice Souter cited *Cleburne v. Cleburne Living Center*, 473 U.S. 432, 451 (1985) (Stevens, J. concurring, joined by Burger, C.J.), a case in which the Supreme Court invalidated a municipal classification under the equal protection clause after applying a reasonableness standard of review.

131. *See id.* at 268–69 (*Adarand* does not reduce scope of congressional power under § 5 of Fourteenth Amendment).

132. *See id.* at 269–70 (Constitution permits remedies for continuing effects of past discrimination).

133. *See id.* at 271 (Ginsburg, J., dissenting, joined by Breyer, J.).

134. *See id.* (stressing areas of agreement in *Adarand* opinions).

135. *See id.* at 272–74 (discussing continuing discrimination).

136. *Id.* at 275 (quoting *id.* at 239 (Scalia, J., concurring in part and concurring in judgment)) (distinguishing between benign and invidious discrimination).

137. *See id.* at 276 (stressing need for careful scrutiny, which *Adarand* program would survive).

138. *See id.* at 271, 276 (concluding that there was no need for Supreme Court intervention in *Adarand*).

139. Podberesky v. Kirwan, 38 F.3d 147 (4th Cir. 1994), *cert. denied*, 514 U.S. 1128 (1995).

140. Hopwood v. Texas, 78 F.3d 932 (5th Cir. 1996), *cert. denied*, 518 U.S. 1033 (1996).

141. Taxman v. Piscataway Township Bd. of Educ., 91 F.3d 1547 (3d. Cir. 1996) (en banc), *cert. granted*, 117 S. Ct. 2506 (1997), *cert. dismissed*, 118 S. Ct. 595 (1997).

142. Coalition for Econ. Equity v. Wilson, 122 F.3d 692 (9th Cir.), *cert. denied*, 118 S. Ct. 397 (1997).

143. *See* FALLON ET AL., *supra* chapter 1, note 1, at 1698–99; STERN ET AL., *supra* chapter 1, note 1, at § 5.7 (7th ed. 1993) (both discussing significance of denials of certiorari).

144. Podberesky v. Kirwan, 38 F.3d 147 (4th Cir. 1994), *cert. denied*, 514 U.S. 1128 (1995).

145. *See* Podberesky v. Kirwan, 764 F. Supp. 364, 366–67 (D. Md. 1991) (discussing history of segregation at University of Maryland).

146. *See Podberesky*, 38 F.3d at 152 (stating facts of case).

147. *See Podberesky*, 764 F. Supp. 364 (D. Md. 1991) (opinion of Motz, J.). The district court held, *inter alia*, that the Banneker program did not violate the equal

protection clause of the Constitution, or the coterminous provisions of Title VI of the Civil Rights Act of 1964 providing for equality in federally funded educational programs. *See id.* at 371–77.

148. *See Podberesky,* 956 F.2d 52, 55–57 (4th Cir. 1992) (opinion of Restani, J., joined by Widener & Hamilton, JJ.) (rev'g and remanding 764 F. Supp. 364 (D. Md. 1991)).

149. *See Podberesky,* 838 F. Supp. 1075, 1083–99 (D. Md. 1993) (upholding program after remand).

150. *See Podberesky,* 38 F.3d at 161–62 (opinion by Widener, J., joined by Wilkins & Hamilton, JJ.) (4th Cir. injunction preventing continued use of racial restriction in Banneker scholarship program).

151. *See id.* at 152–53 (Banneker program did not survive strict scrutiny).

152. *See id.* (quoting City of Richmond v. J.A. Croson Co., 488 U.S. 469, 500 (1989), and citing Wygant v. Jackson Bd. of Educ. 476 U.S. 267, 277 (1986) (plurality opinion) [brackets in original; internal quotation marks omitted]). The *Croson* decision is discussed in chapter 3, part 1, and the *Wygant* decision is discussed in chapter 2, part 4, section i.

153. *See id.* at 153–54 (district court showed too much deference to university findings).

154. *See id.* at 154 (rejecting adequacy of poor reputation in black community).

155. *See id.* at 154–55 (citing *Croson,* 488 U.S. at 498; *Wygant,* 476 U.S. at 276) (hostile climate resulted from general societal discrimination for which race-conscious remedies are impermissible).

156. *See id.* at 155–57 (factual disputes made grant of summary judgment improper).

157. *See id.* at 157–58 (Banneker program was not narrowly tailored remedy).

158. *See id.* at 158 (discussing high achievers).

159. *See id.* at 158–59 (discussing nonresidents).

160. *See id.* at 159–60 (discussing underrepresentation).

161. *See id.* at 159–60 (citing *Wygant,* 476 U.S. at 276, for proposition that race-conscious remedies cannot be used to provide role models).

162. *See id.* at 160 (citing *Croson,* 488 U.S. at 498, for proposition that race-conscious remedies cannot be used to promote racial balance).

163. *See id.* at 160–61 (discussing race-neutral alternatives).

164. *See id.* at 161–62 (directing summary judgment for plaintiff).

165. *See* Greene v. Podberesky, 63 U.S.L.W. 3793 (U.S. Mar. 30, 1995) (No. 94-1621) (*cert. denied,* 514 U.S. 1128 (1995)); Kirwan v. Podberesky, 63 U.S.L.W. 3779 (U.S. Mar. 29, 1995) (No. 94-1620) (*cert. denied,* 514 U.S. 1128 (1995)).

166. *See Greene,* 63 U.S.L.W. at 3793; *Kirwan,* 63 U.S.L.W. at 3779 (citing Regents of the Univ. of Cal. v. Bakke, 438 U.S. 265 (1978)) (describing arguments raised in petitions for certiorari). *Bakke* is discussed in chapter 2, part 2.

167. *See* Kirwan v. Podberesky, and Greene v. Podberesky, 514 U.S. 1128 (1995) (denying certiorari).

168. Hopwood v. Texas, 78 F.3d 932 (5th Cir. 1996), *cert. denied*, 518 U.S. 1033 (1996).

169. *See Hopwood*, 78 F.3d at 935 (prohibiting consideration of race).

170. Regents of the Univ. of Cal. v. Bakke, 438 U.S. 265, 311–15 (1978) (opinion of Powell, J., asserting that diversity is factor that university may properly consider).

171. *See Hopwood*, 78 F.3d at 941–48 (prohibiting consideration of race even to promote student diversity).

172. *See id.* at 934–38 (stating facts of case).

173. *See id.* at 938. The plaintiffs also claimed that the Texas affirmative action program violated Title VI of the Civil Rights Act of 1964, which prohibits discrimination in schools receiving federal funds. *See id.*

174. *See id.* at 938–39 (describing district court opinion); *see also* Hopwood v. Texas, 861 F. Supp. 551 (W.D. Tex. 1994) (district court opinion).

175. *See Hopwood*, 78 F.3d at 934–35 (reversal and remand by 5th Circuit); *id.* at 962 (Wiener, J., concurring specially).

176. *See id.* at 939–41 (analyzing district court's application of strict scrutiny).

177. *See id.* at 941–44 (discussing Justice Powell's opinion in *Bakke*).

178. *Id.* at 944 (student diversity is not a compelling interest).

179. *See id.* at 944–45 (citing Adarand Constructors v. Pena, 515 U.S. 200, 225–29 (1995)); *id.* at 240 (Thomas, J., concurring in part and concurring in judgment); City of Richmond v. J.A. Croson Co., 488 U.S. 469, 493 (plurality opinion) (1989). *Adarand* is discussed in chapter 3, part 4, and *Croson* is discussed in chapter 3, part 1.

180. *Id.* at 945–46 (race cannot be considered even as one of a number of factors).

181. *See id.* at 947–48 (race cannot be used as proxy for diversity factors).

182. *See id.* at 949–51 (citing *Wygant*, 476 U.S. at 274–77 (plurality opinion), and *Croson*, 488 U.S. at 499, 505, for proposition that racial classifications could not be used to remedy general societal discrimination).

183. *See id.* at 950–52 (law school was appropriate unit for past-discrimination analysis).

184. *See id.* at 952 (citing Podberesky v. Kirwan, 38 F.3d 147, 152–54 (4th Cir. 1994), *cert. denied*, 514 U.S. 1128 (1995)). *Podberesky* is discussed in chapter 3, part 5, section i.

185. *See id.* at 952–53 (perceptions of racial hostility were products of general societal discrimination).

186. *See id.* at 953 (law school program did not address perceptions of hostility in minority community).

187. *See id.* at 953–54 (program could not be justified as remedy for low minority student attainment).

188. *See id.* at 954–55 (educational context did not permit broader affirmative action remedies).

189. *See id.* at 955 (no need to consider narrow tailoring).

190. *See id.* at 955–59 (discussing relief).

191. *See id.* at 959–61 (denying intervention).

192. *See id.* at 962 (Wiener, J., concurring specially).

193. *See id.* (summarizing special concurrence of Judge Wiener).

194. *See id.* at 963–64 (arguing that Supreme Court never held that diversity could not be compelling state interest).

195. *See id.* at 964–65 (discussing *Adarand,* 515 U.S. at 237–38).

196. *See id.* at 967–68 (arguing that decision should be narrow).

197. *See id.* at 965–66 (concluding that program was not narrowly tailored).

198. *See id.* at 966 n.24 (discussing Catch-22).

199. *See id.* at 966–67 (discussing remedy).

200. *See* Texas v. Hopwood, 64 U.S.L.W. 3845 (U.S. Apr. 30, 1996) (No. 95-1773) (*cert. filed*). Two black student organizations supporting the Texas program also filed a petition for certiorari, seeking review of the Fifth Circuit denial of their motion to intervene. *See* Thurgood Marshall Legal Society v. Hopwood, 64 U.S.L.W. 3013 (U.S. May 13, 1996) (No. 95-1845).

201. *See Hopwood,* 64 U.S.L.W. at 3845 (describing petition for certiorari).

202. *See id.* (listing signers of petition).

203. *See* Texas v. Hopwood, 518 U.S. 1033 (1996) (denying certiorari); *see also* Thurgood Marshall Legal Society v. Hopwood, 518 U.S. 1033 (1996) (denying certiorari to review denial of motion to intervene filed by black student organizations).

204. *See id.* at 1033–34 (statement of Ginsburg, J., joined by Souter, J., accompanying denial of certiorari).

205. Taxman v. Piscataway Township Bd. of Educ., 91 F.3d 1547 (3d. Cir. 1996) (en banc), *cert. granted,* 117 S. Ct. 2506 (1997), *cert. dismissed,* 118 S. Ct. 595 (1997). The case will be referred to hereinafter as *Piscataway.*

206. *See Piscataway,* 91 F.3d at 1549–50 (describing lower court outcomes).

207. *See, e.g., Affirmative Action Settlement; Excerpts, supra* chapter 1, note 1; Bearak, *supra* chapter 1, note 1; Biskupic, *supra* chapter 1, note 1; Goodnough, *supra* chapter 1, note 1; Greenhouse, *Affirmative Action Settlement: The Overview, supra* chapter 1, note 1; Holmes, *supra* chapter 1, note 1.

208. *See Piscataway,* 118 S. Ct. at 595 (dismissing writ of certiorari after settlement, pursuant to Supreme Court Rule 46.1).

209. *Piscataway,* 91 F.3d at 1550 (quoting affirmative action policy).

210. *See id.* at 1550–51, 1563 (describing affirmative action policy, and noting stipulation that policy was not remedial).

211. *See id.* at 1551–52 (describing facts of case).

212. *See id.* at 1552 (describing district court decision); *see also* United States v. Board of Educ. of the Township of Piscataway, 832 F. Supp. 836, 851 (D.N.J. 1993) (district court opinion granting summary judgment for United States and Taxman).

213. *See Piscataway*, 91 F.3d at 1552 (United States changed sides and withdrew from appeal).

214. *See id.* The three-judge panel consisted of Chief Judge Sloviter and Judges Mansmann and McKee. The en banc judges were Chief Judge Sloviter and Judges Becker, Stapleton, Mansmann, Greenberg, Scirica, Cowen, Nygaard, Alito, Roth, Lewis, McKee, and Sarokin. *See id.* at 1547 (listing argument dates); *id.* at 1549 (listing judges).

215. *See id.* at 1549 (en banc opinion of Mansmann, J.)

216. *See id.* at 1547 (listing opinions).

217. *See id.* at 1553–55 (citing United Steelworkers of Am. v. Weber, 443 U.S. 193, 206–08 (1979), for proposition that Title VII permits some voluntary affirmative action in employment context). *Weber* is discussed in chapter 2, part 5, section i.

218. *See id.* at 1555–56 (citing Johnson v. Transportation Agency, 480 U.S. 616 (1987), for proposition that Title VII permits affirmative action designed to correct for racial imbalance without terminating existing employees). *Johnson v. Transportation Agency* is discussed in chapter 2, part 5, section iv.

219. *See id.* at 1556–58. (Title VII requires affirmative action plans to have remedial purpose).

220. *See id.* at 1558–59 (neither Title VII nor 1972 amendments recognize diversity goal as justification for racial classification).

221. *See id.* at 1559–60 (Title VII liability not limited to standards for equal protection liability).

222. *See id.* at 1560–61 (citing, for proposition that diversity goal does not satisfy equal protection standards, Wygant v. Jackson Bd. of Educ., 476 U.S. 267, 270–78 (1986) (O'Connor, J., concurring in part and concurring in judgment)); *id.* at 294–95 (White, J., concurring in judgment); *id.* at 306 (Marshall, J., dissenting); *id.* at 267–68 (Stevens, J., dissenting). *Wygant* is discussed in chapter 2, part 4, section i.

223. *See id.* at 1561 (citing cases arising in educational context that Third Circuit deemed remedial cases).

224. *See id.* at 1561 (discussing Regents of the Univ. of Cal. v. Bakke, 438 U.S. 265 (1978), and Metro Broadcasting v. FCC, 497 U.S. 547 (1990)). *Bakke* is discussed in chapter 2, part 2, and *Metro Broadcasting* is discussed in chapter 3, part 2.

225. *See id.* at 1561–62, 1562 n.13 (distinguishing *Bakke*, and citing Hopwood v. Texas, 78 F.3d 932, 944 (5th Cir. 1996), *cert. denied*, 518 U.S. 1033 (1996)).

226. *See id.* at 1562–63 (arguing that diversity holding of *Metro Broadcasting*

had been overruled by Adarand Constructors v. Pena, 515 U.S. 200 (1995)). *Adarand* is discussed in chapter 3, part 4.

227. *See id.* at 1563 (discussing *Wygant,* 476 U.S. at 286 (O'Connor, J., concurring), and *Johnson v. Transportation Agency,* 480 U.S. at 647 (Stevens, J., concurring)).

228. *See id.* at 1563–64 (*Piscataway* policy could not satisfy first prong of *Weber* test).

229. *See id.* at 1564 (citing *Weber,* 443 U.S. at 208, for proposition that affirmative action plan cannot "unnecessarily trammel" nonminority interests).

230. *See id.* (finding "utter lack of definition and structure").

231. *See id.* (citing *Weber,* 443 U.S. at 208, and *Johnson v. Transportation Agency,* 480 U.S. at 639–40, as plans with limited remedies).

232. *See id.* at 1564–65 (layoffs imposed impermissible burden under second prong of *Weber* test).

233. *See id.* at 1565 (*Piscataway* policy also violated New Jersey statute).

234. *See id.* at 1565–66 (awarding full back pay).

235. *See id.* at 1566–67 (awarding prejudgment interest but denying punitive damages).

236. *See id.* at 1567 (desirability of diversity not dispositive).

237. *See id.* at 1567 (Stapleton, J., concurring).

238. *See id.* at 1567 (Sloviter, J., dissenting, joined by Lewis & McKee, JJ.).

239. *See id.* at 1567 (arguing that *Piscataway* policy was not really divisive affirmative action policy).

240. *See id.* at 1567–68 (arguing that *Piscataway* case presented clear legal issue under Title VII).

241. *See id.* at 1568–69 (stressing that both teachers were equal in all relevant respects except for their contribution to diversity).

242. *See id.* at 1570–71 (citing *Weber,* 443 U.S. at 208, and *Johnson v. Transportation Agency,* 480 U.S. at 642 (Stevens, J., concurring and characterizing majority opinion) for proposition that those cases did not establish outer boundaries of permissible affirmative action under Title VII).

243. *See id.* at 1571 (Title VII permits efforts to eliminate causes of continuing or future discrimination).

244. *See id.* at 1571–74 (citing legislative history of 1972 amendments to Title VII, and language from several Supreme Court opinions).

245. *See id.* at 1572 (finding it ironic to read Title VII as precluding diversity considerations).

246. *See id.* at 1572–73 (arguing that court of appeals should not reject Supreme Court endorsements of diversity).

247. *See id.* at 1574 (quoting *Johnson v. Transportation Agency,* 480 U.S. at 638).

248. *See id.* (noting similarities to *Johnson v. Transportation Agency,* 480 U.S. at 638).

249. *See id.* at 1574–75 (distinguishing *Wygant,* 476 U.S. at 282, 284).

250. *See id.* at 1575 (discussing *Weber* and *Johnson v. Transportation Agency*).

251. *See id.* (*Piscataway* policy was quite limited).

252. *See id.* at 1575–76 (noting irony in reading Title VII as precluding efforts to eradicate discrimination).

253. *See id.* at 1576 (arguing that Title VII *permits* diversity to be considered).

254. *See id.* at 1576 n.1 (damages should be limited to 50 percent of back pay).

255. *See id.* at 1576 (Scirica, J., dissenting, joined by Sloviter, J.).

256. *See id.* at 1576–77 (citing *Bakke,* 438 U.S. at 265, in support of claim that Title VII permits consideration of diversity in educational context).

257. *See id.* at 1577 (Lewis, J., dissenting, joined by McKee, J.).

258. *See id.* at 1577–78 (arguing that Title VII does not require recourse to coin toss rather than business judgment).

259. *See id.* at 1578 (McKee, J., dissenting, joined by Sloviter & Lewis, JJ.).

260. *See id.* at 1578–79 (arguing that majority's reading of Title VII undermines integration objectives of Title VII).

261. *See* Piscataway Township Bd. of Educ. v. Taxman, 65 U.S.L.W. 3375 (U.S. Oct. 31, 1996) (No. 96-679) (*cert. filed*).

262. *See id.* (describing petition for certiorari).

263. *See* Piscataway Township Bd. of Educ. v. Taxman, 117 S. Ct. 763 (1997) (inviting solicitor general to file brief).

264. *See supra,* text accompanying chapter 3, note 213 (describing change of position by United States); *see also* Biskupic, *supra* Chapter One, note 1, at A8 (same); Greenhouse, *Affirmative Action Settlement: The Overview, supra* chapter 1, note 1, at B4 (same).

265. *See Employment Discrimination—Race: Clinton Administration Switches Stance on Use of Race as Factor in Teacher's Layoff,* supra chapter 1, note 1, at 2134; Greenhouse, *Affirmative Action Settlement: The Overview, supra* chapter 1, note 1, at B4.

266. *See* Piscataway Township Bd. of Educ. v. Taxman, 117 S. Ct. 2506 (1997) (*cert. granted*).

267. *See Employment Discrimination, supra,* chapter 1, note 1, at 2134; Greenhouse, *Affirmative Action Settlement: The Overview, supra* chapter 1, note 1, at B4.

268. *See Affirmative Action Settlement; Excerpts, supra* chapter 1, note 1; Bearak, *supra* chapter 1, note 1; Biskupic, *supra* chapter 1, note 1; Goodnough, *supra* chapter 1, note 1; Greenhouse, *Affirmative Action Settlement: The Overview, supra* chapter 1, note 1; Holmes, *supra* chapter 1, note 1.

269. *See* Piscataway Township Bd. of Educ. v. Taxman, 118 S. Ct. 595 (1997) (dismissing writ of certiorari pursuant to Supreme Court Rule 46.1, which provides for dismissal after settlement).

270. Coalition for Econ. Equity v. Wilson, 122 F.3d 692 (9th Cir.), *cert. denied,* 118 S. Ct. 397 (1997). A more thorough discussion of the Proposition 209 litigation is contained in Spann, *Proposition 209, supra* chapter 1, note 1, at 187.

271. *See Coalition for Econ. Equity,* 122 F.3d at 696, 697.

272. *See id.* (Court of appeals opinion quoting California Ballot Pamphlet prepared by nonpartisan California Legislative Analyst's Office to describe Proposition 209 to California voters).

273. *See, e.g.,* William Claiborne, *Affirmative Action Ban Is Upheld; California Proposition Constitutionally Valid, U.S. Appeals Panel Says,* WASH. POST, Apr. 9, 1997, at A1 (commenting on effect that Proposition 209 might have on anti-affirmative action proposals under consideration by Congress and by other states); Ellis Cose, *After Affirmative Action: Proposition 209 May Become Law, But Californians Are In No Rush To End All Racial Preferences,* NEWSWEEK, Nov. 11, 1996, at 43 (same); Maura Dolan, *U.S. Panel Upholds Prop. 209 Affirmative Action: Three 9th Circuit Justices Rule That Measure To Eliminate Preferences For Women And Minorities In College Admissions And Government Employment Is Constitutional; Opponents Will Appeal, But Some Analysts Believe They Face An Uphill Battle,* L.A. TIMES, Apr. 9, 1997, at A1 (same); *Not Over Till It's Over,* THE ECONOMIST NEWSPAPER, Nov. 16, 1996, at 27 (same); Tim Golden, *Federal Appeals Court Upholds California's Ban On Preferences,* N.Y. TIMES, Apr. 9, 1997, at A4 (same); Lemann, *supra* chapter 1, note 1, at 36 (same).

Proposition 209 has also attracted scholarly attention. *See, e.g.,* Vikram D. Amar & Evan H. Caminker, *Equal Protection, Unequal Political Burdens, and the CCRI,* 23 HASTINGS CONST. L.Q. 1019 (1996); Robert S. Chang, *Reverse Racism!: Affirmative Action, the Family, and the Dream That Is America,* 23 HASTINGS CONST. L.Q. 1115 (1996); Erwin Chemerinsky, *The Impact of the Proposed California Civil Rights Initiative,* 23 HASTINGS CONST. L.Q. 999 (1996); Neil Gotanda, *Failure of the Color-Blind Vision: Race, Ethnicity and the California Civil Rights Initiative,* 23 HASTINGS CONST. L.Q. 1135 (1996); Neil Gotanda et al., *Legal Implications of Proposition 209—The California Civil Rights Initiative,* 24 W. ST. U. L. REV. 1 (1996); Pamela A. Lewis, *Debunking the Myth That Subdivision (c) of the California Civil Rights Initiative Lessens the Standard of Judicial Review of Sex Classifications in California,* 23 HASTINGS CONST. L.Q. 1153 (1996); Yxta Maya Murray, *Merit-Teaching,* 23 HASTINGS CONST. L.Q. 1073 (1996); David Benjamin Oppenheimer, *Understanding Affirmative Action,* 23 HASTINGS CONST. L.Q. 921 (1996); Catherine A. Rogers & David L. Faigman, *"And to the Republic for Which It Stands": Guaranteeing a Republican Form of Government,* 23 HASTINGS CONST. L.Q. 1057 (1996); Spann, *Proposition 209, supra* chapter 1, note 1; Winkfield F. Twyman, Jr., *A Critique of the California Civil Rights Initiative,* 14 NAT'L BLACK L.J. 181 (1997); Volokh, *supra* chapter 1, note 1.

274. *See Coalition for Econ. Equity,* 122 F.3d at 697 (9th Circuit opinion describing lawsuit); Coalition for Econ. Equity v. Wilson, 946 F. Supp. 1480, 1488–91, 1520–21 (N.D. Cal. 1996) (district court opinion describing lawsuit).

275. *See Coalition for Econ. Equity,* 946 F. Supp. at 1493–99 (finding irreparable injury).

276. *See id.* at 1499–1510 (finding likelihood of success on merits).

277. *See id.* at 1499, 1504–08 (Proposition 209 singled out race and gender for imposition of special political burdens).

278. *See id.* (proponents of affirmative action were relegated to statewide initiative process).

279. Hunter v. Erickson, 393 U.S. 385 (1969).

280. Washington v. Seattle School District No. 1, 458 U.S. 457 (1982).

281. *See Hunter,* 393 U.S. at 390–93 (invalidating anti-fair housing amendment).

282. *See Seattle,* 458 U.S. at 462–63, 470–82 (invalidating antibusing initiative).

283. *See Coalition for Econ. Equity,* 946 F. Supp. at 1499–1506 (Proposition 209 was race and gender classification).

284. *See id.* at 1506–10 (Proposition 209 could not survive strict scrutiny).

285. *See id.* at 1511–17 (finding likelihood of preemption under Title VII).

286. *See Coalition for Econ. Equity,* 122 F.3d at 710–11 (O'Scannlain, J., joined by Leavy & Kleinfeld, JJ.).

287. *See id.* at 699–700 (proper to consider challenge to Proposition 209 prior to state court interpretation).

288. *See id.* at 700–01 (discussing standard of review).

289. *See id.* at 701 (no doubt that Proposition 209 was constitutional under "conventional" equal protection analysis).

290. *See id.* at 701–02 (Proposition 209 merely restated equal protection prohibition on race and gender discrimination).

291. *See id.* at 702 (rejecting claim that Proposition 209 was race and gender classification).

292. *See id.* (special treatment of race and gender classifications was warranted under equal protection clause).

293. *See id.* (finding no conventional equal protection violation "as matter of law and logic").

294. *See id.* at 703–09 (Proposition 209 did not entail a "political structure" equal protection violation).

295. *See id.* at 704–05 (expressing skepticism about whether majority could violate its own equal protection rights).

296. *See id.* at 705–07 (Proposition 209 was race and gender neutral).

297. Crawford v. Board of Educ. of the City of Los Angeles, 458 U.S. 527 (1982).

298. *See Coalition for Econ. Equity,* 122 F.3d at 705–06 (noting that *Crawford* upheld constitutionality of antibusing amendment).

299. *See id.* at 706–07 (Proposition 209 was not controlled by *Hunter* and *Seattle*).

300. *See id.* at 707–09 (Proposition 209 did not restructure political process in discriminatory manner).

301. *See id.* at 709 (Fourteenth Amendment does not require preferences).

302. *See id.* (district court erroneously found likelihood of equal protection violation).

303. *See id.* at 709–10 (Title VII did not preempt Proposition 209).

304. *See id.* at 710–11 (Proposition 209 did not violate Constitution).

305. *See id.* at 711 (denying rehearing en banc).

306. *See id.* at 711 (Schroeder, J., dissenting from denial of rehearing en banc, joined by Pregerson, Norris, & Tashima, JJ.).

307. *See id.* (offering reasons for granting rehearing en banc).

308. *See id.* at 712 (arguing that prospective restructuring of political process violated *Seattle*, 458 U.S. at 483).

309. *See id.* (Proposition 209 prohibited remedies that were permissible under equal protection clause).

310. *See id.* (district court decision should have been affirmed to check majoritarian excesses).

311. *See id.* at 712 (opinion of Norris, J., joined by Schroeder, Pregerson, & Tashima, JJ.).

312. *See id.* (quoting *Seattle*, 458 U.S. at 470, and *Hunter*, 393 U.S. at 395 (Harlan, J., concurring), for proposition that Proposition 209 was an impermissible racial classification).

313. *See id.* at 712–13 (Proposition 209 permitted race and gender interests from securing political change at levels of political process open to other special interests).

314. *See id.* at 713–14 (panel improperly injected its own subjective preferences into equal protection clause).

315. *See id.* at 715 (issue was not whether Constitution required affirmative action).

316. *See id.* (fact that Proposition 209 disadvantaged minorities at every level of political process did not make Proposition 209 neutral).

317. *See id.* at 716 (rejecting claim that Proposition 209 did not offend Constitution because women and minorities adversely affected by Proposition 209 collectively constituted majority).

318. *See id.* (*Crawford* did not govern Proposition 209, which prohibited future affirmative action programs).

319. *See id.* at 716–17 (panel disregarded precedent in name of conservative judicial activism).

320. *See id.* at 717 (opinion of Hawkins, J.).

321. *See id.* at 717–18 (lower courts should follow precedent rather than predict Supreme Court abandonment).

322. *See* Coalition for Econ. Equity v. Wilson, 122 F.3d 718, 719–20 (9th Cir. 1997) (9th Circuit denial of stay).

323. *See* Coalition for Econ. Equity v. Wilson, 118 S. Ct. 17 (1997) (Supreme Court denial of emergency stay).

324. *See* Coalition for Econ. Equity v. Wilson, 66 U.S.L.W. 3181 (U.S. Aug. 29, 1997) (No. 97-369) (*cert. filed*).

325. *See id.* at 3181–82 (describing petition for certiorari).

326. *See* Coalition for Econ. Equity v. Wilson, 118 S. Ct. 397 (1997) (*cert. denied*).

NOTES TO CHAPTER 4

1. *See* The Voting Rights Act of 1965, Pub. L. No. 89-110, 79 Stat. 445 (codified as amended at 42 U.S.C. § 1973c (1994)).

2. *See* U.S. CONST. amend. XV.

3. *See* Shaw v. Reno, 509 U.S. 630, 641, 649 (1993) (articulating discriminatory purpose *and* effect test). Justice O'Connor's opinion does not explain why the discriminatory intent test of *Washington v. Davis* should be supplemented by an effects test in the voting rights context. *See id.* However, Justice White's dissenting opinion in *Shaw v. Reno* suggests that an effects test is appropriate in the voting rights context because the legislature is *always* aware of racial considerations when it makes districting decisions. The effects test, therefore, helps to distinguish permissible from impermissible consideration of race. *See id.* at 659–64 (White, J., dissenting); *cf.* Palmer v. Thompson, 403 U.S. 217, 224–26 (1971) (pre-*Washington v. Davis* case emphasizing race-neutral effect rather than intent in upholding decision to close municipal swimming pool rather than comply with court-ordered integration); *see generally* STONE ET AL. *supra* chapter 1, note 1, at 616–22 (discussing discriminatory intent and effect under *Washington v. Davis* test). *See also infra*, text accompanying chapter 4, notes 171–181 (discussing *Shaw v. Reno* consideration of effects test in voting rights context).

4. *See* U.S. CONST. amend. XV, § 2 (authorizing Congress to enforce Fifteenth Amendment through appropriate legislation).

5. *See* Shaw v. Reno, 509 U.S. at 640–41 (discussing § 2 vote dilution, citing Thornburg v. Gingles, 478 U.S. 30 (1986)).

6. Thornburg v. Gingles, 478 U.S. 30 (1986).

7. *See id.* at 50–51 (stating three-pronged test for vote dilution).

8. *See* Lopez v. Monterey County, 119 S. Ct. 693, 697 (1999) (discussing § 5 preclearance requirement); *Shaw v. Reno,* 509 U.S. at 634–35 (same).

9. For useful introductions to the conceptual problems posed by the interaction of the equal protection clause and the Voting Rights Act see Samuel Issacharoff and Pamela S. Karlan, *Standing and Misunderstanding in Voting Rights Law,* 111 HARV. L. REV. 2276 (1998), and Samuel Issacharoff and Richard H. Pildes, *Politics As*

Markets: Partisan Lockups of the Democratic Process, 50 STAN. L. REV. 643, 700–08 (1998). For a more thorough discussion, see the secondary authorities cited in those articles.

10. *See* The Voting Rights Act of 1965, Pub. L. No. 89-110, 79 Stat. 445 (codified as amended at 42 U.S.C. § 1973c (1994)).

11. Voinovich v. Quilter, 507 U.S. 146 (1993).

12. Growe v. Emison, 507 U.S. 25 (1993).

13. *See Voinovich*, 507 U.S. at 153–58 (rejecting "packing" claim).

14. *See Growe*, 507 U.S. at 37–42 (rejecting fragmentation claim).

15. Holder v. Hall, 512 U.S. 874 (1994).

16. Johnson v. De Grandy, 512 U.S. 997 (1994).

17. *See Holder*, 512 U.S. at 884–85 (rejecting challenge to single- or multimember nature of scheme).

18. *See De Grandy*, 512 U.S. at 1005–06 (rejecting vote-dilution claim in context of population proportionality).

19. Young v. Fordice, 520 U.S. 273 (1997).

20. Reno v. Bossier Parish School Bd., 520 U.S. 471 (1997).

21. City of Monroe v. United States, 118 S. Ct. 400 (1997) (per curiam).

22. *See Young*, 520 U.S. at 281–90 (requiring preclearance for minor discretionary voting changes).

23. *See Bossier Parish*, 520 U.S. at 477 (§ 5 preclearance is governed by nonretrogression, rather than vote-dilution, standard).

24. *See City of Monroe*, 118 S. Ct. at 400–02 (finding constructive preclearance under § 5).

25. Lopez v. Monterey County, 119 S. Ct. 693 (1999).

26. *See id.* at 696 (preclearance required for changes mandated by noncovered state).

27. Voinovich v. Quilter, 507 U.S. 146 (1993).

28. *See id.* at 149–52, 157–58 (rejecting "influence dilution" claim).

29. *See id.* at 150, 160 (discussing political support for plan).

30. *See id.* at 149–52 (district court invalidation of plan). The race of the plaintiffs is disclosed in the Appellees' Brief. *See id.*, Appellees' Brief, at 1.

31. *See id.* at 151–52 (district court finding constitutional violation of one-person, one-vote principle).

32. *See id.* at 152–57 (state legislature has broader discretion than federal court in formulating districting plans).

33. *See id.* at 157–58 (white crossover voting precluded finding of vote dilution).

34. *See id.* at 157 (declining to address Fourteenth Amendment validity of majority-minority districts). Justice O'Connor also expressly declined to consider whether the Fifteenth Amendment itself precluded race-conscious redistricting, *see id.* at 160, and rejected the district court's holding that large discrepancies in district

size could not be justified for Fourteenth Amendment purposes by the desire to preserve political subdivision boundaries. *See id.* at 160–62.

35. Growe v. Emison, 507 U.S. 25 (1993).

36. *See id.* at 37–42 (finding failure to satisfy political cohesiveness requirement of *Gingles*).

37. *See id.* at 32–37 (district court should have abstained). Justice Scalia preferred to use the term "deferral" to describe the type of abstention under which a federal court does not dismiss a claim but, rather, delays adjudication pending state-court clarification of an unclear issue of state law pursuant to *Railroad Commission of Texas v. Pullman Co.,* 312 U.S. 496 (1941).

38. *See Growe,* 507 U.S. at 37–42 (district court plan was not required by Voting Rights Act).

39. *See id.* at 27–31, 37–39 (stating facts).

40. *See id.* at 32–37 (requiring abstention). Justice Scalia would have preferred for the federal court to adjudicate the validity of the state-court plan under the Voting Rights Act once the state-court plan had become final. *See id.* at 34–37.

41. *See id.* at 37–42 (citing Thornburg v. Gingles, 478 U.S. 30 (1986) for proposition that racially cohesive minority bloc voting was required as prerequisite to creation of supermajority-minority district).

42. Holder v. Hall, 512 U.S. 874 (1994).

43. *See id.* at 874–85 (§ 2 does not permit challenge to single- or multimember character of governmental system).

44. *See id.* at 876–79 (stating facts).

45. *See id.* at 877–79 (describing lower court decisions).

46. *See id.* at 875–76 (opinion of Kennedy, J., joined by Rehnquist & O'Connor, JJ.).

47. *See id.* at 881 (vote-dilution claim requires deviation from some ascertainable baseline).

48. *See id.* at 881–82 (rejecting claim that five-member commission constituted baseline).

49. *See id.* at 882–85 (opinion of Kennedy, J., joined by Rehnquist, J., distinguishing between § 2 and § 5 challenges). Justice Kennedy distanced himself from the Supreme Court's earlier decision in Chisom v. Roemer, 501 U.S. 380, 401–02 (1991), which suggested that coverage under §§ 2 and 5 was the same. *See Holder,* 512 U.S. at 882–83 (discussing *Chisom*).

50. *See id.* at 885–91 (O'Connor, J., concurring in part and concurring in judgment, finding absence of baseline).

51. *See id.* at 886–87 (§ 2 and § 5 were conterminous, and § 2 could encompass vote-dilution challenge to size of governing body).

52. *See id.* at 889–91 (finding inability to select alternative size for governing body).

53. *See id.* at 891 (Thomas, J., concurring in judgment, joined by Scalia, J., arguing that § 2 did not encompass vote-dilution claims).

54. *See id.* at 891–93, 912–14 (arguing that § 2 challenges should be limited to restrictions on access to ballot).

55. *See id.* at 905–08 (arguing that § 2 claims were unworkable and that they segregated voters by race).

56. *See id.* at 896–912 (arguing that federal judges should not make political theory).

57. *See id.* at 915–16 (emphasis in original). It is unlikely that Justice Thomas intended his plain-meaning argument to be taken literally. Certainly, a state decision to give each white voter two votes while giving each minority voter only one vote would be a "standard, practice or procedure with respect to voting." If a state intentionally achieves the same result by manipulating voting district lines or governing-body sizes, it is not clear why such manipulations should be any less a "standard, practice or procedure with respect to voting." Indeed, Justice Thomas's interpretation of the statutory text as "a sort of catch-all provision . . . phrased with an eye to eliminating the possibility of evasion," *see id.* at 917 (footnote omitted), relies on statutory context and legislative intent in a way that would seem to be precluded by the plain-meaning interpretation that Justice Thomas purports to conduct. It also seems to argue for including vote-dilution techniques within the scope of the statute in order to prevent the precise evasions that Justice Thomas reads the statute to prohibit. Justice Thomas also concedes that the statute defines "voting" to include "'. . . all actions necessary to make a vote *effective,*'" *id.* at 919 (quoting § 14(c)(1) of the act, 42 U.S.C. § 1973*l*(c)(1) (1994) (emphasis in original)), and that "an 'effective' vote is . . . one that has been cast and fairly counted," *see id.* (citing Allen v. State Bd. of Elections, 393 U.S. 544, 590 (1969) (Harlan, J., concurring in part and dissenting in part)), but he makes no effort to explain why vote dilution does not undermine the requirement that a minority vote be "fairly counted." *See id.*

58. *See id.* at 931–36 (objecting to use of legislative history).

59. *See id.* at 936–46 (arguing that *stare decisis* did not require reading § 2 to encompass vote-dilution challenges).

60. *See id.* at 946 (Blackmun, J., dissenting, joined by Stevens, Souter, & Ginsburg, JJ., arguing that § 2 prohibition on vote dilution encompassed challenges to size of governing body).

61. *See id.* at 947 (quoting Allen v. State Bd. of Elections, 393 U.S. 544, 567 (1969), and citing Chisom v. Roemer, 501 U.S. 380, 403 (1991) (quoting South Carolina v. Katzenbach, 388 U.S. 301, 315 (1966)).

62. *See id.* at 947 (relying on Supreme Court precedents interpreting § 2 to encompass wide variety of election and voting practices).

63. *See id.* at 947–49 (relying on Supreme Court precedents interpreting § 5 to encompass size of governing body).

64. *See id.* at 949 (arguing that 1982 amendments ratified expansive coverage of Voting Rights Act).

65. *See id.* at 951 (arguing that five-member county commission constituted reasonable alternative benchmark).

66. *See id.* at 952–54 (arguing that reasonableness requirement would eliminate specious challenges).

67. *See id.* at 955. In this regard, Justice Blackmun noted that Bleckley County had had a history of official segregation in all aspects of local government prior to the enactment of the federal civil rights laws, and that even today, Bleckley County had only one polling place for the entire county—which was located in an all-white civic club. *See id.* at 954 n.6.

68. *See id.* at 956 (Ginsburg, J., dissenting).

69. *See id.* at 956. Justice Ginsburg cited the tension in Title VII between the goal of prohibiting race and gender discrimination on the one hand, and the goal of using race- and gender-conscious affirmative action remedies to eliminate the lasting effects of past discrimination on the other. *See id.* at 956–57.

70. *See id.* at 957 (arguing that job of federal judiciary was to accommodate competing policy objectives).

71. *See id.* (Stevens, J., dissenting, joined by Blackmun, Souter, & Ginsburg, JJ.).

72. *See id.* at 957–63 (Voting Rights Act amendments had ratified use of act to redress vote-dilution claims).

73. *See id.* at 963–66 (arguing that *stare decisis* precluded Justice Thomas's claim that § 2 did not encompass vote-dilution challenges).

74. Johnson v. De Grandy, 512 U.S. 997 (1994).

75. *See id.* at 1000–04. The black and Latino plaintiffs also made Fourteenth and Fifteenth Amendment claims, but those claims were voluntarily dismissed. *See id.* at 1002 n.3.

76. *See id.* at 998, 1024. Although Justices Thomas and Scalia labeled their opinion a dissent, they too would have invalidated the remedial reapportionment plan adopted by the district court—on the grounds that there was no violation of the Voting Rights Act. *See id.* at 1031–32 (Thomas, J., dissenting, joined by Scalia, J.).

77. *See id.* at 999 (majority opinion of Souter, J., joined by Rehnquist, Blackmun, Stevens, O'Connor, Ginsburg, & Kennedy, JJ.).

78. *See id.* at 1005–16 (finding lack of minority vote dilution).

79. *See id.* at 1014 n.11 (proportionality was relevant, although not dispositive).

80. *See id.* at 1015–17 (district court error was to assume that § 2 required maximum number of majority-minority districts possible).

81. *See id.* at 1017–21 (population proportionality does not preclude liability for subtle forms of voting discrimination).

82. *See id.* at 1025 (O'Connor, J., concurring, stressing importance of considering totality of circumstances).

83. *See id.* at 1026 (Kennedy, J., concurring in part and concurring in judgment).

84. *See id.* at 1030–31 (arguing that population proportionality was not relevant to vote-dilution claims, and consideration of population proportionality was inconsistent with goal of race neutrality).

85. *See id.* at 1031 (Thomas, J., dissenting, joined by Scalia, J., reiterating view that § 2 did not encompass vote-dilution claims).

86. Young v. Fordice, 520 U.S. 273 (1997).

87. *See id.* at 281–91 (requiring preclearance under § 5).

88. *See id.* at 275–76 (discussing National Voter Registration Act).

89. *See id.* at 276–81 (describing factual context). Although only the private plaintiffs appealed the three-judge district court decision to the Supreme Court, the United States appeared before the Supreme Court as an *amicus curiae. See id.* at 280.

90. *See id.* at 282 (provisional plan not part of baseline).

91. *See id.* at 284 (citing cases requiring preclearance for minor policy changes and changes designed to comply with Voting Rights Act).

92. *See id.* at 285 (preclearance required regardless of who is favored or disfavored).

93. *See id.* at 285–86 (discussing discretion).

94. *See id.* at 286–90 (rejecting effectiveness of provisional approval).

95. *See id.* at 290–91 (§ 5 preclearance requirement must be applied in context).

96. *See id.* at 291 (enjoining use of plan prior to preclearance).

97. Reno v. Bossier Parish School Bd., 520 U.S. 471 (1997).

98. *See id.* at 472–73, 476–85 (actual retrogression, and not mere vote dilution, required for denial of § 5 preclearance).

99. *See id.* at 486–90 (vote dilution relevant to retrogressive intent inquiry).

100. *See id.* at 474–76 (discussing facts).

101. *See id.* at 472, 476–85 (affirming district court).

102. *See id.* at 473 (listing votes of justices)

103. *See id.* at 476–77 (citing Holder v. Hall, 512 U.S. 874, 883 (1994) (plurality opinion)).

104. *See id.* at 478 (citing City of Rome v. United States, 446 U.S. 156, 183 n.18 (1980) for proposition that state bears burden of proof).

105. *See id.* at 477 (quoting Beer v. United States, 425 U.S. 130, 141 (1976) for proposition that § 5 requires retrogression).

106. *See id.* at 478–80 (requiring decrease in minority voting strength).

107. *See id.* at 479–80 (citing Thornburg v. Gingles, 478 U.S. 30, 50–51 (1986)).

108. *See id.* at 481–82 (federalism concerns indicate that § 2 violation does not establish § 5 violation).

109. *See id.* at 481–83 (§ 2 effects test broader than constitutional prohibition).

110. *See id.* at 483–85 (Justice Department regulation not authorized by Voting Rights Act).

111. *See id.* at 485 (rejecting economy and equity arguments).

112. *See id.* at 486–90 (§ 2 dilutive intent relevant to § 5 retrogressive intent).

113. *See id.* at 485 (reserving question of other issues that might be relevant to § 5)

114. *See id.* at 490 (Thomas J., concurring). The views of Justice Thomas in *Holder v. Hall* are described in the text accompanying chapter 4, notes 53–59.

115. *See id.* (§ 2 problems would be exacerbated in § 5 inquiries).

116. *See id.* at 490–92 (discussing indeterminacy inherent in concept of vote dilution).

117. *See id.* at 492–93 (arguing against deference to Justice Department regulations). The views of Justice O'Connor are discussed in the text accompanying chapter 4, note 110.

118. *See id.* (arguing against attorney general interference with district court independence).

119. *See id.* at 493 (Breyer, J., concurring in part and concurring in judgment, joined by Ginsburg, J.)

120. *See id.* at 493–95 (discussing issue expressly reserved in Justice O'Connor's majority opinion). Justice O'Connor's reservation of this issue is discussed in the text accompanying chapter 1, note 113.

121. *See id.* at 495–97 (arguing that § 5 encompassed unconstitutional intent, as illustrated by Shaw v. Hunt, 517 U.S. 899, 911–13 (1996) and Miller v. Johnson, 515 U.S. 900, 927–28 (1995)).

122. *See id.* at 497 (Stevens, J., dissenting in part and concurring in part, joined by Souter, J.)

123. *See id.* at 497, 507–09 (concurring in remand but dissenting from majority's statement of governing standard).

124. *See id.* at 497–500 (discussing § 2 discrimination).

125. *See id.* at 501–03 (arguing that § 5 preclearance was intended to enhance federal protections).

126. *See id.* at 504–07 & n.9 (discussing text, precedents, and legislative history).

127. *See id.* at 507 (arguing that § 5 intent inquiry encompasses more than mere intent to retrogress).

128. *See* Bossier Parish School Bd. v. Reno, 7 F. Supp. 2d 29 (D.D.C. 1998) (three-judge court), *probable jurisdiction noted,* 119 S. Ct. 899 (1999) *set for reargument,* 67 U.S.L.W. 3783 (U.S. June 24, 1999) (Nos. 98-405 & 98-406).

129. City of Monroe v. United States, 118 S. Ct. 400 (1997).

130. *See id.* at 400–01 (discussing facts of case).

131. *See id.* at 405 (Breyer, J. dissenting, discussing adverse effect of majority-vote requirement on minority voting strength).

132. *See id.* at 400 (per curiam opinion, joined by all but Scalia, Souter, & Breyer, JJ.).

133. *See id.* at 401 (precleared 1968 default rule governed).

134. *See id.* at 401–02 (quoting City of Rome v. United States, 446 U.S. 156, 169 n.6 (1980) [brackets in original; internal quotation marks omitted]).

135. *See id.* at 402 (Scalia, J., concurring in judgment).

136. *See id.* at 402–03 (attorney general notice adequate for finding of preclearance).

137. *See id.* at 403 (Souter, J., dissenting, joined by Breyer, J.).

138. *See id.* at 403–04 (quoting *City of Rome*, 446 U.S. at 169–70 n.6 [internal quotation marks omitted]).

139. *See id.* at 404–05 (attorney general lacked sufficient notice for finding of preclearance).

140. *See id.* at 405 (Breyer, J., dissenting, joined by Souter, J.).

141. *See id.* at 405 (discussing similarities between *City of Rome* and *City of Monroe*).

142. *See id.* at 405–06 (*City of Rome* governed *City of Monroe*).

143. *See id.* at 406–07 (attorney general would not have intended to approve voting change).

144. *See id.* at 407 (attorney general gave facial preclearance but not as-applied preclearance).

145. *See id.* at 407–08 (ambiguities should be resolved against submitting jurisdiction).

146. Lopez v. Monterey County, 119 S. Ct. 693 (1999).

147. *See id.* at 696 (preclearance required for changes mandated by noncovered jurisdiction).

148. *See id.* at 696–99 (describing changes in judicial election districts).

149. *See id.* at 699 (discussing prior Supreme Court decision in Lopez v. Monterey County, 519 U.S. 9 (1996), reversing interim election order).

150. *See Lopez*, 119 S. Ct. at 700 (discussing district court dismissal on remand and subsequent Supreme Court reversal).

151. *See id.* at 696 (majority opinion of O'Connor, J., joined by Stevens, Scalia, Souter, Ginsburg, & Breyer, JJ.).

152. *See id.* at 700–02 (citing United Jewish Orgs. v. Carey, 430 U.S. 144 (1977), for proposition that "partially covered" states must comply with § 5).

153. *See id.* at 703–04 (federalism does not preclude applying preclearance requirement to noncovered states).

154. *See id.* at 703–05 (exercise of independent discretion not required to trigger preclearance requirement).

155. *See id.* at 705 (Kennedy, J., concurring in judgment, joined by Rehnquist, C.J.).

156. *See id.* at 705–06 (arguing that Court should not reach question of whether exercise of discretion is required to trigger § 5).

157. *See id.* at 706 (Thomas, J., dissenting).

158. *See id.* at 706–08 (arguing that § 5 preclearance requirement is limited to policy decisions made by perpetrators of voting discrimination).

159. *See id.* at 708–10 (arguing that § 5 should be read to avoid federalism problems).

160. Shaw v. Reno, 509 U.S. 630 (1993), is discussed in part 2 of this chapter.

161. United Jewish Orgs. v. Carey, 430 U.S. 144 (1977).

162. *United Jewish Orgs.* is discussed in chapter 2, part 1, section ii.

163. Shaw v. Reno, 509 U.S. 630 (1993).

164. *See id.* at 657 (applying strict equal protection scrutiny to voter reapportionment plan).

165. *Croson* and *Metro Broadcasting* are discussed in chapter 3, parts 1 and 2 respectively.

166. *See Shaw v. Reno,* 509 U.S. at 633–39 (stating facts of case).

167. *See id.* at 641–42 (quoting Plessy v. Ferguson, 163 U.S. 537, 559 (1986) (Harlan, J., dissenting) for proposition that Constitution should be color-blind).

168. *See id.* at 641–49. Justice O'Connor emphasized the unusual shape of the voting district that was at issue in *Shaw v. Reno,* stating that "redistricting legislation that is so bizarre on its face that it is 'unexplainable on grounds other than race,' . . . demands the same close scrutiny that we give other state laws that classify citizens by race. *See id.* at 644 (quoting Arlington Heights v. Metropolitan Housing Development Corp., 429 U.S. 252, 266 (1977)).

169. *See id.* at 646 (emphasis in original) (permitting *awareness* of race).

170. *See id.* at 647 (racial gerrymandering reinforces racial stereotypes).

171. The other vote-dilution discrimination cases that Justice O'Connor cited were Rogers v. Lodge, 458 U.S. 613 (1982) (challenge to vote dilution in at-large system of representation); Mobile v. Bolden, 446 U.S. 55 (1980) (same); White v. Regester, 412 U.S. 755 (1973) (challenge to vote dilution in multimember districts); Whitcomb v. Chavis, 403 U.S. 124 (1971) (same). *See Shaw v. Reno,* 509 U.S. at 649.

172. *See Shaw v. Reno,* 509 U.S. at 649–50 (distinguishing between vote dilution and classification of voters by race).

173. United Jewish Orgs. v. Carey, 430 U.S. 144 (1977). *United Jewish Orgs.* is discussed in chapter 2, part 1, section ii.

174. *See Shaw v. Reno,* 509 U.S. at 651–52 (distinguishing *United Jewish Orgs.* as case that did not involve bizarrely shaped voting district).

175. *See id.* at 53–58 (benign plans subject to strict scrutiny to ensure that they are really benign).

176. *See id.* at 657 (declining to reach certain constitutional questions).

177. *See id.* at 659 (White, J., dissenting, joined by Blackmun & Stevens, JJ.).

178. *See id.* at 659 (arguing that it was not plausible to conclude that white voters had chosen to violate their own equal protection rights). Justice White also stressed that it was not until adoption of the revised reapportionment plan that North Carolina had sent its first black representatives to Congress since Reconstruction. *See id.*

179. *See id.* at 659–64 (arguing that inevitable race consciousness in reapportionment decisions was not enough to establish equal protection violation).

180. *See id.* at 661 (quoting White v. Regester, 412 U.S. 755, 766 (1973)) (arguing that discriminatory effect was required to establish equal protection violation).

181. *See id.* at 661–62 (quoting Whitcomb v. Chavis, 403 U.S. 124, 154–55 (1971)) (arguing that, in order to establish equal protection violation, whites would have to possess less opportunity than racial minorities to participate in political process).

182. *See id.* at 667–70 (arguing that *United Jewish Orgs.* was controlling).

183. *See id.* at 670–74 (arguing that odd shape of voting district is inconsequential).

184. *See id.* at 674–75 (compliance with Voting Rights Act is compelling state interest).

185. *See id.* at 676 (Blackmun, J., dissenting, objecting to creation of new cause of action for racial gerrymandering).

186. *See id.* at 676–79 (Stevens, J., dissenting, asserting three objections to majority opinion).

187. *See id* at 678 n.3 (citing Thornburg v. Gingles, 478 U.S. 30, 50–51 (1986)) (arguing that Justice O'Connor's views about racial stereotyping are inconsistent with requirements for establishing vote-dilution claim under Voting Rights Act).

188. *See id.* at 679–82 (Souter, J., dissenting, arguing that race consciousness was inevitable in redistricting).

189. *See id.* at 682–85 (arguing that strict scrutiny should be triggered only by substantial reduction in white voting strength).

190. *See id.* at 685–87 (arguing that shape of voting district does not offend Constitution).

191. United States v. Hays, 515 U.S. 737 (1995).

192. *See id.* at 739–42 (stating facts of case).

193. *See id.* at 741, 749 (discussing procedural history of case).

194. *See id.* at 742 (discussing remand).

195. *See id.* at 742 (quoting FW/PBS, Inc. v. Dallas, 493 U.S. 215, 230–31 (1990) (brackets in original; citations omitted in original)) (discussing obligation to consider issue of standing).

196. *See id.* at 742–46 (jurisdictional prohibition on adjudication of generalized grievances precludes finding standing for all voters in state).

197. *See id.* at 744–45 (discussing representational injuries on district residents inflicted by racial gerrymandering).

198. *See id.* at 745–46 (mere legislative awareness of race does not injure voters).

199. *See id.* at 745–47 (mere racial composition of district does not violate Constitution).

200. *See id.* at 746–47 (standing requires direct, personal injury).

201. Powers v. Ohio, 499 U.S. 400 (1991).

202. *See Hays*, 515 U.S. at 746–47 (distinguishing *Powers v. Ohio*).

203. *See id.* at 747 (vote dilution not required for standing).

204. *See id.* (Ginsburg, J., concurring in judgment).

205. *See id.* at 750 (Breyer, J., concurring, joined by Souter, J.).

206. *See id.* at 750–52 (Stevens, J., concurring in judgment, finding no injury because there was no vote dilution).

207. Note that on the same day that *Hays* was decided, the Supreme Court invalidated a similar affirmative action redistricting plan on the merits in Miller v. Johnson, 515 U.S. 900 (1995), and summarily affirmed a lower court decision upholding a similar affirmative action redistricting plan on the merits in DeWitt v. Wilson, 515 U.S. 1170 (1995), *aff'g* DeWitt v. Wilson, 856 F. Supp. 1409 (E.D. Cal. 1994) (three-judge court). *Miller* and *DeWitt* are discussed in chapter 4, parts 4 & 5, respectively.

208. Miller v. Johnson, 515 U.S. 900 (1995).

209. *See id.* at 904 (citing *Adarand* for strict-scrutiny standard).

210. *See id.* at 905–10 (stating facts of case).

211. *See id.* at 902 (listing votes of justices).

212. *See id.* at 909 (upholding standing of plaintiffs).

213. *See id.* at 910–11 (bizarre shape not necessary for constitutional violation).

214. *See id.* at 911 (quoting *Shaw v. Reno*, 509 U.S. at 652) (distinguishing between vote-dilution claim and racial gerrymandering claim).

215. *See id.* (quoting Mobil v. Bolden, 446 U.S. 55, 66 (1980)) (describing vote-dilution claim).

216. *See id.* at 910–12 (describing racial gerrymandering claim).

217. *See id.* at 912 (quoting *Shaw v. Reno*, 509 U.S. at 647) (states may not segregate voters in voting districts).

218. *See id.* (quoting *Shaw v. Reno*, 509 U.S. at 657) (remedial classifications pose risk of balkanization).

219. *See id.* at 913–14 (bizarre shape of district is relevant to motive, but is not required for constitutional violation).

220. *See id.* at 914–15 (quoting *Shaw v. Reno*, 509 U.S. at 652) (distinguishing *United Jewish Orgs.* as vote-dilution case).

221. *See id.* (*United Jewish Orgs.* not controlling to the extent that it prescribes anything less than strict scrutiny).

222. *See id.* at 916–17 (articulating "predominant factor" test).

223. *See id.* at 915–20 (affirming district court finding of racial motivation).

224. *See id.* at 920 (race cannot be considered shared community of interests without engaging in impermissible stereotyping).

225. *See id.* (strict scrutiny applies to Georgia redistricting plan).

226. *See id.* at 920 (articulating strict-scrutiny test).

227. *Id.* (quoting *Shaw v. Reno,* 509 U.S. at 656).

228. *See id.* at 922 (compliance with attorney general's preclearance requirement of maximizing majority-minority districts does not constitute compelling interest).

229. 5 U.S. (1 Cranch) 137, 177 (1803) ("It is emphatically the province and duty of the judicial department to say what the law is.").

230. *See Miller,* 515 U.S. at 923 (strict scrutiny precludes judicial deference to executive interpretation of Voting Rights Act).

231. *See id.* (Voting Rights Act did not require third majority-minority district).

232. *See id.* at 923–28 (attorney general's interpretation of § 5 poses constitutional difficulties that Congress did not intend).

233. *See id.* at 928 (O'Connor, J., concurring, favoring high threshold requirement for equal protection violation).

234. *See id.* at 928–29 (asserting that constitutionality of existing districts is not thrown into doubt).

235. *See id.* at 929 (*Shaw v. Reno* was intended to focus on extreme instances of gerrymandering).

236. *See id.* (Stevens, J., dissenting, arguing that plaintiffs lacked standing).

237. *See id.* at 929–31 (discussing majority's distinction of racial gerrymandering from vote dilution).

238. *See id.* at 930 (quoting *id.* at 912 (majority opinion)) (finding inconsistency in majority's view of representational harm and majority's aversion to racial stereotyping).

239. *See id.* at 931–32 (distinguishing between inclusion and exclusion of racial minorities).

240. Allen v. Wright, 468 U.S. 737 (1984).

241. *See Miller,* 515 U.S. at 932 (arguing that it has become easier to perpetuate racial bias than to promote integration).

242. *See id.* at 933 (differential treatment of racial groups and other groups constitutes invidious discrimination).

243. *See id.* at 934 (Ginsburg, J., dissenting, joined by Stevens & Breyer, JJ., joined in part by Souter, J.).

244. *See id.* at 934–38 (enumerating points of agreement among all justices).

245. *See id.* at 939–40 (arguing that *Shaw v. Reno* focused on shape of voting district).

246. *See id.* at 940–44 (arguing that *Miller* record did not show bizarre shape or disregard of traditional districting principles).

247. *See id.* at 943 (arguing that Georgia legislature did not merely acquiesce in attorney general's policy of maximizing majority-minority districts).

248. *See id.* at 944 (arguing that Georgia plan recognized shared political interests of black population).

249. *See id.* at 946 n.11 (arguing that *United Jewish Orgs.* controlled *Miller*).

250. *See id.* at 946–47 (districting is inherently about groups rather than individual merit).

251. *See id.* at 947–48 (Ginsburg, J., dissenting, joined by Stevens & Breyer, JJ., distinguishing between plans that enhance and dilute minority voting strength).

252. *See id.* at 949 (Ginsburg, J., dissenting, joined by Stevens, Souter, & Breyer, JJ., cautioning against enlargement of judicial role in districting process).

253. DeWitt v. Wilson, 515 U.S. 1170 (1995).

254. *See id.*, *aff'g* DeWitt v. Wilson, 856 F. Supp. 1409 (E.D. Cal. 1994) (three-judge court). Although the Supreme Court summarily affirmed the district court decision on the redistricting issues, the Court dismissed the appeal with respect to term-limit challenges that were also raised by the plaintiffs. *See DeWitt*, 515 U.S. at 1170; *see also* DeWitt v. Wilson, 63 U.S.L.W. 3201 (Sept. 27, 1994) (enumerating questions presented in jurisdictional statement).

255. *See DeWitt*, 515 U.S. at 1170 (summary affirmance).

256. Unlike denials of certiorari, which technically have no precedential value, *see supra* chapter 1, note 143 and accompanying text, summary affirmances constitute decisions on the merits. As such, they are necessarily entitled to some precedential value. However, it is now generally conceded by both the Supreme Court and commentators that summary affirmances have less precedential value than decisions rendered after full briefing and argument. *See* Edelman v. Jordan, 415 U.S. 651, 670–71 (1974); FALLON ET AL., *supra* chapter 1, note 1, at 647–49; STERN ET AL., *supra* chapter 1, note 1, at §§ 4.28 & 4.29 (all discussing significance of summary affirmance); *see also* Bush v. Vera, 517 U.S. 952, 996 (1996) (Kennedy, J., concurring, noting that Supreme Court summary affirmances do not endorse lower court reasoning); Fusari v. Steinberg, 419 U.S. 379, 391 (1975) (Burger, C.J., concurring) ("When we summarily affirm, without opinion, the judgment of a three-judge District Court we affirm the judgment but not necessarily the reasoning by which it was reached." [footnote omitted]).

257. *See Bush*, 517 U.S. at 958 (opinion of O'Connor, J., citing *DeWitt* for proposition that strict scrutiny did not apply to intentional creation of compact majority-minority district).

258. *See DeWitt*, 856 F. Supp. at 1410 (discussing facts of case, citing Wilson v. Eu, 823 P.2d 545 (Cal. 1992) (approving redistricting plan)).

259. *See DeWitt*, 856 F. Supp. at 1410–11 (discussing facts).

260. *See Wilson*, 823 P.2d at 549–50 (discussing effort to maximize minority participation). The opinion does not state how many majority-minority districts the plan created. *See id.*

261. *See DeWitt*, 856 F. Supp at 1413–14 (discussing challenge to plan). The plaintiffs also challenged the constitutionality of California statutory provisions imposing term limits on political candidates, but neither the district court nor the Supreme Court resolved that claim on the merits. *See id.* at 1410; *see also DeWitt*, 515 U.S. at 1170.

262. *See DeWitt*, 856 F. Supp. at 1410, 1412, 1415 (upholding plan).

263. Miller v. Johnson, 515 U.S. 900 (1995).

264. Shaw v. Hunt, 517 U.S. 899 (1996).

265. Bush v. Vera, 517 U.S. 952 (1996).

266. *See DeWitt*, 515 U.S. at 1170 (summary affirmance).

267. *See DeWitt*, 856 F. Supp. at 1411–15 (distinguishing *Shaw v. Reno*).

268. *See id.* at 1413 (quoting *Shaw v. Reno*, 509 U.S. at 641).

269. *See id.* (California plan did not fit within narrow holding of *Shaw v. Reno*).

270. *See id.* (quoting *Shaw v. Reno*, 509 U.S. at 649).

271. *See DeWitt*, 856 F. Supp. at 1413–14 (citing United Jewish Orgs. v. Carey, 430 U.S. 144, 168 (1977)).

272. *See DeWitt*, 856 F. Supp. at 1414–15 (finding no constitutional violation).

273. *See id.* at 1415 (discussing need for deference to states and compliance with applicable level of scrutiny).

274. *See DeWitt*, 515 U.S. at 1170 (summary affirmance).

275. *See supra* text accompanying chapter 4, notes 255 & 256 (discussing precedential effect of summary affirmance).

276. *See Bush*, 517 U.S. at 1003–05 (Stevens, J., dissenting) (compliance with Voting Rights Act satisfies strict scrutiny); *id.* at 1008–09 (race-conscious districting is not alone sufficient to trigger strict scrutiny); *id.* at 1014–32 (challenged district did not have sufficiently bizarre shape and race did not predominate over traditional districting principles); *id.* at 1034–35 (federalism requires deference to primary role of state in making reapportionment decisions); *id.* at 1045–50, 1066–70 (Souter, J., dissenting) (federalism permits states to use traditional districting principles that recognize communities of shared interests including racial interests); *id.* at 1065 (compliance with Voting Rights Act satisfies strict scrutiny, and Voting Rights Act is not itself unconstitutional); *Shaw v. Hunt*, 517 U.S. at 930–39 (Stevens, J., dissenting) (race did not predominate over traditional districting principles); *id.* at 940–45 (compliance with Voting Rights Act satisfies strict scrutiny); *id.* at 946–51 (federalism requires deference to primary role of state in making reapportionment decisions); *Miller*, 515 U.S. at 940–44 (Ginsburg, J., dissenting) (challenged district did not have bizarre shape and race did not predominate over traditional districting principles); *id.* at 945–48 (*United Jewish Orgs.* authorizes

race-conscious districting); *Shaw v. Reno*, 509 U.S. 674–75 (White, J., dissenting) (compliance with Voting Rights Act satisfies strict scrutiny).

277. *Shaw v. Reno*, 509 U.S. 630 (1993), is discussed above, in part 2 of this chapter.

278. Shaw v. Hunt, 517 U.S. 899 (1996).

279. *See id.* at 902 (North Carolina redistricting plan could not survive strict scrutiny).

280. *See id.* at 901–03 (discussing facts).

281. *See id.* at 900–01 (listing votes of justices).

282. *See id.* at 904 (finding standing only for district residents).

283. *See id.* (citing *Shaw v. Reno*, 509 U.S. at 657–58, and *Adarand*, 515 U.S. at 200) (even benign consideration of race is constitutionally suspect).

284. *See id.* at 906 (race was predominant factor).

285. *See id.* (traditional districting principles had been subordinated to race).

286. *See id.* at 908 (citing *Miller*, 515 U.S. at 920, articulation of strict-scrutiny test).

287. *See id.* Justice Rehnquist also rejected three interests asserted by Justice Stevens in his dissenting opinion, emphasizing that only an actual legislative purpose—not a speculative one—could constitute a compelling state interest. *See id.* at n.4.

288. *See id.* at 909 (requiring high degree of specificity for past discrimination).

289. *See id.* at 910 (desire to remedy past discrimination was not actual motive).

290. *See id.* at 911 (leaving open question of whether compliance with Voting Rights Act constituted compelling state interest).

291. *See id.* at 911–13 (§ 5 preclearance standard would have been satisfied by single majority-minority district).

292. *See id.* at 909, 914 (discussing state interest in complying with § 2).

293. *See id.* at 914; *Gingles,* 478 U.S. at 50–51. The *Gingles* requirements are discussed above, in the text accompanying chapter 4, notes 6 & 7.

294. *See Shaw v. Hunt*, 517 U.S. at 916 (challenged district lacked geographically compact minority population).

295. *See id.* at 916–17 (discussing state argument that remedial majority-minority district could be created anywhere in state).

296. *See id.* at 916–18 (remedial majority-minority districts must be in area where vote dilution occurs).

297. *See id.* at 918 (Stevens, J., dissenting, joined in part by Ginsburg & Breyer, JJ., distinguishing between efforts to benefit and to oppress minorities).

298. *See id.* at 918–21 (Stevens, J., dissenting) (arguing that *Shaw v. Reno* cause of action was misguided).

299. *See id.* at 929–51 (Stevens, J., dissenting, joined in part by Ginsburg & Breyer, JJ., arguing that strict scrutiny should not be applied, but if it were, the challenged plan satisfied strict scrutiny).

300. *See id.* at 918–21 (Stevens, J., dissenting, arguing that racial gerrymandering claims can be used to mask political gerrymandering objections).

301. *See id.* at 921–22 (challengers were complaining of racial integration rather than racial segregation).

302. Reynolds v. Sims, 377 U.S. 533, 561 (1964).

303. Palmer v. Thompson, 403 U.S. 217, 225 (1971).

304. *See Shaw v. Hunt*, 517 U.S. at 923 (citing *Reynolds v. Sims* and *Palmer v. Thompson*). Justice Stevens also cited Lujan v. Defenders of Wildlife, 504 U.S. 555, 573–74 (1992), for the proposition that a generalized grievance about government was not a sufficient basis for standing under the Article III case or controversy provision.

305. *See Shaw v. Hunt*, 517 U.S. at 924 (distinguishing between geographic and racial discrimination).

306. *See id.* at 928 (citing Brown v. Board of Educ., 347 U.S. 483, 495 (1954)) (challenging distinction between residents and nonresidents for standing purposes).

307. *See id.* at 929–51. (Stevens, J., dissenting, joined in part by Ginsburg & Breyer, JJ., arguing that challenged plan did not trigger strict scrutiny, but that it could nevertheless satisfy strict scrutiny).

308. *See id.* at 929–30 (favoring remand for application of different legal standard).

309. *See id.* at 931–33 (arguing that race can be considered as long as it does not subordinate traditional districting principles).

310. *See id.* at 933 n.9 (arguing that majority-minority districts contained communities of shared interests).

311. *See id.* at 935 (arguing that shape of district complied with state constitution).

312. *See id.* at 936–37 (arguing that district shape indicated nonracial factors had been considered).

313. *See id.* at 936 n.13 (arguing that district shape was irrelevant).

314. *See id.* at 937 (identifying two race-neutral districting criteria).

315. *See id.* at 938–39 (discussing two race-neutral districting criteria).

316. *See id.* at 939 n.16 (arguing that strict scrutiny interferes with goals of Voting Rights Act).

317. *See id.* at 940–45 (identifying three compelling state interests).

318. *See id.* at 946–50 (arguing that desire to avoid § 2 vote-dilution violation was narrowly tailored).

319. *See id.* at 951 (Souter, J., dissenting, joined by Ginsburg & Breyer, JJ., reiterating views expressed by Justice Souter in *Bush v. Vera*).

320. Bush v. Vera, 517 U.S. 952 (1996) (plurality opinion of O'Connor, J.).

321. *See id.* at 956–57 (stating facts of case).

322. *See id.* at 956 (opinion of O'Connor, J., joined by Rehnquist & Kennedy, JJ.).

323. *See id.* at 957–58 (citing *United States v. Hays,* 515 U.S. 737 (1995)) (granting standing only to residents of challenged district).

324. *See id.* at 959 (quoting articulation of predominant factor standard from *Miller,* 515 U.S. at 916 [emphasis and brackets in Justice O'Connor's opinion]).

325. *See id.* at 959–65 (characterizing case as mixed motive case).

326. *See id.* at 965–76 (applying strict scrutiny).

327. *See id.* at 968 (use of race as proxy for political affiliation entails racial stereotyping).

328. *See id.* at 977 (challenged plan could not survive strict scrutiny).

329. *See id.* at 976–81 (challenged plan was not narrowly tailored effort to avoid § 2 vote-dilution liability).

330. *See id.* at 981–82 (challenged plan did not advance compelling state interest in providing remedy for history of voting discrimination).

331. *See id.* at 982–83 (challenged plan was not narrowly tailored effort to avoid § 5 retrogression liability).

332. *See id.* at 983–86 (declining to distinguish between invidious and benign racial classifications).

333. *See id.* at 990 (O'Connor, J., concurring).

334. *See id.* at 990–92 (arguing that compliance with § 2 "results" test constituted compelling state interest).

335. *See id.* at 993–95 (emphasis in original) (arguing that states could not create bizarrely shaped districts in order to comply with § 2 results test).

336. *See id.* at 996 (Kennedy, J., concurring).

337. *See id.* (arguing that all race-conscious districting should trigger strict scrutiny).

338. *See id.* at 994–99 (arguing that Constitution permitted only that race-conscious districting necessary to comply with § 2).

339. *See id.* at 999 (arguing that § 2 did not require noncompact majority-minority districts).

340. *See id.* (Thomas, J., concurring in judgment, joined by Scalia, J.).

341. *See id.* at 999–1003 (arguing that race was factor in formulating challenged plan, and challenged plan could not survive strict scrutiny).

342. *See id.* at 1003 (Stevens, J., dissenting, joined by Ginsburg & Breyer, JJ.).

343. *See id.* at 1003–05 (offering three reasons for upholding challenged plan).

344. *See id.* at 1005–06 (arguing that challenged plan was product of political rather than racial gerrymander).

345. *See id.* at 1008–09 (arguing that race-conscious districting was not alone sufficient to trigger strict scrutiny).

346. *See id.* at 1009 n.8 (arguing that Voting Rights Act sometimes requires race-conscious creation of majority-minority districts).

347. *See id.* at 1008–11 (arguing that strict scrutiny should not apply to benign racial classifications).

348. *See id.* at 1011–12 (arguing that strict scrutiny applies only when traditional districting principles have been subordinated to race).

349. *See id.* at 1012–14 (arguing that deference to state legislature was appropriate).

350. *See id.* at 1014–19. Justice Steven also pointed out that bizarre shapes were a necessary consequence of political gerrymandering in urban areas, where high population densities and few open spaces made it difficult to ensure the desired political concentration of voters without drawing districts that had jagged edges. *See id.* at 1017 n.15.

351. *See id.* at 1018–23 (arguing that shape of challenged district was not bizarre).

352. *See id.* at 1024–25 (arguing that racial considerations did not predominate).

353. *See id.* at 1025–26 (arguing for deference to state views about existence of communities of interest).

354. *See id.* at 1027–29 (arguing for deference to state claim that districts were drawn to protect incumbents).

355. *See id.* at 1030–32 (arguing that race had not been used as proxy for political affiliation, but even if it had been, race was accurate proxy).

356. *See id.* at 1033 (arguing that challenged districts were able to survive strict scrutiny).

357. *See id.* at 1033–35 (arguing that compliance with Voting Rights Act constituted compelling state interest).

358. *See id.* at 1035 (arguing that racial gerrymandering decisions created perverse incentives).

359. *See id.* at 1036–37 (arguing that racial gerrymandering cases discriminatorily permitted majority-white, but not majority-minority, districts to be irregularly shaped).

360. *See id.* at 1038 (arguing that racial gerrymandering cases improperly infused federal courts into districting process).

361. *See id.* at 1038–39 (distinguishing between inclusion and exclusion of racial groups).

362. *See id.* at 1040–41 (highlighting lingering effects of past voting discrimination in South).

363. *See id.* at 1045 (Souter, J., dissenting, joined by Ginsburg & Breyer, JJ.).

364. *See id.* at 1045–46 (arguing that *Shaw v. Reno* cause of action resulted from basic misconception about relationship between race and districting).

365. *See id.* at 1047 (citing U.S. Const. art. I, § 1, cl. 2 and art. I, § 4, cl. 1).

366. *See id.* at 1048–49 (stressing importance of recognizing communities of shared interests).

367. *See id.* at 1050–53 (arguing that prior to *Shaw v. Reno*, Court had not displaced traditional districting principles in absence of substantial harm to identifiable group of voters).

368. *See id.* at 1051 n.5 (arguing that race consciousness is not inappropriate in context of districting, where racial interests are obviously relevant).

369. *See id.* at 1053 (citing *Shaw v. Reno*, 509 U.S. at 647–48, and quoting Pildes & Niemi, *supra* chapter 1, note 1, at 506–07) (discussing abstract expressive and representational harms).

370. *See id.* at 1054 (arguing that abstract harms fell on majority and minority voters alike).

371. *See id.* at 1055 (citing Pamela S. Karlan, *Our Separatism: Voting Rights as an American Nationalities Policy*, 1995 U. CHI. LEGAL F. 83, 94).

372. *See id.* at 1055–56 (arguing that *Shaw v. Reno* frustrates remedial use of majority-minority districts to remedy real racial bloc voting).

373. *See id.* at 1056–57 (arguing that Court had failed to provide manageable standard for permissible race consciousness).

374. *See id.* at 1058–60 (citing Piles & Niemi, *supra* chapter 1, note 1, at 585–86) (emphasizing difficulties inherent in applying *Miller* "predominant factor" test).

375. *See id.* at 1058–62 (arguing that permissible factors can correlate with impermissible consideration of race).

376. *See id.* at 1063–64 (arguing that states and lower courts lack adequate guidance).

377. *See id.* at 1065 (arguing that avoidance of Voting Rights Act violation was compelling state interest).

378. *See id.* at 1065 (arguing that it has now become more difficult for states to protect minority incumbents than to protect white incumbents).

379. *See id.* at 1067–69 (arguing that current law violates principles of federalism).

380. *See id.* at 1070–71 (listing options for clarifying meaning of *Shaw v. Reno*).

381. *See id.* at 1073; *but cf. id.* at 996 (Kennedy, J. concurring, suggesting that any race-conscious districting would be subject to strict scrutiny).

382. *See id.* at 1073–77 (arguing that *Shaw v. Reno* should be overruled).

383. Miller v. Johnson, 515 U.S. 900 (1995). *Miller* is discussed in chapter 4, part 4.

384. *See id.* at 902–28 (invalidating majority-minority district on basis of *Shaw v. Reno*).

385. Abrams v. Johnson, 521 U.S. 74 (1997).

386. *See id.* at 77–79 (no increase in majority-minority districts required).

387. *See id.* at 77–85 (stating facts of case); *see also Miller*, 515 U.S. at 905–10 (same).

388. *See Abrams*, 521 U.S. at 77–85 (stating facts of case).

389. *See id.* at 76–77 (listing votes of justices).

390. *See* Affirmative Action Voting Chart, *infra* pages 162–63.

391. *See id.* at 78–79 (summarizing rejected objections to district court plan).

392. Upham v. Seamon, 456 U.S. 37 (1982).

393. *See Abrams,* 521 U.S. at 85–90 (describing challenge to district court plan).

394. *See id.* at 85–86 (precleared plan was not owed deference because it was unconstitutional).

395. *See id.* at 85–90 (district court was not required to create multiple majority-minority districts).

396. *See id.* at 90–91 (citing *Shaw v. Reno,* 509 U.S. at 656) (district court plan would not result in vote dilution).

397. *See id.* at 91–95 (*Gingles* conditions for § 2 vote dilution were not satisfied).

398. *See id.* at 95 (§ 5 is relevant to equitable discretion).

399. *See id.* at 95–98 (district court plan was not retrogressive).

400. *See id.* at 97–98 (1 percent decrease in minority voting strength did not constitute § 5 retrogression).

401. *See id.* at 98–101 (district court plan did not violate one-person, one-vote principle).

402. *See id.* at 103 (Breyer, J., dissenting, joined by Stevens, Souter, & Ginsburg, JJ.)

403. Upham v. Seamon, 456 U.S. 37 (1982).

404. *See Abrams,* 521 U.S. at 103 (summarizing Justice Breyer's dissenting arguments).

405. *See id.* at 103–05 (Georgia policy favoring multiple majority-black districts was entitled to deference as matter of fact).

406. *See id.* at 105–09 (Georgia policy favoring multiple majority-black districts was entitled to deference as matter of law).

407. *See id.* at 110 (quoting, *inter alia,* Bush v. Vera, 517 U.S. 952, 994 (1996) (O'Connor, J., concurring). Justice O'Connor's concurring opinion in *Bush* is discussed above in the text accompanying chapter 4, notes 333–335.

408. *See Abrams,* 521 U.S. at 110 (there was a "strong basis in the evidence" for second majority-black district).

409. *See id.* at 110–14 (district court applied wrong legal standard).

410. *See id.* at 115 (*Abrams* did not involve claim that majority vote would be diluted).

411. *See id.* at 116 (discussing dissents in other Voting Rights Act cases).

412. *See id.* at 116–17(enumerating objections to "predominant racial motive" test).

413. *See id.* at 117–19 (objecting to recent cases prohibiting consideration of race in redistricting process).

414. Lawyer v. Department of Justice, 117 S. Ct. 2186 (1997).

415. *See id.* at 2189–90 (stating facts of case).

416. Johnson v. De Grandy, 512 U.S. 997 (1994). *Johnson v. De Grandy* is discussed in chapter 4, part 1, section iv.

417. Miller v. Johnson, 515 U.S. 900 (1995).

418. *See Lawyer*, 117 S. Ct. at 2190–91 (describing modified plan). The Supreme Court opinion does not explain the discrepancy between its first reference to the challenged district as being 45.8 percent black, *see id.* at 2190, and its subsequent reference to the district as being 45.0 percent black. *See id.* at 2191.

419. *See id.* at 2191–92 (describing district court approval of settlement plan).

420. *See id.* at 2189 (listing votes of justices).

421. *See* Affirmative Action Voting Chart, *infra* pages 162–63.

422. Growe v. Emison, 507 U.S. 25, 34 (1993). *Growe v. Emison* is discussed in chapter 4, part 1, section ii.

423. *See Lawyer*, 117 S. Ct. at 2192 (describing claim that original plan had to be declared unconstitutional before settlement plan could be approved).

424. *See id.* at 2192–93 (state preferences were embodied in settlement agreement).

425. *See id.* at 2193–94 (Lawyer had no right to have constitutionality of original plan adjudicated).

426. *See id.* at 2194–95 (upholding constitutionality of settlement plan).

427. *See id.* at 2196 (Scalia, J., dissenting, joined by O'Connor, Kennedy, & Thomas, JJ.).

428. *See id.* at 2196–98 (district court could not impose redistricting plan in absence of constitutional violation).

429. *See id.* at 2196–98 (quoting *Voinovich v. Quilter*, 507 U.S. 146, 156 (1993) [brackets and emphasis in Justice Scalia's opinion]).

430. *See id.* at 2198–99 (Florida legislature should have been given first opportunity to devise new plan).

431. Hunt v. Cromartie, 119 S. Ct. 1545 (1999).

432. Shaw v. Reno, 509 U.S. 630 (1993), is discussed in chapter 4, part 2.

433. Shaw v. Hunt, 517 U.S. 899 (1996), is discussed in chapter 4, part 6.

434. *See Hunt v. Cromartie*, 119 S. Ct. at 1547–48 (stating facts).

435. *See id.* at 1547 (listing votes of justices).

436. *See id.* at 1549 (assessment of motive is complex).

437. *See id.* at 1548–52 (summary judgment was inappropriate).

438. *See id.* at 1554 (Stevens, J., concurring in judgment, joined by Souter, Ginsburg, & Breyer, JJ.).

439. *Compare id.* at 1549 n.3 (majority opinion of Thomas, J., arguing that racial motivation is more likely than political motivation to create unusual shape) *with id.* at 1554 (Stevens, J., concurring in judgment, arguing that racial and political motivations are equally likely to create unusual shape).

440. *See id.* at 1554–55 (Stevens, J., concurring in judgment, arguing that evidence did not support claim of racial motivation).

441. Department of Commerce v. United States House of Representatives, 119 S. Ct. 765 (1999).

442. *See* U.S. CONST. art I, § 2, cl. 3 ("Representatives . . . shall be apportioned among the several States . . . according to their respective Numbers. . . . The actual Enumeration shall be made within three Years after the first Meeting of the Congress of the United States, and within every subsequent Term of ten Years, in such Manner as they shall by Law direct."); *see also Department of Commerce*, 119 S. Ct. at 768–69 (quoting census clause).

443. The Census Act is codified as amended at 13 U.S.C. § 1 *et seq* (1994).

444. *See Department Of Commerce*, 119 S. Ct. at 774–75, 778 (discussing uses of census data).

445. *See id.* at 768–71 (describing origin of sampling plan).

446. The Voting Rights Act is discussed in chapter 4, part 1.

447. *See Department of Commerce*, 119 S. Ct. at 771–72 (describing lower court challenge in Clinton v. Glavin, 19 F. Supp. 2d 543 (E.D. Va. 1998) (three-judge court).

448. *See Department of Commerce*, 119 S. Ct. at 772 (describing lower court challenge in Department of Commerce v. United States House of Representatives, 11 F. Supp. 2d 76 (D.D.C. 1998) (three-judge court).

449. *See Department of Commerce*, 119 S. Ct. at 779 (affirming three-judge district court decision in *Glavin* and dismissing appeal in *Department of Commerce*).

450. *See id.* at 768 (majority opinion of O'Connor, J., joined at least in part by Rehnquist, Scalia, Kennedy, Thomas, & Breyer, JJ.).

451. *See id.* at 772–75 (majority opinion of O'Connor J., joined by Rehnquist, Scalia, Kennedy, Thomas, & Breyer, JJ., finding standing).

452. *See id.* at 775 (majority opinion of O'Connor, J., joined by Rehnquist, Scalia, Kennedy, & Thomas, JJ., finding violation of Census Act).

453. *See id.* at 776 (quoting § 141(a) of the Census Act, 13 U.S.C. § 141(a)) (1994).

454. *See id.* at 777 (quoting § 195 of the Census Act, 13 U.S.C. § 195) (1994).

455. *See id.* at 777–79 (§ 195 of Census Act prohibits use of sampling for apportionment purposes).

456. *See id.* at 779 (opinion of O'Connor, J., joined by Rehnquist & Kennedy, JJ., drawing inference from lack of partisan debate).

457. *See id.* at 779 (declining to address constitutional question and dismissing *Department of Commerce* appeal).

458. *See id.* at 779 (Scalia, J., concurring in part, joined by Thomas, J., and joined in part by Rehnquist & Kennedy, JJ).

459. *See id.* at 780 (Scalia, J., concurring in part, joined by Thomas, J., objecting to use of legislative silence as interpretive tool).

460. *See id.* at 780 (Scalia, J., concurring in part, joined by Rehnquist, Kennedy, & Thomas, JJ.).

461. *See id.* at 780–81 (arguing that there was no conflict entailed in majority's reading of Census Act).

462. *See id.* at 781 (quoting "actual Enumeration" language of art I, § 2, cl. 3).

463. *See id.* at 781–82 (arguing that Census Act should be read to prohibit sampling for apportionment purposes in order to avoid constitutional difficulties).

464. *See id.* at 782 (Breyer, J., concurring in part and dissenting in part).

465. *See id.* (agreeing that at least some plaintiffs had standing).

466. *See id.* (agreeing with Justice Stevens that § 195 did not bar sampling for apportionment purposes).

467. *See id.* (arguing that § 195 prohibits sampling as substitute for, but not as supplement to, traditional enumeration methods).

468. *See id.* at 782–84 (arguing that statutory language, legislative history, and agency practice supported proposed use of sampling for 2000 census).

469. *See id.* at 786 (Stevens, J., dissenting, joined in part by Souter, Ginsburg, & Breyer, JJ., arguing that sampling was permitted by the Census Act and by the Constitution).

470. *See id.* at 786–88 (Stevens, J., dissenting, joined by Souter & Ginsburg, JJ., arguing that § 141 authorized sampling for any purpose and § 195 required sampling for nonapportionment purposes).

471. *See id.* at 788–89 (Stevens, J., dissenting, joined by Souter, Ginsburg, & Breyer, JJ.).

472. *See id.* (arguing that Constitution permits sampling).

473. *See id.* at 789 (Stevens, J., dissenting, joined by Breyer, J., arguing that both *Glavin* and *Department of Commerce* should be reversed).

474. *See id.* at 789 (Ginsburg, J., dissenting, joined by Souter, J.).

475. *See id.* (objecting to resolution of unnecessary standing issues, but otherwise agreeing with Justice Stevens).

476. The eight constitutional affirmative action cases that the Supreme Court has decided since 1993 are *Hunt v. Cromartie, Lawyer, Abrams, Bush, Shaw v. Hunt, Miller, Adarand,* and *Shaw v. Reno. See* Affirmative Action Voting Chart, *infra* pages 162–63.

477. The seven constitutional affirmative action cases that the Supreme Court has decided since 1993 that involve redistricting claims are *Hunt v. Cromartie, Lawyer, Abrams, Bush, Shaw v. Hunt, Miller,* and *Shaw v. Reno. See* Affirmative Action Voting Chart, *infra* pages 162–63.

478. The five constitutional redistricting cases that were decided in a way that was adverse to the affirmative action claim at issue were *Abrams, Bush, Shaw v. Hunt, Miller,* and *Shaw v. Reno.* The two constitutional redistricting case that were not decided in a way that was adverse to the affirmative action claim at issue were *Hunt v. Cromartie* and *Lawyer. See* Affirmative Action Voting Chart, *infra* pages 162–63. *But see infra* chapter 5, note 49 (explaining why *Lawyer* was arguably not a real affirmative action decision).

479. The eight statutory cases that the Supreme Court has decided under the Voting Rights Act since 1993 are *Lopez, City of Monroe, Bossier Parish, Young, De*

Grandy, Holder, Voinovich, and *Growe. See* Affirmative Action Voting Chart, *infra* pages 162–63.

480. The six Voting Rights Act cases decided since 1993 in which the Supreme Court ruled in a way that was adverse to the affirmative action claim at issue were *City of Monroe, Bossier Parish, De Grandy, Holder, Voinovich,* and *Growe.* The two Voting Rights Act cases decided since 1993 in which the Supreme Court ruled in favor of the affirmative action claim at issue were *Lopez* and *Young. See* Affirmative Action Voting Chart, *infra* pages 162–63.

NOTES TO CHAPTER 5

1. The thirty-two racial affirmative action cases to which the Supreme Court has given plenary consideration since 1974 are Hunt v. Cromartie, 119 S. Ct. 1545 (1999); Department of Commerce v. United States House of Representatives, 119 S. Ct. 765 (1999); Lopez v. Monterey County, 119 S. Ct. 693 (1999); City of Monroe v. United States, 118 S. Ct. 400 (1997); Lawyer v. Department of Justice, 117 S. Ct. 2186 (1997); Abrams v. Johnson, 521 U.S. 74 (1997); Reno v. Bossier Parish School Bd., 520 U.S. 471 (1997); Young v. Fordice, 520 U.S. 273 (1997); Bush v. Vera, 517 U.S. 952 (1996); Shaw v. Hunt, 517 U.S. 899 (1996); Miller v. Johnson, 515 U.S. 900 (1995); United States v. Hays, 515 U.S. 737 (1995); Adarand Constructors v. Pena, 515 U.S. 200 (1995); Johnson v. De Grandy, 512 U.S. 997 (1994); Holder v. Hall, 512 U.S. 874 (1994); Shaw v. Reno, 509 U.S. 630 (1993); Northeastern Fla. Chapter of the Associated Gen. Contractors of Am. v. City of Jacksonville, 508 U.S. 656 (1993); Voinovich v. Quilter, 507 U.S. 146 (1993); Growe v. Emison, 507 U.S. 25 (1993); Metro Broadcasting v. FCC, 497 U.S. 547 (1990); City of Richmond v. J.A. Croson Co., 488 U.S. 469 (1989); Johnson v. Transportation Agency, 480 U.S. 616 (1987); United States v. Paradise, 480 U.S. 149 (1987); Local 93, Int'l Ass'n of Firefighters v. Cleveland, 478 U.S. 501 (1986); Local 28, Sheet Metal Workers Int'l Ass'n v. EEOC, 478 U.S. 421 (1986); Wygant v. Jackson Bd. of Educ., 476 U.S. 267 (1986); Firefighters Local Union No. 1784 v. Stotts, 467 U.S. 561 (1984); Fullilove v. Klutznick, 448 U.S. 448 (1980); United Steelworkers of Am. v. Weber, 443 U.S. 193 (1979); Regents of the Univ. of Cal. v. Bakke, 438 U.S. 265 (1978); United Jewish Orgs. v. Carey, 430 U.S. 144 (1977); and De Funis v. Odegaard, 416 U.S. 312 (1974). *See* Affirmative Action Voting Chart, *infra* pages 162–63. The affirmative action program at issue in one of these cases contained both race and gender preferences, but the Supreme Court's consideration and ultimate approval of the plan arose in the context of a gender-based Title VII challenge rather than a race-based challenge. *See* Johnson v. Transportation Agency, 480 U.S. 616 (1987).

Technically, the post–*Brown v. Board of Education* school desegregation cases that permitted race-conscious pupil assignment are affirmative action cases because of the Supreme Court's intent to benefit minority students by issuing those

262 | *Notes to Chapter 5*

decisions. *See, e.g.,* North Carolina State Bd. of Educ. v. Swann, 402 U.S. 43, 45–46 (1971) (effectively requiring race-conscious pupil assignment to remedy prior school segregation). However, because those cases are not typically treated as affirmative action cases, they have not been included in the present compilation of statistics concerning the Court's affirmative action cases.

2. The case in which the Supreme Court summarily affirmed a lower court decision that upheld an affirmative action plan was DeWitt v. Wilson, 515 U.S. 1170 (1995), *aff'g* DeWitt v. Wilson, 856 F. Supp. 1409 (1994) (three-judge court). *De-Witt* is discussed in chapter 4, part 5.

3. The four cases in which the Supreme Court denied or dismissed certiorari were Coalition for Econ. Equity v. Wilson, 122 F.3d 692 (9th Cir.), *cert. denied,* 118 S. Ct. 397 (1997); Taxman v. Piscataway Township Bd. of Educ., 91 F.3d 1547 (3d Cir. 1996) (en banc), *cert. granted,* 117 S. Ct. 2506 (1997), *cert. dismissed,* 118 S. Ct. 595 (1997); Hopwood v. Texas, 78 F.3d 932 (5th Cir. 1996), *cert. denied,* 518 U.S. 1033 (1996); and Podberesky v. Kirwan, 38 F.3d 147 (4th Cir. 1994), *cert. denied,* 514 U.S. 1128 (1995). These four cases are discussed in chapter 3, part 5.

4. The nineteen cases raising constitutional challenges to affirmative action plans are *Hunt v. Cromartie, Lawyer, Abrams, Bush, Shaw v. Hunt, Miller, Hays, Adarand, Shaw v. Reno, Northeastern Fla., Metro Broadcasting, Croson, Paradise, Sheet Metal Workers, Wygant, Fullilove, Bakke, United Jewish Orgs.,* and *DeFunis. See* Affirmative Action Voting Chart, *infra* pages 162–63.

5. The four Title VII cases are *Johnson v. Transportation Agency, Firefighter v. Cleveland, Stotts,* and *Weber.* Of these four cases, one involved a gender-based challenge to an affirmative action plan that contained both race- and gender-based preferences. *See* Johnson v. Transportation Agency, 480 U.S. 616 (1987). *See also* Affirmative Action Voting Chart, *infra* pages 162–63.

6. The eight statutory Voting Rights Act cases are *Lopez, City of Monroe, Bossier Parish, Young, De Grandy, Holder, Voinovich,* and *Growe. See* Affirmative Action Voting Chart, *infra* pages 162–63.

7. The one Census Act case was *Dept. of Commerce.*

8. The structure of the Voting Rights Act is discussed in the introductory section of chapter 4.

9. The eleven cases that arose in an employment context are *Adarand, Northeastern Fla., Croson, Johnson v. Transportation Agency, Paradise, Firefighters v. Cleveland, Sheet Metal Workers, Wygant, Stotts, Fullilove,* and *Weber.* Of these eleven cases, one involved a race- and gender-based affirmative action plan that was challenged in an employment context on the grounds of unlawful gender discrimination in violation of Title VII. *See* Johnson v. Transportation Agency, 480 U.S. 616 (1987).

10. The two student cases that arose in an educational context are *Bakke* and *DeFunis.*

11. The eighteen cases that arose in a voting rights context are *Hunt v. Cromartie, Dept. of Commerce, Lopez, City of Monroe, Lawyer, Abrams, Bossier Parish, Young,*

Bush, Shaw v. Hunt, Miller, Hays, De Grandy, Holder, Shaw v. Reno, Voinovich, Growe, and *United Jewish Orgs.*

12. The one case that arose in the context of preferential broadcast license programs is *Metro Broadcasting.*

13. *See supra* chapter 5, note 1 (citing thirty-two affirmative action cases given plenary consideration by Supreme Court).

14. The eighteen cases in which the Supreme Court frustrated affirmative action efforts after plenary consideration are *Dept. of Commerce, City of Monroe, Abrams, Bossier Parish, Bush, Shaw v. Hunt, Miller, Adarand, De Grandy, Holder, Shaw v. Reno, Northeastern Fla., Voinovich, Growe, Croson, Wygant, Stotts,* and *Bakke. See* Affirmative Action Voting Chart, *infra* pages 162–63.

15. The fourteen cases in which the Supreme Court facilitated affirmative action efforts after plenary consideration are *Hunt v. Cromartie, Dept. of Commerce, Lawyer, Young, Hays, Metro Broadcasting, Johnson v. Transportation Agency, Paradise, Firefighters v. Cleveland, Sheet Metal Workers, Fullilove, Weber, United Jewish Orgs.,* and *DeFunis. See* Affirmative Action Voting Chart, *infra* pages 162–63. The affirmative action program at issue in one of these cases contained both race and gender preferences, but the Supreme Court's consideration and ultimate approval of the plan arose in the context of a gender-based Title VII challenge rather than a race-based challenge. *See* Johnson v. Transportation Agency, 480 U.S. 616 (1987).

16. The three cases resolved on justiciability grounds are *Hays, Northeastern Fla.,* and *DeFunis. See* Affirmative Action Voting Chart, *infra* pages 162–63.

17. The two justiciability cases in which the Court declined to invalidate affirmative action programs are *Hays* and *DeFunis. See* Affirmative Action Voting Chart, *infra* pages 162–63. In *Hays,* the Supreme Court unanimously found that the challengers to an affirmative action redistricting plan lacked standing, thereby permitting the affirmative action redistricting plan formally to remain in place. *Hays* is discussed in chapter 4, part 3. Note that on the same day that *Hays* was decided, the Supreme Court invalidated a similar affirmative action redistricting plan on the merits in *Miller,* and summarily affirmed a lower court decision upholding a similar affirmative action redistricting plan on the merits in *DeWitt. Miller* and *DeWitt* are discussed in chapter 4, parts 4 & 5. In *DeFunis,* the Court ruled 5–4 that a constitutional challenge to a law school affirmative action program should be dismissed on the grounds of mootness, thereby permitting the affirmative action plan formally to remain in place. *DeFunis* is discussed in chapter 2, part 1, section i.

18. In *Northeastern Fla.,* the Supreme Court held 7–2 that the challengers to an affirmative action construction contract program had standing to maintain the challenge. *See* Affirmative Action Voting Chart, *infra* pages 162–63. *Northeastern Fla.* is discussed in chapter 3, part 3.

19. The twenty-nine affirmative action cases that the Court resolved on the merits are *Hunt v. Cromartie, Dept. of Commerce, Lopez, City of Monroe, Lawyer, Abrams, Bossier Parish, Young, Bush, Shaw v. Hunt, Miller, Adarand, De Grandy,*

Holder, Shaw v. Reno, Voinovich, Growe, Metro Broadcasting, Croson, Johnson v. Transportation Agency, Paradise, Firefighters v. Cleveland, Sheet Metal Workers, Wygant, Stotts, Fullilove, Weber, Bakke, and *United Jewish Orgs. See* Affirmative Action Voting Chart, *infra* pages 162–63. The affirmative action program at issue in one of these cases contained both race and gender preferences, but the Supreme Court's consideration and ultimate approval of the plan arose in the context of a gender-based Title VII challenge rather than a race-based challenge. *See* Johnson v. Transportation Agency, 480 U.S. 616 (1987).

20. The seventeen cases in which the Supreme Court rejected affirmative action claims are *Dept. of Commerce, City of Monroe, Abrams, Bossier Parish, Bush, Shaw v. Hunt, Miller, Adarand, De Grandy, Holder, Shaw v. Reno, Voinovich, Growe, Croson, Wygant, Stotts,* and *Bakke. See also* Affirmative Action Voting Chart, *infra* pages 162–63.

21. The twelve cases in which the Court upheld affirmative action claims are *Hunt v. Cromartie, Lopez, Lawyer, Young, Metro Broadcasting, Johnson v. Transportation Agency, Paradise, Firefighters v. Cleveland, Sheet Metal Workers, Fullilove, Weber,* and *United Jewish Orgs. See* Affirmative Action Voting Chart, *infra* pages 162–63. Of these twelve cases, one involved a challenge to a race- and gender-based affirmative action plan that was upheld by the Court after a challenge that asserted unlawful gender discrimination in violation of Title VII. *See* Johnson v. Transportation Agency, 480 U.S. 616 (1987).

22. The sixteen cases decided on constitutional grounds are *Hunt v. Cromartie, Lawyer, Abrams, Bush, Shaw v. Hunt, Miller, Adarand, Shaw v. Reno, Metro Broadcasting, Croson, Paradise, Sheet Metal Workers, Wygant, Fullilove, Bakke,* and *United Jewish Orgs. See* Affirmative Action Voting Chart, *infra* pages 162–63.

23. The nine constitutional cases in which the Court invalidated or frustrated implementation of the challenged affirmative action plans are *Abrams, Bush, Shaw v. Hunt, Miller, Adarand, Shaw v. Reno, Croson, Wygant,* and *Bakke. See* Affirmative Action Voting Chart, *infra* pages 162–63.

24. The seven constitutional cases in which the Court upheld the challenged affirmative action plans are *Hunt v. Cromartie, Lawyer, Metro Broadcasting, Paradise, Sheet Metal Workers, Fullilove,* and *United Jewish Orgs. See* Affirmative Action Voting Chart, *infra* pages 162–63.

25. The four Title VII cases that the Court resolved on the merits are *Johnson v. Transportation Agency, Firefighters v. Cleveland, Stotts,* and *Weber. See* Affirmative Action Voting Chart, *infra* pages 162–63. Of these four cases, one involved a challenge to a race- and gender-based affirmative action plan that was upheld by the Court after a challenge that asserted unlawful gender discrimination in violation of Title VII. *See* Johnson v. Transportation Agency, 480 U.S. 616 (1987).

26. The three Title VII cases in which the Court upheld the challenged affirmative action plans are *Johnson v. Transportation Agency, Firefighters v. Cleveland,* and *Weber. See* Affirmative Action Voting Chart, *infra* pages 162–63. One of these three cases involved a challenge to a race- and gender-based affirmative action plan that

was upheld by the Court after a gender-based Title VII challenge. *See* Johnson v. Transportation Agency, 480 U.S. 616 (1987).

27. The one Title VII case in which the Court rejected the affirmative action claim is *Stotts. See* Affirmative Action Voting Chart, *infra* pages 162–63.

28. The eight Voting Rights Act cases that the Court decided on the merits are *Lopez, City of Monroe, Bossier Parish, Young, De Grandy, Holder, Voinovich,* and *Growe. See* Affirmative Action Voting Chart, *infra* pages 162–63.

29. The six Voting Rights Act cases in which the Court rejected the affirmative action claims are *City of Monroe, Bossier Parish, De Grandy, Holder, Voinovich,* and *Growe. See* Affirmative Action Voting Chart, *infra* pages 162–63.

30. The two Voting Rights Act cases in which the Court upheld the affirmative action claims are *Lopez* and *Young. See* Affirmative Action Voting Chart, *infra* pages 162–63.

31. The one Census Act case in which the Court rejected the affirmative action claim on the merits is *Dept. of Commerce.*

32. *See supra* text accompanying chapter 5, notes 20 & 21 (Supreme Court overall record in affirmative action cases). *See also* Affirmative Action Voting Chart, *infra* pages 162–63.

33. *See supra* text accompanying chapter 5, notes 23 & 24 (Supreme Court record in constitutional cases). *See also* Affirmative Action Voting Chart, *infra* pages 162–63.

34. *See supra* text accompanying chapter 5, notes 29 & 30 (Supreme Court record in Voting Rights Act cases). *See also* Affirmative Action Voting Chart, *infra* pages 162–63.

35. *See supra* text accompanying chapter 5, notes 26 & 27 (Supreme Court record in Title VII cases). *See also* Affirmative Action Voting Chart, *infra* pages 162–63.

36. *See supra* text accompanying chapter 5, note 22 (citing sixteen constitutional cases decided by Supreme Court on merits).

37. *See supra* text accompanying chapter 5, notes 23 & 24 (Supreme Court record in constitutional cases decided on merits).

38. The nine constitutional cases resolved on the merits in which the Supreme Court was able to issue majority opinions are *Hunt v. Cromartie,* 119 S. Ct. at 1547 (majority opinion by Thomas, J.); *Lawyer,* 117 S. Ct. at 2189 (majority opinion by Souter, J.); *Abrams,* 521 U.S. at 77 (majority opinion by Kennedy, J.); *Shaw v. Hunt,* 517 U.S. at 901 (majority opinion by Rehnquist, J.); *Miller,* 515 U.S. at 903 (majority opinion by Kennedy, J.); *Adarand,* 515 U.S. at 204 (majority opinion by O'Connor, J.); *Shaw v. Reno,* 509 U.S. at 633 (majority opinion by O'Connor, J.); *Metro Broadcasting,* 497 U.S. at 550 (majority opinion by Brennan, J.); and *Croson,* 488 U.S. at 475 (majority opinion by O'Connor, J.). There is a sense in which *Adarand* is more like a plurality than a majority opinion. Justice Scalia, whose vote was necessary to the five-vote majority, signed the majority opinion, *see Adarand,* 515 U.S. at 202–03 (listing votes of justices), but joined that opinion only to the

extent that it was not inconsistent with his concurring opinion. *See id.* at 2118 (Scalia, J. concurring in part and concurring in judgment). *See also* Affirmative Action Voting Chart, *infra* pages 162–63.

39. The six constitutional cases resolved on the merits by majority opinions in which the Supreme Court rejected the affirmative action claims are *Abrams, Shaw v. Hunt, Miller, Adarand, Shaw v. Reno,* and *Croson.* The three constitutional cases resolved on the merits by majority opinions in which the Supreme Court upheld the affirmative action claims are *Hunt v. Cromartie, Lawyer,* and *Metro Broadcasting. See* Affirmative Action Voting Chart, *infra* pages 162–63.

40. The first six constitutional affirmative action cases resolved on the merits— all by plurality opinions—are *Paradise,* 480 U.S. at 152 (1987) (plurality opinion of Brennan, J.); *Sheet Metal Workers,* 478 U.S. at 424 (1986) (plurality opinion of Brennan, J.); *Wygant,* 476 U.S. at 268 (1986) (plurality opinion of Powell, J.); *Fullilove,* 448 U.S. at 452 (1980) (plurality opinion of Burger, C.J.); *Bakke,* 438 U.S. at 267 (1978) (opinion of Powell, J.); and *United Jewish Orgs.,* 430 U.S. at 146 (1977) (plurality opinion of White, J.). *See* Affirmative Action Voting Chart, *infra* pages 162–63. Justice Powell's opinion in *Bakke* was technically not a plurality opinion because the bulk of the opinion was not joined by any other justice. *See Bakke,* 438 U.S. at 267 (opinion of Powell, J.). Nevertheless, subsequent Supreme Court opinions and scholarly commentary have regularly treated Justice Powell's opinion as if it were a plurality opinion that stated a widely held rationale for the *Bakke* Court's decision. *See, e.g., Miller,* 515 U.S. at 904 (citing opinion of Powell, J., in *Bakke* as authoritative); *Adarand,* 515 U.S. at 218, 224 (same); *Croson,* 488 U.S. at 493–94, 496–98 (plurality opinion of O'Connor J.) (same).

41. The seventh constitutional affirmative action case resolved on the merits by a plurality opinion is *Bush,* 517 U.S. at 956 (1996) (plurality opinion of O'Connor, J.).

42. *See supra* text accompanying chapter 5, note 22 (citing sixteen constitutional cases decided by Supreme Court on merits).

43. The twelve constitutional cases resolved on the merits by 5–4 decisions are *Lawyer, Abrams, Bush, Shaw v. Hunt, Miller, Adarand, Shaw v. Reno, Metro Broadcasting, Paradise, Sheet Metal Workers, Wygant,* and *Bakke. See* Affirmative Action Voting Chart, *infra* pages 162–63.

44. The two constitutional cases resolved on the merits by 6–3 decisions are *Croson* and *Fullilove. See* Affirmative Action Voting Chart, *infra* pages 162–63.

45. The one constitutional case resolved on the merits by a 7–1 decision is *United Jewish Orgs. See* Affirmative Action Voting Chart, *infra* pages 162–63.

46. The one constitutional case resolved by a unanimous decision is *Hunt v. Cromartie.* Although unanimous, the decision showed evidence of the same 5–4 split that has now become common on the current Court in affirmative action cases. The majority opinion, holding only that a factual dispute precluded the entry of summary judgment invalidating a redistricting plan, was signed by the five jus-

tices in the conservative bloc, who typically vote against affirmative action programs. *See Hunt v. Cromartie*, 119 S. Ct. at 1547 (majority opinion of Thomas, J., joined by Rehnquist, O'Connor, Scalia, & Kennedy, JJ.). A separate opinion concurring in the judgment was signed by the four justices in the liberal bloc, who typically vote to uphold affirmative action programs. *See id.* at 1554 (Stevens, J., concurring in judgment, joined by Souter, Ginsburg, & Breyer, JJ.). The affirmative action voting blocs on the Supreme Court are discussed in chapter 5, part 1, section i.

47. The eight 5–4 decisions ruling against affirmative action are *Abrams, Bush, Shaw v. Hunt, Miller, Adarand, Shaw v. Reno, Wygant,* and *Bakke. See* Affirmative Action Voting Chart, *infra* pages 162–63.

48. The four 5–4 decisions ruling in favor of affirmative action are *Lawyer, Metro Broadcasting, Paradise,* and *Sheet Metal Workers. See* Affirmative Action Voting Chart, *infra* pages 162–63.

49. In *Lawyer,* the Supreme Court permitted the consideration of race in a voter redistricting context. However, the Court upheld a court-approved settlement that did not add any majority-minority voting districts, but rather eliminated a majority-minority voting district that had previously existed. *See Lawyer,* 117 S. Ct. at 2189–92, 2194–95. *Lawyer* is discussed in chapter 4, part 9.

50. In *Lawyer,* Chief Justice Rehnquist voted with the Court's liberal voting bloc rather than its conservative voting bloc. *See* Affirmative Action Voting Chart, *infra* pages 162–63. The affirmative action voting blocs on the Supreme Court are discussed in chapter 5, part 1, section i.

51. The seven constitutional affirmative action cases that the present Court has resolved on the merits are *Hunt v. Cromartie, Lawyer, Abrams, Bush, Shaw v. Hunt, Miller,* and *Adarand. See* Affirmative Action Voting Chart, *infra* pages 162–63.

52. The five constitutional cases in which the present Court has ruled against the affirmative action claims on the merits are *Abrams, Bush, Shaw v. Hunt, Miller,* and *Adarand. See* Affirmative Action Voting Chart, *infra* pages 162–63.

53. The two constitutional cases in which the present Court has upheld the affirmative action claims on the merits are *Hunt v. Cromartie* and *Lawyer. See* Affirmative Action Voting Chart, *infra* pages 162–63.

54. *See supra* chapter 5, note 49 and accompanying text (explaining why *Lawyer* was arguably not a real affirmative action decision).

55. *See supra* chapter 5, note 46 (explaining that *Hunt v. Cromartie* involved only issue of whether summary judgment was proper).

56. Chief Justice Rehnquist participated in sixteen affirmative action cases that were decided on constitutional grounds. He voted against the affirmative action claims at issue in thirteen of these cases. *See Abrams,* 521 U.S. at 76 (joining majority opinion); *Bush,* 517 U.S. at 955 (opinion of O'Connor, J., joined by Rehnquist, C.J.); *Shaw v. Hunt,* 517 U.S. at 900 (author of majority opinion); *Miller,* 515 U.S. at 902 (joining majority opinion); *Adarand,* 515 U.S. at 202 (joining majority opinion); *Shaw v. Reno,* 509 U.S. at 633 (joining majority opinion); *Metro Broad-*

casting, 497 U.S. at 602 (O'Connor, J., dissenting, joined by Rehnquist, C.J.); *Croson,* 488 U.S. at 476 (joining majority opinion); *Paradise,* 480 U.S. at 196 (O'Connor, J., dissenting, joined by Rehnquist, C.J.); *Sheet Metal Workers,* 478 U.S. at 500 (Rehnquist, J., dissenting); *Wygant,* 476 U.S. at 268 (opinion of Powell, J., joined by Rehnquist, J.); *Fullilove,* 448 U.S. at 522 (opinion of Stewart, J., joined by Rehnquist, C.J.); *Bakke,* 438 U.S. at 408 (opinion of Stevens, J., joined by Rehnquist, J.). He voted in favor of the affirmative action claims at issue in three of these cases. *See Hunt v. Cromartie,* 119 S. Ct. at 1547 (majority opinion of Thomas, J., joined by Rehnquist, CJ.); *Lawyer,* 117 S. Ct. at 2189 (majority opinion of Souter, J., joined by Rehnquist, C.J.); *United Jewish Orgs.,* 430 U.S. at 165 (opinion of White, J., joined by Rehnquist, J.). *See* Affirmative Action Voting Chart, *infra* pages 162–63.

Chief Justice Rehnquist's vote to uphold the affirmative action redistricting plan at issue in *Hunt v. Cromartie* was provisional, deeming the presence of disputed factual issues sufficient to preclude the entry of summary judgment invalidating the plan at that stage of the litigation—a plan that eliminated rather than added a majority-minority district. *Hunt v. Cromartie* is discussed in chapter 4, part 10. Chief Justice Rehnquist's vote in *Lawyer* is a similarly modest endorsement of affirmative action because *Lawyer* too is difficult to view as a real affirmative action case. In *Lawyer,* the Supreme Court permitted the consideration of race in a voter redistricting context. However, the Court upheld a court-approved settlement that did not add any majority-minority voting districts, but rather eliminated a majority-minority voting district that had previously existed. *Lawyer* is discussed in chapter 4, part 9. In *United Jewish Orgs.,* then-Justice Rehnquist voted to uphold a New York redistricting plan that was designed to enhance black voting strength by diluting the voting strength of Hasidic Jews. However, he may have viewed that dispute as a contest between affirmative action for blacks and affirmative action for Hasidic Jews. *United Jewish Orgs.* is discussed in chapter 2, part 1, section ii. It should also be noted that Chief Justice Rehnquist has never voted to uphold a racial classification after strict scrutiny. *See Hunt v. Cromartie,* 119 S. Ct. at 1547, 1548–52 (majority opinion of Thomas, J., joined by Rehnquist, C.J., holding that summary judgment record did not establish that race was predominant factor in adoption of redistricting plan, as is necessary to trigger strict scrutiny under *Miller,* 515 U.S. at 916); *Lawyer* 117 S. Ct. at 2186 (majority opinion of Souter, J., joined by Rehnquist, C.J., holding that race did not predominate over traditional districting principles, as is necessary to trigger strict scrutiny under *Miller,* 515 U.S. at 916); *United Jewish Orgs.,* 430 U.S. at 165–68 (opinion of White, J., joined in part by Rehnquist, J., upholding race-conscious redistricting plan without applying strict scrutiny).

57. Justice O'Connor participated in thirteen affirmative action cases that were decided on constitutional grounds. She voted against the affirmative action claim at issue in twelve of these cases. *See Lawyer,* 117 S. Ct. at 2196 (Scalia, J., dissenting, joined by O'Connor, J.); *Abrams,* 521 U.S. at 76 (joining majority opinion); *Bush,*

517 U.S. at 956, 990 (opinion of O'Connor, J., and O'Connor J., concurring); *Shaw v. Hunt*, 517 U.S. at 900 (joining majority opinion); *Miller*, 515 U.S. at 902 (O'Connor, J., concurring); *Adarand*, 512 U.S. at 202 (author of majority opinion); *Shaw v. Reno*, 509 U.S. at 633 (1993) (author of majority opinion); *Metro Broadcasting*, 497 U.S. at 602 (O'Connor, J., dissenting); *Croson*, 488 U.S. at 476 (author of majority opinion); *Paradise*, 480 U.S. at 196 (O'Connor, J., dissenting); *Sheet Metal Workers*, 478 U.S. at 489 (O'Connor, J., concurring in part and dissenting in part); *Wygant*, 476 U.S. at 284 (O'Connor, J., concurring in part and concurring in judgment). She voted in favor of the affirmative action claim at issue in one of these cases. *See Hunt v. Cromartie*, 119 S. Ct. at 1547 (majority opinion of Thomas, J., joined by O'Connor, J.). *See also* Affirmative Action Voting Chart, *infra* pages 162–63.

58. Justice Scalia participated in eleven affirmative action cases that were decided on constitutional grounds. He voted against the affirmative action plans at issue in ten of these cases. *See Lawyer*, 117 S. Ct. at 2196 (Scalia, J., dissenting); *Abrams*, 521 U.S. at 76 (joining majority opinion); *Bush*, 517 U.S. at 955 (Thomas, J., concurring in judgment, joined by Scalia, J.); *Shaw v. Hunt*, 517 U.S. at 900 (joining majority opinion); *Miller*, 515 U.S. at 902 (joining majority opinion); *Adarand*, 515 U.S. at 202 (Scalia, J., concurring in part and concurring in judgment); *Shaw v. Reno*, 509 U.S. at 663 (joining majority opinion); *Metro Broadcasting*, 497 U.S. at 602, 631 (O'Connor, J., dissenting, joined by Scalia, J., and Kennedy, J., dissenting, joined by Scalia, J.); *Croson*, 488 U.S. at 520 (Scalia, J., concurring in judgment); *Paradise*, 480 U.S. at 196 (O'Connor, J., dissenting, joined by Scalia, J.). He voted in favor of the affirmative action claim at issue in one of these cases. *See Hunt v. Cromartie*, 119 S. Ct. at 1547 (majority opinion of Thomas, J., joined by Scalia, J.). *See also* Affirmative Action Voting Chart, *infra* pages 162–63.

59. Justice Kennedy participated in ten affirmative action cases that were decided on constitutional grounds. He voted against the affirmative action claim at issue in nine of these cases. *See Lawyer*, 117 S. Ct. at 2196 (Scalia, J., dissenting, joined by Kennedy, J.); *Abrams*, 521 U.S. at 76 (author of majority opinion); *Bush*, 517 U.S. at 955, 996 (opinion of O'Connor, J., joined by Kennedy, J., and Kennedy, J., concurring); *Shaw v. Hunt*, 517 U.S. at 900 (joining majority opinion); *Miller*, 515 U.S. at 902 (author of majority opinion); *Adarand*, 515 U.S. at 202 (1995) (joining majority opinion); *Shaw v. Reno*, 509 U.S. 633 (joining majority opinion); *Metro Broadcasting*, 497 U.S. at 631 (Kennedy, J., dissenting); *Croson*, 488 U.S. at 518 (Kennedy, J., concurring in part and concurring in judgment). He voted in favor of the affirmative action claim at issue in one of these cases. *See Hunt v. Cromartie*, 119 S. Ct. at 1547 (majority opinion of Thomas, J., joined by Kennedy, J.). *See also* Affirmative Action Voting Chart, *infra* pages 162–63.

60. Justice Thomas participated in eight affirmative action cases that were decided on constitutional grounds. He voted against the affirmative action claims at

issue in seven of these cases. *See Lawyer*, 117 S. Ct. at 2196 (Scalia, J., dissenting, joined by Thomas, J.); *Abrams*, 521 U.S. at 76 (joining majority opinion); *Bush*, 517 U.S. at 955 (Thomas, J., concurring in judgment); *Shaw v. Hunt*, 517 U.S. at 900 (joining majority opinion); *Miller*, 515 U.S. at 902 (joining majority opinion); *Adarand*, 515 U.S. at 202 (Thomas, J., concurring in part and concurring in judgment); *Shaw v. Reno*, 509 U.S. at 633 (joining majority opinion). He voted in favor of the affirmative action claim at issue in one of these cases. *See Hunt v. Cromartie*, 119 S. Ct. at 1547 (majority opinion of Thomas, J.). *See also* Affirmative Action Voting Chart, *infra* pages 162–63.

61. *See Hunt v. Cromartie*, 119 S. Ct. at 1547, 1548–52 (majority opinion of Thomas, J., joined by Rehnquist, O'Connor, Scalia, & Kennedy, JJ.). *Hunt v. Cromartie* is discussed in chapter 4, part 10.

62. *See supra* chapter 5, note 56 (discussing votes of Chief Justice Rehnquist in constitutional affirmative action cases).

63. *See* Affirmative Action Voting Chart, *infra* pages 162–63.

64. Justice Brennan participated in, and voted in favor of the affirmative action plan at issue in, eight affirmative action cases that were decided on constitutional grounds. *See Metro Broadcasting*, 497 U.S. at 550 (author of majority opinion); *Croson*, 488 U.S. at 528, 561 (Marshall, J., dissenting, joined by Brennan, J., and Blackmun, J., dissenting, joined by Brennan, J.); *Paradise*, 480 U.S. at 153 (opinion of Brennan, J.); *Sheet Metal Workers*, 478 U.S. at 426 (author of majority opinion); *Wygant*, 476 U.S. at 295 (Marshall, J., dissenting, joined by Brennan, J.); *Fullilove*, 448 U.S. at 517 (Marshall, J., concurring in judgment, joined by Brennan, J.); *Bakke*, 438 U.S. at 324 (Brennan, J., concurring in judgment in part and dissenting in part); *United Jewish Orgs.*, 430 U.S. at 168 (Brennan, J., concurring in part). *See also* Affirmative Action Voting Chart, *infra* pages 162–63.

65. Justice Marshall participated in, and voted in favor of the affirmative action plan at issue in, seven affirmative action cases that were decided on constitutional grounds. *See Metro Broadcasting*, 497 U.S. at 550 (joining majority opinion); *Croson*, 488 U.S. at 528 (Marshall, J., dissenting); *Paradise*, 480 U.S. at 153 (joining majority opinion); *Sheet Metal Workers*, 478 U.S. at 426 (joining majority opinion); *Wygant*, 476 U.S. at 295 (Marshall, J., dissenting); *Fullilove*, 448 U.S. at 517 (Marshall, J., concurring in judgment); *Bakke*, 438 U.S. at 324, 387 (Marshall, J., concurring in judgment in part and dissenting in part, and separate opinion of Marshall, J.). Although Justice Marshall was on the Court when *United Jewish Orgs.* was decided, he did not participate in that decision. *See United Jewish Orgs.*, 430 U.S. at 146 (1977). *See also* Affirmative Action Voting Chart, *infra* pages 162–63.

66. Justice Blackmun participated in, and voted in favor of the affirmative action plan at issue in, nine affirmative action cases that were decided on constitutional grounds. *See Shaw v. Reno*, 113 S. Ct. at 2843 (1993) (Blackmun J., dissenting); *Metro Broadcasting*, 497 U.S. at 550 (joining majority opinion); *Croson*, 488

U.S. at 561 (Blackmun, J., dissenting); *Paradise*, 480 U.S. at 153 (opinion of Brennan, J., joined by Blackmun, J.); *Sheet Metal Workers*, 478 U.S. at 426 (joining majority opinion); *Wygant*, 476 U.S. at 295 (Marshall, J., dissenting, joined by Blackmun, J.); *Fullilove*, 448 U.S. at 517 (Marshall, J., concurring in judgment, joined by Blackmun, J.); *Bakke*, 438 U.S. at 324, 402 (1978) (Blackmun, J., concurring in judgment in part and dissenting in part, and separate opinion of Blackmun, J.); *United Jewish Orgs.*, 430 U.S. at 147 (1977) (opinion of White, J., joined by Blackmun, J.). *See also* Affirmative Action Voting Chart, *infra* pages 162–63.

67. *See* Affirmative Action Voting Chart, *infra* pages 162–63.

68. *See* STONE ET AL., *supra* chapter 1, note 1, at ii–ciii (specifying terms of Justices Brennan, Marshall, and Blackmun).

69. *See id.* (specifying terms of Chief Justice Rehnquist and Justices O'Connor, Scalia, Kennedy, and Thomas).

70. *See id.* (specifying terms of Justices Stevens, Souter, Ginsburg, and Breyer).

71. *See* Affirmative Action Voting Chart, *infra* pages 162–63.

72. Justice Stevens voted against the affirmative action plans at issue in *Croson*, 488 U.S. at 475 (joining majority opinion); *Fullilove*, 448 U.S. at 532 (Stevens, J., dissenting), and *Bakke*, 438 U.S. at 408 (Stevens, J., concurring in judgment in part and dissenting in part). *See* Affirmative Action Voting Chart, *infra* pages 162–63. Although Justice Stevens joined the majority opinion in *Croson*, he did not agree that strict scrutiny was the appropriate standard of review, *see Croson*, 488 U.S. at 514–15 (Stevens, J., concurring in part and concurring in judgment), or that affirmative action had to be limited to remedies for past discrimination. *See id.* at 511 n.1. Although Justice Stevens voted to invalidate the affirmative action plan at issue in *Bakke*, he voted to do so on statutory Title VI grounds rather than on constitutional equal protection grounds. *See Bakke*, 438 U.S. at 411–21 (Stevens, J., concurring in judgment in part and dissenting in part)

73. Justice Stevens participated in sixteen affirmative action cases that were decided on constitutional grounds. He voted in favor of the affirmative action plans at issue in thirteen of these cases. *See Hunt v. Cromartie*, 119 S. Ct. at 1554 (Stevens, J. concurring in judgment); *Lawyer*, 117 S. Ct. at 2189 (joining majority opinion); *Abrams*, 521 U.S. at 103 (Breyer, J., dissenting, joined by Stevens, J.); *Bush*, 517 U.S. at 1003 (Stevens, J., dissenting); *Shaw v. Hunt*, 517 U.S. at 918 (Stevens J., dissenting); *Miller*, 515 U.S. at 929 (Stevens, J., dissenting); *Adarand*, 515 U.S. at 242 (Stevens, J., dissenting); *Shaw v. Reno*, 509 U.S. at 659 (White, J., dissenting, joined by Stevens, J.); *Metro Broadcasting*, 497 U.S. at 601 (Stevens, J., concurring); *Paradise*, 480 U.S. at 189 (1987) (Stevens, J., concurring in judgment); *Sheet Metal Workers*, 478 U.S. at 426 (1986) (joining majority opinion); *Wygant*, 476 U.S. at 313 (Stevens, J., dissenting); *United Jewish Orgs.*, 430 U.S. at 147 (1977) (opinion of White, J., joined by Stevens, J.). He voted against the affirmative action plans at issue in three cases. *See Croson*, 488 U.S. at 475 (1989) (joining majority opinion); *Fullilove*, 448 U.S. at 532 (Stevens, J., dissenting); *Bakke*, 438 U.S. at 408 (Stevens,

J., concurring in judgment in part and dissenting in part). *See also* Affirmative Action Voting Chart, *infra* pages 162–63.

74. Since 1990, Justice Stevens has voted to uphold affirmative action claims in all nine constitutional cases that he considered. *See Hunt v. Cromartie*, 119 S. Ct. at 1554 (Stevens, J. concurring in judgment); *Lawyer*, 117 S. Ct. at 2189 (joining majority opinion); *Abrams*, 521 U.S. at 103 (Breyer, J., dissenting, joined by Stevens, J.); *Bush*, 517 U.S. at 1003 (Stevens, J., dissenting); *Shaw v. Hunt*, 517 U.S. at 918 (Stevens J., dissenting); *Miller*, 515 U.S. at 929 (Stevens, J., dissenting); *Adarand*, 515 U.S. at 242 (Stevens, J., dissenting); *Shaw v. Reno*, 509 U.S. at 659 (White, J., dissenting, joined by Stevens, J.); *Metro Broadcasting*, 497 U.S. at 601 (Stevens, J., concurring). *See also* Affirmative Action Voting Chart, *infra* pages 162–63.

75. *See* Affirmative Action Voting Chart, *infra* pages 162–63.

76. Justice Souter participated in eight affirmative action cases that were decided on constitutional grounds, and he voted in favor of the affirmative action plans at issue in all eight cases. *See Hunt v. Cromartie*, 119 S. Ct. at 1554 (Stevens, J. concurring in judgment, joined by Souter, J.); *Lawyer*, 117 S. Ct. at 2189 (author of majority opinion); *Abrams*, 521 U.S. at 103 (Breyer, J., dissenting, joined by Souter, J.); *Bush*, 517 U.S. at 1045 (Souter, J., dissenting); *Shaw v. Hunt*, 517 U.S. at 951 (Souter, J., dissenting); *Miller*, 515 U.S. at 934 (Ginsburg, J., dissenting, joined by Souter, J.); *Adarand*, 515 U.S. at 264 (Souter, J., dissenting); *Shaw v. Reno*, 509 U.S. at 679 (Souter, J., dissenting). *See also* Affirmative Action Voting Chart, *infra* pages 162–63.

77. Justice Ginsburg participated in seven affirmative action case that were decided on constitutional grounds, and she voted to uphold the affirmative action plans at issue in all seven cases. *See Hunt v. Cromartie*, 119 S. Ct. at 1554 (Stevens, J. concurring in judgment, joined by Ginsburg, J.); *Lawyer*, 117 S. Ct. at 2189 (joining majority opinion); *Abrams*, 521 U.S. at 103 (Breyer, J., dissenting, joined by Ginsburg, J.); *Bush*, 517 U.S. at 1003, 1045 (Stevens, J, dissenting, joined by Ginsburg, J., & Souter, J., dissenting, joined by Ginsburg, J.); *Shaw v. Hunt*, 517 U.S. at 918, 951 (Stevens, J., dissenting, joined in part by Ginsburg, J., & Souter, J., dissenting, joined by Ginsburg, J.); *Miller*, 515 U.S. at 934 (Ginsburg, J., dissenting); *Adarand*, 515 U.S. at 271 (Ginsburg, J., dissenting). *See also* Affirmative Action Voting Chart, *infra* pages 162–63.

78. Justice Breyer participated in seven affirmative action cases that were decided on constitutional grounds, and he voted to uphold the affirmative action plans at issue in all seven cases. *See Hunt v. Cromartie*, 119 S. Ct. at 1554 (Stevens, J. concurring in judgment, joined by Breyer, J.); *Lawyer*, 117 S. Ct. at 2189 (joining majority opinion); *Abrams*, 521 U.S. at 103 (Breyer, J., dissenting); *Bush*, 517 U.S. at 1003, 1045 (Stevens, J., dissenting, joined by Breyer, J., & Souter, J., dissenting, joined by Breyer, J.); *Shaw v. Hunt*, 517 U.S. at 918, 951 (Stevens, J., dissenting, joined in part by Breyer, J., & Souter, J. dissenting, joined

by Breyer, J.); *Miller*, 515 U.S. at 934 (Ginsburg, J., dissenting, joined by Breyer, J.); *Adarand*, 515 U.S. at 264, 271 (Souter, J., dissenting, joined by Breyer, J., & Ginsburg, J., dissenting, joined by Breyer, J.). *See also* Affirmative Action Voting Chart, *infra* pages 162–63.

79. The Supreme Court has decided eight constitutional affirmative action cases during the time in which both Justices Stevens and Souter have been sitting on the Court. Those eight cases are *Hunt v. Cromartie, Lawyer, Abrams, Bush, Shaw v. Hunt, Miller, Adarand,* and *Shaw v. Reno. See* Affirmative Action Voting Chart, *infra* pages 162–63. Justices Stevens and Souter always voted together in those eight cases. *See* Affirmative Action Voting Chart, *infra* pages 162–63. In those eight cases, Justices Stevens and Souter authored a total of nine opinions, but only two of those nine opinions were joined by both justices. Justice Stevens wrote opinions in five cases. *See Hunt v. Cromartie*, 119 S. Ct. at 1554 (Stevens, J. concurring in judgment, joined by Souter, Ginsburg, & Breyer, JJ.); *Bush*, 517 U.S. at 1003 (Stevens, J., dissenting, joined by Ginsburg & Breyer, JJ.); *Shaw v. Hunt*, 517 U.S. at 918 (Stevens, J., dissenting, joined in part by Ginsburg & Breyer, JJ.); *Miller*, 515 U.S. at 929 (Stevens, J., dissenting); *Adarand*, 515 U.S. at 242 (Stevens, J., dissenting, joined by Ginsburg, J.). Justice Souter wrote opinions in four cases. *See Lawyer*, 117 S. Ct. at 2189 (majority opinion of Souter, J., joined by Rehnquist, Stevens, Ginsburg, & Breyer, JJ.); *Bush*, 517 U.S. at 1045 (Souter, J., dissenting, joined by Ginsburg & Breyer, JJ.); *Shaw v. Hunt*, 515 U.S. at 951 (Souter, J., dissenting, joined by Ginsburg & Breyer, JJ.); *Adarand*, 515 U.S. at 264 (Souter, J., dissenting, joined by Ginsburg & Breyer, JJ.). The only opinions written by either justice that were signed by the other were Justice Stevens's opinion in *Hunt v. Cromartie*, 119 S. Ct. at 1554 (Stevens, J., concurring in judgment, joined by Souter, J.), and Justice Souter's majority opinion in *Lawyer*, 117 S. Ct. at 2189 (majority opinion of Souter, J., joined by Rehnquist, Stevens, Ginsburg, & Breyer, JJ.). Neither Justice Stevens nor Justice Souter has ever joined a dissenting opinion authored by the other in a constitutional affirmative action case.

80. *See supra* chapter 5, note 1 (listing Court's thirty-two racial affirmative action cases).

81. Korematsu v. United States, 323 U.S. 214 (1944).

82. *See id.* at 216 (adopting strict scrutiny standard of review).

83. *See* Loving v. Virginia, 388 U.S. 1, 11 (1967); *cf. Korematsu*, 323 U.S. at 216 (both stating traditional strict-scrutiny test).

84. *See* STONE ET AL., *supra* chapter 1, note 1, at 601; *see also* Fullilove, 448 U.S. at 519 (Marshall, J., concurring in judgment) (strict scrutiny is "strict in theory, but fatal in fact"). *Korematsu's* tolerance of the race-based internment of Japanese-American citizens is now generally regarded as the product of wartime hysteria, and the result is widely discredited. *See* STONE ET AL., *supra* chapter 1, note 1, at 601, and authorities cited therein; *see, e.g., Adarand*, 515 U.S. at 215 n.*, 236 (criticizing result in *Korematsu*); *id.* at 244 (Stevens, J. dissenting) (same). As is discussed below,

Justice O'Connor's majority opinion in *Adarand* stresses that the strict scrutiny that it envisions is not necessarily fatal scrutiny. *See infra*, text accompanying chapter 5, notes 104–126 (discussing issue of whether *Adarand* strict scrutiny is fatal scrutiny).

85. *See* DeFunis v. Odegaard, 416 U.S. 312 (1974) (case in which Supreme Court began considering affirmative action issue).

86. City of Richmond v. J.A. Croson Co., 488 U.S. 469 (1989).

87. *See Croson*, 488 U.S. at 477–86. Justice O'Connor wrote a majority opinion for the Court on many issues, but only four justices signed Part III-A of Justice O'Connor's opinion, which adopted the strict-scrutiny standard of review for non-congressional affirmative action plans. *See id.* at 493–98 (opinion of O'Connor, J., joined by Rehnquist, White, & Kennedy, JJ.). Nevertheless, Justice Scalia provided a fifth vote for the proposition that strict scrutiny should be applied to affirmative action programs. *See id.* at 520 (Scalia, J., concurring in judgment). *See also Adarand*, 515 U.S. at 221–22 (identifying five justices who applied strict scrutiny in *Croson*). Although Justice Stevens declined to sign Part III-A of Justice O'Connor's opinion, which endorsed strict scrutiny in the abstract, he nevertheless joined Parts III-B and IV of her opinion, which actually applied Justice O'Connor's ends/means analysis to invalidate the Richmond set-aside plan. *See Croson* 488 U.S. at 475 (listing votes of justices), *id.* at 498–508 (majority opinion of O'Connor, J., joined by Stevens, J.).

88. *See Croson*, 488 U.S. at 535–36 (Marshall, J., dissenting, joined by Brennan and Blackmun, JJ.) (arguing for intermediate scrutiny); *cf. id.* at 511–12, 514 (Stevens, J., concurring in part and concurring in judgment) (focusing on prospective benefit of racial classification and discounting importance of standard of review). Note, however, that Justice Stevens did vote to invalidate the Richmond set-aside program because it had not been shown to offer sufficient promise of prospective societal benefit. *See id.* at 511–18.

89. Fullilove v. Klutznick, 448 U.S. 448 (1980).

90. *See id.* at 453–54, 468–72 (opinion of Burger, C.J.) (describing federal plan at issue in *Fullilove*). In an effort to ensure the constitutional validity of the Richmond plan, the Richmond City Council had modeled its plan on the congressional set-aside plan whose constitutionality the Supreme Court had previously upheld in *Fullilove. See Croson*, 488 U.S. at 477–80, 505–06 (discussing belief of city's legal counsel that plan would be constitutional under *Fullilove* decision); *id.* at 528–29 (Marshall, J., dissenting) (asserting that Richmond set-aside plan was patterned upon plan upheld in *Fullilove*). The congressional plan that the Court upheld in *Fullilove* contained a 10 percent set-aside, *see Fullilove*, 448 U.S. at 453–56, whereas the Richmond plan that the Court invalidated in *Croson* contained 30 percent set-aside. *See Croson*, 488 U.S. at 477–86. However, the Richmond City Council had apparently selected a larger set-aside percentage to correspond to the larger, 50 percent black population of Richmond. *See id.* at 479–80 (citing 50 percent black population of Richmond).

91. *See Croson*, 488 U.S. at 486–93 (emphasizing special congressional powers under section 5 of Fourteenth Amendment).

92. Metro Broadcasting v. FCC, 497 U.S. 547 (1990).

93. *See id.* at 566, 600–01 (upholding FCC affirmative action plans).

94. *See id.* at 555–58 (describing two affirmative action plans).

95. *See id.* at 563–66 (applying intermediate scrutiny).

96. *See id.* at 564 (describing intermediate scrutiny standard of review).

97. *Cf. supra* text accompanying chapter 5, note 83 (describing strict scrutiny standard of review).

98. *See Metro Broadcasting*, 497 U.S. at 565–66 (distinguishing *Croson* by emphasizing special congressional powers under section 5 of Fourteenth Amendment).

99. *See Croson*, 488 U.S. at 486–93 (distinguishing *Fullilove* by emphasizing special congressional powers under section 5 of Fourteenth Amendment).

100. *See* chapter 5, part 1, section i (describing Supreme Court voting blocs on issue of affirmative action).

101. *See* SPANN, RACE AGAINST THE COURT, *supra* chapter 1, note 1, at 128–29 (discussing Justice White's greater receptivity to federal than local regulation).

102. *Compare Metro Broadcasting*, 497 U.S. at 550, *with Croson*, 488 U.S. at 475 (reporting votes of justices).

103. *See Metro Broadcasting*, 497 U.S. at 601–02 (Stevens, J., concurring) (focusing on prospective benefit of racial classification); *Croson*, 488 U.S. at 511–12 (Stevens, J., concurring in part and concurring in judgment) (same).

104. *See Adarand*, 515 U.S. at 225–27, 235 (overruling *Metro Broadcasting* and applying unitary strict-scrutiny standard).

105. *See id.* at 202–03, 222–23 (listing votes of justices, and discussing *Croson*).

106. *See id.* at 249–55 (Stevens, J., dissenting, joined by Ginsburg, J.) (Congress entitled to special deference); *id.* at 266–71 (Souter, J., dissenting, joined by Ginsburg & Breyer, JJ.) (*Fullilove* deference to Congress controls); *id.* at 271, 276 (Ginsburg, J., dissenting, joined by Breyer, J.) (Congress entitled to deference; nonfatal standard of review appropriate).

107. *See id.* at 236 ("we wish to dispel the notion that strict scrutiny is 'strict in theory but fatal in fact'").

108. *See id.* at 226, 228 (purpose of strict scrutiny is to ascertain whether affirmative action is legitimate).

109. *Missouri v. Jenkins*, 515 U.S. 70 (1995).

110. *See id.* at 112 (O'Connor, J., concurring) ("But it is not true that strict scrutiny is 'strict in theory, but fatal in fact.'").

111. *Regents of the Univ. of Cal. v. Bakke*, 438 U.S. 265, 287–91 (1978) (opinion of Powell, J.) (arguing for strict scrutiny).

112. *See id.* at 272–81 (opinion of Powell, J.) (describing admissions program for Univ. of Cal. at Davis medical school, which reserved sixteen of one hundred seats in entering class for disadvantaged minority applicants).

113. See *Adarand,* 515 U.S. at 258 (Stevens, J., dissenting, joined by Ginsburg, J.) (discussing Justice Powell's position in *Bakke* and *Fullilove*); *cf. id.* at 243 n.1 (objecting to term "strict scrutiny" on grounds that it has traditionally been understood to be fatal).

114. See *id.* at 267–71 (Souter, J., dissenting, joined by Ginsburg & Breyer, JJ.) (arguing that *Adarand* program was still controlled by *Fullilove*).

115. See *id.* at 245–46 (Ginsburg, J., dissenting, joined by Breyer, J.) (distinguishing between invidious and benign racial classifications under strict scrutiny standard of review).

116. See *id.* at 264–71 (Souter, J., dissenting, joined by Breyer, J.); *id.* at 275–76 (Ginsburg, J., dissenting, joined by Breyer, J.).

117. See *id.* at 239 (Scalia, J., concurring in part and concurring in judgment).

118. See *id.* (Scalia, J., concurring in part and concurring in judgment) ("[i]t is unlikely, if not impossible, that the challenged program would survive under this understanding of strict scrutiny").

119. See *Croson,* 488 U.S. at 524–25 (Scalia, J., concurring in judgment) (state can use racial classifications only to compensate actual victims of state's own discrimination).

120. See *infra* chapter 5, note 218 (discussing Justice Scalia's actual-victim position).

121. See *id.* at 518–19 (Kennedy, J., concurring in judgment) (rule limiting racial preferences to what is necessary to compensate actual victims of discrimination is appealing).

122. See *Firefighters v. Cleveland,* 478 U.S. at 535–45 (Rehnquist, J., dissenting) (Title VII remedies that override seniority must be limited to actual victims of discrimination); *Sheet Metal Workers,* 478 U.S. at 500 (Rehnquist, J., dissenting) (same); *Stotts,* 467 U.S. at 578–83 (majority opinion of White, J., joined by Rehnquist, J.) (same).

123. See *Adarand,* 515 U.S. at 240 (Thomas, J., dissenting) (there is no "racial paternalism" exception to principle of equal protection).

124. Missouri v. Jenkins, 515 U.S. 70 (1995).

125. See *id.* at 121 ("Despite their origins in 'the shameful history of state-enforced segregation,' these [historically-black] institutions can be "'both a source of pride to blacks who have attended them and a source of hope to black families who want the benefits of . . . learning for their children.'"" (quoting United States v. Fordice, 505 U.S. 717, 748 (1992) (Thomas, J., concurring)); *see generally Jenkins,* 515 U.S. at 119–22 (discussing benefits of historically black schools).

126. See *id.* at 122–23 (expressing view that historically black schools in black neighborhoods are not unconstitutional).

127. See Adarand Constructors v. Pena, 965 F. Supp. 1556, 1558–59, 1577–84 (D. Colo. 1997), *vacated as moot by* Adarand Constructors v. Slater, 169 F.3d 1292, 1296–99 (10th Cir. 1999).

128. *See supra* chapter 5, note 57 (enumerating votes of Justice O'Connor in constitutional affirmative action cases). Like the other conservative-bloc justices in the *Adarand* majority, Justice O'Connor voted to reverse the entry of summary judgment invalidating the redistricting plan in *Hunt v. Cromartie* because of disputed factual issues. *See supra* text accompanying chapter 5, note 61. Chief Justice Rehnquist also voted to uphold two additional affirmative action redistricting plans, but he has never voted to uphold a racial classification after strict scrutiny. *See supra* chapter 5, note 56 (describing three instances in which Chief Justice Rehnquist voted in favor of an affirmative action program in a constitutional case).

129. *Cf. Adarand,* 515 U.S. at 249–55 (Stevens, J., dissenting) (enumerating reasons that congressional affirmative action programs are entitled to greater deference than state and local programs).

130. *See Croson,* 488 U.S. at 488–89; *see also Metro Broadcasting,* 497 U.S. at 610–12, 613–14 (O'Connor, J., dissenting); *Wygant,* 476 U.S. at 288 (O'Connor, J., concurring); *Johnson v. Transportation Agency* 480 U.S. at 647–53 (1987) (O'Connor, J., concurring in judgment).

131. *See Metro Broadcasting,* 497 U.S. at 566–68 (recognizing broadcast diversity as permissible goal for affirmative action).

132. *See id.* at 564–65 (applying intermediate scrutiny).

133. *See Adarand,* 515 U.S. at 226–27 (overruling *Metro Broadcasting* with respect to standard of review).

134. *See Metro Broadcasting,* 497 U.S. at 601–02 (Stevens, J., concurring, voting to uphold plan on basis of prospective diversity).

135. *See, e.g., Adarand,* 515 U.S. at 258–59 (Stevens, J., dissenting); *Metro Broadcasting,* 497 U.S. at 601–02 (Stevens, J., concurring); *Wygant,* 476 U.S. at 313 (Stevens, J., dissenting) (all viewing prospective benefit as permissible basis for affirmative action).

136. *See Adarand,* 515 U.S. at 243 (Stevens, J., dissenting, joined by Ginsburg, J., favoring prospective benefit).

137. *See id.* at 270–71 (Souter, J., dissenting, favoring need to eliminate present racial skew in operation of public systems).

138. *See id.* (characterizing concern as relevant to remedy for past discrimination).

139. *See id.* at 264 (Souter, J., dissenting, joined by Ginsburg & Breyer, JJ.).

140. *See Wygant,* 476 U.S. at 286 (O'Connor, J., concurring, recognizing legitimacy of prospective diversity).

141. *See id.* at 288 n.* (characterizing "role model" justification for affirmative action as relevant to general societal discrimination rather than prospective diversity).

142. *Compare Croson,* 488 U.S. at 488–89 (*Fullilove* plan was remedy for past discrimination) *with id.* at 498–99 (*Croson* plan was remedy for general societal discrimination).

143. *See Fullilove,* 448 U.S. at 548–54 (Stevens, J., dissenting) (criticizing congressional findings).

144. *See Croson,* 488 U.S. at 498–506 (insufficient evidence of discrimination in Richmond construction trades); *cf. id.* at 561 (Blackmun, J., dissenting,) (emphasizing that Richmond was "cradle of the Old Confederacy"); *id.* at 528 (Marshall, J., dissenting) (emphasizing that Richmond was capital of Confederacy).

145. *See Adarand,* 515 U.S. at 226, 229–30 (citing *Croson,* 488 U.S. at 493 (opinion of O'Connor, J.)) (strict scrutiny needed to distinguish benign from illegitimate discrimination and to ensure tight "fit" between prior discrimination and remedy).

146. *See Croson,* 488 U.S. at 493 (opinion of O'Connor, J.) (strict scrutiny needed to distinguish benign from illegitimate discrimination and to ensure tight "fit" between prior discrimination and remedy).

147. *See Metro Broadcasting,* 497 U.S. at 566–84 (discussing congressional findings).

148. *See Adarand,* 515 U.S. at 263 & n.18 (Stevens, J., dissenting) (describing congressional deliberations preceding adoption of affirmative action program at issue in *Adarand*).

149. *See Fullilove,* 448 U.S. at 548–54 (Stevens, J., dissenting) (criticizing cursory congressional consideration).

150. *See Metro Broadcasting,* 497 U.S. at 569–71 (FCC designed program at issue).

151. *See id.* at 559 n.8, 572–79 (Congress was politically unable to resolve issue).

152. *See* Winter Park Communications v. FCC, 873 F.2d 347, 364 (D.C. Cir. 1989) (Williams, J., concurring in part and dissenting in part, characterizing appropriations riders as mere "mental standstill").

153. *See Metro Broadcasting,* 497 U.S. at 578 n.29 (appropriations riders were not mere "mental standstill").

154. *See id.* at 558–61, 576–77 (discussing FCC inquiry into validity of its own minority preference programs); *see also Winter Park,* 873 F.2d at 350–51 (same).

155. *See* Steele v. FCC, 770 F.2d 1192, 1196 (D.C. Cir. 1985) (FCC had jurisdiction to adopt affirmative action plan); *see also Metro Broadcasting,* 497 U.S. at 559 n.8 (same).

156. *See* Deduction for Health Insurance Costs of Self-Employed Individuals, Pub. L. 104–7, § 2, 109 Stat. 93–94 (1995) (repealing "distress sale" program).

157. *See Race- and Gender-Based Provisions for the Auctioning of C Block Broadcast Personal Communications Service Licensees, Elimination,* 60 Fed. Reg. 34200, 34202, 34205 (Further Notice of Proposed Rulemaking, in light of *Adarand,* to amend 47 C.F.R. Parts 20 & 24, by eliminating race and gender preferences in FCC cellular spectrum auction program).

158. *See Bakke*, 438 U.S. at 307–10 (opinion of Powell, J.) (stressing importance of findings).

159. *See* STONE ET AL., *supra* chapter 1, note 1, at ii–ciii (specifying term of Justice Powell).

160. *See Wygant*, 476 U.S. at 286–93 (O'Connor, J., concurring); *but see Croson*, 488 U.S. at 498–506 (discussing inadequacy of Richmond City Council's informal finding of past discrimination without reaffirming argument that formal findings are unnecessary).

161. *See Adarand*, 515 U.S. at 263 & n.18 (Stevens, J., dissenting) (describing congressional deliberations preceding adoption of affirmative action program at issue in *Adarand*).

162. *See id.* at 239 (remanding for application of strict-scrutiny standard).

163. *See* Stephen Buckley, *Voting Rights Ruling Called Death Knell for Exclusion; Ex-Clinton Nominee Hails Order in Maryland*, WASH. POST, Apr. 7, 1994, at B1; Anthony Lewis, *Abroad at Home; Anatomy Of a Smear*, N.Y. TIMES, June 4, 1993, at A31; Clarence Page, *'Cumulative Voting' Takes Lani Guinier into the Mainstream*, CHI. TRIB., March 30, 1994, at 23.

164. *See Adarand*, 515 U.S. at 264 (Stevens, J., dissenting) (distinguishing *Adarand* and *Fullilove*).

165. *See Croson*, 488 U.S. at 507–08 (opinion of O'Connor, J.) (quotas reflect stereotyped thinking about racial minorities); *Bakke*, 438 U.S. at 272–75, 315–19 (opinion of Powell, J.) (permitting consideration of race but opposing quotas).

166. *See Metro Broadcasting*, 497 U.S. at 599 (FCC preferences did not entail quotas).

167. *See Fullilove*, 448 U.S. at 521 (Marshall, J., concurring in judgment) quoting *Bakke*, 438 U.S. at 375 (opinion of Brennan, J.).

168. *See Croson,* 488 U.S. at 520, 524–28 (Scalia, J., concurring in judgment) (opposing affirmative action not necessary to compensate actual victims of discrimination, and thereby opposing quotas).

169. *See Metro Broadcasting*, 497 U.S. at 630 (O'Connor, J., dissenting, characterizing "distress sale" program as entailing quotas).

170. *See id.* at 599 (rejecting quota characterization); *but cf. Adarand*, 515 U.S. at 226–27 (overruling another aspect of *Metro Broadcasting*, relating to standard of review).

171. *See Paradise*, 480 U.S. at 153–66 (opinion of Brennan, J.) (upholding quota).

172. *See Sheet Metal Workers*, 478 U.S. at 426–40 (upholding quota).

173. *See Fullilove*, 448 U.S. at 453–54, 468–72 (opinion of Burger, C.J.) (upholding quota). *But cf. Sheet Metal Workers*, 478 U.S. at 475–81 (opinion of Brennan, J.) (characterizing hiring goals in *Sheet Metal Workers* as benchmarks rather than quotas).

174. *See United Jewish Orgs.*, 430 U.S. at 155–62 (opinion of White, J., joined by Stevens, Brennan, and Blackmun, JJ.); *id.* at 171–79 (Brennan J., concurring in part).

175. In *Miller*, Justice Kennedy distinguished *Shaw v. Reno–* and *Miller*-type racial gerrymandering claims from the vote-dilution claim that he found to be present in *United Jewish Orgs.* He believed that *Shaw v. Reno* and *Miller* racial gerrymandering claims recognized the rights of voters not to be assigned to voting districts on the basis of race for the same reason that individuals cannot constitutionally be assigned to public schools on the basis of race. However, Justice Kennedy asserted that *United Jewish Orgs.* concerned a cause of action for vote dilution rather than for racial gerrymandering. *See Miller*, 515 U.S. at 910–15. Justice Ginsburg disagreed in her *Miller* dissent, arguing that *United Jewish Orgs.* was a *Shaw v. Reno–* and *Miller*-type racial gerrymandering case rather than a vote-dilution case. She emphasized that the plaintiffs in *United Jewish Orgs.* had never asserted a vote-dilution claim. *See id.* at 946 n.11 (Ginsburg dissenting).

176. *Compare Metro Broadcasting*, 497 U.S. at 599 (rejecting characterization of "distress sale" program as quota) *with id.* at 630 (O'Connor, J., dissenting) (characterizing "distress sale" program as quota).

177. *See Bakke*, 438 U.S. at 272–75 (opinion of Powell, J.) (opposing quotas).

178. A five-justice majority voted to invalidate the particular plan that was before the Court in *Bakke*, while a different five-justice majority voted to uphold the use of racial preferences in appropriate circumstances. Four justices—Justices Stevens, Burger, Stewart, and Rehnquist—declined to reach the constitutional question, finding that the Davis plan violated Title VI of the Civil Rights Act of 1964, which prohibits federally funded programs from excluding or denying benefits to any person on the grounds of race. *See Bakke*, 438 U.S. at 411–21 (Stevens, J., concurring in judgment in part and dissenting in part, joined by Burger, Stewart, and Rehnquist, JJ.). These four justices would have sidestepped the constitutional issue, finding that it was not properly before the Court. *See id.* at 411–12. The fifth vote to invalidate the plan was provided by Justice Powell, who would have invalidated it on equal protection grounds. See *id.* at 305–20 (opinion of Powell, J.). Because Justice Powell found the Title VI prohibition to be coextensive with that of the equal protection clause, he found it necessary to reach the constitutional issue. *See id.* at 281–87. Four justices—Justice Brennan, White, Marshall, and Blackmun—believed that the preference was valid as a racial classification designed to remedy disadvantages imposed upon minorities by past societal discrimination. *See id.* at 324–26, 355–62 (opinion of Brennan, J., concurring in judgment in part and dissenting in part, joined by White, Marshall, and Blackmun, JJ.). Because, like Justice Powell, these four justices found the scope of the Title VI prohibition to be coextensive with the equal protection clause, they too deemed it necessary to reach the constitutional issue. *See id.* Justice White believed that Title VI gave no cause of

action to private litigants to enforce its funding restrictions. *See id.* at 379–87 (opinion of White, J.).

179. *See id.* at 315–20 (opinion of Powell, J.) (approving of Harvard plan).

180. *See, e.g., Adarand*, 515 U.S. at 240–41 (Thomas, J., concurring in part and concurring in judgment); *Metro Broadcasting*, 497 U.S. at 579–84; *id.* at 601–02 (Stevens, J., concurring); *Croson*, 488 U.S. at 493–98 (opinion of O'Connor, J.); *id.* at 526–28 (Scalia, J., concurring in judgment); *Wygant*, 476 U.S. at 313–19 (Stevens, J., dissenting); *Fullilove*, 448 U.S. at 519–21 (Marshall, J., concurring in judgment); *Bakke*, 438 U.S. at 294–99 (opinion of Powell, J.); *United Jewish Orgs.*, 430 U.S. at 165–68 (opinion of White, J.); *id.* at 172–74 (opinion of Brennan, J.); *DeFunis*, 416 U.S. at 343 (Douglas, J., dissenting).

181. *See DeFunis* 416 U.S. at 340–41 (Douglas, J., dissenting).

182. *See United Jewish Orgs.* 430 U.S. at 172–74 (Brennan, J., concurring in part); *see also Bakke*, 438 U.S. at 358–62 (opinion of Brennan, J.).

183. *See Bakke*, 438 U.S. at 298–99 (opinion of Powell, J.).

184. *See Croson*, 488 U.S. at 493–94 (opinion of O'Connor, J.) (discussing stigmatization in dicta rather than holding, in portion of opinion joined only by Chief Justice Rehnquist, and Justices White and Kennedy).

185. *See Metro Broadcasting*, 497 U.S. at 603–04 (O'Connor J., dissenting) (discussing stigmatization and racial stereotyping in dissent).

186. *See Wygant*, 476 U.S. at 313–19 (Stevens, J., dissenting).

187. *See Adarand*, 515 U.S. at 226 (quoting *Croson*, 488 U.S. at 493) (plurality opinion of O'Connor, J.) (discussing need for strict scrutiny).

188. *See Metro Broadcasting*, 497 U.S. at 566–79 (minority ownership will promote broadcast diversity); *but see id.* at 579–84 (acceptance of nexus between broadcast ownership and broadcast diversity does not constitute racial stereotyping).

189. *See Metro Broadcasting*, 497 U.S. at 601–02 (Stevens, J., concurring); *Croson*, 488 U.S. at 514–16 (Stevens, J., concurring in part and concurring in judgment); *Fullilove*, 448 U.S. at 521 (Marshall, J., concurring in judgment); *Bakke*, 438 U.S. at 319–20 (opinion of Powell, J.); *United Jewish Orgs.*, 430 U.S. at 165–68 (opinion of White, J.); *id.* at 174 (opinion of Brennan, J.).

190. *See Croson*, 488 U.S. at 514–16 (Stevens, J., concurring in part and concurring in judgment) (discussing stigmatization of whites).

191. *See, e.g., Bakke*, 438 U.S. at 294–99 (opinion of Powell, J.); *United Jewish Orgs.*, 430 U.S. at 172–74 (both seemingly conflating stigma and burden on whites).

192. *See United Jewish Orgs.*, 430 U.S. at 172–74 (opinion of Brennan, J.) (upholding plan despite arguable stigmatization of whites).

193. *See, e.g., Adarand*, 515 U.S. at 229 (quoting *Croson*, 488 U.S. at 516–17) (Stevens, J., concurring in part and concurring in judgment); *Adarand*, 515 U.S. at

243–47, 253 n.7 (Stevens, J., dissenting); *id.* at 269–71 (Souter, J., dissenting); *Metro Broadcasting* 397 U.S. at 596–600; *id.* at 630–31 (O'Connor, J., dissenting); *Johnson v. Transportation Agency*, 480 U.S. at 637–38; *Firefighters v. Cleveland*, 478 U.S. at 531–35 (White, J., dissenting); *id.* at 535–45 (Rehnquist, J., dissenting); *Wygant*, 476 U.S. at 279–84 (opinion of Powell, J.); *id.* at 294–95 (White, J., concurring in judgment); *id.* at 306–10 (Marshall, J., dissenting); *Fullilove*, 448 U.S. at 484–85 (opinion of Burger, C.J.); *Weber*, 443 U.S. at 208; *Bakke*, 438 U.S. at 294–99 (opinion of Powell, J.); *United Jewish Orgs.*, 430 U.S. at 165–68 (opinion of White, J.); *id.* at 171–79 (Brennan, J., concurring in part).

194. *See Croson*, 488 U.S. at 507–08 (discussing narrowness requirement without discussing burden on innocent whites).

195. *See Metro Broadcasting*, 497 U.S. at 596–600 (discussing burden imposed on nonminorities by FCC affirmative action plans).

196. *See Wygant*, 476 U.S. at 268, 279–84 (opinion of Powell, J., joined by Burger & Rehnquist, JJ.) (objecting to layoff plan as insufficiently narrow); *id.* at 294–95 (White, J., concurring in judgment) (objecting to layoff of white teachers in order to retain minority teachers).

197. The deprivation of an economic opportunity such as a prospective salary is the same whether it was first promised and then denied or never promised at all. This point was recognized by Justice Stevens in *Wygant. See Wygant*, 476 U.S. at 319 n.14. Outside economic circles, it is probably true that deterioration of the status quo is psychologically viewed as more serious than lost expectations. *See, e.g.,* Lon L. Fuller & William R. Perdue, Jr. *The Reliance Interest in Contract Damages I*, 46 YALE L.J. 52, 53–57 (1936) (under "ordinary standards of justice," restitution and reliance claims are stronger than lost expectation claims). Nevertheless, although differential levels of reliance might arguably accompany the two types of deprivations, reliance would seem to be unjustifiable whenever there is advance notice of a future deprivation, as there is under most affirmative action plans. Moreover, it is unclear why the legislature should not be able to conclude that the public interest in promoting affirmative action outweighs the public interest in protecting the reliance of its citizens.

198. *See, e.g., Wygant*, 476 U.S. at 294–95 (White, J., concurring in judgment); *id.* at 282–84 (opinion of Powell, J., joined by Burger & Rehnquist, JJ.); *cf. Stotts*, 467 U.S. at 574–76 (majority opinion of White, J., joined by Burger, Powell, Rehnquist, & O'Connor, JJ.) (arguing in favor of protecting seniority); *but see Firefighters v. Cleveland*, 478 U.S. at 531–35 (White, J., dissenting) (arguing that Title VII precludes prospective race-conscious promotions when not necessary to benefit actual victims of discrimination); *id.* at 535–45 (Rehnquist, J., dissenting) (same). *See also Weber*, 443 U.S. at 208 (majority opinion of Brennan, J., joined by Stewart, White, Marshall, & Blackmun, JJ.) (emphasizing that preferential training plan did not require discharge of white workers).

199. *See Firefighters v. Cleveland*, 478 U.S. at 535–45 (Rehnquist, J., dissenting)

(arguing that Title VII precludes prospective race-conscious promotions when not necessary to benefit actual victims of discrimination); *Wygant,* 476 U.S. at 282–84 (opinion of Powell, J., joined by Rehnquist, C.J.) (expressing aversion to layoffs); *cf. Stotts,* 467 U.S. at 574–76; (majority opinion of White, J., joined by Rehnquist, J.) (arguing in favor of protecting seniority under Title VII).

200. *See Wygant,* 476 U.S. at 293–94 (O'Connor, J., concurring) (discussing layoff provisions and hiring goals).

201. *See Johnson v. Transportation Agency,* 480 U.S. at 637–40 (considering burden on innocent whites); *Firefighters v. Cleveland,* 478 U.S. at 515–24 (remedial powers of court in approving burdens contained in voluntary consent decree are broader than court's power to issue remedy itself); *Stotts,* 467 U.S. at 576–83 (invalidating affirmative action layoff plan that interfered with nonminority seniority rights); *Weber,* 443 U.S. at 208–09 (Title VII permits voluntary affirmative action plans that do not unnecessarily trammel interest of whites); *see also Wygant,* 476 U.S. at 317–18 (Stevens, J., dissenting) (emphasizing fact that burden on whites was voluntarily assumed through full participation in procedures by which plan was adopted).

202. *See Johnson v. Transportation Agency,* 480 U.S. at 632–33 (voluntary affirmative action plan can be adopted without prima facie showing of past discrimination under Title VII); *Firefighters v. Cleveland,* 478 U.S. at 515–30 (court-approved consent decree can exceed scope of permissible court-ordered remedies under Title VII); *Weber,* 443 U.S. at 208–09 (adjudicated Title VII violation is not prerequisite to voluntary affirmative action plan, as it would be for court-imposed remedy).

203. *See Wygant,* 476 U.S. at 317–18 (Stevens, J., dissenting) (emphasizing fact that burden on whites was voluntarily assumed by full participants in adoption procedure).

204. *See supra* text accompanying and following chapter 5, note 130 (discussing permissible justifications for affirmative action).

205. United Steelworkers of Am. v. Weber, 443 U.S. 193 (1979).

206. *See id.* at 208–09 (prior unlawful discrimination not precondition to voluntary affirmative action); *see also Johnson v. Transportation Agency,* 480 U.S. at 632–33 (extending *Weber* to municipal employers).

207. *See Johnson v. Transportation Agency,* 480 U.S. at 647–57 (O'Connor, J., concurring in judgment); *id.* at 657 (White, J. dissenting); *id.* at 669–77 (Scalia, J., dissenting, joined by Rehnquist, C.J.).

208. *See supra* text accompanying chapter 5, notes 59 & 60 (listing votes of justices in affirmative action cases).

209. *See Adarand,* 515 U.S. at 202–03 (listing votes of justices).

210. *See id.* at 2112–13 (overruling *Metro Broadcasting*).

211. For the general views of Justices O'Connor and Kennedy on the doctrine of *stare decisis* see *id.* at 2114–17. It is not clear what inference should be drawn from the refusal of Chief Justice Rehnquist and Justices Scalia and Thomas to join

the *stare decisis* portion of Justice O'Connor's opinion in *Adarand*, but it is likely that those three justices are more rather than less willing to overrule cases than are Justices O'Connor and Kennedy. Both Justices O'Connor and Kennedy were unwilling to overrule *Roe v. Wade* in the joint opinion that they authored with Justice Souter in *Planned Parenthood of Southeastern Pennsylvania v. Casey*, 505 U.S. 833, 845–46 (1992) (joint opinion of O'Connor, Kennedy, and Souter, JJ.). This was true despite their political opposition to abortion. *See Adarand*, 515 U.S. at 233 (explaining decision not to overrule *Roe* in *Casey*). Justice O'Connor has in the past stated that she disagrees with the holding of *Weber* but that it is now so well settled that she would not overrule it. *See Johnson v. Transportation Agency*, 480 U.S. at 647–48. However, that statement was made in 1987, prior to Justice O'Connor's anti-affirmative-action votes in *Dept. of Commerce, Lawyer, Abrams, Bush, Shaw v. Hunt, Miller, Adarand, Shaw v. Reno, Metro Broadcasting*, and *Croson*, and it is not clear that she will continue to embrace the position that she adopted in *Johnson v. Transportation Agency*.

212. *See Adarand* 515 U.S. at 205–10 (describing *Adarand* affirmative action program).

213. *See id.* at 2117–18 (requiring strict scrutiny of *Adarand* financial incentive plan).

214. *Cf. Weber*, 443 U.S. at 208–09 (declining to demarcate line between permissible and impermissible voluntary affirmative action plans).

215. *See Weber*, 443 U.S. at 200–04, 208–09 (focusing on benign nature of affirmative action plan at issue).

216. *See Adarand*, 515 U.S. at 226–31 (benign affirmative action subject to strict scrutiny).

217. *See Firefighters v. Cleveland*, 478 U.S. at 515–28 (authorizing use of race-conscious remedies in Title VII consent decree when not necessary to provide remedy to actual victims of discrimination); *Sheet Metal Workers*, 478 U.S. at 471–75 (opinion of Brennan, J., joined by Marshall, Blackmun, & Stevens, JJ.) (arguing that Title VII authorized court to order race-conscious remedies not intended to provide make-whole relief to actual victims of discrimination); *id.* at 483–84 (Powell, J., concurring in part and concurring in judgment) (arguing that Title VII authorized court to order race-conscious remedies not intended to provide make-whole relief to actual victims of discrimination, at least where defendant's conduct was egregious); *compare Firefighters v. Cleveland with Stotts*, 467 U.S. at 578–83 (suggesting that race-conscious Title VII remedies are limited to actual victims of discrimination).

218. Justice Scalia has argued that a state can use race-conscious remedies to undo discrimination in which the state itself has engaged in the past, as for example when it raises the salaries of minority workers who are being paid less than white workers doing comparable jobs. *See Croson*, 488 U.S. at 522–28 (Scalia, J., concurring in judgment). It is unclear whether Justice Scalia views such a remedy as a race-

based affirmative action plan or as a plan that compensates actual victims of discrimination. In part, this is because it is unclear whether there is ultimately any difference between the two.

219. *See Johnson v. Transportation Agency,* 480 U.S. at 664–68 (Scalia, J., dissenting, joined by Rehnquist, C.J.) (arguing that Title VII precludes race-conscious affirmative action not required to compensate actual victims of discrimination); *Firefighters v. Cleveland,* 478 U.S. 535–45 (Rehnquist, J., dissenting) (same); *Sheet Metal Workers,* 478 U.S. at 500 (Rehnquist, J., dissenting) (same).

220. *See supra* text accompanying chapter 5, notes 57, 59, & 60 (listing votes of justices in affirmative action cases). Justice Kennedy has also expressed some receptivity to the actual-victim limitation. *See Croson,* 488 U.S. at 518–19 (Kennedy, J., concurring in judgment) (rule limiting racial preferences to what is necessary to compensate actual victims of discrimination is appealing).

221. *See Adarand,* 515 U.S. at 224, 225–27 (applying strict scrutiny to federal as well as nonfederal affirmative action programs).

222. *See Croson,* 488 U.S. at 477–86 (applying strict scrutiny to nonfederal affirmative action programs).

223. *See supra* text accompanying chapter 5, notes 104–129 (discussing whether *Adarand* strict scrutiny is fatal in fact).

224. *See Adarand,* 515 U.S. at 237 (strict scrutiny not "fatal in fact").

225. *See supra* text accompanying chapter 5, notes 104–129 (discussing whether *Adarand* strict scrutiny is fatal in fact).

226. The Supreme Court has held that gender-based classifications are subject to intermediate scrutiny rather than the strict scrutiny that is normally applied to race-based classifications. *See* Craig v. Boren, 429 U.S. 190, 197 (1976) (adopting intermediate scrutiny standard); *cf. United States v. Virginia,* 518 U.S. 515, 531 (1996) (modifying intermediate scrutiny to require "exceedingly persuasive" justification for gender classifications). As a result, *Adarand* does not appear to require the application of strict scrutiny to gender-based affirmative action programs, as it does for race-based programs. Justice Stevens pointed out in his *Adarand* dissent that this creates the perverse result of making it easier under the equal protection clause to adopt a valid gender affirmative action plan than it is to adopt a valid racial affirmative action plan, even though the primary purpose of the equal protection clause was to end the history of discrimination against blacks. *See Adarand,* 515 U.S. at 247 (Stevens, J., dissenting). This anomaly takes on added potential significance when one recalls that Justice O'Connor—the author of the majority opinion in *Adarand*—has almost never voted to uphold a nonjudicial race-based affirmative action program on the merits. The only affirmative action programs that she has voted to uphold on the merits were a redistricting plan wrongly invalidated by summary judgment despite the presence of factual disputes, *see Hunt v. Cromartie,* 119 S. Ct. at 1547, 1548–52 (majority opinion of Thomas, J., joined by O'Connor, J.), and an employment-based affirmative action program that was presented to the

Court as a gender-based program. *See Johnson v. Transportation Agency*, 480 U.S. at 647 (O'Connor, J., concurring in judgment).

227. Washington v. Davis, 426 U.S. 229, 238–48 (1976) (requiring intentional discrimination for constitutional violation).

228. *Cf.* Griggs v. Duke Power, 401 U.S. 424, 429–30 (1971) (finding disparate impact sufficient to establish Title VII violation).

229. *See, e.g., Metro Broadcasting* 497 U.S. at 566, 600–01 (racial preferences for minority broadcasters in award of broadcast licenses); *Croson*, 488 U.S. at 477–86 (minority set-aside for construction contracts); *Wygant* 476 U.S. at 270–73 (1986) (opinion of Powell, J.) (preference for minority teachers in avoiding layoffs); *Fullilove* 448 U.S. at 453–54, 468–72 (opinion of Burger, C.J.) (minority set-aside for construction contracts); *Bakke*, 438 U.S. at 272–81 (opinion of Powell, J.) (medical school admissions preference for disadvantaged minority applicants).

230. Statistical studies documenting the continuing prejudice, social disadvantage, and economic disadvantage of women and racial minorities relative to white males are cited and discussed in Spann, *Proposition 209, supra* chapter 1, note 1, at 238–41.

231. Personnel Adm'r v. Feeney, 442 U.S. 256 (1979).

232. *See id.* at 278–80 (knowledge of disparate impact insufficient to establish equal protection violation).

233. *See id.* Although *Feeney* was a gender discrimination case, *see id.* at 261–64 (describing gender-based challenge to veterans preference program), its intent holding seems equally applicable to racial discrimination.

234. *See infra* text accompanying chapter 5, note 342 (discussing relationship between racial and political gerrymandering).

235. *See supra* chapter 5, note 230 (citing statistical references documenting disadvantages suffered by women and minorities).

236. Griggs v. Duke Power, 401 U.S. 424, 429–30 (1971) (finding disparate impact sufficient to establish Title VII violation).

237. United Steelworkers of Am. v. Weber, 443 U.S. 193 (1979).

238. *See id.* at 208–09 (race-conscious affirmative action does not necessarily violate Title VII).

239. *See id.* at 200–04, 208–09; *cf. Adarand*, 515 U.S. at 218–25 (rejecting benign motive as justification for less than strict scrutiny).

240. *See supra* text accompanying chapter 5, notes 204–216 (discussing impact of *Adarand* on *Weber*).

241. *See supra* text accompanying chapter 5, notes 128 & 129 (suggesting that nonfatal strict scrutiny may be functional equivalent of intermediate scrutiny).

242. As has been noted, the increasing conservatism of the American public seems to rest on a deep ambivalence about affirmative action. The American public seems to favor some ill-defined changes in affirmative action, but is not willing to abolish affirmative action completely. *See supra* text accompanying chapter 1, note 24 (discussing and documenting ambivalence about affirmative action).

243. For an argument that the Supreme Court is institutionally incapable of doing anything other than reflecting majoritarian political preferences, see SPANN, RACE AGAINST THE COURT, *supra* chapter 1, note 1.

244. The seven redistricting cases decided by the Supreme Court since 1993 are *Hunt v. Cromartie, Lawyer, Abrams, Bush, Shaw v. Hunt, Miller,* and *Shaw v. Reno.*

245. The Court invalidated the majority-minority districting plans at issue in *Abrams, Bush, Shaw v. Hunt,* and *Miller.* The Court applied strict scrutiny to the majority-minority districting plan at issue in *Shaw v. Reno. See* Affirmative Action Voting Chart, *infra* pages 162–63.

246. In one case, a unanimous Court provisionally upheld the constitutionality of a districting plan that changed the challenged district from a majority-minority district to a district that contained 43 percent black voting-age residents. *See Hunt v. Cromartie,* 119 S. Ct. at 1547–48. In the other case, the Court upheld 5–4 the constitutionality of a redistricting plan that did not increase the number of major-ity-minority districts, but rather eliminated a majority-minority district that had previously existed. *See Lawyer,* 117 S. Ct. at 2189–92, 2194–95. *See also supra* text accompanying chapter 5, note 61 (discussing *Hunt v. Cromartie*); chapter 5, note 49 (discussing *Lawyer*); Affirmative Action Voting Chart, *infra* pages 162–63.

247. Shaw v. Reno, 509 U.S. 630 (1993).

248. *See id.* at 642–49 (applying strict scrutiny to bizarrely shaped districts).

249. United Jewish Orgs. v. Carey, 430 U.S. 144 (1977).

250. *See Shaw v. Reno,* 509 U.S. at 649–52 (distinguishing prior race-conscious districting cases).

251. *See Miller,* 515 U.S. at 910–12 (racial gerrymandering claim is analytically distinct from vote-dilution claim).

252. United States v. Hays, 515 U.S. 737 (1995).

253. *See id.* at 742–49 (granting standing to maintain racial gerrymandering cause of action only to voters residing in challenged district).

254. *See Shaw v. Reno,* 509 U.S. at 642–43, 659 (race-conscious districting re-inforces racial stereotypes and incites racial hostility); *see also Miller,* 515 U.S. at 911–12 (citing *Shaw v. Reno* for same proposition).

255. *See Hays,* 515 U.S. at 742–49; *Shaw v. Reno,* 509 U.S. at 648 (discussing harms suffered by white residents of majority-minority districts).

256. *See Shaw v. Reno,* 509 U.S. at 659–64 (White, J., dissenting, joined by Stevens, J.).

257. *See id.* at 676–79 (Stevens, J., dissenting).

258. *See Miller,* 515 U.S. at 929 (Stevens, J., dissenting).

259. *See id.* at 930 (quoting *id.* at 912 (majority opinion)); *see also* Shaw v. Hunt, 517 U.S. at 927–29, 946–51 (Stevens, J., dissenting, discussing inconsis-tency in majority's treatment of racial stereotypes); *Shaw v. Reno,* 509 U.S. at 678 n.3 (Stevens, J., dissenting) (same).

260. *See Miller*, 515 U.S. at 932–33 (distinguishing between racial inclusion and exclusion).

261. *See Shaw v. Hunt*, 517 U.S. 921–22 (Stevens, J., dissenting) (white voters were really complaining about integration rather than segregation).

262. *See Bush*, 517 U.S. at 1003–04 (Stevens, J., dissenting) (*Shaw v. Reno* cause of action was misconceived).

263. *See id.* at 1035–37 (*Shaw v. Reno* cause of action was discriminatory); *see also Miller*, 515 U.S. at 931–32 (*Shaw v. Reno* invidiously treated racial groups differently than other groups).

264. *See Shaw v. Reno*, 517 U.S. at 679–85 (Souter, J., dissenting).

265. *See id.* at 686–87 (Constitution does not require voting districts to have nonbizarre shapes).

266. See *Bush*, 517 U.S. at 1054–55 (abstract representational harms fall on all races).

267. *See id.* at 1073–77 (arguing that *Shaw v. Reno* should be overruled).

268. *See Miller*, 515 U.S. at 929–32 (Ginsburg, J., dissenting, joined by Stevens, Souter, & Breyer, JJ.).

269. *See id.* at 944–47 (districting necessarily treats voters as members of a group rather than as individuals).

270. *See Abrams*, 521 U.S. at 119 (Breyer, J., dissenting, finding no constitutional cause of action for racial gerrymandering).

271. Shaw v. Reno, 509 U.S. 630 (1993).

272. *See id.* at 641–42, 646–47 (race-conscious districting sometimes, but not always, triggers strict scrutiny); *see also Bush* 517 U.S. at 958–59 (opinion of O'Connor, J.) (same); *Miller* 515 U.S. at 916–17 (same).

273. *See Shaw v. Reno* 509 U.S. at 642–49 (stressing bizarre shape of voting district).

274. Miller v. Johnson, 515 U.S. 900 (1995).

275. *Adarand* was decided on June 12, 1995, *see Adarand*, 515 U.S. at 200, and *Miller* was decided on June 29, 1995, *see Miller*, 515 U.S. at 900.

276. *See Miller*, 515 U.S. at 915–17 (announcing "predominant factor" test).

277. Washington v. Davis, 426 U.S. 229 (1976).

278. Personnel Adm'r v. Feeney, 442 U.S. 256 (1979).

279. *See infra* text accompanying chapter 5, notes 230–233 (discussing *Washington v. Davis* and *Feeney* interpretations of discriminatory intent).

280. *See Miller*, 515 U.S. at 916 (discussing *Feeney*); *see also Shaw v. Reno*, 509 U.S. at 646 (permitting legislatures to be aware of race in making districting decisions).

281. *See Miller*, 515 U.S. at 916 (recognizing difficulty of applying *Feeney* in voting rights context);

282. Justices Stevens, Souter, Ginsburg, and Breyer believe that the *Miller* "predominant factor" standard is unworkable. *See Abrams v. Johnson*, 521 U.S. 74,

116–19 (Breyer, J., dissenting, joined by Stevens, Souter, & Ginsburg, JJ., arguing that *Miller* "predominant racial motive" standard is too imprecise to be workable, and citing other opinions that have reached same conclusion); *Bush*, 517 U.S. at 1057–64 (Souter, J., dissenting, joined by Ginsburg & Breyer, JJ., finding *Miller* "predominant factor" standard to be unmanageable); *Shaw v. Hunt*, 517 U.S. at 929–30 (Stevens, J., dissenting, joined by Ginsburg & Breyer, JJ., emphasizing difficulty in distinguishing between use of race as "substantial" or "motivating" factor and use of race as "predominant" factor).

283. *See Bush*, 517 U.S. at 996 (suggesting that strict scrutiny should always apply to the intentional creation of majority-minority districts).

284. *See id.* at 999–1003 (Thomas, J., concurring in judgment, joined by Scalia, J., arguing that all intentional majority-minority districts should trigger strict scrutiny).

285. *See Miller*, 515 U.S. at 928–29 (O'Connor, J., concurring, arguing for high threshold of race consciousness to trigger strict scrutiny).

286. DeWitt v. Wilson, 515 U.S. 1170 (1995), *aff'g* DeWitt v. Wilson, 856 F. Supp. 1409 (E.D. Cal. 1994) (three-judge court).

287. *Compare Miller*, 515 U.S. at 921–22 (discussing efforts to maximize majority-minority districts), *with* Wilson v. Eu, 823 P.2d 545, 549–50 (1992) (California Supreme Court decision upholding *DeWitt* plan and discussing efforts to maximize majority-minority districts).

288. *Compare Miller*, 515 U.S. at 910 (district court found race to have been "overriding, predominant force") *with DeWitt*, 856 F. Supp at 1413–15 (district court found that race did not predominate over traditional districting principles).

289. *See* Lawyer v. Department of Justice, 117 S. Ct. 2186, 2194 (1997) (upholding under clear-error standard district court finding that race was not predominant factor).

290. *See Miller*, 515 U.S. at 917–20 (deferring to district court findings of fact that were not clearly erroneous).

291. *See Abrams* 521 U.S. at 91–95 (deferring to district court findings of fact that were not clearly erroneous).

292. *See Shaw v. Reno*, 509 U.S. at 658 (reversing district court on question of law).

293. *See Shaw v. Hunt*, 517 U.S. at 903, 918 (reversing district court on question of law).

294. *See Hunt v. Cromartie*, 119 S. Ct. at 1547–48.

295. *See Miller*, 515 U.S. at 928–29 (O'Connor, J., concurring, arguing for high threshold of race consciousness to trigger strict scrutiny).

296. *See Shaw v. Reno*, 509 U.S. at 633 (majority opinion of O'Connor, J.).

297. Justice O'Connor was a member of the 5–4 majority in each of the five Supreme Court cases that ultimately invalidated affirmative action districting plans on constitutional grounds after plenary consideration. *See Abrams*, 521 U.S. at 76

(joining majority opinion); *Bush*, 517 U.S. at 955, 990 (opinion of O'Connor, J., and O'Connor J., concurring); *Shaw v. Hunt*, 517 U.S. at 900 (joining majority opinion); *Miller*, 515 U.S. at 928–29 (O'Connor, J., concurring); *Shaw v. Reno*, 509 U.S. at 633 (1993) (author of majority opinion). *See also* Affirmative Action Voting Chart, *infra* pages 162–63.

298. *See Miller*, 515 U.S. 928–29 (O'Connor, J., concurring, arguing that strict scrutiny should be reserved for extreme districting cases).

299. The six cases in which Justice O'Connor has voted to invalidate an affirmative action districting plan on constitutional grounds are *Lawyer*, 117 S. Ct. at 2196 (Scalia, J., dissenting, joined by O'Connor, J.); *Abrams*, 521 U.S. at 76 (joining majority opinion); *Bush*, 517 U.S. at 955, 990 (opinion of O'Connor, J., and O'Connor J., concurring); and *Shaw v. Hunt*, 517 U.S. at 900 (joining majority opinion); *Miller*, 515 U.S. at 928–29 (O'Connor, J., concurring); and *Shaw v. Reno*, 509 U.S. at 633 (1993) (author of majority opinion). The only redistricting case in which Justice O'Connor voted to uphold a challenged plan was *Hunt v. Cromartie*, 119 S. Ct. at 1548–52 (joining majority opinion), where she agreed that the presence of factual disputes precluded the entry of summary judgment. *See supra* text accompanying chapter 5, note 61 (discussing *Hunt v. Cromartie*); *see also* Affirmative Action Voting Chart, *infra* pages 162–63.

300. The five cases in which the Supreme Court has ruled against affirmative action districting plans on constitutional grounds after plenary consideration are *Abrams, Bush, Shaw v. Hunt, Miller*, and *Shaw v. Reno*. The two cases in which the Court upheld the constitutionality of the challenged districting plans were *Hunt v. Cromartie* and *Lawyer*—neither of which involved the creation of any new majority-minority districts. *See supra* text accompanying chapter 5, note 61 (discussing *Hunt v. Cromartie*); chapter 5, note 49 (discussing *Lawyer*); Affirmative Action Voting Chart, *infra* pages 162–63.

301. *See supra* chapter 5, note 84 (discussing *Korematsu*).

302. *See Adarand*, 515 U.S. at 237 ("we wish to dispel the notion that strict scrutiny is 'strict in theory but fatal in fact'"); *see also supra* text accompanying chapter 5, notes 107–129 (discussing meaning of strict scrutiny after *Adarand*).

303. *See Shaw v. Reno*, 509 U.S. at 633, 653–57 (majority opinion of O'Connor, J., joined by Rehnquist, Scalia, Kennedy, & Thomas, JJ., leaving open question of whether majority-minority districts drawn, *inter alia*, to comply with Voting Rights Act violated equal protection clause).

304. *See Miller*, 515 U.S. at 903, 920–21 (majority opinion of Kennedy, J., joined by Rehnquist, O'Connor, Scalia, & Thomas, JJ., leaving open question of whether compliance with Voting Rights Act constitutes compelling state interest).

305. *See* Shaw v. Hunt, 517 U.S. 899, 901, 911 (1996) (majority opinion of Rehnquist, C.J., joined by O'Connor, Scalia, Kennedy, & Thomas, JJ., expressly leaving open question of whether compliance with Voting Rights Act constitutes compelling state interest).

306. *See Abrams*, 515 U.S. at 77, 91 (majority opinion of Kennedy, J., joined by Rehnquist, O'Connor, Scalia, & Thomas, JJ., assuming without deciding that compliance with Voting Rights Act constitutes compelling state interest).

307. *See Shaw v. Hunt*, 517 U.S. at 901–03 (discussing district court decision).

308. *See id.* at 900, 911–12, 918 (listing votes of justices, and holding that plan did not survive strict scrutiny, even if intended to comply with § 5 or § 2 of Voting Rights Act).

309. *See Abrams*, 521 U.S. at 77, 77–79 (majority opinion of Kennedy, J., joined by Rehnquist, O'Connor, Scalia, & Thomas, JJ., rejecting claim that district court plan violated Voting Rights Act by reducing number of majority-minority districts).

310. *See Bush*, 517 U.S. at 956, 976–82 (opinion of O'Connor, J., joined by Rehnquist & Kennedy, JJ., rejecting Voting Rights Act claims and voting to affirm district court invalidation of majority-minority district; *id.* at 1972–74 (Thomas, J., concurring in judgment, joined by Scalia, J., voting to affirm district court invalidation of majority-minority district).

311. *See Miller*, 515 U.S. at 903, 920–28 (majority opinion of Kennedy, J., joined by Rehnquist, O'Connor, Scalia, & Thomas, JJ., affirming district court invalidation of majority-minority district, and stating that compliance with attorney general's interpretation of § 5 of Voting Rights Act did not constitute compelling state interest).

312. *See supra* text accompanying chapter 5, notes 286–290 (discussing *De-Witt*). Although the three-judge district court in *DeWitt* reasoned that compliance with the Voting Rights Act constituted a compelling state interest, *see DeWitt*, 856 F. Supp. at 1415, the Supreme Court's summary affirmance in *DeWitt* did not necessarily constitute an affirmance of the lower court's reasoning. *See supra* test accompanying chapter 4, notes 255 & 256 (discussing precedential effect of summary affirmance).

313. *See supra* chapter 5, note 300 (discussing *Hunt v. Cromartie* and *Lawyer*).

314. *See Miller*, 515 U.S. at 903, 926–28 (majority opinion of Kennedy, J., joined by Rehnquist, O'Connor, Scalia, & Thomas, JJ., finding that constitutional difficulties would be posed by reading § 5 of Voting Rights Act to incorporate attorney general's preclearance policy of maximizing majority-minority districts).

315. *See id.* (majority opinion of Kennedy, J., joined by Rehnquist, O'Connor, Scalia, & Thomas, JJ., finding that constitutional difficulties would be posed by reading § 5 of Voting Rights Act to incorporate attorney general's preclearance policy of maximizing majority-minority districts).

316. *See supra* text accompanying chapter 5, notes 304–306 (expressly reserving question of whether compliance with Voting Rights Act constitutes compelling state interest); *cf. Shaw v. Hunt*, 517 U.S. at 909–10 (conceding that need to remedy specific acts of past discrimination, that did not constitute mere general societal discrimination, could constitute compelling state interest).

317. *See Abrams*, 521 U.S. at 77, 91 (majority opinion of Kennedy, J., joined by Rehnquist, C.J., assuming without deciding that compliance with Voting Rights Act constituted compelling state interest, in case rejecting need for additional majority-minority district); *Shaw v. Hunt*, 517 U.S. at 901, 911 (majority opinion of Rehnquist, C.J., expressly leaving open question of whether compliance with Voting Rights Act constituted compelling state interest, in case invalidating majority-minority district); *Miller*, 515 U.S. at 903, 921 (majority opinion of Kennedy, J., joined by Rehnquist, C.J., leaving open question of whether compliance with Voting Rights Act constituted compelling state interest, in case invalidating majority-minority district). *See also* Affirmative Action Voting Chart, *infra* pages 162–63.

318. *See Bush*, 517 U.S. at 999–1003 (Thomas, J., concurring in judgment, joined by Scalia, J., arguing that all intentional majority-minority districts should trigger strict scrutiny).

319. *See supra* text accompanying chapter 5, notes 58 & 60 (discussing voting records of Justices Scalia and Thomas in constitutional affirmative action cases).

320. *See Adarand*, 515 U.S. at 204 (author of majority opinion).

321. *See Shaw v. Reno*, 509 U.S. at 633 (author of majority opinion).

322. *See Bush*, 517 U.S. at 990–92 (O'Connor, J., concurring, stating that compliance with § 2 of Voting Rights Act can constitute compelling state interest).

323. *See id.* at 993–95 (majority-minority districts can be created as long as districts are not drawn for "predominantly racial reasons").

324. *See supra* text accompanying chapter 5, notes 107–129 (discussing Justice O'Connor's claim that strict scrutiny is not necessarily fatal).

325. *See supra* text accompanying chapter 5, notes 57 & 128 (discussing Justice O'Connor's voting record in constitutional affirmative action cases).

326. Wygant v. Jackson Bd. of Educ., 476 U.S. 267 (1986).

327. *See id.* at 286 (O'Connor, J., concurring, stating that formal findings are not required and that prospective diversity can constitute compelling state interest).

328. City of Richmond v. J.R. Croson Co., 488 U.S. 469 (1989).

329. *See id.* at 498–506 (majority opinion of O'Connor, J., invalidating affirmative action program for lack of formal findings to show that program was necessary to remedy past discrimination).

330. Metro Broadcasting v. FCC, 497 U.S. 547 (1990).

331. *See id.* at 610–17 (O'Connor, J., dissenting, distinguishing between permissible remedies for past discrimination and impermissible efforts to promote diversity).

332. *See Bush*, 517 U.S. at 996–99 (Kennedy, J., concurring, stating that strict scrutiny permitted race-conscious actions required by § 2 of Voting Rights Act).

333. *See id.* at 996 (arguing for narrow range of circumstances in which race-conscious districting should be permitted).

334. *See supra* text accompanying chapter 5, note 59 (discussing Justice Kennedy's voting record in constitutional affirmative action cases).

335. *See Shaw v. Hunt*, 517 U.S. at 929–39 (Stevens, J., dissenting, joined by Ginsburg & Breyer, JJ.).

336. *See id.* at 940–45 (compliance with §§ 2 & 5 of Voting Rights Act constitutes compelling state interest).

337. *See Bush*, 517 U.S. at 1033–35 (Stevens, J., dissenting, joined by Ginsburg & Breyer, JJ., stating that compliance with Voting Rights Act constituted compelling state interest).

338. *See id.* at 1065 (Souter, J., dissenting, joined by Ginsburg & Breyer, JJ., indicating belief that compliance with Voting Rights Act constituted compelling state interest); *see also Shaw v. Hunt*, 517 U.S. at 951 (Souter, J. dissenting, joined by Ginsburg & Breyer, JJ., adopting same position).

339. *See Dept. of Commerce*, 119 S. Ct. at 775 (majority opinion of O'Connor, J., joined by Rehnquist, Scalia, Kennedy, & Thomas, JJ.). *Department of Commerce* is discussed in chapter 4, part 11.

340. *See supra* chapter 5, note 244 (listing seven redistricting cases).

341. For example, the North Carolina redistricting plan was before the Court three times—in *Shaw v. Reno*, *Shaw v. Hunt*, and *Hunt v. Cromartie*. The North Carolina cases are discussed in chapter 4, parts 2, 6, & 10. The Georgia redistricting plan was before the Court twice—in *Miller* and *Abrams*. The Georgia redistricting cases are discussed in chapter 4, parts 4 & 8. The Florida redistricting plan was before the Court twice, first as a Voting Rights Act case in *De Grandy*, and then as a constitutional case in *Lawyer*. The Florida redistricting cases are discussed in chapter 4, part 1, section iv, and chapter 4, part 9. In addition, the Supreme Court has granted review of the Bossier Parish, Louisiana, redistricting plan twice under the Voting Rights Act, and it has set the second grant of review over for reargument during the 1999–2000 Term. This means that the *Bossier Parish* case will have been argued before the Supreme Court three times. The *Bossier Parish* case is discussed in chapter 4, part 1, section vi.

342. *See Hunt v. Cromartie*, 119 S. Ct. at 1551 (suggesting that it may be constitutionally permissible to use race as a proxy for party affiliation in political gerrymandering). It is by no means clear why the Supreme Court believes that the equal protection clause prohibits gerrymandering based on race, but does not prohibit gerrymandering based on political party affiliation.

343. *See supra* text accompanying chapter 5, notes 254–259 (discussing Supreme Court's aversion to use of racial stereotypes as proxy for other traits).

344. *See* Adarand Constructors v. Pena, 515 U.S. 200, 224–27 (1995) (applying strict scrutiny to all racial affirmative action programs).

345. *See id.* at 224–25 (refusing to distinguish between benign and invidious racial classifications).

346. *See id.* at 237 (strict scrutiny is not necessarily fatal scrutiny).

347. *See* Korematsu v. United States, 323 U.S. 214 (1944); *see also supra* chapter

5, note 84 (discussing *Korematsu* as last case to uphold racial classification after strict scrutiny).

348. *See supra* text accompanying chapter 5, notes 312–313 (discussing nonapplication of strict scrutiny in cases upholding redistricting plans); *see also* Affirmative Action Voting Chart, *supra* pages 162–63.

349. *See* Loving v. Virginia, 388 U.S. 1, 11 (1967); *cf.* Korematsu v. United States, 323 U.S. 214, 216 (1944) (both stating strict scrutiny test).

350. *See* City of Richmond v. J.A. Croson Co., 488 U.S. 469, 488–89 (1989); *see also*, Metro Broadcasting v. FCC, 497 U.S. 547, 610–12, 613–14 (1990) (O'Connor, J., dissenting); Wygant v. Jackson Bd. of Educ., 476 U.S. 267, 288 (1986) (O'Connor, J., concurring); Johnson v. Transportation Agency 480 U.S. 616, 647–53 (1987) (O'Connor, J., concurring in judgment).

351. *See Croson*, 488 U.S. at 498–506 (finding inadequate evidence of past discrimination in Richmond construction trades).

352. *See id.* 498–508 (discussing narrow-tailoring requirement).

353. *See* Adarand Constructors v. Pena, 965 F. Supp. 1556, 1558–59, 1577–84 (D. Colo. 1997) (invalidating *Adarand* presumption on remand for not being narrowly tailored), vacated as moot by Adarand Constructors v. Slater, 169 F. 3d 1292, 1296–99 (10th Cir. 1999).

354. *See supra* chapter 5, note 217 (discussing Supreme Court treatment of actual-victim limitation).

355. *See* Shaw v. Reno, 509 U.S. 630, 642–49 (1993) (applying strict scrutiny to bizarrely shaped, majority-minority districts); *id.* at 649–52 (distinguishing prior vote-dilution cases).

356. *See* Miller v. Johnson, 515 U.S. 900, 910–12 (1995) (describing right not to be assigned to voting district based on race).

357. *See id.* at 915–17 (articulating "predominant factor" test); *see also id.* at 928–29 (O'Connor, J., concurring, stressing that new cause of action for racial gerrymandering did not invalidate existing districts even though race had been factor in drawing district lines).

358. *See id.* at 915–20 (strict scrutiny applies only where race was "predominant factor").

359. *See id.* at 925–28 (finding constitutional difficulties posed by attorney general's reading of Voting Rights Act as requiring maximization of majority-minority districts).

360. *See Hunt v. Cromartie*, 119 S. Ct. at 1551 (suggesting that it may be constitutionally permissible to use race as a proxy for party affiliation in political gerrymandering).

361. *See supra* text accompanying chapter 1, notes 60–62, and chapter 5, notes 254–259 (discussing Supreme Court's aversion to use of racial stereotypes as proxy for other traits).

362. *See* Affirmative Action Voting Chart, *supra* pages 162–63.

363. *See id.* These voting blocs are discussed in chapter 5, part 1, section i.

Bibliography

Affirmative Action Settlement; Excerpts From Statement By School Board Lawyer On Lawsuit's Settlement, N.Y. TIMES, Nov. 22, 1997, at B4.

B. Drummond Ayres, Jr., *University Regents in California Battle Over Affirmative Action*, N.Y. TIMES, July 21, 1995, at A1.

Barry Bearak, *Affirmative Action Settlement: The Reaction; Settlement Ends High Court Case On Preferences: Rights Groups Ducked A Fight, Opponents Say*, N.Y. TIMES, Nov. 22, 1997, at A1.

ALEXANDER BICKEL, THE MORALITY OF CONSENT (1975).

Joan Biskupic, *Rights Groups Pay To Settle Bias Case; High Court Affirmative Action Ruling Avoided*, WASH. POST, Nov. 22, 1997, at A1.

William Booth, *U. of Calif. Ends Racial Preferences: Pioneer in Diversity Adopts Stance Urged by Gov. Pete Wilson*, WASH. POST, July 21, 1995, at A1.

Ethan Bronner, *U. of Washington Will End Race-Conscious Admissions*, N.Y. TIMES, Nov. 7, 1998, at A12.

DeNeen L. Brown, *Gray in the Debate on Color: Many See Both Sides of Affirmative Action*, WASH. POST, June 5, 1995, at A1.

Tom Brune, *Now That I-200 Is Law, What's Next?—UW Alters Admission Policy*, SEATTLE TIMES, Nov. 5, 1998, at A1.

Stephen Buckley, *Voting Rights Ruling Called Death Knell for Exclusion; Ex-Clinton Nominee Hails Order in Maryland*, WASH. POST, Apr. 7, 1994, at B1.

William Claiborne, *Affirmative Action Ban Is Upheld; California Proposition Constitutionally Valid, U.S. Appeals Panel Says*, WASH. POST, Apr. 9, 1997, at A1.

Ruth Colker, *Anti-Subordination Above All: Sex, Race and Equal Protection*, 61 N.Y.U. L. REV. 1003 1986).

Ellis Cose, *After Affirmative Action: Proposition 209 May Become Law, But Californians Are In No Rush To End All Racial Preferences*, NEWSWEEK, Nov. 11, 1996, at 43.

Maura Dolan, *U.S. Panel Upholds Prop. 209 Affirmative Action: Three 9th Circuit Justices Rule That Measure To Eliminate Preferences For Women And Minorities In College Admissions And Government Employment Is Constitutional; Opponents Will Appeal, But Some Analysts Believe They Face An Uphill Battle*, L.A. TIMES, Apr. 9, 1997, at A1.

John Hart Ely, Democracy and Distrust: A Theory of Judicial Review (1980).

Employment Discrimination—Race: Clinton Administration Switches Stance On Use Of Race As Factor In Teacher's Layoff, 66 U.S.L.W. 2134 (Sept. 9, 1977).

Richard H. Fallon et al., Hart and Wechsler's The Federal Courts and the Federal System (4th ed. 1996).

Howard Fineman, *Race And Rage: Affirmative Action: Republicans Hope It Will Drive A Wedge Between Liberal Democrats And White Swing Voters,* Newsweek, Apr. 3, 1995, at 23.

Owen Fiss, *Groups and the Equal Protection Clause,* 5 J. Phil. & Pub. Aff. 107 (1976).

Eric Foner, Reconstruction: America's Unfinished Revolution (1988).

Heath Foster, *Affirmative Action Rules Tossed Out By State Voters,* Seattle Post-Intelligencer, Nov. 4, 1998, at A1.

Lon L. Fuller & William R. Perdue, Jr., *The Reliance Interest in Contract Damages I,* 46 Yale L.J. 52 (1936).

Clifford Geertz, *The Thick Description: Toward An Interpretive Theory Of Culture, in* The Interpretation of Cultures: Selected Essays 3 (1973).

Tim Golden, *Federal Appeals Court Upholds California's Ban On Preferences,* N.Y. Times, Apr. 9, 1997, at A4.

Abby Goodnough, *Affirmative Action Settlement: The Decision; Prospect Of A Costly Loss Led Board To Drop Case,* N.Y. Times, Nov. 22, 1997, at B4.

Linda Greenhouse, *Affirmative Action Settlement: The Overview; Settlement Ends High Court Case On Preferences: Tactical Retreat,* N.Y. Times, Nov. 22, 1997, at A1.

Linda Greenhouse, *By 5-4, Justices Cast Doubts On U.S. Programs That Give Preferences Based Upon Race: Debate Is Fueled; Rigorous Criteria Set For Court's Approval Of Such Programs,* N.Y. Times, June 13, 1995, at A1.

Gerald Gunther & Kathleen M. Sullivan, Constitutional Law (13th ed. 1997).

John F. Harris, *Clinton Avows Support For Affirmative Action: 'Mend It, but Don't End It,' President Says in Speech,* Wash. Post, July 20, 1995, at A10.

John F. Harris, *For Clinton, A Challenge Of Balance,* Wash. Post, June 14, 1995, at A1.

Louis Harris, *Affirmative Action and the Voter,* N.Y. Times, July 31, 1995, at A13.

A. Leon Higginbotham, In the Matter of Color: Race and the American Legal Process (1978).

Steven A. Holmes, *A Dilemma Led To A Deal Over Hiring Tied To Race,* N.Y. Times, Nov. 23, 1997, § 1, at 37.

Aldous Huxley, Brave New World (1932).

Pamela S. Karlan, *Our Separatism: Voting Rights as an American Nationalities Policy,* 1995 U. Chi. Legal F. 83.

Michael Kinsley, *The Spoils Of Victimhood: The Case Against The Case Against Affirmative Action*, NEW YORKER, Mar. 27, 1995, at 62.

Charles R. Lawrence, *The Id, The Ego, And Equal Protection: Reckoning With Unconscious Racism*, 39 STAN. L. REV. 317 (1987).

Nicholas Lemann, *Taking Affirmative Action Apart*, N.Y. TIMES, June 11, 1995, § 6 (Magazine), at 36.

Anthony Lewis, *Abroad at Home; Anatomy Of a Smear*, N.Y. TIMES, June 4, 1993, at A31.

Kevin Merida, *Senate Rejects Gramm Bid to Bar Affirmative Action Set-Asides*, WASH. POST, July 21, 1995, at A13.

Not Over Till It's Over, THE ECONOMIST NEWSPAPER, Nov. 16, 1996, at 27.

Clarence Page, *'Cumulative Voting' Takes Lani Guinier into the Mainstream*, CHI. TRIB., March 30, 1994, at 23.

Richard H. Pildes and Richard G. Niemi, *Expressive Harms, "Bizarre Districts," And Voting Rights: Evaluating Election-District Appearances After* Shaw v. Reno, 92 MICH. L. REV. 483 (1993).

Todd S. Purdum, *President Shows Fervent Support For Goals of Affirmative Action*, N.Y. TIMES, July 20, 1995, at A1.

LAWRENCE ROSEN, THE ANTHROPOLOGY OF JUSTICE: LAW AS CULTURE IN ISLAMIC SOCIETY (1989).

Rene Sanchez, *Washington's New Affirmative Action Question: How to End It*, WASH. POST, Nov. 13, 1998, at A2.

Eric Schnapper, *Affirmative Action And The Legislative History Of The Fourteenth Amendment*, 71 VA. L. REV. 753 (1985).

Girardeau A. Spann, *Color-Coded Standing*, 80 CORNELL L. REV. 1422 (1995).

Girardeau A. Spann, *Proposition 209*, 47 DUKE L.J. 187 (1997).

GIRARDEAU A. SPANN, RACE AGAINST THE COURT: THE SUPREME COURT AND MINORITIES IN CONTEMPORARY AMERICA (1993).

Girardeau A. Spann, *Simple Justice*, 73 GEO. L.J. 1041 (1985).

ROBERT L. STERN ET AL., SUPREME COURT PRACTICE (7th ed. 1993).

GEOFFREY R. STONE ET AL., CONSTITUTIONAL LAW (3d ed. 1996).

David A. Strauss, *Discriminatory Intent and the Taming of* Brown, 56 U. CHI. L. REV. 935 (1989).

Kathleen M. Sullivan, *Comment: Sins of Discrimination: Last Term's Affirmative Action Cases*, 100 HARV. L. REV. 78 (1986).

The Supreme Court, 1977 Term, 92 HARV. L. REV. 57 (1978).

The Supreme Court, 1979 Term, 94 HARV. L. REV. 75 (1980).

Mike Tharp, *Copying California: A New Battleground for Affirmative Action in the Pacific Northwest*, U.S. NEWS & WORLD REPORT, Nov. 9, 1998, at 34.

Abigail Thernstrom, *A Class Backwards Idea: Why Affirmative Action For The Needy Won't Work*, WASH. POST, June 11, 1995, at C1.

LAURENCE H. TRIBE, AMERICAN CONSTITUTIONAL LAW (2d ed. 1988).

Winkfield F. Twyman, Jr., *A Critique of the California Civil Rights Initiative*, 14 Nat'l Black L.J. 181 (1997).

Vagueness of I-200 Could Limit Damage (Editorial), Seattle Times, Nov. 5, 1998, at B8.

Eugene Volokh, *The California Civil Rights Initiative: An Interpretive Guide*, 44 UCLA L. Rev. 1335 (1997).

Legal Authorities

CASES

Abbott Lab. v. Gardner, 387 U.S. 136 (1967).

Abrams v. Johnson, 521 U.S. 74 (1997).

Adarand Constructors v. Pena, 965 F. Supp. 1556 (D. Colo. 1997).

Adarand Constructors v. Pena, 515 U.S. 200 (1995).

Adarand Constructors v. Skinner, 790 F. Supp. 240 (D. Colo. 1992), aff'd 16 F.3d 1537 (10th Cir. 1995).

Allen v. State Bd. of Elections, 393 U.S. 544 (1969).

Allen v. Wright, 468 U.S. 737 (1984).

Arlington Heights v. Metropolitan Housing Development Corp., 429 U.S. 252 (1977).

Beer v. United States, 425 U.S. 130 (1976).

Bossier Parish School Bd. v. Reno, 7 F. Supp. 2d 29 (D.D.C. 1998) (three-judge court).

Brown v. Board of Educ., 347 U.S. 483 (1954) (*Brown I*), 349 U.S. 294 (1955) (*Brown II*).

Bush v. Vera, 517 U.S. 952 (1996).

Chisom v. Roemer, 501 U.S. 380 (1991).

City of Monroe v. United States, 118 S. Ct. 400 (1997) (per curiam).

City of Richmond v. J.A. Croson Co., 488 U.S. 469 (1989).

City of Rome v. United States, 446 U.S. 156 (1980).

Cleburne v. Cleburne Living Center, 473 U.S. 432 (1985).

Clinton v. Glavin, 19 F. Supp. 2d 543 (E.D. Va. 1998) (three-judge court).

Coalition for Econ. Equity v. Wilson, 118 S. Ct. 397 (1997) (*cert. denied*).

Coalition for Econ. Equity v. Wilson, 66 U.S.L.W. 3181 (U.S. Aug. 29, 1997) (No. 97-369) (*cert. filed*).

Coalition for Econ. Equity v. Wilson, 118 S. Ct. 17 (1997) (Supreme Court denial of emergency stay).

Coalition for Econ. Equity v. Wilson, 122 F.3d 718, 719-20 (9th Cir. 1997) (9th Circuit denial of stay).

Coalition for Econ. Equity v. Wilson, 122 F.3d 692 (9th Cir. 1997).

Coalition for Econ. Equity v. Wilson, 946 F. Supp. 1480 (N.D. Cal. 1996).

Craig v. Boren, 429 U.S. 190 (1976).

Crawford v. Board of Educ. of the City of Los Angeles, 458 U.S. 527 (1982).

DeFunis v. Odegaard, 416 U.S. 312 (1974).

Department of Commerce v. United States House of Representatives, 119 S. Ct. 765 (1999).

Department of Commerce v. United States House of Representatives, 11 F. Supp. 2d 76 (D.D.C. 1998) (three-judge court).

DeWitt v. Wilson, 515 U.S. 1170 (1995), aff'g DeWitt v. Wilson, 856 F. Supp. 1409 (E.D. Cal. 1994) (three-judge court).

DeWitt v. Wilson, 63 U.S.L.W. 3201 (Sept. 27, 1994) (enumerating questions presented in jurisdictional statement).

Dred Scott v. Sandford, 60 U.S. (19 How.) 393 (1857).

Edelman v. Jordan, 415 U.S. 651 (1974).

Firefighters Local Union No. 1784 v. Stotts, 467 U.S. 561 (1984).

Franks v. Bowman Transp. Co., 424 U.S. 747 (1976).

Fullilove v. Klutznick, 448 U.S. 448 (1980).

Fusari v. Steinberg, 419 U.S. 379 (1975).

FW/PBS, Inc. v. Dallas, 493 U.S. 215 (1990).

Green v. County School Bd., 391 U.S. 430 (1968).

Greene v. Podberesky, 63 U.S.L.W. 3793 (U.S. Mar. 30, 1995) (No. 94-1621) (*cert. denied,* 514 U.S. 1128 (1995)).

Griffin v. School Bd., 377 U.S. 218 (1964).

Griggs v. Duke Power, 401 U.S. 424 (1971).

Growe v. Emison, 507 U.S. 25 (1993).

Guardians Ass'n v. Civil Serv. Comm'n of the City of N.Y., 463 U.S. 582 (1983).

Hirabayashi v. United States, 320 U.S. 81 (1943).

Holder v. Hall, 512 U.S. 874 (1994).

Hopwood v. Texas, 78 F. 3d 932 (5th Cir. 1996), *cert. denied,* 518 U.S. 1033 (1996).

Hunt v. Cromartie, 119 S. Ct. 1545 (1999).

Hunter v. Erickson, 393 U.S. 385 (1969).

International Bhd. of Teamsters v. United States, 431 U.S. 324 (1977).

Johnson v. De Grandy, 512 U.S. 997 (1994).

Johnson v. Transportation Agency, 480 U.S. 616 (1987).

Keys v. School District No. 1, Denver Colorado, 413 U.S. 189 (1973).

Kirwan v. Podberesky, 63 U.S.L.W. 3779 (U.S. Mar. 29, 1995) (No.94-1620) (*cert. denied,* 514 U.S. 1128 (1995)).

Korematsu v. United States, 323 U.S. 214 (1944).

Lawyer v. Department of Justice, 117 S. Ct. 2186 (1997).

Local 28, Sheet Metal Workers Int'l Ass'n v. EEOC, 478 U.S. 421 (1986).

Local 93, Int'l Ass'n of Firefighters v. Cleveland, 478 U.S. 501 (1986).

Lopez v. Monterey County, 119 S. Ct. 693 (1999).

Loving v. Virginia, 388 U.S. 1 (1967).

Lujan v. Defenders of Wildlife, 504 U.S. 555 (1992).

Lujan v. National Wildlife Federation, 497 U.S. 871 (1990).

Metro Broadcasting v. FCC, 497 U.S. 547 (1990).

Middleton v. City of Flint, 92 F.3d. 396 (6th Cir. 1996).

Miller v. Johnson, 515 U.S. 900 (1995).

Milliken v. Bradley, 418 U.S. 717 (1974).

Missouri v. Jenkins, 515 U.S. 70 (1995).

Mobile v. Bolden, 446 U.S. 55 (1980).

NAACP v. Allen, 340 F. Supp. 703 (M.D. Ala. 1972).

North Carolina State Bd. of Educ. v. Swann, 402 U.S. 43 (1971).

Northeastern Fla. Chapter of the Associated Gen. Contractors of Am. v. City of Jacksonville, 508 U.S. 656 (1993).

Palmer v. Thompson, 403 U.S. 217 (1971).

Personnel Adm'r v. Feeney, 442 U.S. 256 (1979).

Piscataway Township Bd. of Educ. v. Taxman, 118 S. Ct. 595 (1997) (dismissing writ of certiorari pursuant to Supreme Court Rule 46.1, which provides for dismissal after settlement).

Piscataway Township Bd. of Educ. v. Taxman, 117 S. Ct. 2506 (1997) (*cert. granted*).

Piscataway Township Bd. of Educ. v. Taxman, 117 S. Ct. 763 (1997) (inviting Solicitor General to file brief).

Piscataway Township Bd. of Educ. v. Taxman, 65 U.S.L.W. 3375 (U.S. Oct. 31, 1996) (No. 96-679) (*cert. filed*).

Planned Parenthood of Southeastern Pa. v. Casey, 505 U.S. 833 (1992).

Plessy v. Ferguson, 163 U.S. 537 (1896).

Podberesky v. Kirwan, 38 F. 3d 147 (4th Cir. 1994), *cert. denied,* 514 U.S. 1128 (1995).

Podberesky v. Kirwan, 764 F. Supp. 364 (D. Md. 1991).

Powers v. Ohio, 499 U.S. 400 (1991).

Railroad Commission of Texas v. Pullman Co., 312 U.S. 496 (1941).

Regents of the Univ. of Cal. v. Bakke, 438 U.S. 265 (1978).

Reno v. Bossier Parish School Bd., 520 U.S. 471 (1997).

Reynolds v. Sims, 377 U.S. 533 (1964).

Rogers v. Lodge, 458 U.S. 613 (1982).

San Antonio Independent School District v. Rodriguez, 411 U.S. 1 (1973).

Shaw v. Hunt, 517 U.S. 899 (1996).

Shaw v. Reno, 509 U.S. 630 (1993).

Shelley v. Kraemer, 334 U.S. 1 (1948).

Slaughter-House Cases, 83 U.S. (16 Wall.) 36 (1873).

South Carolina v. Katzenbach, 388 U.S. 301 (1966).

Steele v. FCC, 770 F.2d 1192 (D.C. Cir. 1985).

Stotts v. Memphis Fire Dep't, 679 F.2d 541 (6th Cir. 1982).

Swann v. Charlotte-Mecklenburg Bd. of Educ., 402 U.S. 1 (1971).

Taxman v. Piscataway Township Bd. of Educ., 91 F.3d 1547 (3d. Cir. 1996) (en banc), *cert. granted,* 117 S. Ct. 2506 (1997), *cert. dismissed,* 118 S. Ct. 595 (1997).

Teamsters v. United States, 431 U.S. 324 (1977).

Thornburg v. Gingles, 478 U.S. 30 (1986).

Thurgood Marshall Legal Society v. Hopwood, 64 U.S.L.W. 3013 (U.S. May 13, 1996) (No. 95-1845).

TV 9, Inc. v. FCC, 495 F.2d 929 (D.C. Cir. 1973).

United Jewish Orgs. v. Carey, 430 U.S. 144 (1977).

United States v. Board of Educ. of the Township of Piscataway, 832 F. Supp. 836 (D.N.J. 1993).

United States v. Carolene Prods., 304 U.S. 144 (1938).

United States v. Cruikshank, 92 U.S. 542 (1875).

United States v. Fordice, 505 U.S. 717 (1992).

United States v. Harris, 106 U.S. 629 (1882).

United States v. Hays, 515 U.S. 737 (1995).

United States v. Montgomery County Bd. of Educ., 395 U.S. 225 (1969).

United States v. Munsingwear, 340 U.S. 36 (1950).

United States v. Paradise, 480 U.S. 149 (1987).

United States v. Reese, 92 U.S. 214 (1875).

United States v. Students Challenging Regulatory Agency Procedures (SCRAP), 412 U.S. 669 (1973).

United States v. Virginia, 518 U.S. 515 (1996).

United Steelworkers of Am. v. Weber, 443 U.S. 193 (1979).

Upham v. Seamon, 456 U.S. 37 (1982).

Voinovich v. Quilter, 507 U.S. 146 (1993).

Warth v. Seldin, 422 U.S. 490 (1975).

Washington v. Davis, 426 U.S. 229 (1976).

Washington v. Seattle School District No. 1, 458 U.S. 457 (1982).

Whitcomb v. Chavis, 403 U.S. 124 (1971).

White v. Regester, 412 U.S. 755 (1973).

Wilson v. Eu, 823 P.2d 545 (Cal. 1992).

Winter Park Communications v. FCC, 873 F.2d 347 (D.C. Cir. 1989).

Wygant v. Jackson Bd. of Educ., 476 U.S. 267 (1986).

Young v. Fordice, 520 U.S. 273 (1997).

CONSTITUTIONAL PROVISIONS

U.S. CONST. art. I, § 1, cl. 2

U.S. CONST. art. I, § 2, cl. 3

U.S. CONST. art. I, § 4, cl. 1

U.S. CONST. amend. V

U.S. CONST. amend. XIII

U.S. CONST. amend. XIV

U.S. CONST. amend. XIV, § 1

U.S. CONST. amend. XV

U.S. CONST. amend. XV, § 2

STATUTES

Census Act, 13 U.S.C. § 1 *et seq.* (1994).

Census Act § 141(a), 13 U.S.C. § 141(a) (1994).

Census Act § 195, 13 U.S.C. § 195 (1994).

Civil Rights Act of 1964, Title VI, Pub. L. 88-352, 78 Stat. 241, 252 (codified as amended at 42 U.S.C. §§ 2000d, *et seq.* (1994)).

Civil Rights Act of 1964, Title VII, Pub. L. No. 88-352, 78 Stat. 241, 253 (codified as amended at 42 U.S.C. §§ 2000e to 2000e-17 (1994)).

Civil Rights Act of 1964, Title VII, § 703(a), Pub. L. No. 88-352, 78 Stat. 255, as amended, 86 Stat. 109 (codified as amended at 42 U.S.C. § 2000e–2(a) (1994)).

Civil Rights Act of 1964, Title VII, § 703(d), Pub. L. 88-352, 78 Stat. 256 (codified at 42 U.S.C. § 2000e–2(d) (1994)).

Civil Rights Act of 1964, Title VII, § 703(h), Pub. L. 88-352, 78 Stat. 257 (codified as amended at 42 U.S.C. § 2000e-2(h) (1994)).

Civil Rights Act of 1964, Title VII, § 706(g), Pub. L. 88-352, 78 Stat. 261 (codified as amended at 42 U.S.C. § 2000e-5(g) (1994)).

Deduction for Health Insurance Costs of Self-Employed Individuals, Pub. L. 104–7, § 2, 109 Stat. 93-94 (1995).

Public Works Employment Act of 1977, Pub. L. 95-28, 91 Stat. 116 (codified as amended at 42 U.S.C. § 6701 *et seq.* (1994)).

Small Business Act, Pub. L. No. 85-536, 72 Stat. 384 (codified as amended at 15 U.S.C. §§ 631-6201 (1994)).

Small Business Administration Act § 8(a), 15 U.S.C. §§ 637(d)(2), (3) (1994).

Surface Transportation Act § 106(c)(2)(B), 101 Stat. 146 (1987).

Surface Transportation and Uniform Relocation Assistance Act, Pub. L. No. 100-17, 100 Stat. 145 (codified as amended at 23 U.S.C. §§ 101-160 (1994)).

Voting Rights Act of 1965, Pub. L. No. 89-110, 79 Stat. 445 (codified as amended at 42 U.S.C. § 1973c (1994)).

Voting Rights Act of 1965 § 14(c)(1) (codified as amended at 42 U.S.C. § 1973*l*(c)(1) (1994)).

EXECUTIVE ORDERS AND REGULATIONS

Exec. Order No. 10,925, 3 C.F.R. 448 (1959-1963), *reprinted in* 1961 U.S.C.C.A.N. 1274 (1961).

Race- and Gender-Based Provisions for the Auctioning of C Block Broadcast Personal Communications Service Licensees, Elimination, 60 FED. REG. 34200, 34202, 34205

47 C.F.R. Parts 20 & 24

Index

About the Author

Girardeau A. Spann was born in Cleveland, Ohio, and grew up in White Plains, New York. He attended Valhalla High School, Princeton University, and Harvard Law School. After graduating from law school, Spann worked as a staff attorney for Ralph Nader's Public Citizen Litigation Group in Washington, D.C. Spann then joined the faculty of the Georgetown University Law Center, where he is now a Professor of Law.

At Georgetown, Professor Spann teaches Contracts, Torts, Administrative Law, and Constitutional Law. His recent writings have been about race, the Constitution, and the Supreme Court, with an emphasis on the role that postmodern thought should play in legal analysis. Spann is the author of *Race against the Court: The Supreme Court and Minorities in Contemporary America* and is a coauthor of *Constitutional Theory: Arguments and Perspectives* (2d ed.). Professor Spann lives in Washington, D.C.